Sinking into the Honey Trap:
The Case of the Israeli-Palestinian Conflict

For those who desire to know more than they have been told.

SINKING INTO THE HONEY TRAP

THE CASE OF THE ISRAELI-PALESTINIAN CONFLICT

DANIEL BAR-TAL

Tel Aviv University

Translated into English by Barbara Doron

Westphalia Press
An Imprint of the Policy Studies Organization
Washington, DC
2023

Westphalia Press
An imprint of Policy Studies Organization
1367 Connecticut Avenue NW
Washington, D.C. 20036
info@ipsonet.org

ISBN: 978-1-63723-716-8

Cover and interior design by Jeffrey Barnes
jbarnesbook.design

Daniel Gutierrez-Sandoval, Executive Director
PSO and Westphalia Press

Updated material and comments on this edition
can be found at the Westphalia Press website:
www.westphaliapress.org

Contents

Foreword

David N. Myers

The Internet Age once augured the prospect of a new era of global harmony, anchored by the democratization of knowledge and open access to all in search of its rich treasures. But just as the once-grand promise of a globalized world without boundaries has been shattered by the resurgence of an exclusionary local ethno-nationalism, so too has cyber space been chopped up into so many social media silos, many of which enable and proudly propagate disinformation, propaganda, and lies. We avail ourselves of these sites in order to affirm our pre-existing biases, not to inform ourselves of new perspectives that we might not want to hear. Indeed, encountering viewpoints that we like to hear sates us and reinforces our sense of self.

It is volitional acts of this kind that help produce a fragmented social media landscape, but not only they. The very algorithms that drive internet search engines are not neutral mathematical formulae. They promote and perpetuate, as Safiya Noble has powerfully shown in *Algorithms of Oppression*, deeply ingrained prejudices and misconceptions, often of a racist nature.

The world that has resulted is not the utopia of democracy and open access that technology futurists once dreamt of. It is a world of stark epistemological divides between competing versions of truth, with groups of adepts lined up in tense, often violent, opposition to one another. And it is this world into which Daniel Bar-Tal has situated his latest analysis of Israeli society. *Sinking into the Honey Trap of the Intractable Conflict* is the *summa summarum* (to date) of an eminent scholar whose generative and prolific body of scholarship operates at the boundaries of social and political psychology. The book is less about "the case of the Israeli-Palestinian conflict," as the subtitle reads. Rather, it is a profound, searing, and moving probe into the soul of Israeli society from someone who has lived in and devoted a half-century of study to it.

Bar-Tal understands well that the internet did not invent the conflict between Israelis and Palestinians nor the epistemological divide that surrounds representations of Israel. For many Israeli Jews, he shows, Israel has always been a country of unsurpassed virtue—an advanced and progressive democracy with, as is often trumpeted, the most moral army in the world. It comes, for them, at least as close to Ahad Ha-am's vision of "a light unto the nations" as to Theodor Herzl's normalized nation-state like all others.

By contrast, for Palestinians and many around the world, Israel is a rogue state that has systematically deprived Palestinians in its midst of basic rights—expelling, occupying, and imposing an apartheid regime on them. Bar-Tal is duly mindful of this epistemological divide, but where he makes his most important contribution in this book is in exploring the nature of the divide within Israel society itself, and in particular, *within* its Jewish majority.

Indeed, this book, Bar-Tal tell us at the outset, is about "the Israeli-Jewish story." That story, which he expertly tells here, is not of an explosively multicultural and cacophonous society. Rather, it is the story of a black and white world divided between forces of good and forces of evil, with no gray space in between. On one side stands Israel, prominently aligned with the forces of good against the dark forces of evil, symbolized, on the other side, by the Palestinians (and all who support or sympathize with them). Those who fail to recognize this Manichean divide—and who the forces of good are—face serious sanction. They risk ostracization and delegitimization, both within Israel and outside it. As a progressive Jew and historian who has steadfastly resisted the Manichean divide, I know well the wrath and indignation that can fall upon those who are perceived to step out of line.

What is compelling in this book is Bar-Tal's skill in tracing the way the "Israel-Jewish story" has been enshrined in Israeli and Jewish consciousness and promoted as the only possible narrative frame for understanding the relationship between Israelis and Palestinians. *Sinking into the Honey Trap* is, at one level, an account of the marshalling of media resources to promote the story of Israel's virtue, facilitated by the full deployment of state institutions and the mobilization of politically aligned non-profits and print, broadcast, and online news outlets. The effectiveness of this effort has increased in the age of social media when it is possible to malign instantly those who deviate from the story of unblemished virtue. But Bar-Tal shows that this project—once labeled in Israeli parlance as *hasbarah* (propaganda)—has accompanied the Israeli state for decades.

Indeed, this book is, at one level, a careful reconstruction of the centering of a triumphalist narrative of Israeli virtue beginning with the establishment of the state in 1948. Bar-Tal shows how the long-standing guiding narrative was cracked open briefly on a couple of occasions: in the wake of the negotiations between Israel and Egypt that led to the peace treaty of 1979 and, more importantly, in the midst of the Oslo peace process in the 1990s, when it was important for public officials to advance the view—which many in Israel had come to believe—that the Palestinians were now a legitimate and meaningful partner for peace. But that latter opening proved to be evanescent. The collapse of the Oslo process and the outbreak of the Second Intifada in the early 2000s had a devastating impact on Israeli Jewish consciousness, quickly sealing back up the boundaries of the guiding narrative that had briefly allowed for a glimpse of the humanity and even suffering of Palestinians. Since that time, the story of Israeli virtue—and the companion tale of Palestinian genocidal aims—has been fortified in public institutions, messaging, and diplomacy, in step with Israel's growing rightward drift. All who fail to toe the main party line—for example, by questioning Israel's occupation of the West Bank or its human rights record—become subject to withering criticism. Bar-Tal offers up a fascinating case in point when he calls attention to the Israeli Supreme Court, which has proven to be an exceptionally reliable defender of Israel's presence and policies in the West Bank, notwithstanding a rather wide-ranging international consensus about their illegality. "Time after time," Bar-Tal notes, "the Supreme Court has ruled in favor of the state." And yet, on the rare occasions when it has expressed some measure of support for the rights of Palestinians, it has been subjected to ferocious attack by government ministers, parliamentarians, media, and common citizens. This line of assault has been a hallmark of the reign of Benjamin Netanyahu as Israel's Prime Minster, especially his long tenure from 2009 to 2021—and now again, after his re-election in 2022. The Supreme Court, a decidedly conservative institution with respect to the rights of Palestinians in the occupied territories, has been cast as the embodiment of unrestrained left-wing forces seeking nothing less than the destruction of the state of Israel.

How could this kind of claim be made? How could the Supreme Court be considered a traitorous institution, given its function in the Israeli system and, for that matter, its track record? Bar-Tal's historical reconstruction of the entrenchment of the narrative of virtue in Israeli society sets the wider context in which attacks on the Supreme Court have taken place.

But it is really the psychological overlay that Bar-Tal brings to this story that allows us to understand the formation and function of a Manichean narrative that demands total adherence. And there are few better than Bar-Tal to bring analytic depth to this narrative. He has devoted his exceptional career to nuanced work that makes use of the tools of "socio-political psychology." Here he provides readers with a conceptual lexicon to understand how we got to where we are.

The first of the key terms in this lexicon is trauma. Not surprisingly, Bar-Tal takes us back to the Holocaust, which became for Israelis "the ultimate national trauma, still affecting all aspects of life in Jewish society up to the present." It is impossible to grasp the narrative of Israeli virtue and, concomitantly, Palestinian perfidy without comprehending the enormity of this tragedy nor the lingering effects of post-Holocaust trauma. In borrowing from the work of Daphna Canetti and Gilad Hirschberger, Bar-Tal homes in on the "Holocaustization of Jewish consciousness" as it plays out in Israeli society. This sensibility regards ongoing violence and injury—as they emanate from war and terror, for example—as expected features of a world bent on the elimination of Jews. It also justifies violence and injury inflicted on others as essential features of the imperative to survive, which is understood to be one of the most important lessons of the Holocaust. Incidentally, this sensibility seems to operate without regard to the huge and growing power asymmetry between Israel and the Palestinians.

The book argues that trauma has created a socio-psychological "infrastructure" upon which Israeli Jews have constructed their collective identity, armed with a "repertoire" of social-psychological tools that allow them to remain unbending in their faith in the justness of their cause. Perhaps the most important tool, Bar-Tal demonstrates, is the guiding narrative of Israeli Jewish society, premised on an "ethos of conflict" which routinizes strife and enmity as normal features of daily life. This "conflict supporting narrative" transforms a core epistemological divide into an ontological one: Israelis and Palestinians, Jews and Arabs, don't simply see the world in diametrically opposed terms. They *are* different—Jews are good, Arabs are evil. All who reject this juxtaposition risk ceding their place as legitimate members of society.

As a self-described "loyal patriot," Bar-Tal cannot rest passive in support of a psychological repertoire on which his fellow Israeli Jews rely that he regards as deeply unhealthy. Toward the end of the book, Bar-Tal quotes a haunting sentence from George Orwell that captures the dilemma: "War is not meant to be won, it is meant to be continuous." The need for ongoing strife as an organizing principle seems to be unending, part of an inviolable social contract anchoring Israeli Jewish society.

As convincing and disconcerting as his diagnosis is, Bar-Tal surprisingly does not succumb to despair. The great historian Yosef Hayim Yerushalmi spoke of the ability of Jews, honed over the course of their long Diaspora history, to mount a kind of "interim hope" that mediated between total despondency and messianic redemption. Bar-Tal holds out the prospect of arriving at this kind of "interim hope." He neither regards Israeli behavior as unique in modern history (recalling Russia, China, and Turkey among other state actors); nor does he forget that other seemingly intractable conflicts have found a measure of reconciliation, most appositely, that between Catholics and Protestants in Northern Ireland.

History demonstrates that change is possible. The importance of this book is to make the case that what is required to alter the equation is not only a clear plan for conflict resolution but an unsparing analysis of the psychological pillars of a group's collective consciousness. "Every major societal change," Bar-Tal concludes, "must begin with the construction of new narratives." Change of that sort requires, in addition to a transformative leader, a bold willingness to confront one's own pathological adherence to a psychological repertoire at whose core stands conflict.

During his long and productive career, Daniel Bar-Tal has more than contributed his share to the cause. He has used his manifold talents as a scholar to expose the soul of his own society. Here in this book, he offers, through a mix of self-sacrifice and self-analysis (as an Israeli citizen), his own best attempt at a therapeutic intervention for that society. There is no way to know if he will succeed. But we must acknowledge with deep gratitude his courage, honesty, and perspicacity in prodding his fellow Israelis to crack open once again and more forcefully the narrative of exclusion on which their collective identity is built. That, he reminds us with a mix of hard-headed critique and interim hope, is the necessary path toward greater self-awareness, empathy, and openness to the Other.

David N. Myers is Distinguished Professor and holds the Sady and Ludwig Kahn Chair in the UCLA History Department, Los Angeles. He is the director of the UCLA

Initiative to Study Hate, as well as the immediate past President of the New Israel (2018–2023). He is the author or editor of more than fifteen books including *Between Arab and Jew: The Lost Voice of Simon Rawidowicz.*

Preface

This book responds to four questions that have concerned researchers from various realms of knowledge as well as many citizens living in areas of conflict: Why aren't bloody and lasting conflicts solved by peaceful means, despite the heavy price societies must pay for the many years of continuing violence? Moreover, what specific processes develop when this type of conflict has continued over time? What causes these developments? And finally, what are the inevitable consequences?

Unfortunately, not only are these conflicts unsolved, but they frequently escalate and intensify, even when a peace process has begun. Moreover, in addition to the enormous costs in various spheres (loss of lives, harm to emotional wellbeing, considerable economic costs, and more) in countries involved in violent conflict, there is almost always clear harm to democracy and to principles of morality, combined with a descent towards authoritarianism. In my opinion, these outcomes are unavoidable.

In order to answer these questions, I shall document developments which have taken place in Jewish Israeli society, primarily since the beginning of the twenty-first century, by adopting a psychological-social-political approach. Considering the Israeli-Palestinian conflict from the beginning of the 2000s, under rightwing leaders, Jewish society has become more and more extreme in their attitudes both about the conflict and about democratic elements of the state. This began in the 1980s and at the beginning of the 1990s; Jewish society in Israel had enjoyed a period of moderation in their approach to the conflict, as well as an expansion of democracy. It should be noted that in the first three decades after independence, conflict culture had totally dominated Israel, and during that period, democracy had been very deficient as well.

The focus on the Israeli-Palestinian conflict should be treated as a case study, because I deeply believe that engaging in and maintaining a lasting and bloody conflict necessarily leads not only to high costs, but also to the deterioration of democratic and moral principles, as has also taken place in other societies. That has become obvious in Turkey, as conflict with Kurds still rages, and in India and Pakistan, still enmeshed in the Kashmir conflict, and in Morocco, enduring its continuing occupation of Western Sahara.

At this point, it is important to mention that I studied physiological psychology with Professor Yeshayahu Leibowitz immediately upon my entry into Tel Aviv University in November 1967. The eminent professor was then devoting at least ten minutes of every lesson to prophesying what could be expected in Israeli society if it continued to occupy the territories conquered in the Six-Day War in June 1967. Leibowitz's opinions were unequivocal, and they were difficult to hear during that period—a time when the nation was rejoicing after the war and feeling pride that the army had succeeded in "liberating" these areas. Unfortunately, in retrospect, it seems clear that Professor Leibowitz was right. He foresaw what would become of Jewish society much more accurately than many politicians who have shaped society for years to come.

Leibowitz wrote the following, which echoed what he had said in his lessons time after time as a prophetic vision. It eventually appeared in the daily newspaper, *Yedioth Aharonoth* in April 1968:

> **It is not the territory which is the problem but rather the population of about 1.25 million Arabs living in the territories over whom we will have to impose our authority. The inclusion of these Arabs (in addition to the 300,000 who are Israeli citizens) under our control means the annihilation of the State of Israel as the state of the Jewish people, the destruction of the entire Jewish nation and the obliteration of human beings – Jews and Arabs alike … The state will no longer be a Jewish state, but rather a "Canaanite" state.** Its problems, and its needs and functions will no longer be the problems, needs and functions of the Jewish nation in its own land and abroad, but only the interests of the specific government and the administration of that state – the interests of the authority controlling the Jews and Arabs alike. These will be similar to the problems of the state of Lebanon, which is only concerned with the permanent worry about a solution to the problems of relations between the Maronites, the Muslims and the Druze, and others. The state will be harassed by these specific problems and will not be concerned with the Jewish nation. In a short time, the spiritual and emotional ties between the state and the Jewish nation will be severed, and the spiritual and emotional ties be-

tween the state and the historical content of the Israeli nation and Judaism will be terminated. **The total content of the monstrosity called "Greater Israel" will be nothing but its governmental-administrative system.** From the social standpoint, in a short time, there will no longer be a Jewish worker or a Jewish farmer in that state. The Arabs will be the working nation, and the Jews will be managers, supervisors, administrators, police, and primarily, the secret service. **The state, which is ruling a hostile population of 1.4–2 million foreigners, will necessarily be a state based on security services with all that that entails, and with implications for the spirit of education, for free speech and thought and for a democratic government.** The characteristic corruption in every colonialist state will find its place in Israel. The administration will have to deal with suppression of an Arab rebellion, on the one hand, and acquiring Arab quislings, on the other. It is also to be feared that the Israel Defense Forces, which up to now has been an army of the people, will atrophy into an occupation force, and its officers, who will become military rulers, will be like their counterparts in other nations. (My emphasis)

And the writing was engraved upon the wall for the future of Israel.

The conceptual approach used in the book to analyze processes and events is interdisciplinary but based on socio-political psychology. Without a doubt, there are additional approaches which could explain the events in another way. The book's approach has been developed by me for more than 40 years and has been widely accepted by researchers of conflicts throughout the world. This conceptualization enables a comprehensive, all-encompassing, methodical and causative view on the macro level for every society involved in a violent intractable conflict which has lasted more than a generation (25 years), such as Jewish society in Israel. This approach serves as a lens through which anyone may examine the information and interpret it. Nevertheless, I have made every effort not to be captive to its precepts and have also made use of additional ways of thinking from other disciplines to assist in analyzing Jewish society. Thus, the present book uses conceptualizations and research findings from political science, sociology, cultural studies, communications, and education.

It is obvious that the book has been written from a certain perspective and that no small number of Jewish readers will consider the contents of the book as one sided in its critical approach. Of course, there is academic research that illuminates all the developments that have been described in a positive light. However, in contrast, some may maintain that this approach ignores events and developments which are presently perceived as making positive contributions to the state and to society. Indeed, it is true that there are positive occurrences and developments, and they have been described by many writers, especially supporters of the present and past regimes. However, even in the context of at least some of these events, in my opinion, the public does not really know all the details—among them, a comprehensive account of the Camp David Conference of 2000 or the disengagement from Gaza in 2005—and they accept descriptions and interpretations provided by political leaders and most of the media in their wake, who make every effort to construct a certain mindset among the Jewish-Israeli public. These processes also take place in other states involved in lasting violent conflicts.

Nevertheless, the book is about the Israeli Jewish story—the story we have been told, and that most Jews accept and internalize. This is the story that we assimilate in kindergarten and continue to nurture in school, in the military, and in most of the media. This story shapes us, explains the past and present to us, and offers a deceptive vision for the future. It satisfies the basic needs of a people involved in a bloody conflict who do not understand that another story can be told that will satisfy the same needs, like the Protestants, French, or Basques who resolved their conflicts peacefully. We did the same when we signed a peace agreement with Egypt. Instead of *"better Sharm el-Sheikh without peace than peace without Sharm el-Sheikh"* as Moshe Dayan had proclaimed, we realized over time that it is better to have peace with Egypt that guarantees our security, rather than continuing to occupy Sharm el-Sheikh. Moshe Dayan also changed his mind and understood that the conflict with Egypt was senseless.

This story is also told by the Israeli government to many friendly governments, organizations, and citizens of the world. Some of them do not evaluate or examine the story told to them and thus their understanding remains a one-sided presentation that obscures many facts, processes, and events. The sad reality is that in Israel and other parts of the world, anyone who dares to tell a different story is subject to sanctions. Those who offer another way to see reality or point out the injustices done are sometimes punished, or silence themselves and choose to give in and to give up.

The education system in Israel, for the most part, sets clear rules about what is allowed to be said and what is forbidden, and in so doing, it sins against the basic educational goals of openness and criticism. More than a few artists, filmmakers, writers, visual artists, journalists, and opinion makers present critical views to the people, but instead of causing an earthquake, their voices dissolve without leaving a mark. And so, the plane continues to dive.

The book describes, explains, and analyzes the blindness suffered by most of the people. The reality that Isaiah Leibowitz described over half a century ago is coming to pass as a prophecy of wrath. It takes courage and clear vision or perhaps the innocence of a child to shout, "the king has no clothes," to fight for sanity while stepping out of the comfort zone. This is possible and important for future generations who will have to pay for their parents' blindness.

Another issue which may trouble some readers is that the main contribution of the Palestinians to the failure of the peace process has been disregarded as, in the Israeli opinion, the Palestinians bear all of the responsibility for the development of the conflict and its continuation. In the book, there is no attempt to acquit the Palestinians for their part in the conflict or for their contribution to its persistence. And the Palestinians have made a contribution! The Palestinian worldview is quite similar to that of Jewish society, and actually presents an inverted symmetrical mirror image to theirs.

In Israel, there is an abundance of material documenting the contribution of the Palestinians to the fueling of the conflict. The government and other bodies have publicized a large quantity of material and have made sure that it will affect public consciousness among Jews and be disseminated in the international community. The picture is much more complicated than placing the blame on one side alone, and therefore, it is very important to open the eyes of people to information which is less readily available. Unless we take a sober look at the situation, we will continue to drown in the mud of the conflict.

The book focuses on Jewish society in Israel, since the Israeli-Arab conflict, and especially the conflict with the Palestinians, is of great interest as a typical case of intractable conflict; in addition, as an Israeli Jew, I have experienced its effects throughout my life and have even taken an active part in it. I follow its developments with great interest as it affects the very core of my existence and influences me, as well as all Israeli society, which remains an integral part of my identity and the object of my loyalty. Moreover, a great part of my academic career has been devoted to investigating bloody and long-lasting conflicts around the world, and especially, to the investigation of Jewish society in Israel. For more than 40 years, I have accumulated a large amount of information and have collected much data about the Israeli-Palestinian conflict. I believe that this is a clearly asymmetric conflict with great advantage to the Jewish side, considering its large army, as well as its clearly striking economic and technological advantage, and the unequivocal support of a superpower—the United States. Moreover, the Palestinian nation is living under Israeli occupation. Let us clarify, in that context, that even those who are convinced of their right to the actual land and thus, do not consider that it is occupied, cannot deny that the people living on it—the Palestinians—are under an occupation. Finally, Israel has greater possibilities to manage the conflict and the possibility of ending it. Thus, the focus on Jewish society is not surprising as understanding psychological-social processes aids in understanding the realities of the conflict at present. Of course, just as I examine the psychological-social-political dynamics of Jewish society in Israel, it would be similarly possible to examine Palestinian society, and there are already initial studies in that direction that use the conceptual framework presented in this book. There are parallel processes in the two societies which, as noted, often constitute a kind of mirror image. In both societies, the same psychological and social mechanisms operate which maintain the conflict. Furthermore, this book should be seen as an analysis not only of the Jewish-Israeli case, but also as an example of other cases which are occurring in other parts of the world.

The book addresses the reader who is willing to receive information about developments existing in Jewish society in Israel that are not obvious. A critical look demands not only exposure to new material but also to fresh thinking and ideas, to the accumulation of additional information and its examination, and finally, to drawing new conclusions. I certainly do not want the material presented in the book to be accepted as indisputable evidence, but rather as information to be carefully examined. Exposure to new information and the understanding of a different point of view do not necessarily lead to agreement with the arguments. The reader has every right not to agree with the arguments raised. It is important to remember that in no argument will both sides be right (at least in their own eyes); otherwise, the argument would end very quickly. The book presents fundamental research questions about the reasons for the existence of intractable conflicts, their processes and consequences. The reader must judge whether the book answers these questions with accepted and valid scientific tools and whether the analysis offers appropriate responses.

The analytical tools of the social sciences and the humanities enable approaches from different viewpoints about social phenomena, and that is an advantage. Otherwise, we would accept the same analyses again and again. Research studies dealing with diverse views of a phenomenon illuminate it with a variety of viewpoints and thus contribute to an intellectual challenge, enabling people to understand what is happening in their own society. In addition, they assist in comprehending processes and developments in other societies in the world. There is no doubt that this book represents both the knowledge that I have accumulated in my lifetime, the experiences I have gained and the principles and values I have been educated by and which I have internalized. These have determined the choice of my research questions. This is the way scientists throughout the world operate because there is no other way to conduct scientific investigation.

The first two chapters of the book present the background of the conflict development from the time the state was established, but with a focus on conflict developments from the early twenty-first century as, in my view, this was a turning point from a psychological-social standpoint which affected everything that happened later. During this period, a significant retreat from support for a peace process took place among the Jewish public. The psychological-social repertoire among Israeli Jews stabilized, after having experienced a dramatic change in the wake of events which took place in the early 2000s: the failure of the Camp David Conference, the eruption of the second intifada with its episodes of horrific violence and especially in view of the framing of these events by Israeli leaders. This, to a great extent, still dictates Jewish public opinion about the conflict, influences their choice of leadership, and of course, affects the conduct of the conflict. Although during the 1990s it had appeared that the conflict might be solved peacefully, the negotiations conducted in those years did not lead to the wished-for results. Moreover, the failure of negotiations conducted intensively by U.S. Secretary of State John Kerry during 2013-

2014 led to a renewal of violent clashes. The return of Netanyahu in 2022 to rule with the extreme right-religious coalition is the closing chapter of openness and the new stage of the occupation and conflict. At present I understand that, thanks to a series of internal and external circumstances, the early 1990s provided a window of opportunity that has been closed for the time being.

To a certain extent, this book is a continuation of my book *Living with the Conflict*, written in Hebrew and published in 2007. In that book, the psychological-social foundations for an analysis of Jewish society in Israel were set out. In addition, in 2013, Cambridge University Press published my book *Intractable Conflicts: Socio-Psychological Foundations and Dynamics* in English. The book clarifies many of the processes that take place in intractable conflicts, in general, in many different societies.

The present book contains an in-depth analysis of the radicalization of Israeli society in all its institutions and networks, coming on the heels of its former moderation. It has been updated to November 2022. The question of what caused this change has gnawed at me and the book presents an analysis of how this radicalization occurred. The book is based on a Hebrew version entitled *"Comfort Zone of a Society in Conflict"* co-authored with my friend and colleague, Amiram Raviv. The present English version has been significantly expanded conceptually, updated and adapted to readers from the international community.

The book does not offer an optimistic view—perhaps due to my sobriety, knowing how difficult it is to make a societal change, unfreezing well anchored system of beliefs and adopting a new socio-psychological repertoire that supports peacemaking. The present leadership in Israel has gained support for its policies regarding the conflict from most of the Jewish public and there is no meaningful opposition to offer a clear alternative. At this time, there is not even a leader like De Gaulle or Begin on the horizon, who might securely move the nation into a peace process. Nevertheless, I know that it is possible as a number of cases of intractable conflicts eventually embarked on the path to negotiations and have settled their conflict peacefully.

It is difficult to predict how the Israeli-Palestinian conflict will develop in the coming years. There might always be unexpected surprises. Those who aspire to reach a peace agreement with the Palestinians must be prepared for a long period of struggle for the future of Israel, even involving the coming generations. Under present conditions, the path must be paved with the courage to stand up to forces who react with methodical delegitimization of all who choose this path. Only with the assistance of a convincing narrative as to the justness of the path to peace with determination and persistence, can the political direction of Israel be changed. This has taken place in Northern Ireland, in Spain, while coping with the Basque conflict, or in France following the Algerian war. I still believe that the day will come, perhaps after much more bloodshed and other heavy costs which are paid and will be paid by both societies, when the Israeli-Palestinian conflict achieves a solution, and the hoped-for peace will reach our region.

Finally, I would like to note two factors that greatly influenced my life including my professional career. The first is my mother (we call her Zosia), who was responsible for my intellectual upbringing, with complex and critical thinking and open-mindedness. It was she who encouraged me to read numerous works of classical literature during my childhood, adolescence, and early adulthood. It was she who discussed with me various ideas and the books that I read or plays and films that I saw. It was she who implanted in me the liberal values of unconditional acceptance of the other, freedom of expression, and justice. These values have served as a beacon for my personal life and my academic career.

In addition, as the second factor—she was one of nine siblings. But except for her sister and this sister's daughter, who survived the Holocaust hell in Warsaw, the entire family perished in Treblinka. Thus, from my early years I acquired the command of "never again" that characterizes Israeli society. But here the similarity ends to some extent. The State of Israel has mostly adopted the particularistic lesson, saying that Jews must be powerful militarily and exercise their right to defend themselves even without considering the views of the international community. My understanding of "never again" mainly touches upon the conditions that raised the Nazi regime to power and then enabled the regime to carry out the Holocaust. In my view, it is vital to struggle unconditionally against racism, xenophobia, chauvinism, fascism, and militarism. This struggle is essential if civilization, including the Jews, wants to prevent additional genocide, ethnic cleansing, or wide-ranging violations of human rights.

This is the place to thank the Walter Lebach Institute for Jewish-Arab Coexistence at Tel Aviv University for the grant that has enabled publication of the Hebrew version of the book. Ido Oren greatly helped us in gathering information about the costs to Jewish society. Shaul Arieli, Akiva Eldar, and Yehuda Shaul helped in fact checking information about the settlement project. Importantly, all emphasized material throughout the book is my attempt to call attention to the importance of the specific texts.

Daniel Bar-Tal

International Intractable Conflicts: The Turkish-Kurdish Case

On a Tuesday noon, 20 July 2015, a suicide terrorist blew himself up outside the Amara Culture Center in Suruç, Turkey, near the Syrian border. The blast killed 33 people.[1]

At that very moment, a press conference was taking place at the center, held by the Socialist Youth Federations Association (SGDF). Its activists, an alliance of young Turks and Kurds, were presenting a plan to rebuild the Kurdish town of Kobanî on the other side of the Syrian border, a town which had been seriously damaged by the Islamic State of Iraq and the Levant (ISIIL—also known as ISIS) during the Syrian civil war. The youths were planning to cross the border after the meeting and begin the rebuilding.

The blast ended their plans.

This was only one of many violent attacks in the wake of the Syrian civil war, but its ramifications were unusual. The Kurdistan Workers' Party (PKK), which at that time had been involved in complex negotiations with the Turkish government to resolve the demands of the Kurdish minority in Turkey, blamed the Turkish government for cooperation with the terrorists of the Islamic State in planning the attack. Two days later, activists of the PKK murdered two Turkish policemen in the Urfa district of Turkey while they were sleeping, and the bloodshed between the resistance and the government began again. In retaliation, the Turkish air force attacked Kurdish bases and towns in Iraq and killed many civilians. The temporary cease-fire that had been achieved two years earlier collapsed. Violent encounters between the Turkish army and the Kurdish militias in the southeast of the country resumed in all their ferocity.

The conflict re-escalated and the violence had returned.

The dispute between Turkey and the Kurdish minority has persisted for more than 40 years. It revolves around the Kurdish demand to achieve autonomy, granting them political and cultural expression in areas where they are a majority. Turkey, in contrast, refuses to recognize their national

1

aspirations, fearing a spread to other minorities in the state. In 1984, the conflict took a more violent turn when the military arm of the PKK for the first time attacked Turkish army units in the southeast of the country—the most disputed area. Since then, the two sides have been engaged in bloody conflict, while from time to time there is an attempt to reach a peace agreement.

In 2013, it seemed that the violence had finally reached its end. In discussions between the sides, the PKK agreed to hold their fire and to withdraw their forces from Turkey to Iraq. In return, Turkey was supposed to advance constitutional and legal changes towards the recognition of human rights of the Kurds. A wave of optimism hung in the air. But the attack in the border town of Suruç and the chain of events in its wake brought the talks to an end.

As great as expectations had been during the talks, such was the force of the violence that followed their collapse. For the first time, the fighting trickled into neighboring Syria. As this part is being written, more than 30,000 Kurds and 14,000 Turks have died as a result of the dispute. Four thousand villages have been destroyed and three million people have been forced to leave their homes—about 10% of them, as a result of violent expulsion. Up to the present, in economic terms, according to estimates, the cost of the conflict can be calculated as reaching an approximate 150-300 billion dollars for the Turkish side and about 30 billion dollars for the Kurds.[2]

WHY DO CONFLICTS CONTINUE?

These shocking figures, along with the development of the almost arbitrary events that led to the collapse of the talks in 2015, raise an important question: **Why, in fact, aren't conflicts like this brought to a peaceful solution? This question is brought even more sharply into focus when considering the heavy price paid by the societies which conduct the conflicts.** The question is also relevant to other violent conflicts which have lasted for many years, and which are still festering around the world: between Muslims and Hindus in Kashmir, between Sinhalese and Tamils in Sri-Lanka, between Greeks and Turks in Cyprus, between Russians and Chechens in Chechnya, and of course, between Jews and Palestinians in Israel. As in the Turkish story, in some of these instances, the conflict has greatly escalated precisely after the two sides have together formulated a possible solution. In total, in 2019, there were about 54 state-based violent conflicts and about 67 non-state violent conflicts worldwide, according to data on disputes from the Uppsala Conflict Data Program (UCDP) in Sweden. Also, in 2019 alone, about 76,500 people were killed in these conflicts, the great majority in Afghanistan (about 40%). This number indicates a significant decrease in fatalities after the defeat of the Islamic State. Between 1989 and 2019, 2.5 million people were killed in violent conflicts. Rwanda led other states with about 515,793 fatalities during the largest genocide since the Second World War.[3]

In social-psychological terminology, some of the violent and protracted disputes are called "intractable conflicts"[4] and they have a number of fundamental characteristics. They are extremely violent, including loss of both life and property. They revolve around goals that are considered existential for both societies—that is, essential for their physical survival, and thus there is no room for compromise about them. Huge resources are invested in their conduct—both material and non-material—in order not to lose. They continue for at least one generation (25 years), being viewed as unsolvable. And finally, they serve as an important component of the collective identity of the involved societies, and even play a major role in the personal lives of individuals in these societies. These conflicts are termed intractable as members of the involved societies feel that they have no control over their peaceful resolution, and they see no prospect of peace. In contrast, conflicts that are under control are not violent; the two sides make every effort to keep them on a low flame and to solve them quickly via negotiation. The sides moderate public opinion and express the desire to compromise. These disputes do not usually continue for a long period of time and there is no great investment in them. These are the two extremes of the intractable-tractable dimension in evaluating conflicts.

In the study of international conflicts, the Israeli-Palestinian conflict is considered the prototype of an intractable conflict: It perfectly reflects all the necessary criteria. In this book, I will try to explain why it has not been resolved peacefully despite the heavy price demanded from both participating societies.[5] More specifically, the question that should be asked is why Jewish society makes such a significant contribution to the continuation of the conflict, which has escalated in recent years. In addition, it is important to clarify what kinds of societal processes and consequences exist as a result of the continuation of the conflict.

But before beginning the analyses, it must be pointed out, as a side note, that at times the dispute has also been referred to as the Israel-Arab conflict, relating to a wider confrontation, and including not only Israel and the Palestinians, but also a number of additional Arab states. However, despite the dominance of that battlefront between the end of the 1940s and the end of the 1970s, since the signing of the peace treaty with Egypt, the core of the conflict has involved relations between the Israeli-Jewish population and the Palestinian population. In addition, this is the front which has, for decades, been the focus of internal Israeli attention, as well as the center of attention in the international community.

In order to answer the fundamental questions, I will concentrate on the socio-psychological aspect of the Israeli-Palestinian conflict, which proposes an approach focusing on the development of a conflict culture, while analyzing the dynamics generally characteristic of intractable conflicts. **The basic premise regarding such conflicts maintains that, although they have been created as a result of actual events that every member of the group has experienced, in reality, they have continued—and they are still continuing—also on the basis of ideas that have been formulated in people's minds.**[6] Thus, the answer to the question above must be sought also in the psychological repertoire held by members of the involved societies. This baggage is composed of beliefs, attitudes, and feelings, and is organized into narratives that describe, interpret, and explain the conflict. The narratives, for example, outline what the conflict is about; they describe how the conflict broke out; they explain why it is continuing by positioning actual events in a wider historical context; and then explain why no resolution is possible. In a long process, this repertoire and its narratives turn into pillars of conflict culture that become hegemonic in many societies. But additional questions of no less importance seek to understand how these narratives were formed, imparted, and institutionalized.

In simple language, these narratives supply all the reasons and logical bases for continuing the conflict. Thus, in disciplinary terminology, these are called "conflict supporting beliefs." Their institutional foundations, some of which date to even before the conflict broke out, involve the sense among the group members that they have suffered deprivation. At the next stage, the sense of deprivation is attributed to the other, rival society and this intensifies the conflict for as long as it exists.

Accordingly, long-lasting conflicts are resolved when members of society feel at least in a meaningful way that they have received in the conditions of the resolution what they have been deprived of and so the conflict may be ended.

The construction of such narratives is necessary, as human beings tend to consider their own behavior as rational and appropriate to the circumstances. Therefore, these narratives express a sincere attempt by the members of society to organize their experiences and the information flowing to them into a knowledge system (as well as what could be termed a system of beliefs) which fulfills a well-defined role in dealing with reality. In the nature of the process, in time, these narratives become a prism through which society members also interpret the reality of the conflict in all of its complexity. Knowledge that does not fit the narratives is discarded. Alternative knowledge that might dispute the narratives is discredited and even blocked. And because new decisions and choices are made in light of partial and biased information, they reinforce the conflict realities to an even greater extent in a kind of circular feedback. Narratives created on a certain factual basis turn into stories that then create "new facts." Although some stories have a grain of truth, others have no factual basis but are constructed to create a particular reality that serves the course of conflict continuation with the use of violence. In this way, a vicious circle is created.

I do not claim that some of the grievances advanced by groups are not justified or have no moral justification. The world has been full of injustice, beginning with slavery, colonialism, occupation, exploitation, and discrimination. Groups have had to achieve their rights by managing conflicts. Nevertheless, all of them have had to construct narratives to make their case, in order to mobilize supporters. But many of these narratives are presented in a selective, biased and sometimes even distorted form because the major motivation for their construction is the achievement of societal-political goals, even when they are inherently justified. **Well rationalized narratives enable mobilization of society members to participate in a conflict with the readiness to kill and be killed. Intractable conflicts last for years. The side in possession of the commodity (territory, power, status, wealth, or other resources), even when this is immoral according to present international laws or norms, does not yield to the demands of the deprived side and that often leads to use of violence by both sides.**

Viewing reality through the prism of pre-dictated narratives enables society members to live their lives with their own justifying story and without sensing the heavy costs of an intractable conflict. The price is perceived as "part of life," as an unavoidable necessity, because, through the years, a process of routinization has enabled society members to get used to it. In any case, no discussion takes place in public space about how extremely high the price really is, and certainly not whether it is necessary or justified. This all takes place not only while lives are being lost, but also as democracy deteriorates. Violent events are also considered bearable after society members have become accustomed to them through the process of routinization, and thus, they cannot change attitudes, all the more so since they take place at a stable and permanent rate that does not lead to turmoil. The unstable conflict thus becomes the most stable piece of data in social life. This is not surprising, since human beings have always created their own realities for themselves that are the result of their understanding, and then there is not a shadow of uncertainty that this understanding represents the most beneficial or moral reality for themselves.

These are normal processes occurring in every society involved in an intractable violent conflict. They also have clear and unavoidable results. Not only do they fan the flames of the conflict, but the societies involved also pay an intensely heavy price for their involvement. Society members are not even aware of some of these effects. In any case, in every such society, these effects develop in many facets of life because it is impossible to isolate the conflict from everything else that takes place in society. This is especially true when the conflict also includes a long-term occupation and when the occupying population has settled in the occupied territories and establishes a territorial continuum of the occupying nation. **The occupation and the conflict, with its own norms, its deeds, its attitudes, and its values and behavior, penetrate the occupying society and have crucial effects on whatever happens. The occupying society becomes occupied by the occupation.** These effects are principally negative, and they leave their destructive mark on society. I am well aware of this generalization, and view the present book as an in-depth case study which enables us to learn much about what occurs in other societies under similar circumstances. But the argument goes beyond cases of occupation. A violent and lasting conflict takes over the consciousness and soul of the involved society, turning into an addiction to its vicious cycles.

Both people on the Jewish side and on the Palestinian side go through this process, and so both sides contribute to the maintenance of the conflict. However, the contributions are not equal. Israel is much stronger, and in addition, it has the means to achieve a solution. And since Israeli Jewish society is, in my opinion, the main player involved in continuing the conflict—this work will focus on Israel. (For those interested, an analysis of Palestinian society using a similar conceptual framework has recently been made by Ronni Shaked in his Hebrew book, *Behind the Keffiyeh: The Conflict from the Palestinian Perspective*).[7] In the framework of an analysis of Israeli-Jewish society, psychological processes accompanying the conflict which have not been examined up to now through this prism will be described. Not always are these processes visible to the eye: Sometimes prior knowledge is necessary in order to identify them. But pointing them out and examining their ramifications may contribute to a change in viewpoint regarding the conflict, and to the development of a different perspective.

In the coming pages special emphasis will be placed on the internal societal processes which have led to such long-term participation in the conflict. In addition, I will shed light on the often-unnoticed developments that change the nature of a society, its identity, its statehood and its institutions. I will point to the implicit mechanisms which aid in framing media, public and political events in a way that strengthens the conflict, and I will outline the changing perceptions of the conflict in Israeli Jewish society as a result of the outbreak of the Al-Aqsa intifada in September 2000. This uprising marked one of the major turning points in the history of the society and the conflict.

One of the central arguments of this work is that Israeli-Palestinian conflict supporting narratives are the main obstruction to its peaceful resolution.[8] Accordingly, one focus will be on these narratives. I will present their contents, the needs they serve, how they developed, how they were disseminated and acquired, the ways they function in daily life and their effects. We will see how they have penetrated into social institutions, learned by society members, how political forces garner support for them, and which resources are invested to that end. In addition, a second central argument is that the constructions of these narratives, which have become hegemonic in the culture of the conflict, necessarily result in societal processes that change the

structure of society and its identity and penetrate its institutions and organizations. As the third argument, I maintain that the prices paid by Jews in Israel (as well as by societies involved in other intractable conflict) in various realms of life, and especially, the erosion of morality with the deterioration of democracy and the growing authoritarian elements arising from the conflict and the occupation, have been unavoidable and were already "written on the wall" in the Israeli case in 1967. Finally, I argue that Jewish society feels comfortable with the reality that has been created and fears to change it.

These are general arguments that may be verified in every violent intractable conflict. But when the conflict includes an occupation, in which the occupying power settles in the occupied territories, and there is powerful asymmetry between the occupiers and the occupied, all these arguments have even much greater validity. Nevertheless, it is important to remember that there is always someone who benefits from the penetration of these narratives into the blood vessels of society and from the continuing conflict. For them, it is worth its weight in gold, in status, and in maintaining a coherent view of the world. But for progress towards peace, the conflict supporting narrative must be shattered.

This is surely not an easy task, and in order to succeed, we should remember Egyptian President Anwar Sadat who saw through the conflict supporting narratives and recognized that the psychological barriers are what prevented a peace process between his country and Israel. And this is what he said in his historic speech at the Knesset on 20 November 1977, relating to the factors that prevent societies involved in conflict to reach an agreement:

> ...Yet there remained another wall. This wall constitutes a psychological barrier between us. A barrier of suspicion. A barrier of rejection. A barrier of fear of deception. A barrier of hallucinations around any action, deed or decision. A barrier of cautious and erroneous interpretations of all and every event or statement. It is this psychological barrier which I described in official statements as representing 70 percent of the whole problem. Today, through my visit to you, I ask you: Why don't we stretch our hands with faith and sincerity so that, together, we might destroy this barrier? Why shouldn't ours and yours meet with faith and sincerity, so that togeth-

er we might remove all suspicion of fear, betrayal and ill intentions? Why don't we stand together with the bravery of men and the boldness of heroes who dedicate themselves to a sublime objective? Why don't we stand together with the same courage and boldness to erect a huge edifice of peace that builds and does not destroy? An edifice that is a beacon for generations to come—the human message for construction, development and the dignity of man? Why should we bequeath to the coming generations the plight of bloodshed, death, orphans, widowhood, family disintegration, and the wailing of victims?

And we add our own question: Yes, why should we?

In order to answer that question, the next chapter will begin with a brief description of the Jewish-Arab conflict, and in particular, the Israeli-Palestinian dispute, and I will then present and analyze the theoretical framework.

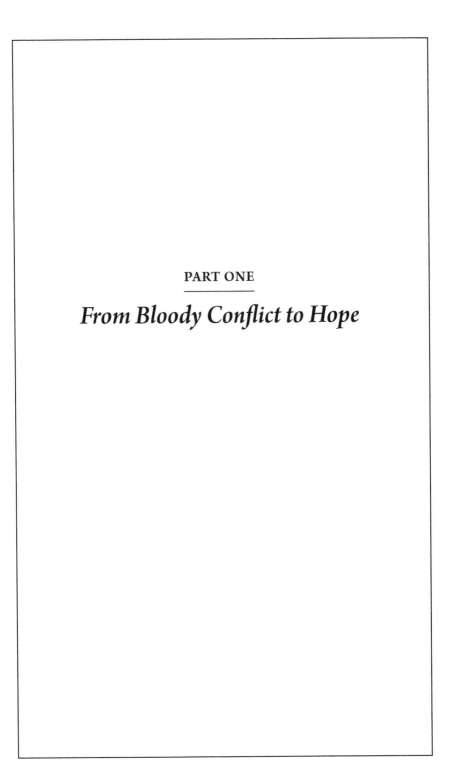

PART ONE

From Bloody Conflict to Hope

CHAPTER 1

An Intractable Conflict

THE SOURCES OF THE CONFLICT: A BRIEF SUMMARY

The Jewish-Arab conflict, the archetype of the Israeli-Palestinian dispute, began at the end of the nineteenth century, with the new waves of Jewish settlement in Palestine, which was then under the control of the Ottoman Empire. At the time, the Jews were a very small minority among an Arab majority —in 1880, before the project began, there were about 27,000–30,000 Jews, making up about four to six percent of the general population living in Palestine. The roots of the conflict were implanted in the conflicting aspirations of these two populations.

The Jews came to Palestine from 1882 under the auspices of the Zionist Movement—a national movement believing that the Jewish nation could only continue to exist if masses of Jews returned to their ancient homeland, establishing a national state within its borders and realizing their legitimate aspirations for national recognition. To that end, the Zionist Movement advocated immigration to the "land of Israel," and its settlement. However, the ancient homeland of the Jews had already been settled by an Arab population who were also developing national aspirations at more or less the same time, and they too wanted to realize those aspirations in the same territory.[9] We can see then that, as in all human conflict, this one began in the heads of the few who formed and disseminated their ideas.

The Arabs wanted to defend their status as inhabitants with rights and as having possession of the land, and simultaneously, to maintain its Arab and Muslim character. In contrast, the Jews wanted to change existing conditions by purchasing land and settling on it in an attempt to transform the land despite its Arab population, and ultimately, to create the Jewish homeland. In that context, it is interesting to note the relatively early observations by Nagib Azoury, a Maronite Christian who served as an official of the Ottoman Empire in Jerusalem and who was affected by the Arab national spirit. In his 1905 book, *Le Réveil de la Nation Arabe* (The Awakening of the Arab Nation), considered one of the first expressions of pan-Arabism, a movement calling for unification of all Arab nations, Azoury wrote:

> *Two important phenomena—of the same nature but op-posed—are emerging at this moment in Asiatic Turkey. They are the awakening of the Arab Nation and the latent effort by Jews to reconstitute on a very large scale the ancient Kingdom of Israel. These two movements are destined to confront each other continually until one of them prevails over the other. The final outcome of this struggle, between two peoples that represent two contradictory principles, may shape the destiny of the whole world.*[10]

Two Conflicting Foundations

Azoury's words were prophetic, as the dispute between the Jews and the Palestinians has continued to smolder with great intensity up to the present. The conflict has obvious other foundations. It does not only revolve around political, economic or territorial issues but, from the beginning, it has also involved religion and cultural differences. **Based on such great gaps in aspirations, the two sides quickly developed ethnocentric and sectarian mindsets regarding their common existence in mandatory Palestine and later in the state of Israel.**

At the beginning of the Jewish Zionist waves of immigration to Ottoman Palestine in 1882-3, there were about 40,000 Jews (about half were orthodox and anti-Zionist) and about 450,000 Arabs. In 1917, the land was conquered by the British in World War I from the Ottoman Empire, and in 1920 Britain was assigned to administer the territory by the League of Nations. On November 2, 1917, the British issued a public statement announcing support for the establishment of a "national home for the Jewish people" in Palestine. The first British population census in 1922 indicated that there were about 84,000 Jews and about 750,000 Arabs. Years later, on 29 November 1947, the General Assembly of the United Nations decided to end the British Mandate in Palestine and to establish two independent states—a Jewish state and an Arab state. According to the plan, Jerusalem and its environs would be under international supervision. The partition plan gave the Jews, who were then 33% (about 650,000) of the total population, a state that included 56% of the territory of Mandatory Palestine, while the Arabs, who were 67% (about 1,350,000) of the population, received 43% of the territory.[11]

Almost all of the Arab leaders rejected the proposal and immediately began violent attacks against the Jewish population. The Declaration of Independence of the State of Israel in May 1948 led to an invasion of Arab state armies into Israeli territory. The war had begun. It ended with a striking Israeli victory, which led to another 22% of the Palestinian territory being annexed, which, according to the partition plan, should have been under Arab control. In addition, during the war, approximately 700,000 Palestinians fled or were expelled and became refugees.[12]

With the outbreak of the War of Independence in November 1947 and the establishment of the State of Israel in May 1948, the Jewish-Palestinian conflict, which had begun as a violent struggle between communities, became an international dispute. As time went on, it even expanded: Participants included many of the regional countries, various international organizations, and even the superpowers. In the following two decades, the conflict—now known as the Israeli-Palestinian conflict—became a major topic of international discussion and of media coverage.

From the establishment of the state and until the mid-1970s, the Israeli-Palestinian dispute retained all the characteristics of an intractable conflict. This was the context in which both societies lived. The conflict was violent and central to the lives of the two involved societies. It was long-lasting and required enormous resources. In addition, with socio-psychological foundations, it was considered unsolvable and revolved around aims that both of the sides perceived as vital to their very existence: These aims focused on questions of the right of the Jewish nation to self-determination, its return to its homeland, the establishment of the Jewish state and in addition, national-cultural-religious control of the space. **When aims like these are considered existential, there is no room for compromises—not even the smallest and most inconsequential concession. Both sides constructed supporting narratives, froze with them and even were digging in their positions. Thus, these worldviews led to the disregard of the needs of the other, to the negation of the identity and narrative of the opponents, and to systematic efforts to delegitimize them. Every concession was perceived as a loss for the conceding side, as in a zero-sum game.** The Arabs absolutely rejected the right of the Jews to self-determination and to an independent state, and even refused to recognize the historical connection of the Jews to their homeland. Contrastingly, in Israel, the perception took hold that the aim of the Arabs was the complete eradication of the Jews, as a kind of continuing version of the Holocaust. And in such a situation of "we or they," the Jews in Israel believed that they had to ensure their existence even if it meant the use of violence, as even one defeat could lead to the destruction of the state.

The dominant feeling on each side was one of "sole legitimacy"—an attitude that views legitimacy as a resource that cannot be shared or divided. It was everything or nothing. The Arabs related to themselves as having the right of "precedence" over the land and thus, viewed the Jews who had arrived as immigrants, or even more severely, as invaders and colonialists. The Jews, in contrast, related to the land as a legacy promised to them by God in the Bible, as their historical-cultural homeland, and as a place of refuge considering the dangers that the Jewish nation had faced and were still facing. They did not recognize the unique national identity of the Palestinians and considered them as part of a larger Arab nation, having the rights to many states and thus, lacking legitimate roots in the country, and as "tenants" on land belonging to the Jews.

Under these conditions, during the early years of the state and later, the solution to the conflict appeared even farther away. All attempts to settle the dispute by peaceful means—and there were such attempts—failed.[13] **The minimum demands on the Palestinian side were greater than the maximum concessions that the Israeli side was willing to make.** Israel, which, at the end of the war in 1948, controlled more land than what had been offered in the Partition Plan and retained a relatively small Arab population under its sovereignty, did not see any reason to change the existing situation. That would have meant withdrawing from the conquered territories and/or bringing back the hundreds of thousands of the Palestinians refugees who had fled during the war. This was considered all the more impossible to the Israeli government considering the Arab hostility and hatred directed towards Israel by both the Arab states and the Palestinians. These negative feelings became even more intense following the Six-Day War, the results of which made the conflict clearly asymmetric: Israel now had an obvious advantage militarily, politically, technologically, and economically, and it held sole domination over all of the assets demanded by the Palestinians—land for a state, national self-determination, political rights, control, and resources. **The combination of aims considered existential, asymmetric power relations and the absence of possibilities for achieving peace led the sides to entrench themselves in their positions and even to justify the use of violence with a good reason to "die for the homeland."**

In actuality, the conflict had been violent almost from the beginning. During the early pre-state years, violence by the Arab side was expressed in economic boycott, demonstrations, strikes, and physical harming of Jews. Later wars broke out, but even the intervening periods were characterized by violent events, such as shelling and bombing from the air, infiltration by hostile forces, terror attacks and more. As a result, many fighters were injured and killed, but in addition, no small number of civilians lost their lives. The political-social-economic systems supplied both sides with reasons and justifications for violence. At the peaks of the conflict, the two sides mobilized all possible resources, both internal and externally from supporting states, aiming to win the conflict. Both sides invested enormous amounts of money in developing and purchasing armaments and ammunition of various types, and even greater investment in educating and preparing wide swaths of the population to participate in the fighting.

The conflict, in all its features, has had significant effects on the lives of all citizens involved, and still does. And not only in the physical sense. From the establishment of the state of Israel and up to the present, the conflict has been a decisive factor in political, military, industrial, economic, social, and educational decision making and has even left its cultural mark. Media discourse covers the conflict on a daily basis, and this often overshadows other topics competing for public attention. The conflict is also a crucial topic in almost every election campaign in Israel and to a great extent, it determines electoral voting trends. It motivates the activities of political parties and other political frameworks and is a critical factor in forming coalitions, and party unifications or splits. Moreover, the conflict is taught in the educational system and is also expressed in all cultural products, as some artists have positioned it at the center of their works. It unceasingly affects the personal worlds of society members, and even their relationships with their close surroundings. There have often been well-known cases in which two family members have stopped speaking to each other because of their differing attitudes toward the essence of the conflict and how it best should be solved.

THE SOCIAL-PSYCHOLOGICAL APPROACH

It is true that the conflict relates to concrete demands by the involved sides and refers to real experiences. However, most of its features and beliefs that have been mentioned and will be further discussed, are based on psychological perceptions, beliefs and attitudes. And that

is a key point. In many senses—it is clearly true that "much is created and exists in one's head." In the book, I use the psychological term "belief"[14] (a basic unit) as referring to a claim that is created in people's thought processes. (Some psychologists call "belief" a cognition or even a schema.) All in all, these assertions represent the total knowledge accumulated by an individual. Some beliefs, called societal beliefs, are shared by people in the same society or group and they characterize the group. They enable a shared view among society members, making it possible for them to communicate, and these beliefs even guide their collective behavior.[15]

It should be stressed that the violent events taking place, the intentions of the players when these are publicly expressed, and the clear attempts which have been made to solve the conflict—all of these are solid data. They serve as a context for the development of the socio-psychological repertoire. But the **interpretation** of the data, the attribution of intentions which are not expressed openly by the players, **their appraisal of conflict attributes, constructing their positions and drawing conclusions—as, for example, the attitude that goals at the basis of the conflict are existential, the view that the conflict cannot be solved, or understanding it as a zero-sum game—these are all learned and inferred subjectively on the basis of the context.** Members of Israeli society are divided in all of these results of psychological activity and even senior army officers who have been working together in the same context for many years are divided in their opinions about the conflict.

Moreover, people are not born with these perceptions, beliefs, and attitudes. They are constructed based on the knowledge society members acquire through the years, the ideologies they hold, the images and stereotypes they adopt and the information constantly flowing to them, shedding light on reality, but with certain emphases. In many cases, it is not possible to establish the measure of "veracity" of these perceptions, as they often express value judgments rather than objective evaluations of reality. But from the moment that these perceptions are experienced as reflecting reality—they become an accurate picture of reality for the people who hold them. And they react according to them. This does not occur only on the basis of concrete experiences (personal and collective), but it is also—and primarily—dependent on education, learning and socialization, as well as exposure to the media, to public opinion and to the political system, and especially to political and military leaders, as a recent study has unequivocally shown.[16] This psychological postulation does not negate the effects on perceptions of events and situations which actually do occur. There is no doubt that the clearer and more striking the actual reality is and the wider the agreement about it, the more equivocal material it provides for perception and evaluation. So, for example, no one doubts the fact that on the 6 October 1973, the Yom Kippur War broke out and Israel was in real danger. However, the more the event falls into the area of societal judgment, which is ambiguous by nature, the greater the disagreement about the event and how it is evaluated. This is so because psychologists have well established that social judgements are often biased and even distortive. The story upon which the classic film Rashomon is based clearly showed that, when being evaluated, even actual events are subject to people's attitudes, motives and values.

The entire range of perceptions, beliefs, attitudes, values, motives and even feelings which connect individuals to their society is part of the so-called *socio-psychological repertoire*. And as we will see, the specific way it has evolved in Israel has had a dramatic effect on the development of the conflict.

How to Deal with the Challenges Posed by the Conflict?

The conditions of the Israeli-Arab/Palestinian conflict that have been described here do not enable individuals to live a normal way of life, as they do in states like the Netherlands or Australia where, when one hears the sound of firing, it is "only the king's birthday." The continuing violence teeming around us leads to a sense of threat, bereavement, pain, insecurity, stress, fear, anger, sorrow, exhaustion, difficulty and misery, as in other intractable bloody conflicts. Of course, these feelings are personal; they differ from one person to another and change from one period to the next. Feelings during the battles of the Yom Kippur War were not similar to those of experienced during the War in Lebanon in 1982. **Nevertheless, Jewish society in Israel may be characterized as living under constant threat which results in chronic fear and anxiety. And there are those who maintain that we live in constant chronic trauma.**[17]

Thus, the reality of the conflict in Israel leads to deprivation of basic needs. This is especially true when relating to insecurity and feelings of fear, in addition to the sense of ambiguousness and uncertainty, and the impossibility of even anticipating what will occur in the near future. In this situation, people must find a way of satisfying their deprived needs. Their deprivation impairs human functioning. For example, an Israeli cannot know where danger is lurking as the possibilities are so numerous and so diverse: indiscriminate shooting in population centers, terror attacks, firing of rockets and in extreme cases, even war. These dangers do not overlook any citizen, nor do they pass over children. Although only in a few cases is there direct physical injury to a member of Jewish society, studies indicate that the very exposure to the violence of the conflict, even if it is "only" on the television screen, affects emotional and physical welfare.[18]

These evils may be accompanied by harm to the positive collective image. First, as in every violent dispute, in the framework of the Israeli-Palestinian conflict, immoral actions may be carried out by Jews, including real injustices, and these do harm to the self-perception of Jewish society members as being moral and humane. Second, and this seems to be the most common case in recent years, even harm suffered by Jewish society could damage its collective positive image, expressed in feelings of helplessness and as an injury to national honor. In both cases there is firm evidence indicating that mental health among Israelis has been deteriorating as a result of these experiences.[19]

Jewish society in Israel, like all societies involved in intractable violent conflicts, must therefore deal with the challenges they face due to conflict conditions. And in order to continue to function as normally as possible, the complex and unclear realities must be invigorated with a sense of meaning and security, strengthening self-confidence and feelings of pride. In addition, a life of constant stress demands fostering strength and resilience—both to prepare for whatever is to come and to cope with present psychological wounds. Finally, on the most practical level, society must mobilize its young Jewish members to participate actively in the conflict, and even to internally develop the willingness to make the ultimate sacrifice of all—their lives and the lives of their children—in order to meet the goals that society has defined for itself. In other words, for as long as the conflict goes on, Israeli society is challenged to be victorious in the continuing violence or at least, not to lose, in any of the frequent confrontations, in order not to lower their level of deterrence and retribution. These are clearly not simple missions.

There are various ways to cope with the challenges and of course, great amounts of resources are required, if only to arm the troops who take an active part in the fighting, or to effectively train and prepare the military units; but this book will focus on the ***psychological measures*** that an intractable conflict demands from society in order to cope with the long-lasting violence: what these measures are; how they are developed; what needs they fulfill; how they function and what the results are.

The Development of a Socio-psychological Repertoire

Thus, one of the central arguments is: in order to meet these challenges, Jewish society—like every society engaged in a difficult and violent conflict—has developed a socio-psychological repertoire conforming to the coping demands. It is composed of a variety of societal beliefs, attitudes, feelings, motives and values, and it fulfills both personal and collective needs. At the basis of the socio-psychological repertoire, there are societal beliefs that, in their entirety tell the complete story (called a narrative), describing contemporary reality with its goals, and portraying the past in order to explain the nature of the conflict—how the conflict began and how it has continued, what we are fighting for and why, who we are, who the enemy is, and what conditions are necessary for us to succeed in this struggle. In fact, we refer to the collective narrative that is shared by society members. It is defined as a social construction that coherently describes, explains and justifies an event or issue based on collective experience. It preoccupies the collective, providing a sequential and causal story that is relevant to the collective agenda, becomes embedded into the societal belief system and often represents collective identity. Finally, it has a function of satisfying the needs of a collective. Narratives can refer to many different subjects, such as specific events, personalities, situations, or even processes. But among them, it is possible to distinguish master narratives that consist of holistic, complete and comprehensive stories that provide a wide-ranging outlook about a group's past, present, or even future.

In our case, as in other societies, these collective narratives pose the goals the conflict is set to achieve and grant them an infrastructure of justifications. They indicate the threats and how to deal with them. They enable the Jews to view themselves as justified, fair, moral, humane, as well as victims and peace seekers. One of the most central of these beliefs, based on negative stereotyping with delegitimizing content, and imbibed by the Jews from early childhood, explains the violence committed by Arabs as resulting from their "inhuman" nature which is permanent and unchanging. At the same time, the narratives also supply an explanation for and legitimization of violence among Jews (giving psychological permission to kill), which is perceived as a preventive measure against the inhumanness of the enemy in the approaching danger.

Indeed, responsibility for the violence is placed completely on the Arab side. And the higher the numbers of Jews who have been killed, the more this serves as tangible evidence in the self-perception of Jews as the victims of the conflict, thus, in turn, justifying the increase in violence that they themselves are committing. In reaction to the great losses suffered by the Jewish side in the conflict, a patriotic belief has also been formed, calling for mobilization and sacrifice, along with the frequent demand for unity and solidarity—both due to the necessity of vanquishing the enemy. In the end, the aspiration for peace is always expressed as an ideal, amorphous, and comprehensive, presenting the Israeli nation as peace-loving.

Added to these narratives is the non-comprehension and complete disregard of the needs and aspirations of the Palestinians, denying their identity and even hurting them physically in different ways. **Indeed, as naturally occurs during protracted and bloody conflicts, perception is binary and over-simplified, one-dimensional, and moralistic, and leads to biases and distortion.** It narrows the range and directs point of view and understanding. It is no wonder that Jews do not make any effort and even refuse to see things from the Palestinian perspective and have not felt the need to put themselves in Palestinian shoes. As a result, they cannot understand why Arabs are not willing to accept Jews as returning to their ancient homeland, why they use violence against Jews, and why they were not ready to make the compromises offered to them during the British Mandate, including the division of the country according to 1947 decision of the UN General Assembly, or why they want all of the land for themselves and even demand that Jews return to their countries of their origin. Instead of pondering these questions, Jews focus on their own aspirations, goals and needs, and the only question they must deal with is how to achieve them.

Conflict-Supporting Narratives: Ethos of Conflict and Collective Memory

The development of the socio-psychological repertoire had already begun during the 1920s and peaked during the end of 1960s. The societal beliefs described here, which were unified into a complete and coherent narrative, formed two central and coherent stories: one refers primarily to the present but also to the future (the ethos), and the second talks about the past (the collective memory). Both evoke strong feelings. In effect, they have provided the conflict supporting narratives, which rationalize and justify the continuation of the bloody struggle against the enemy, without proposing any way to escape from the violence by making any peace that can be considered as fair by the rival.

The first, **the ethos of conflict**, is a kind of ideological story, a master narrative, describing, explaining and interpreting the reality of the conflict systematically, holistically, and comprehensively. It does not refer to specific issues that arise in certain situations but rather constitutes an organized structure of societal beliefs that support an overall view of a general situation of conflict within which society is immersed and outlines future needed steps to continue the conflict. From a functional standpoint, it supplies the narrative that enables society to remain accustomed to a state of violent intractable conflict and makes it possible for society members to withstand its challenges by creating a framework of justifications, explanations and predictions regarding the situation. It enables a common viewpoint for society members, stressing their sense of belonging to Jewish society, and granting a unique character to that society, and thus, it is a central component of the common collective identity of society members.

In addition to the ethos, **a collective memory** of the conflict has been developed in Jewish society, as it has in every society engaged in violent struggle. In this case, it tells the story as a master narrative of the history of the conflict: how it started, why it has continued, what the main milestones have been, and why the conflict does not end. However, it should be noted that there is a difference between popular memory, which is the dominant memory among society members, and official memory, retained by the authorities and institutions of society. These two types of memory can match or contradict each other to one extent or another. In Israeli Jewish society, until the end of the 1970s, these two types were completely identical. Only after the state had been in existence for thirty years did some society members begin to create an opposing collective memory to the one cultivated by state institutions and its leaders. In general, there can be a number of popular collective memories competing each against the other. The collective memories are, by nature, selective and biased, and are not meant to reflect "historical truth," but rather, because they are anchored in a certain political-societal context, their role is to serve society's needs in the present. The socio-psychological repertoire, which is a super-concept that includes both ethos and collective memory narratives, with all their accompanying societal beliefs, always include a range of emotions held by every society involved in violent conflict: fear, anger, and hatred, along with pride in the ability to withstand conflict challenges. All of these emotions developed in Jewish society from the early stages of the conflict.

It is important to note that some of the societal beliefs in the Jewish psychological repertoire have existed in long-standing Jewish tradition. For example, the sense of victimhood has been deeply inherent in Jewish culture, considering Jewish experience throughout history. In addition, Jews bear deeply rooted ethnocentric beliefs tied to the ancient sense of being the "chosen people," and "a light unto the nations." During the formative years of the conflict with the Arabs, the enduring beliefs, those linked to self-perception as victims and the traditional beliefs involving a positive self-image have undergone certain adaptations and have been assimilated into the new collective story. Other beliefs, such as those linked to patriotism or delegitimization of the Arabs have been created and formulated only with the evolvement of the conflict. In the following, we further delve into each of the eight fundamental societal beliefs comprising the Israeli-Jewish socio-psychological repertoire as consolidated during the first twenty years of the state of Israel.

However, even before that, it is important to understand something critical about socio-psychological repertoire in general: After it has taken shape in the minds of society members, it constitutes the main lens through which members view events, interpret reality, evaluate the information flowing to them, make decisions, and choose their actions. This knowledge, as a reflection of their world, constitutes the perspective through which they see and interpret it. In that sense, there is no difference between a leader and any other member of society, even considering the fact that leaders usually have much more information and knowledge about public issues. Moreover, it is very difficult to change perceptions and evaluations that have been assimilated and stored in the brain, when knowledge about a subject (like this conflict) has accumulated from a very early age. It is strengthened through the years by experience, and of course, by a variety of sources, such as parents, teachers, textbooks, the media or leaders. This knowledge is central, is held with great confidence and is ego involving, and thus, mediates the comprehension of all new information and experiences. In order to change the lenses, individuals have to be opened to new knowledge, unfreeze held views and form a new view of the conflict. This process does happen, but usually takes a long time. Commonly, individuals freeze their narratives about the conflict, and it is very difficult to change their views. I will now detail the main themes of the societal beliefs included in the ethos of conflict and collective memory as they developed during the first decades of the existence of the state and became hegemonic in the individual and collective socio-psychological repertoire. Since the concept narrative is very openly defined and used, it is possible to look at each theme as a specific narrative standing by itself.

THE MAIN THEMES OF THE CONFLICT SUPPORTING NARRATIVES IN JEWISH-ISRAELI SOCIETY

Societal Beliefs Justifying the Goals

The most important of the ethos of conflict societal beliefs is justification of the conflict's goals. In the Israeli Jewish case, it concerns the idea of the return of the Jewish people to their land after two thousand years of exile, and the establishment of a Jewish state in their ancestral homeland. This is at the ideological heart of the Jewish national movement, Zionism.

Jewish nationalism developed in the context of the general national awakening among European nations, along with the Jewish distress at the increasing antisemitism in the countries where Jews were living. Moreover, in some countries the antisemitism was accompanied with pogroms. The movement representing the emerging Jewish nationalism—Zionism— took shape in Europe during the second half of the nineteenth century and provided Jews with national goals to which they could aspire. The most important of these goals, the establishment of a Jewish state in the land of Israel, was of crucial importance in the preservation and self-determination of the Jewish nation. According to Zionist ideology, only its creation could bring about national fulfillment, giving full expression to the Jewish societal identity and safeguarding the nation against the dangers it faced.

The justifications for this super-objective were drawn from the fields of history, theology, culture, and nationalism, along with practical politics and the instinct for self-preservation. These rested, inter alia, on the claim that the Jewish nation had been created in the land of ancient Israel, and its early culture developed there while, through all the years of exile, the Jews had maintained their spiritual and physical connection with the land and always aspired to return to it; and the threat of antisemitism in the diaspora intensified the need for the secure existence of the Jewish nation in its ancient homeland. Accordingly, the Holocaust was perceived as expressing the ultimate ordeal that Jews had faced in the diaspora, and in that sense, it was crucial evidence of the justness of the Zionist aspiration that only a Jewish state could prevent further massive harm to the Jews. As such, the solution to be desired was the establishment of a Jewish state that could protect their lives and their personal and collective security. Beliefs in the justness of Jewish goals appear as a narrative in the canonic document of the State of Israel—the Declaration of Independence, formulated in 1948. The declaration opens with the statement: "*The Land of Israel was the birthplace of the Jewish people. Here their spiritual, religious and political identity was shaped. Here they first attained statehood, created cultural values of national and universal significance…*" However, the establishment of a Jewish state was not an abstract objective as it was connected to territorial demands and borders for the state. But the question of state territorial borders was open and remains so even today.

In due course, an additional element was added to the system of beliefs in the justness of Jewish goals: the negation of any rationale for Palestinian self-determination and for the establishment of a Palestinian state. From the 1950s to the 1970s, the prevailing attitude among Jews assumed that there was no Palestinian nation, that the people who considered themselves "Palestinian" actually belonged to the Arab nation. In 1978, only 9% of the Jews supported an establishment of the Palestinian state. In addition, Jews believed that Palestinians did not have a deep-rooted link to the land as most had arrived in the eighteenth and nineteenth centuries and remained thanks to the economic prosperity provided by the Jews. These arguments were based on testimony from people who had visited Palestine in the eighteenth and nineteenth centuries and had been impressed that the land was empty and neglected. Among these visitors was Mark Twain, who included similar sentiments in his book *The Innocents Abroad, or, The New Pilgrims' Progress*, published in 1869. He described the north of the country: "…*These unpeopled deserts, these rusty mounds of barrenness*

... that melancholy ruin of Capernaum, the stupid village of Tiberias, slumbering under its six bereaved plumes of palms..." (Part 5, Chap. 48). In this vein, the phrase "a land without a people for a people without a land" was widely circulated by Zionists in the late nineteenth and early twentieth century as describing the state of the nationhood and the country. As a consequence, in time, these attitudes led to a denial of the fact that a Palestinian national movement was developing, with the argument that this movement was artificial and was a reaction against Zionism, with an intention to expel Jews from their homeland.

The struggle for the land continued for decades, along with the attempt to settle it. Ultimately, the War of Independence, which was constitutive and decisive for the establishment of the State of Israel, served as background for the creation of epistemic support for the right of the Jews to the country and for the design of a clear mindset. The establishment of the State of Israel became the realization of the great objective of the Zionist Movement, having shed much blood to achieve that goal. One percent of the Jewish population (about 6,000) had been killed in the violent struggle for its creation. Even after the state had been established, the violence continued, in a struggle for the state's continued existence. During this period, there were many violent skirmishes and two wars (the Sinai Campaign and the Six-Day War), accompanied by continual threatening rhetoric and a general embargo by the Arab nations. During the 1967 war in June, after being threatened by Egypt, within six days, Israel conquered large expanses of territories, including the Sinai Peninsula and Gaza Strip from Egypt, the West Bank along with East Jerusalem from Jordan, and the Golan Heights from Syria. These years witnessed the solidification of the societal beliefs of the ethos of conflict.

These events and how they were perceived were put to an even more significant test following the Six-Day War. Until 1967 most of the Israeli public were reconciled to the territorial size of the state as determined at the end of the War of Independence, despite the fact that the aspiration to incorporate "both sides of the Jordan" continued to exist among a minority, most of whom identified as supporting the Herut Party (right-wing nationalistic party), the National Religious Party, and a small number of Ahdut HaAvoda (leftist-nationalistic party) supporters. However, the occupation of the West Bank of the Jordan, the Gaza Strip, Sinai and the Golan Heights in the wake of the Six-Day War changed opinions among the public and the leadership regarding the territorial image of the state and significantly strengthened the belief that Jews have the right to maintain their hold over the new territories. Immediately after the war, then-Minister of Defense Moshe Dayan announced: *"We have returned to the holiest of our holy places, never to part from them again."*

Did You Know?

Surveys taken between the Six-Day War and the Yom Kippur War by the Guttman Center for Public Opinion and Policy Research found that about 75% of the Jewish public supported maintaining control over the occupied territories, especially the West Bank, but also the Gaza Strip and the Golan Heights. In the years 1974–1977, more than 60% of Israeli Jews thought that the Palestinians did not constitute a separate nation but were part of the Arab nation and that Jordan fulfilled the function of a state for them. In addition, over 70% agreed with the statement that the Arab-Palestinian nation was an artificial concept that had appeared only in recent years because of developments in the Middle East.[20]

A new consensus developed in the Israeli Jewish society that viewed the territories as "liberated," intimating that they had belonged to Jews in the ancient past. It was argued that Jews had now returned to parts of their homeland that had been promised to them and that they represent a foundation of their cultural and national heritage. This perspective received hegemonic status in Israeli Jewish society after the Six-Day War. It was expressed by most national leaders and political parties, journalists, and many of the political and cultural elite, as well as most Jewish citizens.[21]

As this viewpoint evolved, the belief also developed that Israel must not retreat from the "liberated" territories. This too was based on historical, theological, national and cultural arguments, but added to these were political and security contentions. An expression of this belief, for example, can be found in the declaration published on 27 September 1967, signed by 57 distinguished top public figures from the worlds of politics, culture, and security in Israeli society (for example, Dan Tolkowsky, Rachel Yannait Ben Zvi, Yitzhak Tabenkin, Avraham Yoffe, Natan Alterman, Haim Guri, Moshe Shamir, and Shai Agnon). It determined:

> *The victory of the Israeli Defense Forces in the Six-Day War*
> *has placed the nation and the state in a new and fateful peri-*

od. *The complete Land of Israel is now held by the Jewish nation, and just as we do not have the right to give up the State
of Israel, we are obligated to retain what we have received:
The Land of Israel. We must faithfully maintain the entirety
of our land both by reason of the past of the nation as well as
its future, and no Israeli government has the right to give up
this completeness.*

Acceptance of this perspective made any withdrawal from territories "giving them away" rather than "returning them." The clearest translation of
this belief into actions in the field has been the project to create Jewish
settlements in the occupied territories. Only three days after the end of the
war, the State of Israel destroyed the houses of the Mugrabi neighborhood
in old Jerusalem, opposite the Western Wall and expelled its Palestinian
residents, and a year later, in September 1968, the state established settlements in Gush Etzion, south of Jerusalem, and in April 1969, in Hebron.
At the beginning, Jewish settlement was achieved by military order, that
is, appropriated land was presented as being necessary for building army
camps or posts. The practice was designed by Moshe Dayan ostensibly to
circumvent international law, which prohibits the construction of buildings for civilian use in occupied territory. In reality, land appropriation
was accompanied by a wink—and everyone involved, including the Israeli
public, knew that the real purpose was to establish civilian settlements.
This method was used to establish a number of settlements until it was
banned by the Supreme Court in a ruling in the Alon Moreh High Court in
1979.[22] Through the years, Jewish neighborhoods have been built in East
Jerusalem and many dozens of settlements and outposts have been established on the West Bank, in which hundreds of thousands of Jews have
been settled (about 475,000 by the end of December 2021, not including
those Jews living in East Jerusalem). The settlements faithfully reflected
the basic Zionist perception since 1882 that only by building settlement
on the land could the Zionist ideal be achieved.[23]

Formation of Societal Beliefs about Security

Beliefs related to security are found in all societies involved in bloody conflict, and they are considered of the highest importance in Jewish Israeli
society. In Israel, they are the focus of public discourse; they affect the
way the conflict is managed, and, in fact, they also affect all other areas
of life in Israel. Living in security is considered a necessary condition for

the existence of the Jewish nation in its state. In order to understand how these beliefs operate and the role they play, it is important to first know how they evolved.

Jews have felt insecurity and fear not only during the peak years of their intractable conflict, from the 1950s to the 1970s, but throughout history, which has been fraught with countless dangers and threats. Therefore, for Jews, the concern about their security, both as individuals and as a collective, has dominated their lives for generations and still does.[24] This began in the Biblical era, during which the Jews were described as "a people that shall dwell alone," facing a variety of threats from among hostile nations surrounding them. During this long period, about 1,200 years, the Hebrew nation lived in its homeland, but always under the shadow of occupation and violent struggles for independence. It lost ten tribes during the Assyrian conquest in 721 BC and then the exile following the destruction of the First Temple in 597 BC by the Babylonians. Jews returned to their country with the permit given by the Persian king Cyrus the Great, who conquered Babylon, and they set up a self-governing province. Nevertheless, their sense of insecurity continued during the Greek occupation and then Roman control, culminating in the forced exile of part of Jewish settlement following the Bar-Kochva revolt. Later, during 2,000 years of diaspora, the character of the threats changed and correspondingly, the challenges the Jewish nation was forced to deal with were also different, changing in accord with the period, context and the particular place they resided. In general, during the years of the diaspora, Jews faced expulsions, pogroms, persecution, blood libels, murder, torture, exceptional taxation, and various other restrictions. But the ultimate threat was the organized and methodical attempt by Nazi Germany to destroy the entire Jewish nation during the Second World War. The Holocaust, during which a third of the Jewish nation were murdered, has become the ultimate national trauma, still affecting all aspects of life in Jewish society up to the present, and it has become one of the marks of identification of the Jewish collective.[25]

These experiences, throughout the existence of the Jewish nation, have fatefully affected the content of its collective memory—both popular and official. The conclusion that was drawn is that, due to the unique attributes of the Jewish nation, it has been sentenced to permanently remain under existential threat which will never disappear, as other nations are infected with hatred towards the Jewish nation, expressed in wide-ranging anti-

Semitism. This conclusion has been the point of departure for any discussion about security.

Even since the beginning of the era of renewed Jewish settlement in the land of Israel, the question of security has played a central role in the lives of Jewish society as almost all society members were in agreement that the security of the Jewish settlement, and later, the security of the state of Israel was continually facing a palpable threat—and that one military loss in a war would be a national disaster. From the standpoint of the Jews, the events of the last century supplied clear evidence of the dangers threatening them as individuals and as a societal collective, and thus, they had both the right and the obligation to defend themselves.[26] This also led to the belief held by the great majority of Jews in Israel that the aim of the Arabs was to destroy the state and/or all of the Jews living in it. David Ben-Gurion, the first Prime Minister of Israel, coined the formula still accepted today that *"the problem of Israeli security is unlike the security problems of any other country: It is not a problem of borders or sovereignty—but rather a literal problem of physical existence."*[27]

At this point, it is important to examine the significance of beliefs about security. We usually relate to them as though they express an objective evaluation of reality, usually by asking the question: Is there, or is there not security and how much security is there? However, the answer to that question is far from being objective. There are considerable differences in how Israelis, or people in general, relate to security.

The American psychologists, Richard Lazarus and Craig Smith argue that the experience of insecurity and fear is a psychological manifestation linked to two appraisals: the first relates to the appraisal made by the individual as to the identification of a threat (early evaluation), and the second relates to the appraisal made by the individual of his/her ability to deal with the threat and overcome it. Alternatively, people will feel security and a lack of fear when they do not identify threat, or they do identify a threat but estimate that they are able to overcome it with minimal effort and cost.[28] These appraisals do not relate only to personal security, but also to collective security evaluated by people, including experts, high-ranking officers, and political leaders.

In this analysis we do not claim that a sense of insecurity solely depends on subjective factors alone and is not based on an evaluation of objective reality. But in the practical world, the effect of solid information in supplying important data to assess a threat, is limited. Why is this so? For a number of reasons. First, reality is often unclear and difficult to comprehend, and even the ability of "experts" to predict future events is limited due to the complex factors and the large number of variables that construct "reality." Thus, it is difficult to talk about drawing unequivocal conclusions about a present state of affairs and/or a future situation. Under these circumstances, people tend to rely on perceptions and appraisals that are necessarily subjective. There is no other way to assess the dangers facing the country. Second, in many cases, the public does not hold all of the information necessary to make a credible evaluation of the threat but may only have partial knowledge (and that is even true of political leaders and experts). Finally, there are so many variables affecting assessments made by different people about the two issues posed by Lazarus and Smith. People differ in their beliefs, their ideologies, their feelings, their experiences, and their knowledge about specific topics and thus, they differ widely in their appraisal of a threat and their ability to cope with it.[29]

Although we have tied insecurity to fear, it is important to explain something about the difference between them. While insecurity is a rational-emotional reaction relating to an analysis of reality, that is to say, "a cognitive reaction," fear is an elemental emotional response, that is to say, "a gut reaction." Let us focus on fear for a moment. Fear is aroused in situations of threat and danger to an organism (in our case, to a human being) and/or to the environment (in our case, to society), and it enables an immediate adaptive response to threat as, in many cases, it is activated automatically and spontaneously. But fear may also lead to immediate action, as defensive responses are adopted according to learned signals testifying to immediate threat or direct danger: for example, recognition of a person sitting in a bus as an Arab or identification of an unattended bag in a shop. It is no wonder that Israeli Prime Minister Golda Meir did not respond positively to the messages sent by Egyptian President Anwar Sadat at the beginning of the 1970s signaling that he desired negotiations with Israel. She had learned through experience about the nefarious intentions of the Egyptians through the years. And the commanders of the army also identified danger in Sadat's willingness to land at Ben Gurion airport, while all the government representatives awaited him in November 1977, and they warned Prime Minister Begin of a trap. Fear, as an automatic physiological reaction, takes control of the person even before he succeeds in evaluating the situation as it exists using rational thinking. Finally, there are significant ramifications to long-term experience of fear, some of which have a negative effect on thinking processes: Fear intensifies sensitivity to indications of threat; it grants disproportional predominance to information about potential threats and leads to an extension of associative information networks about threat; it causes exaggerated appraisal of danger and threat, and even increases expectation that they will appear. The result is a tendency to adhere to well-known situations and to avoid the risky or unknown, or in other words, stagnation of thinking that prevents openness to new ideas. Moreover, fear often generates aggressive reactions when the "fight or flight" response takes control of the frightened people. In Israel, the dominant response is "fight."[30]

In the context of the Israel-Palestinian conflict, there are recurring signs pointing to threat, both to the collective and to the members of society as individuals; these date from the founding of the state up to the present. Israelis live in a realty of war, violent military clashes, rocket attacks on the civilian population and a variety of terrorist attacks. In addition, the various media outlets constantly report intentions to harm the state and the Jewish population as individuals, using the rhetoric of threat and danger. And the security beliefs held by the public are also affected by what has been learned in years past, as well as being influenced by the Israeli collective memory, bequeathed to and internalized by all Israeli Jews.[31] Thus, societal beliefs regarding insecurity serve as a guarding tower because they prevent sudden and unpleasant surprises in all societies involved in a violent conflict.

What Are the Main Security Beliefs in Israeli Society?

There are a number of predominant security beliefs which have become enrooted in Israeli society from the time of the establishment of the state. The most prominent of them maintains that the Israeli security problem is unique and existential, and only the Jews precisely understand the security dangers and challenges facing them. This premise was invalidated more than once, but it still is used as a dogma by the Israeli Jewish public and its leaders.[32] As time passed, an additional premise developed, asserting that Israel had the right and the obligation to deal with these threats self-reliantly, without depending on foreign military aid or international bodies. This obligation has been expressed in the right to use deterrence, to punish and to forcefully prevent violent activity, and therefore, at times,

Israel must be the first to initiate operations, including defensive wars, in order to prevent dangerous situations. This worldview leads to the sense that maintaining security is the most important of public priorities, and the great majority of Jews in Israel share the societal belief that security concerns must be evaluated before any other consideration.

The perpetual concern with security beliefs has turned Israeli society into a "society in uniform." The army is perceived as its central institution, having enabled the establishment of the state in the past, and maintaining its existence in the present. However, this special status is not only a consequence of its formal role in ensuring security, but also its status as a social institution (as a sociological concept), as all society members make up the army. Let me explain. In Israel, there is no clear division between civil society and military society, especially among Israeli secular, traditional and even national-religious sectors, as exists in other Western societies. The Israeli military and Israeli society are interwoven and linked by inseparable bonds, forming a unified space and a unified identity. What does this mean in actuality? Most society members do compulsory military service (with the exception of most of the ultra-Orthodox and the Arab minorities) and many also continue with long-lasting annual reserve service, while a small minority adopt an army career. This turns the army into an inseparable part of family life, as the family's sons and daughters, like their parents, continue to serve in the army. This in turn creates dense social networks involving many members of Jewish society, creating a societal-military community whose members have one foot in civilian life and the other, in the military. It is based on personal relations as well as common values, norms and perceptions, at least in issues connected to security, the status of the army and the conflict. The positive social attitude towards the army has thus become part of personal identity and is strongly linked to collective identity. Regardless of their political positions, almost all the serving sector is proud when their children pass the very difficult selection to serve as pilots in the air force, in commando units, in the paratrooper's brigades and in the top intelligence branch.

Under these conditions, concern for security has become a kind of religious ritual, and at the same time, the substrata of this concern may be seen everywhere in the general culture. It is expressed in every area of social life (specifically, in the institutionalization and routinization of military elements in daily life);[33] in the overwhelming presence of military speech and terminology in civil life; in the modes of thinking and forms of action identified with military service; in the militaristic features of general culture and the admiration for the army and everything connected with it, in particular; and in the inability to accept criticism of immoral military behavior.[34] The army is viewed as the best effective institution that can fulfill many different roles in the Israeli society, as it is also the most trusted. Military footprints are found in every aspect of life in Israel: societal, economic, industrial, and even in the educational, health, cultural, and artistic arenas.

But above all else, Israeli society has accepted living by the sword and has assented to the constant waiting, for some segments of the population, sometimes even with enthusiasm, for the next war. Thus, security holds a central status in the Israeli agenda, certainly in comparison to other threats, such as social, political and economic dangers, religious threats, or even health dangers.[35] It is no wonder that Israel has often been characterized as an army that has a state, rather than a state that has an army.

Societal Beliefs about Delegitimization of the Palestinians

An intractable conflict is also a greenhouse for the development of the most egregious stereotypes, and particularly, societal beliefs negating the humanity of the opposing group, resulting in psychological approval to harm its members. Thus, delegitimization in all its forms, including dehumanization, gives covert expression to the violent long-lasting conflict between Jews and Arabs in Israel, as is true in other conflicts.[36] The views of Arabs and the behavior towards them shaped David Ben Gurion, who determined in the early 1950s that *"[t]he Arabs in Israel must be judged by what they can do and not by what they have done."* With this statement, he formulated the fundamental attitude of the state towards the Arab minority in Israel and later towards the Palestinians in general, implicitly expressing an underlying basic distrust of them that became an explicit consensual view.

The early meeting between Jews, mostly of European descent, and the Arab natives living in Israel, provided "facilitating" conditions for the creation of negative stereotypes, distrust and animosity. The Israeli Jews viewed Arabs as primitive, lacking in culture, and savage, and as time went on and the conflict became deeper and more violent, Arabs began to be perceived as violent, murderers, bloodthirsty, lawbreakers, rabble, traitors, cruel, easily incited, and unreliable.[37] This view has been shared by Jews who arrived from Arab countries after the establishment of the state. At a certain stage, the delegitimization and its characteristics began to be perceived by the Jews as permanent and stable, as they were supposedly inborn. In an opinion poll in 1968, 60% of Israeli Jews agreed with the statement: *"Arabs can improve considerably, but they will never be as advanced as the Jews."*[38] Along with these attitudes, negative emotions developed, such as hostility, hatred and anger, which accompanied the characterizations of delegitimization.

In addition, the Arabs have been presented as having initiated **all** acts of violence against Jews from the beginning of the conflict, including initiating the wars, and are seen as responsible for ceaseless murder of Jews.[39] In opinion polls continuing from 1973–1977, more than 75% of Jews maintained that the real aim of the Arabs was "to destroy the state of Israel." In addition, at least until the 1980s, almost all Jews customarily termed the Palestinians as "Arabs" (and some still commonly use this term of reference in the present)—a generalization that demonstrates how Jewish society has not distinguished between the Palestinian population and other Arab nations who are living in their own countries. The slogan "Death to the Arabs" is still heard today on the part of extremist individuals and groups. The distinct national identity of the Palestinians has been denied and with it, their right to self-determination.

Delegitimization has also been supported by the connection often made between the harm done to Jews by Arabs in Israel, and the harm and persecution of the Jews by other nations in the diaspora (and especially the mass murder of Jews by the Nazis during the Second World War).[40] A special effort was made to revile the Palestine Liberation Organization and Yasser Arafat, its head, and to attribute to them the ultimate epithet of delegitimization as an organization of terrorist murderers, including direct comparisons to the Nazis. And because the PLO represents the political aspirations of the great majority of Palestinians, this has meant the delegitimization of the entire Palestinian nation.[41]

Nevertheless, it is important to note that following the occupation of the West Bank and the Gaza Strip during the Six-Day War, many Palestinians began to work inside Israel—and this continued at least until 1993. It is difficult to estimate the number of Palestinians who were employed in Israel during those years because many of them were working illegally, but according to various estimates, the number was in many tens of thousands. They worked in gas stations, on building sites, in restaurants or in agriculture, and in a variety of other cleaning or gardening jobs, enabling them to get to know their employers, their coworkers, and Jewish customers. This meeting certainly affected the perceptions of Palestinians by the Jewish public, as proposed by Gordon Alpert's "contact theory," suggesting that interaction between members of two hostile groups could change their negative attitudes.[42] Many stories appeared, even in newspapers, about interpersonal trust relations and closeness that had evolved, indicating the development of a positive attitude towards the Palestinians by many Jews. But, as in many other cases around the world, the Jewish public were able to build positive relations with individuals, but at the same time, continued to view the abstract general Palestinian entity with extreme negativity.

Societal Beliefs about Collective Positive Self-image

Jewish-Israeli society also developed societal beliefs expressing a collective positive self-image on the basis of the Jewish ethos. But this view was strengthened and also changed somewhat with the advent of Zionism as Zionist Jews considered themselves the vanguard of a "new nation" which had achieved a rebirth in its homeland, and the Jews in general were and are presented as courageous, industrious, decisive, cultured, advanced, wise and intelligent (for evidence, references to "people of the book" or at present, "a start-up nation"). At least for some of the public, and based on Jewish sources, the Jews, as part of their covenant with God, have been chosen for a specific mission- to be "a light unto the nations." Of course, this positive self-image is a complete contrast to the delegitimization beliefs attributed to Arabs, and even to other nations.

As these societal beliefs developed, many myths and narratives were created in the process of constructing a new reality. These emphasized the struggles of the pioneers, "making the desert bloom," "building the land," absorbing immigrants, and of course, the military victories.[43] In addition, the allegedly humane and compassionate treatment of the Arab population in Israel was emphasized, as part of the wider perception that the Jews are peace loving, but have been forced to participate in a violent conflict against their will. Even as the conflict continued, Jews in Israel presented themselves as being ready to end the hostilities immediately by peaceful means, but, to their sorrow, they have constantly been met by an enemy who is determined to destroy them, and who has rejected every solution.

Golda Meir expressed this well in saying, *"We can forgive the Arabs for killing our children, but we can never forgive them for forcing us to kill their children. Peace will come only when they love their children more than they hate us."*[44]

As part of the efforts to maintain this myth, many stories have circulated about the moral behavior of Israeli soldiers who have treated Palestinian civilians and soldiers with mercy and consideration, and this has sometimes even endangered their lives. Some have even paid the highest price of all—they have sacrificed their own lives. In addition to emphasizing positive deeds by Jews, maintaining these beliefs has also demanded that the negative acts carried out by Jews during the years of conflict be kept hidden. As Judah Leib Gordon, a Jewish poet of the Enlightenment, wrote in his poem, Scenes of Pain: *"We are blind bats to our own faults, but eagle-eyed towards the defects of our comrades."* Jews used terror during the British Mandate, which included throwing hand grenades into Arab markets, looting, killing, and even carrying out a number of massacres in Arab villages during the War of Independence, expelling Arabs from their homes and killing prisoners during other wars. We will touch upon some of these deeds later in the book. The myths and narratives which have been part of the education of every Israeli Jew were a result not only of the vital need for a positive self-perception and construction of collective identity, but also stemmed from the desire to sharpen the difference between Jews and Arabs as much as possible and to make it possible to present Jews in a positive light to the international community.

Societal Beliefs about a Collective Self-perception as a Victim

The combination of beliefs we have cited above—beliefs referring to the justice of Israeli Jewish ways and their positive self-image—have served as a basis for the creation of the perception of Israeli Jewish society as the sole victim in the conflict.[45] Jews came to settle their homeland innocently and honestly, hoping to realize their historical right and to create a refuge from persecution in the diaspora, but there they encountered the unjustified aggression of the Arabs. Thus, the Jews were the clear victims of the conflict. Accordingly, the strong opposition of the Arab states to the Zionist ideal was viewed as a continuation of traditional antisemitism.[46]

The self-perception of Jews as victims surrounded by a hostile environment was greatly strengthened by the total opposition of the Arabs to the establishment of a Jewish state even during the British Mandate and then, immediately following the establishment of the state, when the armies of the Arab countries invaded Israel in an attempt to occupy it. As time went by, the perception of Israeli Jews as victims became more powerful as the Arab states made every attempt to harm the young state in a variety of ways, including terror attacks against Israelis which started in the 1950s and the Arab boycott, beginning immediately after the 1948 war. And while the aggressive acts on the Arab side were all perceived as well-planned in advance and unjustified, the wars and Israeli military operations were all perceived as acts of self-defense and "no choice" situations, such as retaliation attacks, during the 1950s and 1960s, the Sinai Campaign, and the Six-Day War.

These attitudes did not appear one day out of the blue; they are based on Jewish self-perception through the generations, as a nation persecuted by a hostile world. As noted, the hostility peaked with the Holocaust. The mass killings in cities and towns, the railroad trains carrying people to their deaths, and the millions murdered in the gas chambers have all become canonic impressions that perpetually accompany Jews and act as a lighthouse guiding their way. This paramount event constitutes a trauma which cannot be expunged and dwarfs everything else undergone by Jews for hundreds of years and anything experienced by other nations.[47] It is the chosen trauma of Jews, defined as shared societal mental representation of a historical event in which the group suffered a catastrophic and traumatic loss and humiliation at the hands of its enemies. It has a determinative effect on the shared societal feeling of being a victim by society members. Of importance is the fact that the group did not heal from this experience and is unable to mourn it properly. Therefore, the event becomes externalized, leaving indelible imprinting upon the psyche of the group, marking its memory and even shaping its collective identity. It is embedded in the culture, passed down from generation to generation and, thus, can be "re-activated" during times of threat and stress to ensure the continued support of its members.[48] As the chosen trauma, the Holocaust is recreated and reconstructed not only on Holocaust Remembrance Day, but also throughout the year, and it is proliferated via a wide range of channels. These include visits to the death camps in Poland by Israeli youth.[49]

The youth journeys to Poland began at the end of the 1980s and became institutionalized in the 1990s. Since then, tens of thousands of young people in the eleventh and twelfth grades (nearly an entire generation) have traveled to Poland in droves, from almost every high school in Israel, for a journey mainly devoted to visiting death camps, former ghettoes, and the killing fields, and preceded by an intensive period of preparation. This "death journey" by Israeli youth has become an educational venture of initiation ceremony, as most Israelis and their leaders believe that the Holocaust could return and that the enemies, who are generally termed "Nazis" wishing to annihilate the Jewish nation, have only changed form.[50] Thus, the journey, as one lasting crucial ceremony, establishes and solidifies the beliefs that Jews were the ultimate victims in the Holocaust, that the victimhood continues, that there are at present nations that wish to annihilate Jewish people and then only the state of Israeli with its strong army is the safe haven for them. In essence, the perception has become enrooted that views time and fate as determining possible persecution, destruction, and eradication. Moreover, during the long years of conflict between the Jews and Arabs in Israel, the link between the wars with the Arabs and the destruction by the Nazis during the Second World War is frequently cited. The Arabs have been depicted as aspiring to destroy the State of Israel and to cast its Jewish population into the sea.[51]

In fact, all the experiences noted above, beginning with the pogroms and the Holocaust and continuing to the wars and terror attacks in Israel, have led to a broader mindset than merely the sense of victimhood. They have caused a "Jewish siege mentality," asserting that all nations are hostile to the Jewish nation.[52] This mentality has become deeply ingrained in Jewish culture. Each year, during the Passover Seder, the participants repeat:

> *That which stood for our ancestors applies to us as well.*
>
> *For it was not only one individual who stood up against us,*
> *to destroy us.*
>
> *Rather, in every generation they stand up against us, to destroy us.*
>
> *But the holy one, blessed be he, redeems us from their hands.*

And the Talmudic midrash (explication) explains that *"all of the nations hate Israel"* (Beraishit Rabba, 63, 7). This is a framework that encompasses all enemies, whether Egyptian, Persian, Greek, Roman, Muslim, Christian, anti-Semitic European, Nazi or Arab—there is no distinction between nations and states, and among the various political and historical factors. The Jewish collective is forever facing "the children of darkness," the nations of the world who are not distinguished from one another. The popular song written by Yoram Taharlev in the 1960s best expresses this siege mentality: "*The whole world is against us/ it is an ancient tune/which our forefathers taught us/to sing and also to dance.*" (From the song "The Whole World is Against Us.") This attitude fits in well with a fatalist outlook, still common among the Israeli-Jewish public, according to which the realities of the Israeli Palestinian conflict are a historical continuation of hatred of Jews in the present generation in which the hateful enemy is the Arabs and their leaders who aspire to annihilate Israel.

Did You Know?

A study carried by Schori-Eyal, Halperin, and Bar-Tal found that Jews in Israel carry three layers of sense of victimhood that have a hierarchal order, interacting among them. The first layer and the basic one is the sense of victimhood based on the experiences in the long history of Jews and the Jewish cultural tradition. The second layer has been constructed on the basis of the protracted and bloody conflict with Arabs in general and specifically with the Palestinians. The third layer refers to specific violent encounters with Arabs like, wars, battles, or terror attacks. In all these events, Jews felt that they are the victims because they were perceived as in-justful, forced on Jews, in which Jews were hurt because of Arab intentional violence. This sense of victimhood has prevailed even when Jews eventually achieved unequivocal victory in the violent events.[53]

Almost all Israeli leaders, from every part of the political spectrum, have held beliefs reflecting the siege mentality. They have viewed Israel as an isolated state in a world hostile to it, and to which only a small number of states are friendly. David Ben Gurion, Israel's first Prime Minister, well expressed this siege mentality in an article he wrote for the *Davar* newspaper on 17 February 1953:

> *In its long journey on the stage of world history, for four thousand years, in most of the lands of the universe, in the east and in the west, in the north and in the south, our nation has forever encountered hatred and hostility, libel and denunciation, persecution and torture, destruction and massacre ... the hatred and loathing during thousands of years has taken various forms, but its content has not very much changed ...*

Similar statements can be found as expressed every Prime Minister from David Ben Gurion to Binyamin Netanyahu.

Societal Beliefs about Patriotism

One of the necessary challenges facing Jewish society in Israel, as any society involved in a long-lasting intractable conflict, is the need to mobilize society members to support the conflict and even to actively participate in it, including making the ultimate sacrifice—loss of their children's lives. Without that, it would be impossible to maintain the conflict over time.

Members of the new Jewish society settled in Palestine as pioneers who were aspiring to realize the Zionist ideal. For dozens of years, from the beginnings of immigration in 1882, tens of thousands of people arrived in Israel, settled in various places, tilled the soil, set up settlements and contended with the local Arab population, which reacted with hostility. Patriotic sacrifice was a central value in Israeli culture during that period, as well as during the first twenty years of statehood. After the establishment of the state, there was a certain change in the tenor of patriotism: There was greater stress placed on the army and on the Israeli-Jewish fighter and less emphasis on the pioneering myth of the founding generations that emphasized settling the land. However, loyalty to the society and to the land remained a priority, even though the emphasis had changed.[54]

During the first two decades of the state, military service was considered fundamental and was not to be avoided. Combat service was the aspiration of very many of the enlistees, and volunteers for special combat units received respect and honor. Those who were recruited to pilot training, commando units and paratroopers received special recognition. Sacrificing one's life was thus viewed as a legitimate price that patriotic citizens could be asked to pay, and those who lost their lives while serving received homage and esteem. Furthermore, death of a family member in battle or in a terror attack was accepted as an occurrence that had taken place during an existential national struggle and no questions were asked about its necessity.[55] As in the poem Cornerstone (Rosh Pina) by Beitar revisionist youth movement member Moshe Skolsky, *"The mountain peak cannot be conquered without a grave waiting at its base."* It is no wonder then that research conducted by the Guttman Center for Public Opinion and Policy Research found that, between 1967–1977, more than 60% of Jews in Israel thought that there was need for self-sacrifice for the state. Another expression of patriotism could be found in feelings of complete certainty among almost all society members that emigration from the homeland was forbidden (and was termed negatively as "descending" in Hebrew). Those who did leave Israel were vilified and met with hostility. In 1976, Prime Minister Yitzhak Rabin called those who had avoided military service "waste material of weaklings."

During the 20 years following the establishment of the state, there was almost total blind patriotism.[56] The Jewish public accepted every demand by the leadership to mobilize and self-sacrifice without objection or criticism, and the narratives supplied by political and military leaders were accepted without asking too many questions about their validity. Therefore, for example, the public accepted the expulsion of Arabs and the destruction of Arab villages, the military government imposed on the remaining Arabs, the manipulated Sinai Campaign in 1956, the acts of retaliation on the Jordanian and Egyptian borders, or the violent events on the border with Syria. The leadership, on its part, stringently controlled the communications media and prevented public discussion or even leaks of any details that might harm support for their policies.

Patriotic beliefs explained acceptance of the heavy price demanded by life under the shadow of the conflict and justified it. It was almost impossible to find an Israeli who had not heard of Joseph Trumpeldor, a national hero (a Zionist activist and a commander who was killed by Arabs, defending a Jewish settlement in the north, Tel Hai, in 1920), and the words attributed to him as he lay dying: "*It is good to die for our country.*" In addition, patriotic beliefs encouraged a sense of national unity which softened the effects of loss, as well as mitigating other bitter events. It is no wonder that the most respected patriots after 1947 were those who took part in the struggles for national independence and then in wars or other military encounters.

Societal Beliefs about National Unity

Every society invests great efforts to achieve internal unity and solidarity, but these values are particularly important in times of intractable conflict. In Israel, the violent confrontations with the Arabs, the external threats and other factors, termed "a national emergency," led Jewish society of the 1950s and 1960s to consolidate around security concerns, alongside expressions of routine patriotism that are characteristic of other nations. Simultaneously, challenging national unity was perceived—as in other societies in conflict—as doing real damage to the country's ability to stand up to the threats, and this was especially true during times of security tensions.

During the early years of the state, reinforcing the sense of cooperation and belonging was especially called for considering the differences in origin among the Jewish population, who immigrated from dozens of countries. During the waves of immigration, various groups of Jews had arrived in Israel for different reasons, with different values, attitudes and behavioral norms and with different cultural backgrounds. The leaders of the state made every effort to establish a "melting pot" for the new immigrants in order to create unity and uniformity, and to establish the widest possible societal consensus regarding the conflict, its causes and its expected solution. Sanctions were applied to those Jewish society members who deviated and did not conform to the norms and the consensual views. In this context, it is interesting to examine the words of Menachem Begin in a speech to the Knesset immediately after the occupation of Sinai during the 1956 Sinai campaign. Begin, the leader of the oppositional Herut party, was an ideological and personal rival of Prime Minister David Ben Gurion, and Ben Gurion even excluded him from involvement in enacting policy decisions. In his speech of 7 November 1956, Begin stated:

> *The moral and historic meaning of the mighty campaign of our glorious and heroic army … is legal national self-defense. We have a special reason to rejoice at the fact that this awareness is now shared by the whole nation. […] At this time, when our hearts are overflowing with both joy and concern, we turn first to our nation, to the men, women and children, to the old and young in Israel. With all proud modesty we can say, after we have withstood the supreme test: a small nation but a great one; there are those who are stronger; there are those who are richer; there are those who are cleverer, but there is none which is braver or more steadfast than we.*

Begin's speech illustrates that even those who were bitterly ideologically and politically opposed to the establishment, still made an effort to fall into line in times of military crisis. In fact, it can be said that, during the first 20 years following the establishment of the state, despite political disagreements between the parties and although there were deep class and sectorial rifts, Jewish society almost totally stood united behind the leadership in everything related to the conduct of the conflict.[57] Israeli leaders and society members had unified views regarding ways of managing the violent conflict.

Societal Beliefs about Peace

The subject of peace appears in the narratives of most societies involved in conflict and it plays a number of important roles First, it presents the society as looking forward to peace, as pursuing peace, and as loving peace; these qualities are not only important for society's self-image, but also to present the society in the best possible light to the international community. In addition, the aspiration for peace grants a small hope for peace to a society entangled in a difficult and violent situation; in a certain sense, it serves as a light at the end of the tunnel.[58]

For most of the years of conflict, in fact, until very recently, the principle of peace represented the ultimate aspiration of Jewish Israeli society. Peace was perceived as a central value, and its achievement was determined as the supreme goal. But the attitude towards peace among Israeli Jews, like other societies immersed in conflict, was not specific and did not include practical proposals to achieve peace. The opposite was true; peace was presented in utopian, idealistic images and as amorphous and abstract. It was presented as a dream and not as a reality that must be advanced. This was made clear by Prime Minister David Ben Gurion in a speech to the Knesset in 1956: *"There is not a people in the world so deeply concerned for the principles of peace and justice contained in the United Nations Charter as is the Jewish people."* But the same leader had very clear red lines that prevented the possibility of settling the conflict peacefully after the War of Independence in 1949 and he adopted a militaristic policy during his terms of office.

Among the many other examples of the utopian attitude towards peace, we may point to the songs about peace which appeared after the Six-Day War, at the height of the conflict. The two songs sung by the Army Entertainment Troupe, "Tomorrow" by Naomi Shemer and "The Song for Peace" by Yankele Rosenblit became the most popular of these as the years passed. The chorus of "The Song for Peace," which became a kind of anthem for the peace movements of later years, proclaims: *"So, just sing a song for peace/ Don't whisper a prayer/ Better just sing a song for peace/ In a loud shout."* However, in the field, the picture was very different. An opinion poll from the early 1970s indicated that a huge majority among the Jewish

Israeli public (ranging from 80–90%), were not at all willing to consider a significant compromise in order to achieve a peace agreement.[59]

As in many other cases, this dissonance—the self-image of Jewish society as seeking peace, at the same time as their absolute refusal to support the possibility of a solution that requires compromise—has been explained as resulting from the behavior of the Arabs.[60] They have been presented as the side that rejects peace, and denies every attempt to reach agreement, and thus, they have forced the Jews into this violent conflict. As such, the perception has taken hold that the only way to reach peace is by "deterrence," that is, using power and punishment. Peace, under these conditions, has become an aspiration that is not limited in time, and achieving peace is uncertain, whether in the near future or at all.

CULTURE OF CONFLICT

Described above are the eight themes that stand at the heart of the Jewish-Israeli narrative regarding the conflict: societal beliefs relating to the justness of the conflict goals, beliefs relating to security, beliefs relating to the delegitimization of the Arabs, beliefs relating to a positive self-image of Israeli Jewish society, beliefs relating to the Israeli Jewish perception of itself as victim, beliefs relating to patriotism, beliefs relating to national unity, and beliefs relating to peace. All these beliefs have been integrated into a narrative supporting the continuation of the conflict.

During the 1950s and 1960s, a period when all prerequisites of the intractable conflict evolved with great intensity, a culture of conflict developed, consisting of a conflict supporting narrative containing the themes described above, along with shared emotions.[61] At present, almost all the national institutions are still mobilized in order to impart these principles to Jewish citizens. This begins in kindergartens and continues in schools, in youth movements and of course, during army service (while family life also contributes to the process). The state has cultivated myths, symbols and heroes through all possible socialization channels under their authority in order to enable Jewish society to stand up to the threats of the Arab nations and to justify cases of loss and pain. Among others, the myths of Masada, the Warsaw ghetto uprising, the Maccabean uprising against the Greeks, the Bar-Kochva revolt against Romans, and the defense of Tel Hai have been given special attention as symbols of sacrifice and defense of the homeland. Without a doubt, some of these symbols and narratives have been developed by society members as a necessity while living in the shadow of the conflict, and this pertains especially to those citizens who are concerned about the deaths of soldiers in battle. Family members of the fallen have felt a strong and obvious need to justify their ultimate sacrifice. Thus, the situation was perceived as having "no alternative," and that includes the violence and the wars. This motive represents a cornerstone of every intractable conflict. "No alternative" means that there are no other choices; there is only one option and that is to continue to struggle for existence and to survive. In fact, most conflict supporting beliefs strengthen the "no alternative" premise. This provides motivation and resilience, but it also limits and narrows thinking processes. If the Arabs want to kill us and do not want peace, we clearly have no alternative but to fight them.

During the first two decades following the establishment of the state, expressions of conflict culture were clearly dominant in all national institutions, in the wide range of cultural products, in school textbooks, in official texts, leaders' speeches, national ceremonies, and more. One of the main sites for these expressions was the mass media-in this period- radio and the printed newspapers and magazines. On the one hand, the media, being representative of a society involved in an intractable conflict, were affected by the ethos of conflict and transmitted its messages. On the other hand, as a central channel for information dissemination to society members, the media also aided in **creating** the ethos of conflict and implanting its societal beliefs.[62]

During that period, the communications media were under the control of the political leadership, to the extent that they became an inseparable part of the state political structure. The very close relationship between the political and the media establishments was a result of both the societal and ideological proximity between them, and due to the fact that a large sector of the communications media was owned by political parties. The political establishment viewed the media as an extension of itself which could be used to advance national and ideological objectives, especially in relation to security concerns, and thus, it applied strict censorship. The newspapers, on their part, accepted the establishment role which the government had designated for it and cooperated. As a result, a number of formal and informal structures were created to organize and arrange the cooperation between the media and the government, among which were the military censorship system, an editors' committee (an informal body in which government leaders and senior journalists met and were given "off the record" information), an agreement with military reporters, and other daily practices of news control and briefings, applied to the media by the political echelon.

Hebrew literature, theater, movies and textbooks presented the conflict as an existential issue during those early years, and they almost always expressed the conflict supporting narrative. The Jews were praised as those who were struggling to live a normal life, but at the same time, were forced to bear arms in order to defend themselves, and they were depicted heroically as being highly moral, and particularly, as the only victims of the conflict. In contrast, the Arabs were often delegitimized: They were not presented as human beings, but rather as abstract forces of evil, and were generally described in nightmarish terms.[63]

The hegemonic ideological narrative was instilled by indoctrination covering most political, social, cultural, and educational products during those first decades. This narrative, which served as the foundation of the conflict culture, was selective, biased and distorted. It was based for the most part on supportive information which was usually intensified, while any information which was not supportive, was concealed. So, for example, the significance of the killing of many inhabitants of the village of Dir Yassin in April 1948, during the War of Independence, was minimized among the Jewish population, and then later, by the government of the State of Israel, with the argument that the killing had been done by groups of dissidents from the Lehi and Etzel, the underground movements that acted separately from the major resistance and did not represent the general Jewish population. Other massacres carried out during the War of Independence in 1948 were hidden and omitted like the ones in Tantura, Reneh, Hula, and other places.[64] Other examples are the concealment of information about the massive expulsion of Arabs during the War of Independence and hiding the fact that the three to five thousand Arabs who had been killed in the 1950s, while illegally entering Israel, were mostly just peasant farmers trying to take back possessions that they had left behind in Israel. In addition, the reports about violent confrontations between Israel and Syria did not provide reliable information either about the causes of the conflict or about the nature of the violence.[65] **Viewing the situation broadly, it can be said that, during the height of the conflict, in the 1950s and 1960s, the main societal beliefs that appeared in the narratives of Jewish society in Israel were aimed at enabling the state to deal with the challenges it was facing.** They were helpful in mobilizing society for the most important national goals, and simultaneously they enabled to satisfy individual and collective psychological needs. This was a period in which the leadership and the public did not see any possibility for a peace process that would lead to an end to the conflict with the Arab states. **However, the same narratives that were nurtured through the years and were imparted in all social institutions through every possible channel, in time became significant barriers to a peace process, making it more difficult for any attempt to reach an agreement.**

SUMMARY: WHAT HAVE WE LEARNED ABOUT THE FIRST PERIOD AFTER THE ESTABLISHMENT OF THE STATE?

The first two decades of the existence of the State of Israel, and even to some extent, the third decade, considerably shaped the character of Jewish society in Israel. It was a period in which the conflict was at its peak, extremely violent and accompanied by hostile rhetoric on the part of all the Arab states, who were threatening the destruction of the State of Israel. **Many of the key norms, fundamental assumptions, and basic principles were formed in this period and have been serving since then as a compass for the behavior of the Israeli leadership and the Israeli Jewish public in general.**

In this difficult period, the political leadership of the State of Israel conducted the conflict adopting the following basic premises which were valid until the Six-Day War in 1967:

1. The Arab states are interested in destroying the State of Israel and are not interested in reaching a peace agreement with it.

2. Arabs cannot be trusted because of their innate tendency towards violence and their lack of trustworthiness.

3. We should not accept proposals to return the Palestinian refugees to the State of Israel, even if this is included in the draft for a peace agreement.

4. A unique situation has developed in the realm of security. There

are immediate threats to the security of the State of Israel and its inhabitants.

5. A strong army must be maintained, an army that will be able to deal with the threats of the Arab states and the internal societal challenges. It will be the "nation's army" and will play an important role in social integration, as well as other societal tasks.

6. Operations initiated by Israel and retaliatory raids should be carried out to deter the enemy.

7. The ultimate deterrence should be developed against the desire to destroy Israel.

8. In defending the homeland, all possible means should be used without considering the opinions of the international community which abandoned the Jews during the Holocaust.

9. Jews from all over the world should be brought to Israel in order to build a strong state and the entire nation will be its army.

10. A united society should be established regarding security issues in order to deal with the conflict challenges.

11. The nation should be educated to accept the possibility of living for a long period of time in the shadow of the conflict.

12. Opportunities for military, political and economic cooperation with nations of the world should be used.

With the occupation after the Six-Day War, a number of basic premises were added which stemmed from the dramatic changes taking place after the war. Israel had occupied the West Bank, the Gaza Strip, the Sinai Peninsula, and the Golan Heights. Despite the wishes of many society members and government leaders who wanted to remain in the occupied territories for various reasons, the government did not decide on annexing all the territories, but rather Israeli law was applied over East Jerusalem in 1967, and in 1980 a bill was passed uniting East and West Jerusalem as the unified capital of the State of Israel. In 1981 a Basic Law was enacted to apply Israeli law, jurisdiction and administration over the Golan Heights. The other territories were perceived as a kind of trust in the event negotiations took place between the Arab states and Israel. During that period, the basic assumption took root that Israel would never retreat to the Green Line, the internationally recognized border, on the West Bank. Under the pretext of solidifying security, new settlements were built in the occupied territories of the West Bank, Sinai, Golan Heights and the Gaza Strip.

Considering these basic premises, the revised attitudes towards the conflict demanded the investment of great resources in order to fulfill the individual and collective needs of Jewish society members. For example, resilience had to be developed in order to enable society members to experience a routine life of never-ending stress and new conditions were required to enable Jewish society to successfully stand up against the Arab enemy, with preference for a complete military victory that would end the conflict once and for all.

Managing an intractable conflict demands socio-psychological resources. The Jewish leadership knew that it had to have a clear, convincing and organized rationale that would not only describe and explain the existence and the continuation of the conflict, but also one that would enable continued daily living in the shadow of the conflict, with everything that entailed. Thus, an ethos of conflict was developed along with the collective memory, whose main themes supplied the psychological conditions necessary to face the challenges of the conflict. The narrative that resulted transmitted and cultivated all the themes that can be found in all conflicts of this type throughout the world. In addition, the government made every effort to suppress information contradictory to these narratives and prevent it from reaching the public. On the direct order of Ben Gurion even letters of soldiers were censored. **Thus, the public lived under Spartan conditions, within a fortified wall, lacking openness or access to criticism, and without the democratic values of a free flow of information or equality for all citizens: The free flow of information was blocked by the government.**

The Arab citizens of Israel were discriminated against institutionally and legally by the national authorities. Many were expelled during the 1948 war and some, even immediately after it ended. About 500 villages were systematically destroyed, and most of their land was confiscated. About 150,000 of the Arabs who remained were placed under the jurisdiction of a military government.[66] **Newly revealed documents in the state archive show how the Israeli security and governmental apparatus in the 1950–60s implemented policies that kept the Arab minority in Israel under direct control and maintained their low status by discrimination, preventing higher education, and**

preserving their traditional social structure. The formal government discussions even touched upon the possibility of their expulsion.[67]

Moreover, the security apparatus was used by the leadership to supervise Jewish opposition, and the institutions of checks and balances as well of the legal system were staffed by individuals close to the government's political views. In addition, Jews who immigrated to Israel from North Africa and Asia and members of the political opposition were discriminated against by the governing systems. In fact, Israel, during the first decades if its existence was more similar to an authoritarian state than to a democratic one. Ben Gurion, as a powerful leader, believed that the enormous challenges that were facing the young state justified his autocratic style of leadership.[68] But at the same time, he and the formal institutions were imparting the view that Israel was a bastion of democracy. He set conventions about the nature of the conflict, Arabs, security, Jewish past victimhood, relationship between religion and the state, and the view of democracy with the authoritarian practices that were well absorbed by the political culture of the state and can be clearly detected in the present days.

Closure and government supervision were appropriate for conditions that made it necessary to maintain the narratives of the ethos of conflict and collective memory. All official and unofficial societal institutions were mobilized to achieve this objective and were directed to inculcate and support these values. In this reality, a conflict culture developed which became hegemonic and was dominant and remained unchallenged until the beginning of the 1970s. This is not surprising in view of the evidence that almost all states begin their conflict with consensual mobilization to cope with the enemy.

The next chapter will deal with the second period of psycho-societal developments in Jewish society, which started with the beginning of the peace process with Egypt, and which was characterized by feelings of hope, evolving at least among part of the Jewish public.

CHAPTER 2

A Spark of Hope

CONSTITUTIVE EVENTS OF THE 1970s
AND THE CONSEQUENT CHANGES

On 9 November 1977, a light appeared at the end of the tunnel of intractable conflict between the Arabs and Jews. On that day, following secret talks in Romania and Morocco, Egyptian President Sadat announced in a public speech before the People's Council of the Egyptian parliament that he was ready to go to the Knesset in Jerusalem to discuss peace with Israel. In his speech, Sadat declared: *"I am ready to go to their home, to the Knesset itself, to argue with them..."* And on 19 November 1977, at 9:00 in the evening, the Egyptian President's plane landed at Ben Gurion Airport, and there, waiting for him, was Israel's entire political elite, including Prime Minister Menachem Begin (who had been elected just six months previously), Israeli President Ephraim Katzir, and the heads of the opposition. At that moment, an alternative to the conflict supporting narrative was created: Arabs could be trusted and could be partners to a peace process. Later, in the 1980s and the early 1990s, this new narrative became legitimized and even institutionalized.[69] In truth, the first signs of the alternative narrative had already appeared during the 1960s, when the conflict was at its climax, with left-wing groups that supported peacemaking with Arabs like Matzpen, New Outlook and Siach—all very small left organizations. But the real credit for its development must primarily be attributed to the War of Attrition (1969-1970) which claimed the lives of so many (in total, about 1,000 soldiers were killed) and led to increasing soberness about the striking victory in 1967. Cracks began to appear in the widely accepted consensus about national goals: The status of existing narratives was gradually undermined and new narratives, which had not succeeded in penetrating consciousness during the 1950s and 1960s, began to seep into the public space.

Although the Six-Day War victory revived long-standing territorial aspirations held by mainstream groups of Jewish society, in contrast, voices of a small minority were heard unequivocally opposing these aspirations. The conflict between these two political positions aroused important public discourse, evaluating, inter alia, basic political, social, and military assumptions which had guided Israeli society for the previous two decades; but primarily, the discussion raised questions about the nature of the occupation and its effects on Jewish society, as well as the issue of a stable political solution to the conflict that would ensure the existence of the State of Israel.

On 28 April 1970, some 70 twelfth grade students, mostly from Jerusalem, had sent a letter to Prime Minister Golda Meir, a letter which was later known as the "first letter from high school seniors." The young people signing the letter, who were on the point of being recruited into the army, protested against Israeli policies in the occupied territories, against the continuation of the War of Attrition, and against the refusal of the Israeli government to respond to the initial contacts by mediators attempting to spark discussion of a peace agreement with the Arab states. Almost simultaneous to the protests at home, dramatic events were taking place elsewhere in the Middle East. In the autumn of 1970, President Gamal Abdul Nasser of Egypt died, and he was replaced by Anwar Sadat. On a number of occasions, Sadat had expressed his willingness to sign an agreement with the State of Israel, but he was not taken seriously by the Israeli leadership and his comments were ignored. Israeli mental closure, inflexibility, and deep distrust inspired greater approval for the frozen conception of continuing the conflict. But at the beginning of the 1970s, artists began to protest Israeli intransigence and the occupation, and to cast doubt on the morality of Jewish conduct in the conflict. This worldview appeared in Israeli theatrical plays (for example, in plays (such as *Queen of the Bathtub* by Hanoch Levin, in 1970, *Fashkolnik* by Rami Rozen in 1975, and *Cherli Ka-Cherli* by Danny Horowitz, 1978, in the plastic arts (in works by Micha Ullman, Pinhas Cohen-Gan, Motti Mizrahi, and Shraga Weil) and in literature (in the story "Early in the Summer" by A.B. Yehoshua in 1974). The contents of the artistic works referred to Israeli militarism, violation of human rights, victimization of the Palestinians, and the unnecessary sacrifices of the Israeli soldiers. This mindset of protest had, until then, been unknown to most members of Jewish society in Israel.

The Yom Kippur War, initiated by Sadat in October 1973, intensified the protest—the war was perceived as proof of the justness of the alternative narrative supporting peace making. In 1975, the Israeli Council for Israeli-Palestinian Peace was established by respected figures in Israeli society, including Reserve General-Major Matti Peled, one of the heroes of the Six-

Day War; former director-general of the Finance Ministry Yaacov Arnon; former Secretary-General of the Labor Party Lova Eliav; journalist Uri Avneri; and Reserve Colonel Meir Pail. The open discourse about what had previously been consensual positions, dominant for decades, intensified in the 1970s and signaled that a peace ethos had begun to claim legitimacy. The new messages, like the people who transmitted them, became a legitimate part of public discourse in Israel. The eight beliefs composing the ethos of conflict and collective memory began to lose their complete hegemonic dominance.

Peace with Egypt

There is no doubt that the constitutive event of this period was the arrival of the Egyptian president in Israel. **A constitutive event** is defined as a very important occurrence that takes place in society; Society members experience this event directly (by participating) and/or indirectly (when watching it, hearing or reading about it). The event receives great resonance and is relevant to the well-being of society members and society as a whole. It involves society members, takes a central place in public discussions and on the public agenda, and produces information that makes society members reevaluate their psychological repertoire and may often move them even to change it. This **constitutive event** is an example of a very positive step with favorable consequences. Not all constitutive events are positive. Some have had negative results with severe implications.

Sadat's visit was a rare historic turning point that had been accomplished in an extremely short period of time. Egypt had for so many years been considered the most dangerous enemy of Israel and only some few months prior to this moment, a large puppet of Sadat, dressed as a Gestapo officer, had led one of the Purim parades. And here, within an unusually short period of time, without pressure from the Israeli public, in a secretly arranged process by the leadership, the ultimate enemy of yesterday had turned into a respected partner for peace. It is difficult to imagine a similar top-down development taking place as quickly as this one did. Indeed, the world had not experienced similar cases, especially one that did not involve external pressure, as many other cases of peacemaking have shown. **This teaches us that when the leaders of the government unite with the leaders of the opposition and unequivocally inform the public that a past enemy can be a partner for peace and that it is possible to reach conflict resolution, society members accept this message. Indeed,** on that fateful evening in November, Israeli citizens were glued to their television screens, almost refusing to believe that this was actually happening. **The very foundations of their accepted beliefs were being shaken. This significant event forced many Jewish Israelis to reevaluate the socio-psychological repertoire that they had always taken for granted. For the first time, they were really seeing an event that contradicted everything they had ever heard, learned, and thought for years, which testified to the fact that peace with the Arabs was possible.**

The peace agreement with Egypt was finally signed on 26 March 1979, and unequivocally proved that the Arabs could be partners to a successful peace process. The agreement removed the strongest Arab state militarily from the cycle of violence and significantly weakened the existential threat to Israel. Moreover, it also proved that the basic need for security could be achieved by peacemaking rather than only by occupying territory and managing a violent conflict. Suddenly new hope was born. Importantly, "hope" is not only a flowery phrase but also a concept describing a certain reality: It is defined as *"a feeling of expectation and desire for a certain thing to happen."* It enfolds the image of a goal, characterized as positive, and the ways to achieve this goal.[70] Now, such hope for the first time existed in Israeli public discourse. It found expression in the incipient establishment and development of a meaningful peace movement, Peace Now, which succeeded in attracting tens of thousands of Israeli Jews. The movement was established to advance the peace process with Egypt and after the signing of the peace agreement, it actively supported initiating a similar process with the Palestinians as well.[71]

These years witnessed a series of momentous events. As discussed above, Sadat's trip to Jerusalem in 1977 resulted in the signing of a historic peace agreement two years later in return for full evacuation of the Sinai Peninsula. The War in Lebanon in 1982, considered the first Israeli-initiated "war by choice," aroused unprecedented protest and opposition; and the first intifada, erupting in December 1987 was the initial expression of widespread Palestinian opposition to life under occupation, and in time, became a stubborn popular rebellion. All these events considerably expanded and deepened the alternative narrative of supporting peace making. Each of them in turn created cracks in the accepted belief that the essence of the conflict was an existential struggle (in contrast to a dispute over goals which were not vitally important, but merely circumstantial).

This led to a reexamination of the possibility of conducting a peace process with Arab leadership and even a reevaluation of the "Arab character." The cracks spread and created a fracture of the dominant ethos of conflict, a fissure in the central narrative of the collective memory, and in the myths it had engendered. This served to accelerate the development of new societal beliefs—the hegemonic image of little David struggling against Goliath began to change, along with a reexamination of the acceptance that war was a necessity, that the fighters were defending our homes, and that they were more humane and more moral than their adversaries. The memory of the hundreds of thousands of Israelis who participated in a demonstration organized by Peace Now to protest the massacre under the observing eyes of the Israeli army in the Palestinian refugee camps of Sabra and Shatila in Beirut by the Lebanese Christians (who were allowed by the Israeli army to enter the camps) and the commission of inquiry in its wake, epitomizes how deep the fracture was and how immense the polarization in Israeli society had developed.

In the late 1980s, two important events became extremely significant vis-à-vis Israeli control of the West Bank. On 31 July 1988, Hussein, the king of Jordan, announced the administrative separation of the West Bank from Jordan and the renunciation of any claim to that territory, ending the possibility that the West Bank would be returned to Jordan, as some Israeli leaders had hoped. And on 15 November 1988, the head of the Palestine Liberation Organization, Yasser Arafat, proclaimed the establishment of a Palestinian state, and actually recognized the State of Israel within its 1967 borders, paving the way for a division of the area into two states.

The "New Historians"

The group of "new historians" who appeared in Israeli academia during the 1980s, hold a special place in the formation of the new alternative discourse. They were academic researchers who reexamined the findings of accepted historiography about the Zionist movement and the establishment of the State of Israel, from the beginning of the twentieth century up to the 1960s, particularly on the basis of new documentation which had been released in the 1970s and 1980s. Their objective was to investigate what had actually taken place during that period, without bias, and as such, to put all of the accepted beliefs of the official Zionist narrative to the test. The main researchers of the group were Tom Segev, Benny Morris, Ilan Pappe, Gershon Shafir, Baruch Kimmerling, Yoel Migdal, Simha Flappan, and Avi Shlaim. Their works revealed basic flaws in research of the history of the state and the history of the conflict—flaws which had been accepted not only by official state institutions, like the educational system, but also in academia. They discovered, *inter alia*, that, until the 1930s, the British had tried to prevent the establishment of a Palestinian state and, behind the scenes, had clearly supported the creation of a Jewish state. This contradicted the official narrative according to which Britain did everything in its power to prevent the possibility of a Jewish state. In addition, it was found that the violent events of 1936–1939 were not directed against the Jews, but rather were an armed Arab rebellion primarily in protest against the British who were ruling the country. It was also revealed that no small number of Palestinian refugees had been expelled from Israel by the Jewish army, in stark contradiction to the accepted narrative according to which most, if not all the refugees "fled willingly" following instructions from the Supreme Muslim Council. Furthermore, considering the War of Independence, it now became clear that Israel had been at an advantage in human resources and military materials, at least from a certain stage of the war. This was also completely contradictory to the official version stating that the local Arabs, with the support of the Arab nations, were numerically superior and the war represented "the few against the many." Atrocious acts committed by Jewish forces against Arabs during the war were also exposed. Finally, again in contrast to the official narrative, it became clear that Israel had not taken advantage of all the opportunities to achieve peace with the Arabs.[72] Despite these discoveries, it should also be noted that these research studies outraged other historians who disagreed with the findings and methods of these scholars.[73] Nevertheless, they not only uncovered new information about the conflict, but also revealed how deep the formal censorship and self-censorship had penetrated academia.

The Events of the 1990s

Additional important events which deepened the process of change included the Gulf War in January–February 1991, which left its scar on society in the wake of the difficult experiences of the Israeli population, who spent much time sitting in sealed rooms and shelters, wearing protective gas masks, helplessly waiting for rocket attacks from Iraq. As result of American pressure, in November 1991, an international peace conference assembled in Madrid, with the participation of an Israeli delegation, and delegations from Arab states and additional countries. This was followed by bilateral talks between the sides, focusing on political topics. In addition, multilateral talks also began, dealing with regional subjects, including water, economic cooperation, and the refugee problem. In Washington, bilateral talks took place between an Israeli delegation and a joint Jordanian–Palestinian delegation. All these events ultimately led to indirect negotiations between Israel and the Palestine Liberation Organization (PLO), after the Likud had lost the 1992 elections and Yitzhak Rabin, representing the Labor Party, had become prime minister.

On 13 September 1993, a Declaration of Principles (the Oslo 1 Accord) was signed between Israel and the PLO, with each side recognizing the other. The accord goals included Israeli withdrawal from the Gaza Strip and from Jericho, and the creation of the Palestinian National Authority. The PLO recognized Israel's right to exist in peace and security, obligated itself not to engage in terror or in other violent activity, and promised to seek a peaceful solution to the conflict. The mutual recognition between Israel and the PLO went into effect with the signing of the Declaration of Principles which determined a framework for the administration of Palestinian autonomy in the Gaza Strip and on the West Bank. This was also a surprise, like the visit of the Egyptian president had been, 16 years earlier. But this time the reactions were different. The rightist opposition led by the Likud party expressed strong resistance towards the agreement because it negated the realization of its main objective to establish a "Greater Israel," including the West Bank and the Gaza Strip (Eretz Yisrael Hashlema in Hebrew).

In 1994 Israel began to carry out the first stage of the Declaration of Principles and withdrew its forces from the Gaza Strip and from Jericho, and the Palestinian Authority was established under the auspices of Yasser Arafat, the head of the PLO. The Oslo II Accords were signed in Taba, Sinai, on 27 September 1995, giving the Palestinians independent authority over Palestinian cities on the West Bank and Gaza, as well as 450 Palestinian villages. It was agreed that elections would be conducted in the areas controlled by Palestinian Authority. The West Bank was divided into three categories: A, B, and C.[74] In spite of these significant achievements, it is important to note that the Oslo Agreements did not relate to or solve central issues that constituted the heart of the conflict: the establishment of a Palestinian state, its borders, the division of Jerusalem, the security safeguards, the question of the return of refugees and the status of the Jewish settlements in the occupied territories, among others. It was determined that discussions about these central issues would begin no later than 1996 and would end before May 1999. These discussions never took place. But the Oslo Agreements led to a number of changes among part of the Jewish public in Israel. The agreements contributed to the legitimization and the humanization of the Palestinians and enabled people to see them as partners to peace talks, at least among a majority of Israeli Jews. Moreover, they aided in recognizing the unique Palestinian national identity and raised the possible establishment of a Palestinian state.

However, the agreement with the Palestinians aroused deep disagreements in the political arena and in Jewish society, and the Likud, the second largest party in the Knesset in this period, expressed extreme and unequivocal opposition to that dramatic step. In the end, the accords were passed by the Knesset, but the great polarization between supporters and opponents led to a bitter struggle for public opinion which was accompanied by demonstrations and protests.[75] In February 1994, Baruch Goldstein, a resident of Hebron and an active member of the extreme rightwing Kach political organization, entered the Cave of the Patriarchs in Hebron and shot 29 Muslim Palestinians to death and wounded 125 more during their prayers. This constitutive event for Palestinians precipitated a deadly wave of terror in Israel, which was carried out by the opposition to the Palestinian Authority—the Hamas[76] and the Jihad[77] movements—in which dozens of Israeli citizens were killed. (Until the terror attack by Goldstein, Hamas had only conducted two acts of terrorism in the occupied territories, with no Jewish dead). The Palestinian terror attacks heightened the rift in the Jewish public, which peaked with the signing of the Oslo II Accords, and a wave of demonstrations against the accord broke out, some of which were violent and included incitement against the government and its policies. These events represented a difficult state of polarization, with one side perceiving real signs of a peace process on the ground, while for the other side, the Palestinian violence provided evidence of a continuation of the intractable conflict. Under these circumstances, Prime Minister Yitzhak Rabin had to navigate the state and supply the basic needs of the Jewish public, and most importantly, the need for security.[78]

In order to stop the erosion of support for the peace process, the Israeli heads of state decided to hold a demonstration of support for the process, which took place at the main square of Tel Aviv on 4 November 1995. At the end of the demonstration, as he was leaving the square, Prime Minister Rabin was assassinated by Yigal Amir, a religious-nationalist Jewish student who opposed the peace process policies. In February, Palestinian terror attacks struck Israeli cities with great intensity following the Israeli assassination of the "engineer," Yahya Ayyash (one of the architects of the wave of suicide bombing attacks of the 1990s) on the orders of the new prime minister, Shimon Peres, who had assumed the position after the assassination of Yitzhak Rabin.

In May 1996, the rightwing Likud Party won the elections, and their candidate for prime minister, Benjamin Netanyahu, put together a rightwing government. During the election campaign, Netanyahu had obligated himself to honor the agreements signed by Israel, and although he delayed the implementation of the interim agreement, in 1997, he signed the agreement to determine Israeli army deployment in Hebron and in 1998, he signed the Wye River Memorandum, which detailed steps to implement the Oslo Agreements, while maintaining reciprocity. However, as evidenced in later years, it appears that he actually did everything in his power to revoke, or at least to delay, the Oslo peace process.

In principle, even during Netanyahu's term as prime minister, the basic assumptions that had guided the Rabin government had not changed, at least not publicly or officially.[79] This held true even though Netanyahu considered the Palestinians, under Yasser Arafat, only fulfilling their obligations in part; and he coined the slogan, "If they give, they'll receive; if they don't give, they won't receive." During his term of office, a violent confrontation broke out between the Israeli army and the forces of the Palestinian Authority, following the opening of the Western Wall tunnel in Jerusalem in September 1996 on the order of the prime minister. The Israeli act was considered a strike against a place sacred to Islam, Temple Mount. In the violence that erupted, 17 Israeli soldiers and close to 100 Palestinians lost their lives.

Along with the changes that took place during this second period, the settlement project in the occupied territories, which had begun immediately after the Six-Day War during the term of a Labor Party government, was considerably expanded. Construction progressed intensively on the West Bank, the Gaza Strip, and the Golan Heights. But the most dramatic increase in the number of settlers began only after the Likud, led by Menachem Begin, gained control of the government. Immediately after the elections in 1977, there were 38 settlements with 1,900 settlers. A decade later, in the 1980s, the number of settlers had jumped to about 50,000, who were living in more than 100 different settlements, including in new Jewish cities established in occupied areas. Netanyahu significantly increased the Jewish settlements on the West Bank and in the Gaza Strip, after Yitzhak Rabin had restricted them to what he called "security settlements" (settlements along the borders of the 1967 line) and had promised that they would not be expanded. In 1999 there were already 183,900 settlers, in addition to Jewish residents of East Jerusalem. These settlements, which continued to expand, greatly affected the course of the conflict and relations with the Palestinians, although the government repeatedly made the misleading and propagandist statement that "the settlements are not an obstacle to peace."

In the elections for prime minster in 1999, Ehud Barak, the nominee of the Labor Party, was victorious and he promised to implement peace policies and to continue the legacy of Yitzhak Rabin, who had established the meaningful peace process with the Palestinian nation. The term of Barak began with hope. At first, he began negotiations with Syria. But he got cold feet and decided to turn to negotiation with Palestinians. In May 2000 Israel withdrew from Lebanon after being there since 1982, although the IDF had withdrawn to southern Lebanon in 1985. The deadly attacks of Hezbollah on Israeli forces and the constant demonstrations of the Four Mothers organization deminading withdrawal forced Barak to make the decision. We will discuss Barak's term of office in the next chapter.

As noted, the effects of the events that have been described above, starting from the visit of Egyptian President Sadat to Jerusalem, resulted in clear lines of disagreement in Jewish-Israeli society. They marked two opposing camps, termed the left and the right, or doves and hawks—a division which still exists and expresses the split, and even fracture of Israeli society when relating to the conflict. At the end of the 1970s and the beginning of the 1980s, the minority alternative position gained legitimacy and was gradually seen as moral and therefore acceptable, and this aroused lively public debate. The existence of more than one alternative was significant for a society that, until then, had punished any minority who had dared to disagree with the official narrative by ostracism and sanctions. The next stage, the institutionalization of these narratives and viewpoints took place during the 1980s when they penetrated the social establishment, including political parties such as Ratz and the Labor Party, the media and cultural and academic elites. The alternative narrative was also adopted by civil society organizations like Yesh Gvul ("There's a Limit"), which was established during the War in Lebanon, and Women in Black and B'Tselem (The Israeli Information Center for Human Rights in the Occupied Territories), formed during the first intifada, in 1988 and in 1989 respectively. All of them expressed resistance to the continuation of the occupation from a moral point of view.

When considering the perception of reality expressed through the narratives held by society members, it is important to note that the described constitutive events which led to new, difficult, and intensive public discussion, also exposed significant rifts on a wide range of other matters in Israeli society. The deepest prohibitions and taboos began to rise to the surface, and profound disagreements developed about a variety of issues, beginning with the morality of Jewish behavior at the time the state was being established, the nature of Zionism and ending with the future of the occupied territories and lines of the peace settlement. In addition, deep analysis reveals specific changes in the issues relating to the narrative of ethos of conflict and collective memory, which we will now detail.

CHANGES IN THE CONFLICT-SUPPORTING NARRATIVES

Changes in the Belief of the Justness of Our Goals

The belief in the justness of the demand for "greater Israel" lost its absolute character and raised doubts among different sectors of the public. More and more society members were no longer ready to automatically accept the decisions of the government, and many did not view every initiative involving the use of power as necessarily serving Israeli goals. The 1990s witnessed a dramatic turn of direction in attitudes among both the leadership and the public. At the beginning of the decade, there was a gradually increasing willingness to return sections of the West Bank as part of the developing peace process, and public opinion polls showed a reduction in the number of people who considered that holding on to the territories was of supreme importance.[80] At the same time, the belief that the Palestinians actually constituted a nation gained legitimacy, and there was in Israel a decline in popularity of beliefs among certain segments that denied their claims to human rights. The alternative ethos began to flourish, an ethos that supports a peace process. In the beginning of the nineties the support for the establishment of the Palestinian state started ascending, reaching its climax of 55% by 1999. Correspondingly, the basic beliefs of the conflict supporting narrative were starting to change among some sectors of the public.[81]

Changes in Security Beliefs

Even at the beginning of the 1970s, changes in security beliefs could already be identified. For example, the limits of using military power to create security was increasingly being recognized, and more and more Jewish Israelis adopted the belief that peaceful relations with the Arab states was more important to maintain security than stubbornly insisting on holding on to territory. The successful withdrawal from Sinai supplied decisive evidence that this was so, and as the years passed, willingness to exchange territories for peace increased.

An article published in the daily newspaper *Ha'aretz* on 24 June 1988, presented the opinions of a number of generals in the Israeli army on central security issues, and there was disagreement among them about the future of the territories. Zvi Ayalon, who had served as deputy commander-in-chief, stated that *"the security of a state is composed of a number of factors, and these are mainly military power, the economy and industry, education and societal conditions ... In my opinion, our control of the Palestinian entity first of all harms three of the components of security: society, the economy and education..."* He summarized, *"Everything I have said leads to the conclusion that there is no security advantage in holding on to territories."* Yishayahu Gavish, the former commander of the IDF Southern Command, asserted that *"it [was] not necessary to hold on to territories for security needs, but there is no doubt that there are territories that we will have to hold on to. And that is already a subject for negotiation."* And of course, there were generals who thought that continuing to hold onto all the territories was vital.[82]

Additional changes also appeared in beliefs referring to relations between security institutions and society. The viewpoint that sanctified the security establishment and granted its members full trust was gradually being challenged. Demands began to be heard for increasing civilian control over security institutions, for supervision of the enormous security budget, for reduction of military censorship, and in general—for public-civilian discussion of security issues. Demands of this type and the resulting open discussion were expressed, for example, in newspaper investigations touching upon Israeli failures in military combat which had occurred through the years or tragedies during training accidents, in requests that the civilian courts discuss military operations and decisions of the military echelons, in publishing soldiers' complaints about improper conduct by the army, and in public demands to reduce the defense budget.

From the moment these issues were critically raised, more and more failures, misappropriations, moral misdeeds, and even violations of law were exposed, which somewhat lowered the prestige of the military establishment. The image of the fearless fighter was also shattered in the years following the Yom Kippur War, as the cases of post-traumatic stress syndrome and the scars left by combat experiences rose to the surface. Even the image of Israel as a dauntless nation always willing to go into battle began to crack, and during the War in the Gulf in 1991, a fairly wide-ranging public discussion took place as to the legitimacy of residents leaving the rocket-struck area around Tel Aviv for safer areas.[83]

But despite all these changes in the content of security beliefs, their continued presence in the Israeli ethos remained central during the 1980s and 1990s. The war in Lebanon, the first intifada and the massive terror attacks of the 1990s that claimed many victims, led most Jewish-Israelis to continue to believe that the security of the state and its citizens remained under significant threat. In September 1997, an opinion poll conducted by Gallop and published in the daily newspaper, *Yedioth Ahronoth*, found that only 33% of Jews in Israel considered that their personal safely was satisfactory ("very good" or "good"). Nevertheless, trust in the Israeli army remained very high among the Jewish public in Israel. The level of trust in the army has always remained above 75% and it has continually been rated higher than any other institution in Israel.[84] In 2019, the IDF trust level even reached 90%.

Contributing to these tendencies in society—again—were the Israeli mass media. Despite certain changes occurring in their ethos during these years and the expanding media criticism of security areas that had, in the past, been considered taboo, in general, the media continued to express the official positions of the political and military establishments, which of course continued to emphasize the **dangers** facing Israel. This tendency actually increases in times of crisis, as characteristic of an intractable conflict. The sense of anxiety which has been nurtured through the years and is still being nurtured as these lines are being written, creates adherence to security beliefs and is an important obstacle to developing beliefs of reconciliation necessary for achieving a solution to the conflict.

Changes in Beliefs about Arabs

The events of the Yom Kippur War for the first time led to the image of Arab soldiers as those who were able to surprise and even to triumph against the Israeli army in battle. From being cowards, primitive, and easily incited, as Jewish Israelis had imagined them, they had now become brave, and resolute. Moreover, Sadat's visit to Jerusalem also gave Israelis a more positive view of Arabs. A few years later, the war in Lebanon presented the Palestinians in a way that Israeli Jews had not considered them previously—as a determined nation conducting a struggle for self-determination and independence against the might of a powerful army, many times stronger than they were. The same image was reflected during the first intifada, at least in the eyes of some Jewish Israelis. who understood that most of this struggle was not carried out violently, and thus perceived of Palestinians as strong-willed, courageous, persevering, and united in their efforts. And finally, the peace process with the Palestinians in the 1990s fundamentally changed the relationship between the two nations and affected many Israeli Jews in the way they viewed their enemy of long decades. This change also held true for Jordanians, who signed a peace agreement with the State of Israel in 1994 and thus, "came out of the closet," as unofficial relations had been carried on with Israeli leaders since 1948. All the experiences cited above changed the accepted stereotypes about Arabs among the Israeli Jews. Even the relations that developed on a personal level with Palestinians from the occupied territories who crossed the Green Line border to work in Israel, as well as contacts with Palestinians who were Israeli citizens, reduced the negative stereotypes.[85]

During these years, changes also took place in the beliefs about delegitimization. From 1993, the year Oslo I was signed, Palestinian leaders began to appear in person in the Israeli media, or alternatively, had meetings with Jewish leaders; especially memorable in this context are the handshakes between Rabin and Arafat and then later, between Netanyahu and Arafat, transmitting a clear message to the Jewish public about Palestinian humanization and legitimacy. This enabled Israelis to view the Palestinians as behaving within the boundaries of international norms. Simultaneously, the process of Palestinian personalization was also developing and made it possible to see them as individuals, as human beings, with characteristics similar to those of Israeli Jews. In addition, during this period, the Arab leaders who appeared in the media authentically explained Palestinian behavior, aspirations, and needs, and thus, the Jewish public, for the first time, heard the side of their opponent in the conflict without mediation or filtering.

Another important way that the delegitimization belief began to change during these decades relates to the decline of the general categorization term, "Arabs." The Israeli Jews began to refer separately to Egyptians, Lebanese, Syrians, Palestinians, and even to different groups of Palestinians. The reduction in the use of the "Arab" category reflected the differentiation created at that time in the Jewish Israeli attitude towards the various Arab nations and as mentioned, even Palestinians were seen as consisting of various groups, with some supporting the peace process, and there were also differences among those who opposed it.[86]

There were, of course, many sectors of the Jewish public who continued to hold a very negative image of Arabs in general, and of Palestinians in particular. Even during the peace process, in these sectors, the Palestinians were considered as having negative intentions. On average, between 1986 and 2005, more than 50% of the Jewish public in Israel believed that the real objective of the Arabs was to destroy the state of Israel, and among them, about 25% believed that the Arabs also aspired to annihilate most of the Jews in Israel.[87] The violent terrorist attacks against Jews took place while the political process was going on, and contributed to those feelings, and these attacks created facilitating grounds for the spread of negative stereotypes as well as public campaigns led by the opposition which painted the Palestinians as untrustworthy and as dishonest about their real intentions. The important fact was that the consensual and dominant opinion had been broken and public opinion had become heterogeneous, as a sizable minority held opinions which were very different from the accepted opinions among almost all society members during the first decades following the establishment of the state. The opinion of the minority that viewed Palestinians as partners to peace making was well grounded in political parties, civil society and societal groups like artists, or academia.

Changes in the Self- Perceptions of Jews

Parallel to the changes in beliefs about Arabs, changes also took place among some of the Jewish public in their beliefs about Jews, in a kind of mirror image. The trust in beliefs relating to Israelis as moral and humane began to erode and this was true as well of perceptions about Jewish courage and determination. The facts themselves illustrated that Israelis had carried out immoral acts, that they had been defeated in battle and that they had missed opportunities to solve the conflict with Arabs peacefully—and some sectors of the public actually accepted the information and changed their views.

Following the Yom Kippur War, there was already a reduction in estimation of Israeli soldiers' courage and determination in comparison to soldiers in Arab countries; in the War in Lebanon, on the other hand, the perception of the nation as moral and humane was deeply damaged, after the publication of controversial actions by the Israeli army including the bombing of residential neighborhoods in Beirut, and of course, the fact that the Israelis had turned a blind eye to the massacre carried out by Christian-Maronites in the Palestinian refugee camps of Sabra and Shatila. For the first time in the history of Israel's wars, sectors of the public, including some political leaders, openly came out against the war, and the phenomenon of conscientious objection to army service began to appear. Of special note was the case of Colonel Eli Geva as the only high-ranking officer in the history of Israel who, during the war, resigned from his role as commander of an armored brigade in protest of the way Israel was managing the war.

The positive self-image continued to erode during the first intifada and the attempt to suppress it by force, using the military; the response of "breaking the Palestinians arms and legs"—in accord with the directives of then-Minister of Defense, Yitzhak Rabin—had a particularly negative effect as, at the time, the Palestinians were conducting a struggle without extreme violence. During those years, another belief that was becoming more prevalent was that Israeli presence in the occupied territories had a negative effect on military morality and was sometimes leading "our children" to behave with great brutality, unwarranted in dealing with an occupied population.

Despite the groups in Jewish society who, during the 1980s and 1990s, began to show interest in the criticism that came to light about Israeli actions in the occupied territories, most Israeli citizens remained indifferent and continued to hold a positive self-image. This public developed various kinds of defensive strategies, such as denial, rationalization, projection, or repression, making it easier for them to cope with the realities of the occupation and with information that countered the collective positive self-image of Jews in the context of the conflict.[85]

Changes in Victimhood Beliefs

As described above, for many years, Jewish society in Israel maintained the self-image of being the sole victims of the conflict with the Arabs in general and with the Palestinians in particular; it was the War in Lebanon that first fractured the strong belief among Jews in their victimhood, and that crack deepened during the violent suppression of the first intifada. Only in the 1990s, when the severe wave of suicide terrorism broke out, did the perception of self-victimization again intensify.

What was it, then, that changed the sense of self-victimhood for a bit more than a decade? During the war in Lebanon, Israeli soldiers witnessed Palestinian victimization with their own eyes, whether in their home neighborhoods that soldiers had forcibly entered, or in Palestinian refugee camps. As mentioned above, the massacre in the Sabra and Shatila refugee camps, which the Jewish soldiers did not do anything to prevent, represented the ultimate disillusionment. Later, a similar picture became clear in the occupied territories when the Israeli army tried to use force to overcome the Palestinian popular uprising. (It appears that the Israeli choice to adopt the Arab term, *intifada*, exposed a desire to cover up the real nature of what was happening—a revolt or a popular uprising.) As a result of the soldiers' experiences, the general Israeli public discovered what was taking place in the territories, whether directly from the soldiers themselves or with the mediation of the media.

As this information became public knowledge, two complementary processes developed in Jewish Israeli society—the first was an intensification in the perception of Palestinians as victims of the conflict, and the second was the deterioration of the sense of sole victimization of Jews. These changes, of course, took place only among a part of the Jewish population. Many Jews continued to view themselves as the only victims of the conflict—a fixation stemming from deep internalization, both personal and cultural, of the perception that the Jews have been victims from the dawn of history.

Changes in Beliefs about Patriotism

Beliefs relating to patriotism remained part of the Israeli ethos during those years, but their centrality diminished considerably. Some groups among Israeli Jews began to question the necessity of sacrificing one's life in confrontation with the Arabs (just as the Biblical attempt to sacrifice Isaac was unnecessary). They also expressed less willingness to volunteer for national missions or to suffer continuing hardship for the sake of the state. From 1987 to 1994, the National Security and Public Opinion Project surveyed Israelis as to whether they agreed with the statement that "it is good to die for our country." In 1987 a striking majority of about 70% agreed with the statement, but by 1994, agreement had decreased to about 60%, a fall of 10%.[86]

Simultaneous to the fall in support for myths and beliefs glorifying patriotic behavior, new beliefs began to flourish in certain segments of the society, including the aspiration for individualism and self-actualization. Because of these new beliefs, avoiding military service, and emigrating from Israel were becoming more and more legitimate and correspondingly, they became more and more normative. A survey taken among Jews in Israel in 1986 found that about 50% of respondents viewed emigration from Israel as unacceptable, in comparison to 70% three years earlier. Surveys conducted by the Public Opinion Project indicated that in March 1984, 5.3% of the population viewed themselves as possibly emigrating from Israel, while in August 1985, the percentage had risen to 7.7% and in December 1986, 9% responded in the affirmative.[87] From the mid-1990s, the percentage of people who said that they were convinced that they wanted to live in Israel in the long term fell—in 1996, 84% replied that they were convinced; in 1997, 70% responded that they were; in 1999, the percentage had fallen to 64%; and in 2000, only 58% concurred with the statement.

Public protests like the first "letter from high school seniors," which conditioned readiness to serve the country on government actions, expressed the futility of automatic obedience. This was something that Israel had never experienced until then, and it indicated the development of a new kind of patriotism—no longer blind patriotism that obeyed the orders of the government or the army, but rather, constructive patriotism for the benefit of the country, patriotism that demanded an investigation of policies, political aims and military orders, while safeguarding moral values.

Changes in Beliefs about Unity

The democratization process taking place during Prime Minister Levi Eshkol's term of office in the late 1960s provided opportunities to express positions in opposition to the majority opinion in a variety of areas. This also held true for opinions about the Israeli-Arab-Palestinian conflict, which had reflected broad consensus from the late 1940s until the mid-1970s. But the great change occurred with the development of new societal beliefs that legitimized the prominence of alternative narratives in Jewish Israeli society, emphasizing the right to express different views than those of the majority. This change, which was not encouraged by the establishment, gradually developed after the Six-Day War in 1967, gained intensity during the Yom Kippur War, and accelerated and even became institutionalized during the War in Lebanon in 1982. Finally, in the 1990s, the polarization between the rightwing and the leftwing became solidified and stabilized, climaxing during the term of Prime Minister Yitzhak Rabin, when the rightwing camp, which opposed the Oslo Accords, conducted a campaign of resistance, including demonstrations, protest watches, distributing explanatory pamphlets and more. The most extreme example of this campaign was the comparison of Rabin to Hitler and Mussolini. An infamous demonstration in Jerusalem in October 1995 featured a poster of Rabin dressed in a black SS uniform, alongside a photo of Himmler. The poster was the work of Kach members, but many rightwing party leaders (among them, Benjamin Netanyahu) who were present on the stage ignored the slander.

In this context, the right began to label the peace process with the Palestinians, requiring withdrawal from the occupied territories, considered the ancient homeland of the Jewish people, as treason. Additionally, rightists repeatedly asserted that approval of the Oslo Agreement in the parliament (Knesset) was illegitimate because it lacked the backing of a Jewish majority—that is, the accord could get a majority of votes only with the support of the Arab parties and the Arab Knesset members. In addition to the political dispute between left and right, there was deep dissent between religious and secular Jews, leading to a broad disintegration of national unity, while, in addition, during the 1980s and 1990s significant ethnic and class discord also appeared.

Changes in Beliefs about Peace

Although peace still remained a desired objective in Israeli society, during the 1970s striking changes in the content of peace beliefs were taking place. The simplistic idealistic, utopian and amorphous perception of peace was replaced by realistic, concrete, and more complex concepts including, inter alia, recognition of the need to negotiate with the enemy and to compromise in order to reach agreement. This sparked a hope for peace which was real and concrete by nature; not vague yearnings and wishes but rather, realistic goals and plans. The new vision of peace, more substantive as well, now included painful compromises that led to national polarization and a social-political struggle on the very attempt to reach a solution.

This was, by nature, a result of circumstances in the field. During those years, Israel was for the first time, conducting negotiations with its enemy states—first, for a separation of forces agreement with Syria and Egypt in 1974 and 1975, and then for a peace agreement with Egypt between 1977–1979. The negotiations for separation of forces initially created the recognition that relations with neighbors were not necessarily binary—peace or conflict—but that they were rather multidimensional and could take many forms. It also became clear that negotiations for a peace agreement with Egypt involved many complex details that aroused intense disagreements. In any case, the results of both negotiations led to turmoil in societal beliefs about peace. Concerning peace with Egypt, the price Israel would have to pay aroused dissention among different groups in the nation. In addition, the later negotiations and agreement with the Palestinians included many details and stages and demanded an Israeli withdrawal from territories considered part of the "homeland" by a large number of Israeli Jews.

Did You Know?

Surveys show that the Jewish public differentiated among the Arab nations when evaluating the chances for achieving peace. From the mid-1970s, a majority of society members believed that it was possible to make peace with Egypt and Jordan, but not with Syria. Regarding Palestinians, only a minority of about 20% believed that peace could possibly be achieved with them, but in the mid-1990s, those who thought peace with Palestinians was possible increased to 40%. In 1999, the number of believers even reached about 57%. In other

**words, during the peace process with the Palestinians, a firm major-
ity believed in the possibility of achieving peace with them, and between 1996 and 1999 a majority of Jews (above 50%) supported the
Oslo Accords.**[88]

In spite of the turmoil, the utopian image of peace refused to disappear—
peace continued to be considered an unachievable ideal, and this view was
still accepted by large sectors of the Jewish public, primarily by rightwing
hawks. In contrast, other groups in Jewish society, the doves, began to
doubt the belief that Israel actually aspired to peace, and distrusted the
assumption that the road to peace was thwarted only by the intransigence
of the Arabs. More and more of these groups viewed the State of Israel as
unwilling to compromise and pay the price for peace and for that reason,
its government avoided entering serious negotiations by setting various
conditions, and this was especially true in the Palestinian context.

CHANGES IN THE CULTURE OF CONFLICT

More specifically and concretely, changes in the artistic and educational
realms also began to develop.

Changes in the Arts

In cultural and artistic spaces, during the 1970s, Israeli authors, play-
wrights, and filmmakers began to focus on the lives of Arabs as individuals, and this was especially true regarding Arab citizens of Israel, who
had been invisible for more than 20 years, since the establishment of the
state. In literature, in the theater, and in the cinema, a new image of Arabs
began to appear—the image was undergoing powerful humanization and
the Arab was now presented more holistically as having doubts, aspirations, and daily worries. Some of the works even prominently featured an
Arab-Palestinian individual, whether within Israel or on the West Bank,
and multi-dimensionally outlined his/her complaints, thoughts, feelings,
needs and worries.

Along with the changes being made in the presentation of Arabs and
Palestinians, there was a similar change in the depiction of Jews and the
representation of the essence of the conflict; it was sometimes illustrated
by analogies to interpersonal conflict between real people, hinting that it
was a conflict that could be solved. In general, subjects that were almost
completely absent from cultural life in the 1950s and 1960s, such as dis-

crimination, repression, violence, pride in Palestinian identity, and others were brought up and became topics of animated discussion. Many artists did not only view Palestinians as victims, but also expressed empathy with their anger, frustration and with the legitimate national Palestinian struggle. The first ice breakers, as noted, appeared at the beginning of the 1970s in plays, the visual arts, and literature. Breaking through all the conventions was not easy. The satirical review by Hanoch Levin, *Queen of the Bathtub*, was presented at the Cameri Theater in 1970. It ridiculed the arrogance, and immorality of the Jews in Israel after the Six-Day War. The play was canceled by the Israeli Film and Theater Ratings Board, but they reversed themselves when asked to give reasons for their decision. However, the public had their say in demonstrations of opposition, and the play closed after only 19 performances.

During the 1980s and the 1990s, there was increased preoccupation in art with the conflict, including a growing level of criticism and greater frequency of representations opposed to the official narrative. The First War in Lebanon, which was termed by critical groups as a "war of choice," and later as a "war of deception," consolidated strong artistic opposition to the policies of the rightwing government, and then, to the policies of the national unity government which followed it. The theater, the cinema, literature, art, satiric radio programs, and rock music, alongside the popular culture that developed from the "bottom" and included, *inter alia*, soldiers' protest songs (for example, the paraphrase of a children's song: "Pick us up, plane/ Take us to Lebanon/ We will fight for [Arik] Sharon, and we'll come home in a casket"). All of these contained expressions of protest against aggressive policies, along with demands for compromise with the Palestinians. The first intifada was seen by many Israeli artists as a serious political and moral problem that raised substantial questions about the blindness of the leadership and a society that had lost its way. From the mid-1990s, in cultural and artistic fields, discussion expanded about Israeli policies in the occupied territories of oppressing the Palestinian population, and the destructive potential of Jewish settlements that could prevent division of the land. These policies were deemed a massive historical error and as harming the foundations of the Israeli state and its society.

Noteworthy among the works of literature reflecting this new approach were the novels *The Lover* (1977) by A.B. Yehoshua, *Refuge* (1977) and *A Trumpet in the Wadi* (1987) by Sami Michael, *A Locked Room* (1980) by

Shimon Ballas, *The Smile of the Lamb* (1983) by David Grossman, and *A Good Arab* (1984) by Yoram Kaniuk; the plays *The Last Hope of Nahmani Street* (1974) by Hillel Mittelpunkt, *The Ruler of Jericho* by Yosef Mundi, *The Return* (1975) by Miriam Keini, *Cherly ka-Cherly* (1978) by Danny Horowitz, *Palestinian Girl* (1985) by Yehoshua Sobol, and *A Surrogate's Womb* (1990) by Shulamit Lapid; and the movies *Eagles* (1981), *Hamsin* (1982), *Soldier of the Night* (1984), *Rage and Glory* (1984), *Beyond the Walls* (1985), *Avanti Popolo* (1985), and *One of Us* (1989), among many other works. The mythological satiric radio program, *A Fly on Your Head*, beginning in 1968 on the army radio station, should also be mentioned.

In order to clearly and concretely illustrate the openness that was developing in the Israeli cultural climate during the years of hope, we compare two historical documentary television series that were broadcasted on the official Israeli television channel: *Amud Ha'esh* (*Pillar of Fire: The Rebirth of Israel*) and *Tkuma* (*Revival: The First 50 Years*). *Pillar of Fire* was produced by Yigal Lousin at the end of the 1970s in order to festively celebrate 25 years of statehood, and the series was ultimately broadcast in 1981. It included 19 episodes of about one hour each, focusing on the history of Zionism between 1896–1948. *Revival* was produced by Gideon Drori to commemorate the 50th anniversary of the state, and was first broadcast on Israeli television in 1998. The series included 22 episodes dealing with the history of Israel between 1948–1995. A comparison between the two series is particularly interesting as the first three episodes of *Revival* present a review of the events that had taken place between 1936–1948, and these events were at the center of the narrative presented in *Pillar of Fire*. Master thesis research in the Hebrew University by Moshe Nuriel carried out in 2015 discusses the depth and the extent of change taking place between the 1970s and the 1990s. It is helpful to delve more deeply into this research as the two programs were produced by the Israel Broadcasting Authority, one of the official governmental bodies supervising state institutions and therefore representing state policy.

The findings of the comparison indicated that *Pillar of Fire* powerfully presented the conflict-supporting Zionist narrative. The delegitimization of the Arabs was predominantly carried out by de-humanizing them. They were presented as inhuman, including recurrently portraying them as uncivilized, as an Arab mob, and as fanatical extremists. The terms used to describe them emphasized their desire to harm Jews for no reason, but just because of their treacherous, violent, and murderous characters. This presentation was contrasted to the humane character of the Jews. Moreover, in *Pillar of Fire*, the clash between the Jews and the Arabs in Israel was portrayed as a meeting between a culture and a sub-culture on a lower level. Arab society was described as lazy, primitive, superstitious, easily inflamed, and continually plotting. In this framework, Arabs were shown as ungrateful, and unwilling to be thankful to the culture that had rescued them from their backwardness.

In contrast to *Pillar of Fire*, *Revival* presented a different narrative, complex and multidimensional. One of the salient features of *Revival*'s portrayal of the Arab is the focus on the human-individual aspect of the character, the presentation of different and complex layers of Arab-Palestinian identification, and the formation of Arab identity, while relating to different points of view about the Israeli-Palestinian conflict. The first episodes of the series are full of descriptions of personal contacts that have existed between Jews and Arabs. Even when Arab opposition to Jewish settlement is presented, the point of reference in *Revival* enables reasonable inclusion of the needs and desires of the Arab individual. Moreover, the design of the *Revival* series and its moral-humanistic approach towards the Arab is manifested by a description of the complicated relations between Jews and Arabs, focusing on the desires and difficulties of the individuals, and even presenting Arabs as humane and empathic. The series directly confronts the Jewish viewer with the distress of the Arab population in Israel, even when this distress is a result of the national aspirations of the Zionist movement. The unique features of the characters can be understood and accepted as the episodes detail the links between cause and effect, between factors that existed in reality and the ways the Arabs acted and reacted to them. In other words, Arab violence is no longer a result of an automatic barbaric instinct embedded in the Arab character, as described in *Pillar of Fire*, but rather human and rational reactions by the Arab population to the threat to their very physical and symbolic existence, as individuals and as a group, due to the activities of the Zionist movement. As a result, Arab violence is no longer described as behavior that cannot be restrained, but as an expression of an existential need. The complex point of view in *Revival* is also expressed in its approach to the two sides as victims of the conflict. As such, it confronts its audience with scenes perceived as unjust and immoral, both from the Arab side and from the Jewish side. This contrast in approach clearly shows the revolutionary change undergone by at least a section of the Jewish public in Israel. This change came from the top down, a change affecting the highest levels of society that is perhaps difficult for many to understand at present, when, at the beginning of the 2020s, Jewish society is in complete conscious retreat from a complex view of the situation.

Changes in the Educational System

In the mid-1980s, a significant change in the approach to the question of Jewish-Arab relations could also be identified in the Israeli educational system. The Ministry of Education adopted an open and daring approach that led to a number of changes in teaching the historical narrative of the conflict, in the way Arabs were presented and with regard to teaching democracy.[89]

The first signs of education for peace appeared in new instructions published by the Ministry of Education in 1984, under the leadership of the then-Minister of Education Yitzhak Navon, a representative of the Ma'arach, a center-left political party. It involved a curriculum focusing on Jewish-Arab coexistence and considering a number of aspects of the Jewish-Arab and the Israeli-Palestinian conflict. The curriculum attempted to advance values such as multiculturalism, respect, tolerance, and equality. The Director General's circular issued that year by the Ministry of Education declared that there was "an existential need" for the educational system to deal with relations between Jews and Arabs in Israel and in the wider region. It thus determined that the history of the Arab nations, their culture, their art, their language and their religion would *"be taught in schools, and the subject of relations between Israelis and Arabs would be integrated into the educational system from kindergarten until the end of high school."* Two years later, in 1986, the Unit for Democracy and Coexistence was established in the Ministry of Education, dedicated to advancing subjects like active citizenship and improving relations between various groups in Israeli society. That year, Education Minister Yitzhak Navon decided to focus on education for democracy as the central topic of study for that school year.

These trends intensified in the 1990s, while the peace process with the Palestinians was in progress, during Prof. Amnon Rubinstein's term as minister of education. For the first time since the establishment of the state, a comprehensive program was published requiring education for peace, focused on the conflict between Israel, the Arab nations, and the Palestinians, in the framework of the attempt to advance an education revolution on this issue. In a special issue of the Director General's circular published in May 1994 by the Ministry of Education, Rubenstein wrote the following:

> *We should present the achievement of peace between us and our neighbors, the Palestinians and the Arab nations, as an agreed-upon goal and to explain its essential importance, its contribution to the security, the strength and the prosperity of Israel. However, we must present the range of opinions existing in Israeli society relating to political arrangements, the legitimate debate being conducted at present on this issue, the explanations of the two sides. [...] The educational system [...] accepts the responsibility to deal with the process taking place at this time within Israeli society and to be part of it.*

The public education system, thus, accepted the responsibility, in practice, to consolidate support for the peace process among students, as an educational activity that was designed to accompany the political process. The objective was to advance the chances of acceptance of the process, without ignoring the forces opposed to it. The greater goal that was defined in this program was described as "*developing a citizen who was tolerant, aware of the principles of peace, sensitive, involved, knowledgeable and with a reasoned and well-based political worldview, with the ability to conduct a cultured dialogue with others of different political views, and to develop empathy and understanding, without the need for agreement with others of different political views from theirs.*"

The subjects advanced by the program were the concept of peace, the history of the Israeli-Arab-Palestinian conflict, the Arab world, the Middle East, the peace process, and others. However, the real test for the educational system, as specified in the program, would be its ability to accompany the students and to support them through the significant changes expected in the coming years, in which the enemy of the past would become a partner for discussion, and thus, to strengthen Israeli society as a whole. In order to achieve this, according to the Director General's circular, the educational system must "*develop a new viewpoint, among the students, a view that is anchored in the ethos of peace,*" while also recognizing the difficulties involved in dealing with peace in the educational system, as a topic so complex, so sensitive and so fraught with risks. The author of this book, who served as the advisor to the Minister of Peace Education, directed all units of the Education Ministry to prepare peace education programs for the short and long terms. Some of these programs were activated on various levels—for example, in-training courses for teachers; work plans for the various departments of the Education Ministry, school districts, and schools; wide-ranging activities by non-governmental organizations in educational institutions; and more. As mentioned, the minister also decided that peace education would be the central topic of the school year. One of the most significant activities that year was the publication of a large number of educational materials for kindergarten, elementary, and high school teachers and students, dealing with Arabs and the peace process.

In comprehensive research, Professor Eli Podeh examined history textbooks published from 1948 to 2000.[90] He identified far-reaching changes that had taken place through the years. In comparison to textbooks of the 1950s and 1960s, which were written with the objective of indoctrination and depicted a simplistic, superficial, and selective version of the conflict and of Arabs, textbooks written in the 1990s presented a new view of the conflict, more open, nuanced and critical, and portrayed Arabs in general and Palestinians in particular in a more complex, multidimensional, and differentiated way. Nevertheless, all of the textbooks transmitted the Zionist narrative—as ostensibly necessary for textbooks studied in the framework of the public school system.

Over ten years later, a study that compared Israeli and Palestinian school textbooks used in 2011 found that (1) dehumanizing and demonizing characterizations of the Other are rare in both Israeli and Palestinian books; (2) both Israeli and Palestinian books present unilateral national narratives that portray the Other as enemy, chronicle negative actions by the Other directed at the self-community, and portray the self-community in positive terms with actions aimed at self-protection and goals of peace; (3) there is lack of information about the religions, culture, economic and daily activities of the Other, or even of the existence of the Other on maps.[91]

SUMMARY: A CHANGE IN DIRECTION

Between 1977 and 1999 there was a change of direction in Jewish-Israeli society, from a psychological-societal-political standpoint. The cultural alternative described earlier, which developed and crystallized among artists, academics, and civil society, gradually permeated to most social and political institutions. This created a new context on the basis of which a narrative evolved that competed with the ethos of conflict and collective memory—a narrative supporting a peace process. Such a change has also been observed in societies that have embarked on the road to peace after a long bloody conflict, as in the Northern Ireland or in the Basque country.

In Israel during the first period, most major events that took place represented corroborating evidence for old conflict narratives of ethos of conflict and collective memory. In contrast, during the second period, a series of events took place—first and foremost, the peace treaty with Egypt—undercutting previous understandings. The characteristics of intractable conflict, which were most dominant during the first period, began to lose their intensity, and the conflict, although continuing to exist, acquired new aspects of relative moderation. The first period had witnessed a freezing of the conflict supporting beliefs that were accepted uncritically and dogmatically. The second period saw the beginnings—at least among some of the Jewish public in Israel—of an unfreezing, that is, a willingness to re-examine societal positions and conflict supporting beliefs of the ethos of conflict and the collective memory and to consider alternative beliefs supporting a peace process.[92]

However, it is important to clarify that, during the second period, there were not only changes in the relations between Israel and the Arab states, but also changes in the political-societal climate in general in Israeli society. After two decades during which a pseudo-democracy had existed in Israel, as fundamental principles of democracy had been violated (for example, the military government prevented civic equality; freedom of expression was saliently limited by open and concealed censorship and of course, by self-censorship, and any opposition was supervised by the government), during the following years, Israeli society became more open and more democratic. A series of significant changes taking place in the 1970s lent support to this process— information was flowing more freely than in the past; independent media platforms appeared, at the beginning in printed newspapers and later, on television; the new leadership was less dogmatic and civil societal institutions developed. Of special note was legislation in 1992 of two Basic Laws to guarantee fundamental rights and liberties. One law, *Basic Law: Human Dignity and Liberty*, attempts to protect human dignity and freedom in order to establish the values of the State of Israel as a Jewish and democratic state. The other, *Basic Law: Freedom of Occupation*, holds that every citizen or resident of the state is entitled to engage in any occupation, profession, or line of work, and that every governmental agency must respect the freedom of occupation for every citizen or resident.

This new climate was also expressed in the establishment of various organizations and non-profit associations, some of which were even formed with the express purpose of opposing government policy, such as Peace Now, the Peace and Security Council, Women in Black, and B'tselem— The Israeli Information Center for Human Rights in the Occupied Territories. There was also a rise in the numbers of visits by Israelis abroad and that contributed to increasing exposure to information, experiencing different ways of life and types of political patterns. In addition, globalization reached Israel approximately during those years and brought new standards of political behavior and the freer flow of information. As a result, a critical spirit began to develop, relatively open debate ensued, and the possibility of disagreeing with the establishment about its goals, policies, and narratives about conflict management gained legitimacy. These changes did not herald the establishment of an Israeli liberal democracy in the full sense of the concept, but it certainly signaled an important change from events of the first twenty-five years of independence. To generalize, the developments described in this chapter indicate that when intractable conflicts deescalate, an open climate develops in society. Societal closure and illiberalism are closely related to situations of escalated bloody conflicts that require antidemocratic steps in order to preserve conflict supporting narratives as hegemonic.

Yet it seems that the most powerful change took place thanks to the decision by Israeli state leaders and the Palestine Liberation Organization to begin a political process in 1993, which would end the Israel-Palestinian conflict. This step, which only three years earlier would have seemed completely impossible, was enabled primarily by the development of a new Israeli worldview according to which, it would be possible under certain conditions, to settle the Israeli-Palestinian conflict by peaceful means. This view, advanced by the political echelon led by Prime Minister Yitzhak Rabin and Foreign Minister Shimon Peres, was fundamentally revolutionary, as it flew against the accepted Israeli premises until that point, which considered the conflict as unresolvable and as requiring conflict management, mainly by violent means. This outlook had been ascendant from the establishment of the state and had been accepted by every prime minister up to Yitzhak Shamir, who had left office in 1992 and was replaced by Yitzhak Rabin.

"Our gaze is today turned toward the good opportunities; toward days without fear and nights without trepidation; toward a growing economy and a society that wants for nothing...," stated Rabin on 21 September 1993. At the signing of the Declaration of Principles, setting out the interim arrangements of Palestinian autonomy, he continued: *"If and when the peace which we so desire comes here, our lives will be completely transformed. We will no longer live by our swords alone ... There is a chance that we will merit good neighborly relations, the end of the bereavement which has existed in our homes, the end of the wars."*

A few months later, on 4 May 1994, during the signing of the Cairo Agreement regarding the Gaza Strip and Jericho, he added:

> *"We are convinced that our two peoples can live on the same patch of territory, 'every man under his vine and under his fig tree,' as the Prophets foretold, and bring to this country—a land of rocks and of tombstones—the taste of milk and honey that it deserves.[...] On this day, I turn to you, the Palestinian people, and say: Our Palestinian neighbors, a century of bloodshed has forged in us a core of mutual enmity [...] Today we are both extending a hand in peace. Today we are inaugurating a new age."*

In these two last speeches—both made in Hebrew to a Jewish audience on Israeli soil—Prime Minister Rabin had broken with many hegemonic agreed-upon conventions of the ethos of conflict and had expressed a number of themes that completely contradicted the propagated dominant assumptions supporting the continuation of the conflict. In addition, he even expressed strong opposition to the siege mentality, according to which "the whole world is against us," which was dominant in Jewish society.

Thus, in a process that went on for a number of years, the leaders of the Labor Party, who had been elected in 1992, developed new political as-

sumptions (which were detailed by Yaacov Bar-Siman-Tov, Ephraim Lavie, Kobi Michael, and Daniel Bar-Tal in 2007). The following are a number of these assumptions:

1. The Palestinian nation cannot by subdued by military means and
    thus, the conflict cannot be ended in this way.

2. Israeli rule of the Palestinians will do harm to the Jewish nation,
    and thus, it is in the Israeli interest to part ways with them by find-
    ing a solution using negotiation.

3. Negotiations can only be conducted with the Palestine Liberation
    Organization headed by Yasser Arafat, as under present circum-
    stances, the organization has abandoned the principles of "armed
    struggle" and the "phased doctrine," and is ready to recognize Is-
    rael and to reach an agreement to end the conflict with the follow-
    ing conditions: the establishment of a Palestinian state within the
    1967 borders, with East Jerusalem as its capital, and a solution to
    the refugee problem on the basis of United Nations Resolution
    194.

4. The PLO is ready to accept Israel's position that the political pro-
    cess must be gradual and conducted in stages, with the problem-
    atic issues—such as the status of Jerusalem, the refugee problem,
    the borders, and the Jewish settlements—to be discussed only at
    the time of the final-status settlement.

5. The PLO's commitment to abstain from and prevent terrorism
    will enable Israel to transfer conduct of the war against Palestinian
    terrorism to the PLO.

6. Mutual trust can be created by an ongoing peace process.

7. The establishment of a Palestinian Authority will lead to respon-
    sible behavior by the Palestinians, as the creation of formal insti-
    tutions creates a proto state which, from that moment, has some-
    thing to lose, and thus it will negotiate with Israel responsibly to
    achieve a "fair compromise."

Of course, the changes in direction described in this chapter did not include all society members. Many still adhered to the central themes of the
ethos of conflict and the collective memory (narratives supporting the
continuation of the conflict) and continued to hold views delegitimiz-

ing the Arabs, persisting in collective self-aggrandizing, and considering Jews as the only victims of the conflict. In addition, there were those who still desired maximum implementation of the conflict objectives, that is, holding on to all of the territories considered part of the land of Israel, including Jewish settlements throughout the occupied territories. In short, conflict supporting beliefs continued to throb in the hearts of some sectors of the Jewish public and to determine the path for some of the leaders in their approach to the Israeli-Palestinian conflict—and this in spite of the pressures of *realpolitik* exerted by other nations, primarily the United States, as well as international organizations, often preventing these aspirations from being realized.

In any case, developments from the 1970s to the 1990s led to a new socio-psychological reality in Israeli Jewish society, in which at least two narratives representing different worldviews were competing equally and still are—but today the competition is quite asymmetrical because the conflict supporting narratives have become hegemonic. These views are expressed in a socio-psychological repertoire that includes not only societal views but also attitudes, motives, values and feelings. Of course, this societal reality is not dichotomous, but rather, organized in a kind of continuum, from left to right, on which society members are placed. At one end, the leftwing, there are society members for whom the goals of Zionism were realized with the establishment of the State of Israel, and now, the main goal is achieving peace and normalization. The feeling that, even though Israel is threatened, these are not existential threats and therefore, the enormous sums invested in defense should be reduced and should be diverted to other needs. In addition, they believe that military force should not be used in an attempt to solve a variety of problems, but that more effort should be invested in finding other solutions. They would like to promote Israel's standing in the international community and to relate to the Jewish nation like any other, and as such, they criticize Jewish conduct towards the Palestinian minority—both Palestinian citizens of Israel and those who live in the occupied territories—and they demand fundamental changes. In this alternative worldview, the Jewish nation is not the only victim of this conflict, but shares that status with the Palestinians, who are struggling under occupation (which is, by nature, brutal). As the Palestinians are human beings, just like the Jews, they should not be humiliated with treatment that delegitimizes them, but rather, should be related to humanely, distinguishing between those who support violence and those who do not. Finally, this outlook considers that there is a partner for a peace process and Israel must enter into serious negotiations and ultimately, accept painful compromises. Expansionist policies of building new settlements must be stopped in order to reach an agreement that will end the bloodshed and lead to the prosperity of both nations. Finally, they distinguish other prices paid by society for the continuation of the conflict, and particularly the deterioration of democracy and the harm to human rights.

At the other end of the continuum, the rightwing, there are society members who identify numerous existential threats to the Jewish nation in Israel. They believe that the Arabs will not be satisfied with less than the destruction of the state, and there are nations in the world (except for the Americans, and Israel cannot even be sure of their support which depends on the policies of the president), whose deep-seated antisemitism means that not only will they not help us in our time of need but will even be happy to see Israel disappear. In this reality, only Israel's military, technological, and economic might will enable it to successfully deal with the threats surrounding it from all sides. Thus, we should not recoil from using force to deter, to punish and to prevent harm to Israel and its inhabitants. The Arabs have not changed since Jewish settlement began and thus cannot be trusted. They are violent and unreliable; they have no respect for human life and most importantly, they are incapable of changing as these characteristics are in their genes. In comparison, the Jewish nation is moral and is different from other nations, and especially the Arab nations, because Jewish Israeli behavior is rational and considers the lives of its citizens. The Jews are actually the sole victims of the conflict and this victimhood is only another instance in the history of persecution and pogroms experienced by Jews and carried out by the nations of the world from time immemorial. We must never forget the Holocaust, an eternal reminder of Jewish fate, and make sure that it is never repeated. The Jews of Israel must be strong, united and ready for sacrifice, including sacrificing one's life. Finally, the Jews desire peace and aspire to it with all their hearts, but Israel's neighbors agitate for war and are not ready for reasonable negotiations. Until they learn that the Jewish nation is eternal and cannot be harmed, the nation will have to live by the sword. Most of the rightwing public do not care much about the harm to democratic values and principles, and human rights and are content with Israeli conduct.

This outline clarifies that, while the first worldview represents the basis of an ethos and culture of peace, the second worldview clearly represents the ethos and culture of conflict. Of course, between the two fundamental worldviews, there are many intermediate views on the continuum that integrate themes different from those which have been presented, with varying levels of intensity. In general, it may be said that, due to the many relevant issues involved when evaluating the conflict, the Jewish public in Israel represents a mosaic of diverse views, some of which are surprising in the elements they combine.

The development of the alternative ethos, which gained considerable support, caused a schism and led to increasing polarization in Jewish society. In the 1980s and 1990s, the two political camps were almost equal in size, and identification with one of them became an indicator of societal identification and membership. Beyond the fact that it determined party affiliation and voting identity, it also signaled a political-societal worldview on a wide variety of issues, like attitudes towards human rights, minorities, other groups, government and law, the principles and values of democracy, nationalism, racism, militarism and sometimes even the approach to religion and its institutions. In effect, from the 1980s on, all political-societal life was organized around this continuum. And one's place on the continuum also affected personal life and interpersonal relations.

A great change took place in the 2000s. Constitutive events occurring at the very beginning of the millennium served as turning points in the socio-psychological dynamic among the Jewish public in Israel and designed the societal-political map that generally holds true for the present, as well. The next chapter analyses this dynamic, and we will present the socio-psychological repertoire that developed in its wake.

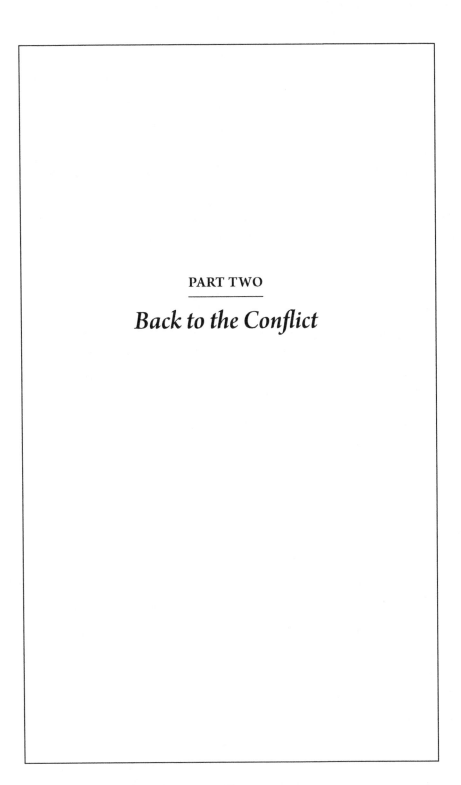

PART TWO

Back to the Conflict

CHAPTER 3

The Conflict Escalates in 2000

In 2000, a profound change in public opinion took place among the Jewish public, and its effects can still be felt. The dramatic events that escalated the conflict, and their interpretation by most Israeli leaders, the mass media, and official institutions, led to a loss of hope by many Jews. In its place pessimism developed about any possibility of a solution and about the "real" intentions of the Palestinians. In other words, the spirit of the rightwing became dominant in Israeli Jewish society, and leftist attitudes became unacceptable. The conflict culture returned to take its dominant hegemonic place. This was primarily the result of two constitutive events that took place in the space of two months: the failure of political talks at Camp David in July 2000, and the Second *Intifada* that broke out two months later, in September of that year—along with the third constitutive event, the evacuation of the Gaza Strip and its consequences.

I suggest evaluating these events as examples of constitutive events that have served as determinants of escalation. These types of constitutive events have also occurred in other intractable conflicts, as between Turks and Kurds, Hindus and Muslims in Kashmir, or between Turkish and Greek Cypriots. In all of these cases, the two rival sides were close to settling their conflict peacefully, but various constitutive events broke off the negotiations and the sides returned to their conflicts. In all these cases, however, there was one more element that played a major role, as also holds true in the Israeli case—constitutive information provided by the leaders or other epistemic authorities who framed events for society members. This is defined as information supplied by an epistemic authority about a matter of great relevance and importance to society members and to society as a whole. It has wide resonance, involves society members, occupies a central position in public discussion and on the public agenda, and forces society members to reconsider and change their psychological repertoire. The information can be about an event that has already taken place, will take place in the future or even an event which will never take place. It can also be fake news. This information is usually selective, biased and distorted, as we will see, for example, in the Israeli case. It is often meant to serve the source that provides the information. For instance, U.S.

89

President George W. Bush, Jr. provided constitutive information about weapons of mass destruction in Iraq, information which was false, and he then initiated a devastating war in Iraq. In Israel, any number of times, leaders have provided misleading constitutive information regarding wars and violent activities that have been instrumental in constructing political views as, for example, the information that the first Prime Minister of Israel David Ben Gurion supplied about the Sinai war in 1956. It was a secret adventure orchestrated by Britain, France and Israel to control the Suez Canal that was nationalized by the president of Egypt, Gamal Nasser. Society members often have no direct access to political or military information, and therefore must rely mostly on information provided by their leaders and by other sources, such as the mass media.

Leaders, as one of the most influential sources of information, use the media as a mediator in order to reinforce their impact on public opinion. Hence, in many cases, the media not only reflects the existing changes in public opinion, but also plays a role in creating them by providing new information and knowledge from leaders and then amplifying them.[93] The role of the mass media becomes even more pivotal in times of peace negotiations or war, especially when changes take place in the political environment. Then, the media tend to provide temporal and narrative structure by constructing a framework and later validating it. It is this framework that provides the particular meaning to the information provided.[94] By framing the information in a specific way, the presentation suggests a particular organizing storyline which points to its scope and essence, its underlying causes, and possible consequences, and thus provides a particular clarifying view that is often accepted as truthful, by at least part of the society.

Considering this explanation, this chapter will present two constitutive events and their framing (constitutive information) that served as the turning points in the complex peace process between Israeli Jews and Palestinians

THE CAMP DAVID CONFERENCE AS A CONSTITUTIVE EVENT

The first constitutive event, the Camp David Conference, took place from 11–24 July 2000. High level delegations of Israelis and Palestinians and their political leaders met in the United States at the presidential country retreat at Camp David, with mediation by an American team headed by President Bill Clinton. The delegations were working on the formulation of a historic final-status agreement which would proclaim the end of the Israeli-Palestinian conflict. However, they did not succeed in reaching agreements in the time they had allotted, and then Prime Minister of Israel, Ehud Barak, hastened to dramatically announce that the summit had failed and that the Palestinians were not partners for negotiations in a peace process.

Considering that the summit had been closed to the media and that the discussions were secret, the information transmitted to the public by the leaders about the reasons for the failure was decisively influential. And indeed, as time went by, it became clear that this constitutive information had become firmly solidified in public consciousness as a central narrative that, even today, still dominates Israeli Jewish society. In short, the narrative outlined by Barak determined that the prime minster had done "everything" in his power to reach an agreement, without leaving a stone unturned; he had been ready to make broad concessions that represented a revolution in the Israeli approach to a solution to the conflict, while the leader of the other side, Yasser Arafat, had refused to accept Barak's proposals and did not suggest alternative proposals. It became clear to Barak, as he had himself said after the conference had been adjourned, that *"Arafat is no longer a partner for negotiations"* and that the summit negotiations had *"revealed his true face"* as someone not interested in peace. This constitutive information was supported in real time by almost all the members of the Israeli delegation and even by President Clinton—who had persuaded Arafat to come to the summit only after he had promised that, in the event of failure, he would not place blame on the Palestinian side. Arafat had thought that the sides were not yet ready for a summit conference and that preliminary discussions and preparations should be conducted in advance. In summary, almost all the political leaders of Israel, as well as the great majority of Israeli media figures, repeated the themes supplied by Ehud Barak and aided in affirming them as absolute truth. Furthermore, after the Camp David Conference, some of the Israeli negotiators even concluded that the Palestinians did not want to end the conflict, not only because they did not want to compromise on the issues of Jerusalem, Temple Mount, and the return of the refugees, but because they wanted to continue the violent struggle and even to destroy Israel. Most Israeli Jews, as we will see, placed the responsibility for the failure of the summit exclusively and absolutely on the Palestinian side.[95]

A Complex Depiction of What Transpired at Camp David

Through the years, there have been many publications dealing with the events at Camp David, written by political figures with differing worldviews. The resulting reports are still greatly disputed. In general, each side has made supreme efforts to place the blame for the summit failure on the other side. This has not only stemmed from the subjective interpretations that each delegation accorded to the events, but also from the comprehension that it is of the greatest importance to convince one's own society members of the good intentions of their side, and of the other side's responsibility for the failure. Furthermore, the participants understood that these accusations held great weight with the international community which would condemn the side considered "guilty" for being inflexible and uncompromising.[96]

Despite Barak's success in having his narrative assimilated in Israel (as well as succeeding in the international community, at least in the first years after the conference), various publications about the negotiations that had occurred during the conference have raised important criticism. They have argued that the Israel proposals were "unsatisfactory" and raised doubts about the way Barak conducted them. It has been contended that he arrived without being prepared for negotiations as he assumed omnipotently that he would be able to convince the Palestinian delegation to accept his proposals. Additional criticism asserts that the Americans had not prepared the management of these difficult negotiations (in contrast to President Jimmy Carter who had managed the first Camp David negotiations between Israel and Egypt in 1978). Moreover, in contrast to the claim that the Palestinians did not offer any proposals at the conference and did not move from the positions they had arrived with, it became clear that they too made a number of significant steps to advance a possible solution, for example, relinquishing the demand for neighborhoods in East Jerusalem where Jewish neighborhoods had been built.[97] The Dror Moreh documentary film *The Human Factor* (2019), in which the major American mediation figures (Dennis Ross, Martin Indyk, Gamal Helal, Aaron David Miller, Daniel Kurtzer and Robert Malley) were interviewed, provides unequivocal testimony to the significant shortcomings of the Barak story that was imparted to the Israeli public.

Of special importance is the indication that, even before the conference began, the leaders of the two sides had lost trust in each other, especially

Arafat, since Barak had broken two promises that he had given to him regarding the transfer of three villages to Palestinian authority and the release of Palestinian prisoners—and trust is the determinative factor in the negotiation with Palestinians. In addition, Barak had also begun negotiations with Syria, and only when that had failed, he had turned to the Palestinians. But the most important insight arising from what has been written about the conference is that while, from the Israeli standpoint, Barak's proposals were far-reaching and generous, from the Palestinian standpoint, they were far from satisfactory.[98] First, merely considering principles, the Palestinians demanded that the starting point of the negotiations would be the future implementation of UN General Assembly Resolution 194 regarding the refugee problem and Security Council Resolutions 242 and 338 regarding the existence of the occupation and the division of the land on the basis of the 1967 borders—all of which had received international legitimacy—as the basis of negotiations which would lead to achieving their rights. In contrast, the Israelis aspired to a compromise that would be based on the existing situation, particularly in the context of security arrangements and the Jewish settlements—that is, they wanted the normalization of most unilateral activity that they had conducted since 1967.[99] For example, according to conditions proposed by the Israelis at Camp David in 2000, the future Palestinian state would not have full territorial contiguity, but would be connected via narrow passages, or bridges and tunnels. Barak proposed, at the first stage, to establish a Palestinian state on 87% of the West Bank and 100% of the Gaza Strip, but not including the Jordan Valley. Only after 10–25 years would the territory of the Palestinian state grow to about 92% of the West Bank. In any case, Israel would have control of the eastern border on the Jordan River. It is clear from this proposal that the existing Jewish settlements determined the proposed map and took preference over the contiguity of the Palestinian state. Thus, in accord with Israeli proposals, all the settlements and all of the army bases had to be connected to Israel by roads with full Israeli control. But from a Palestinian standpoint, they were ready to relinquish only 78% of the territory (the State of Israel according to the Green Line border) they considered their homeland (whole country) and keep 22% (West Bank and the Gaza Strip) for the Palestinian state, with a minor swap of land. Thus, Barak's proposal was not acceptable to them. Before Barak left for Camp David, the then-head of the Intelligence Branch, Amos Malka, presented Barak with his unequivocal appraisal that Arafat would demand a full 22%

of the land remaining in what they considered their historic homeland with minor territorial exchanges, because Malka thought that the Palestinians wouldn't compromise on less than that.[100] General Malka, as head of intelligence, has stated:

> At that time, Yasser Arafat was determined to reach a decision in 2000. His determination stemmed not from the symbolism of that year, but rather from his aspiration to achieve, at least to the greatest extent possible, his strategic vision based on four components: a. an independent state, b. a return to the 1967 borders with minimal adjustments and concessions, and in compensation, territorial exchanges, c. determining East Jerusalem as the capital of the Palestinian state, d. finding a suitable solution to the refugee question. These components represented four red lines and they clarified how narrow the space for compromise was.

An identical opinion was presented at the time from the Advisor on Palestinian Affairs to the Head of the General Security Services, Matti Steinberg.[101] These appraisals disappeared from the published notes following the failure of the conference.

The fundamental disagreement about the size of the area allotted for the Palestinian state was and still remains one of the obstacles for a solution to the conflict—but it was not the only one at Camp David. The lack of agreement primarily about the issue of Jerusalem and especially about sovereignty over the Muslim quarter, the Palestinian neighborhoods adjoining the Old City, and most importantly, sovereignty over the Temple Mount, were all direct factors in the collapse of the talks.[102] However, in time, the primary reason for the collapse that was disseminated to the Israeli public was the alleged demand by the Palestinians to return refugees to the State of Israel, even though that issue was barely touched upon during the conference. Ultimately, the gaps between the sides were fundamental, and that was the reason the conference failed. The entire political negotiation process between Israel and the Palestinians, which had begun seven years earlier, was now at the edge of an abyss. Arafat and the Palestinian negotiating team asserted that Barak's proposals at Camp David were not deserving acceptance, and they represented Israeli-American collusion designed to force an unjust and unfair agreement on the Palestinians. **And Barak was completely prepared for such a scenario.**

Did You Know?

There is abundant evidence that the well-timed campaign by Ehud Barak to place the blame on the Palestinians was drawn up in advance and that he had prepared a plan to impress his narrative upon Israelis and on the other nations of the world in the event of a failure. Gadi Baltiansky, who served as Barak's media advisor, testified that already on the eve of the conference, Barak had decided on a binary line of action: either he would leave with an agreement, or he would leave with an indictment against the Palestinian Authority. There was no middle course. This has also been confirmed by Barak's then-advisor, Eldad Yaniv. Contrastingly, immediately upon the end of the conference, Saab Erekat, one of the senior Palestinian representatives at the negotiations, in an interview with CNN, stated that although no agreement had been achieved, there had been progress. He repeated this several days later in an article he wrote for *The Washington Post*. Barak, who appeared immediately afterwards, maintained that the opposite was true. He blamed the Palestinians for the failure and began his intensive campaign against Arafat—and this reaction actually surprised the Palestinians.

Thus, directly after the failure of the summit, Barak and his allies opened an intense and methodical offensive to implant the narrative that he had prepared in advance, both to the Israeli public and to the international community. For Israeli Jews this was **constitutive information** that forced society members to reexamine their psychological repertoire and adjust it in accord with the narrative they had been told by the prime minister. In contrast, the Palestinians had not prepared a similar program and for long weeks remained silent in reaction to the series of claims issued by the Israelis. The Palestinians believed that the summit had attained certain achievements and that negotiations should be continued intensively in other forums. So, after the conference, in September, Barak hosted Arafat at his home in Kochav Yair, and additional attempts were made to continue negotiations in Paris, Sharm-el-Sheikh, Cairo, Washington, and Taba. However, none of these attempts led to the desired agreement despite progress on some points.

Nevertheless, it may be asked whether Israel really did "go all the way" at Camp David, at a time when Barak argued that his intentions had been sincere. Israel's acceptance of the Clinton Plan in December 2000 (despite expressing certain reservations) and the fact that, in the framework of negotiations taking place at Taba in 2001, Israel proposed additional concessions (for example, expanding the territory that would be transferred to the Palestinians in the context of territorial exchange, and accepting, in principle, the division of Jerusalem) to those offered at Camp David, are both evidence that the proposals made at the summit in July 2000 had not been the maximum that Israel could offer, even in its own estimation.[103]

THE OUTBREAK OF THE AL-AQSA *INTIFADA* AS A CONSTITUTIVE EVENT

The second constitutive event that led to a dramatic change in Israeli public opinion began on 28 September 2000, with the outbreak of the second *intifada*. The match that ignited the violence was the provocative and controversial decision by the then-head of the opposition, Ariel Sharon, to go up to the area of Temple Mount accompanied by Likud Knesset members, in order to check the repairs being carried out there by the Waqf. In reaction, Palestinian demonstrations erupted, involving stone throwing and rifle fire. These were met by the toughest possible response of Israeli military forces. On the first day there were no serious casualties (no one was killed), but the next day, with the eruption of the riots, seven Palestinians were killed and 300 were wounded. Seventy Israeli policemen were also injured in the clashes that spread over the Old City of Jerusalem. These violent clashes signaled the beginning of the second *intifada*.

The Israelis and the Palestinians remember the reasons for the outbreak of the intifada completely differently. These are the undisputed facts: During the first month of the *intifada*, the Palestinian uprising included mostly disturbances which were met by intense and heavy Israeli fire, almost without limitation. Regarding terror attacks, Palestinians fired mainly at soldiers and at Israeli cars in the West Bank. Data gathered by the Palestinian Red Crescent and the Israeli Foreign Ministry indicates that, by the end of October, the first month of the riots, 141 Palestinians had been killed and more than 500 had been injured, while on the Israeli side, there were 11 deaths and one person wounded. In general, during the first thirty days of the *intifada*, the Israel army fired more than a million bullets.[104] On 2 November 2000, for the first time during the second *intifada*, a car bomb exploded near the Machane Yehuda food market in Jerusalem and three weeks later, another exploded in Hadera, a small town south of Haifa. From that point, the number of Israeli deaths increased. But that was also true of the number of Palestinian deaths. From November to December 2000, for example, 186 Palestinians were killed and 540 were injured, while, during the same period, 31 Israelis were killed and 84 were injured. The first suicide terror attack took place on 28 March 2001 in east Kfar Saba, a town east of Tel Aviv. At that point, from the beginning of the *intifada*, 409 Palestinians had been killed and 1,740 had been injured, while on the Israeli side, 70 citizens had been killed and 183 had been injured.

The great number of victims on the Palestinian side during the first days of the *intifada* testify to the policy of using maximum force by the army, which was, in many cases, indiscriminate. This was because the IDF had been prepared for this confrontation and operated with military might, making use only of military considerations in order to subdue the Palestinians and to teach them a lesson.[105] The result was tragic, even in the view of Israeli political and defense figures. In September 2002, an investigation of the Israeli reaction to the *intifada*, written by Ben Caspit and published in the daily *Ma'ariv* newspaper, found that *"in the political and military echelons, the opinion is that perhaps the devastating reaction of the IDF and the blows suffered by the Palestinians during the first weeks, led to a deterioration in the situation and escalated the confrontation."*[106]

There is no doubt about one piece of data: From the day the violence broke out, the army received wide room to maneuver, enabling it to use great force. However, even while granting this wide area for action, the political echelon sometimes felt that military activity was too severe and tried to moderate it. But in these cases, the army chose to ignore the orders.[107] The military was so easy on the trigger that Shlomo Ben Ami, at that time serving as minister of internal security and for part of that time, also foreign minister, made the following point about the violent confrontation in the autumn of 2000 in his memoir, published in 2004: *"There was a gap between the instructions of the political echelon and their translation in the field. It was a structural failure expressed both in the political-military axis and the political-police force axis regarding the ability of the political level to control and supervise the dynamic of events in the field and the reaction at the operational levels."*[108] Ben Ami even argued later in his memoir that the military reaction was sometimes ten times stronger than what had been approved.

The gap in the approach between the political and the military echelons was mainly a result of the army ignoring the fact that the government had not intended to "subdue" the Palestinians or cause the Palestinian Authority to collapse. Israel had really aspired to continue the political process, even if it was just for the sake of appearances, because, *inter alia*, negotiation was viewed by the government as the most effective means to end the violence or at least to restrain it, and because it feared internationalization of the conflict. These assumptions were supported by the Israeli intelligence organizations and by the National Security Council, which maintained that there was no military solution to the violent confrontation with the Palestinians and even if they were subdued militarily, the violence would eventually erupt again. They had also argued that the military blows, as painful as they might be, would not change the minimum conditions of the Palestinians for signing a peace agreement. In any case, until Arik Sharon became prime minister in March 2001, the two sides related to the violent confrontation as a "**bargaining dispute**." In other words, it was not necessarily a zero-sum conflict, but rather a struggle to improve the Palestinian bargaining chips for negotiations. This approach was formulated partially on the basis of the evaluation of a number of figures in the security apparatus, including the head of the Military Intelligence Branch and the head of the Palestinian Department of the Military Intelligence Branch, both of whom believed that Arafat actually was interested in reaching an agreement and that, in the right scenario, an agreement could possibly be reached.

So the leadership, headed by Barak, that had blamed Arafat for the failure at Camp David but had also recognized the necessity of continuing the political process, was now, following the return from the conference, forced to do so under fire. The result was a failure of the "policy of containment," as it was termed by the government. The large number of casualties on the Palestinian side contributed in turn to an additional escalation, considering the wish by Palestinian organizations to equalize the "balance of bloodshed," and the cycle of violence was more brutal than could be imagined. In December 2000, the popular Palestinian uprising became a real armed confrontation. The military branch of Fatah, the Tanzim, and later, Hamas and other organizations, took the initiative and the violent confrontations expanded to include attacks on civilians, firing at military vehicles on the roads, shooting at settlements and at army camps, as well as murderous attacks by suicide terrorists on population centers in Israel. According to the calculations of the Israeli General Security Services, during the five years of violent confrontations, 1,060 Israelis were killed (two-thirds of whom were civilians) and 6,089 were injured. There were about 140 attacks by suicide terrorists, causing the deaths of 500 people and about 3,400 people were injured. Among the terrible acts of terror, it is possible to cite the suicide attack at the Tel Aviv Dolphinarium in 2001, killing 20 young people, and the attack at the Park Hotel where 30 people were murdered at a Seder on Passover eve in 2002. As time went on, these attacks took on critical significance in the crystallization of the new perception of the conflict and the attitudes towards it by the Jewish public in Israel. With regard to Palestinian casualties, there are disagreements. The estimation is that during the five years of the *intifada*, about 3,250 Palestinians were killed, including assassinations of Palestinian political and military figures.[109] There is considerable disagreement about the proportion of uninvolved civilians who were killed. Estimates range between 40 to 66 percent.[110]

In retrospect, one of the main reasons for the Palestinian violence was the disillusion among growing numbers of Palestinians at the authoritarian and corrupt character of the Palestinian Authority from the very day it was established. This was added to the growing bitterness that the Oslo Agreement had not only failed to improve the economic situation in the West Bank, but that it had even considerably worsened. After the agreements had been signed, the Palestinians were no longer able to work in Israel on a large scale, and movement within the area became more difficult for them as the West Bank had been divided into three separate sectors—areas A, B, and C—each of them with different authorities and rules. In the end, the agreements did not end the sense of occupation, with limitations on movement, with the erection of dozens and even hundreds of roadblocks and with the constant presence of the Israeli army, along with a continuation of construction in the Jewish settlements, land expropriation from the Palestinians, and the paving of bypass roads for Jews only. And when it became clear to the Palestinian public, following the Camp David conference, that the political agreement that had been expected to remove the occupation completely had not been achieved by the Palestinian Authority, Palestinians undertook, just as they had in 1987, to support the leadership in breaking through the diplomatic stalemate by resorting to violence. Thus, the events of September 2000 were, to a great extent, an expression of distress and frustration among most of the Palestinian public, directed both at the Authority and at Israel.[111]

In this context of general disillusionment, it should be said that the Jewish public deeply felt the failure of negotiations as well. The political process had been expected to bring a halt to Palestinian violence, but that had not happened. The opposite had occurred; the *intifada* had led to a peak in the most terrible type of terror activity—suicide terrorism, which caused heavy loss of life. At the time, there were almost no similar cases of terrorism throughout the world—the terror was very frequent and was carried out by those who were willing to commit suicide, and it claimed the lives of so many people, even going about their daily lives at city centers. What sharpened Jewish reactions of rage and hostility towards the Palestinians was the fact that the acts of terror took the lives of "innocents"—civilian men, women and children, and this intensified Israeli expressions of Palestinian delegitimization. The Jewish public did not receive what they needed most from the Oslo Agreements—a sense of security. **That is what happens in all conflicts when the peace process not only does not supply society members' needs but even intensifies their deprivation—the political process collapses, and the sides return to violent confrontation. In all conflicts that have been resolved peacefully, at least the majority of the participating societies thought that the most important needs were satisfied in the conflict resolution. This has been the case in peacefully resolved conflicts in Northern Ireland, Algeria, the Basque country, and El Salvador, as examples.**

The second *intifada* finally came to an end at the Sharm el-Sheikh summit, on 8 February 2005, a summit that included the leaderships of Israel and the Palestinians. The chair of the Palestinian Authority, Mahmoud Abbas (Abu-Mazen), who had taken the place of Arafat (after his death), announced officially that the *intifada* had ended. Prime Minister Arik Sharon, on his part, agreed to withdraw the IDF from Palestinian cities and to stop the assassinations of Palestinian leaders and the destruction of Palestinian homes.

Constitutive Information Regarding the Beginning of the Al-Aqsa **Intifada**

A short time after the violence had begun in September 2000, Prime Minister Barak, other members of the coalition, and senior army officers, including the then-Commander in Chief Shaul Mofaz, his deputy, Moshe Yaalon, and the head of the Research Division of the Intelligence Branch Amos Gilad, began to disseminate the contention that the intifada had been initiated and well planned by Arafat and the Palestinian Authority, without concrete evidence. At that point, many security and government officials openly and fully supported this version of the events, and it was repeated constantly by the media, which echoed it again and again. As time elapsed and the violence continued and even escalated, the government, the security forces and most of the communications media sharpened this message, and it began to be argued that the intentions of the Palestinian Authority were to destroy Israel; the country, they insisted, was now fighting for its very existence. In addition, security and government sources continued to publicize the information that Arafat was personally responsible for all the terror attacks, and that the Palestinian leadership was not a partner for negotiation because of their involvement with terror and their refusal to stop it.

Did You Know?

In contrast to the prevailing belief disseminated by Barak and the head officers of the IDF (the commander-in-chief and his deputy), all professional bodies which investigated the issue rationally with special investigatory committees—the Intelligence Branch of the IDF and the assessment panels of the General Security Services, the Mossad (the Israeli national intelligence agency) and the Foreign Ministry—all supported a different narrative according to which Arafat did not plan the intifada, but rather that it broke out spontaneously and escalated due to the combination of the forceful reaction of the Israeli army, on the one hand, and the absence of political incentives to stop it, on the other. In addition, the Mitchell Committee, the investigative body set up by the United States and others in late 2000, rejected the view that Arafat and the Palestinian Authority orchestrated the outbreak of the Second Intifada.[112]

As the ex-head of the General Security Services, Ami Ayalon asserted in 2004, when he was already a civilian: "*At the beginning, the Al-Aqsa intifada was an unplanned popular uprising that was not motivated by any specific political goal ... The chair of the Palestinian Authority was carried along in this violent struggle, as in order to stop it, he would have had to create some kind of political expectation of change.*"[113] Reserve Major-General Amos Malka, who had been the head of military intelligence at the time, cast doubt on the professional integrity of the then-head of the Research Division, Amos Gilad. In an interview to the national daily newspaper, *Haaretz*, in 2004, he stated: "*I say with full responsibility that throughout my term as the head of military intelligence, there was not even one document from the Research Division expressing the appraisal that Gilad claims that he presented to the prime minister. As required by the work procedures no document could have left the Research Division without receiving the approval of the head of the military intelligence.*" He added: "*I did everything in my power. I testified before the Knesset Committee on Foreign Affairs and Security several times and I presented reports to the chief of staff. At no time did I say that I accepted the conspiracy theory that Oslo was a plot to destroy Israel. Unfortunately, Mofaz as chief of staff, and Bogie (Ya'alon) as his deputy, ignored what I said. What Gilad said suited them better.*"[114] This view was also supported by the deputy head of GSS at the time, Yuval Diskin; GSS advisor for Palestinian affairs, Matti Steinberg; and senior Mossad officer, Yossi Ben Ari, who was asked to investigate the reasons for the outbreak of the second intifada.[115] Later, the head of the GSS during that period, Avi Dichter, expressed a similar reaction: "*I also don't accept the thesis about a multi-stage plan by the Palestinians, led by Yasser Arafat, for the intifada of September 2000 ... Neither Yasser Arafat, nor those who first ignited the demonstrations, nor others who participated, knew that there was going to be an intifada.*"[116] The recent analysis of the second *intifada* events and interviews of the participants in them comes to the unequivocal conclusion: "*The outbreaks of riots in both the PA territories and inside the Green Line were spontaneous uprisings that had not been orchestrated. PA Chairman Arafat was surprised by the outbreak of the Second Intifada in Judea and Samaria and the Gaza Strip after Sharon went to the Temple Mount. He tried to prevent the riots from spreading but was unsuccessful and eventually gave up. The outbreak of the intifada in the Palestinian territories and the riots in Israel were a diffused surprise for Israel.*"[117]

It should be emphasized that at no point did the Al-Aqsa intifada present a significant threat to the IDF. In Operation Defensive Shield in 2002, the aim of which was to defeat the Palestinian Authority and to stop the terror, within a month and a half, a number of Israeli army divisions had recaptured all of the West Bank cities.

All this reliable information did not prevent the Israeli media from presenting the version put forward by Barak and his team for the failure of the summit and the outbreak of the *intifada*, which became the dominant narrative. Thus, the Israeli public was primarily exposed to this version which served as constitutive information, having crucial influence on the public viewpoint.

A Dramatic Change in Public Opinion

The year 2000 represented a sharp turning point and the beginning of a dramatic shift among the Jewish public in Israel.[118] In order to describe this change in public opinion, brought about by the second intifada and the failure of the Camp David negotiations, I will cite the findings of research that I conducted with Amiram Raviv and Rinat Abromovich (who is also a political psychologist) in 2002–2003, at the end of the *intifada*.[119] It included in-depth interviews with a group of 98 Jewish Israelis, aged 51–75 (born in Israel or immigrated to Israel in childhood, and had not left the country for more than two years); they were representative of the general public in economic status, gender, geography, and ethnic group. They were divided into three main ideological groups, hawks (rightwing), center, and doves (leftwing). This population was chosen because it had a long-term perspective of the conflict with the Palestinians, as the respondents were already old enough to remember the 1967 Six-Day War and its aftermath. The aim of the research was to investigate the changes that had taken place in the beliefs of the ethos of conflict and the collective memory following the events of 2000. The findings indicated a clear picture—in Jewish Israeli society, there had been a significantly sharp change. The interviewees expressed a critical change in their attitudes towards the Palestinians and their leaders, primarily those who had identified themselves as center and leftwing. The Palestinians were now perceived by most as "not a partner" to a peace process and they were considered violent and unreliable. In addition, there was an intensified sense of threat both on personal and collective levels, due to a growing sense that the Palestinians actually wanted to destroy the state of Israel.

For example, one of the interviewees who had defined himself as "leftwing" described the reasons for the outbreak of violence: "*They wanted an excuse, that if [Ariel] Sharon had not gone up to 'Temple Mount, nothing would have happened. But they had been planning something like this for a long time.*" Another interviewee, who identified himself as "center" said, "*Barak himself was harmed by lack of trust [...] by Arafat. That lying scoundrel. He made fun of Barak in front of the whole world. How could he do such a thing? Really humiliated him.*"

The Peace Index surveys, conducted at that time by the Steinmetz Center for Peace Research at Tel Aviv University, examined public opinion in Israel regarding the conflict and also investigated other matters on the public agenda in Israel and still does. These surveys have been carried out since June 1994. In November 2000, the survey found that 80% of Jewish Israeli citizens believed that the Palestinians were the only ones responsible for the outbreak of violence in the second *intifada*.[120] In 2002, 84% of Jewish respondents agreed that the Palestinians were the only ones to blame for the deterioration in relations between the two nations, or that they bore the most responsibility for this drop, while only five percent thought that Israel was completely to blame.[121] In October 2000, 71% of the Jewish public considered that Arafat *"was behaving like a terrorist"* while two years earlier, only 41% had agreed with that statement.[122] Another survey, conducted in March 2001 and published in the *Yedioth Aharonoth* daily newspaper, found that 58% of the Jewish Israeli public had changed their opinion about Palestinians and were more negative, and 37% reported that they had become more "hawkish" because of the events of 2000.[123] In addition, according to the Peace Index, in 1999, 51% of the Jewish population in Israel supported the Oslo Accords, while in 2001, support had fallen to 36%. Furthermore, survey participants were asked, *"To what extent do you believe that the Oslo Accords will lead to peace between Israel and the Palestinians in the coming years?"* They were asked to respond on a scale of one to one hundred. In 1999, with the election of Ehud Barak as prime minster, the result was at its peak—an average of 50.3. But in June 2001, it had steeply dropped to 24, and after that, it continued to decline.[124] **In other words, within two years, trust in the Palestinians and in the peace process had completely shattered.** Research conducted by Asher Arian in 2001 indicated a similar tendency. The percentage of Israelis who said that they believed that *"peace would be secured within the coming years"* fell from 68% in 1999 to 35% two years later, in 2001.[125]

Another crucial change that signaled increasing polarization refers to political self-identification among Jewish Israelis on a left-right continuum. While throughout the 1990s the Jewish public was more or less stable in their ideological identities, the events following the Camp David summit led to a sharp shift in opinion. **Here are the numbers: in the 1980s, about 40% defined themselves as leftwing; during the early 1990s, 36% identified as such; in March 2000, about 30% viewed themselves on the left; and in January 2001, after the Camp David conference and the outbreak of the Al-Aqsa *intifada*, the leftwing had dropped to 23%.**[126] **In May 2002, in a survey appearing in the *Maariv* daily newspaper, only 19% identified as leftwing, while 48% stated that they** were rightwing. The other respondents defined themselves as center, or alternatively, did not know how to define themselves.[127] A decade and a half later, in the Peace Index of 2019, only 12.5% of the Jewish public categorized themselves as leftwing, 22% said that they were center, and 64% classified themselves as rightwing. A similar picture was found in the March 2022 survey.[128] This distribution has been stable for a number of years, with only minimal movement. In short, a dramatic shift in public opinion took place early in the 2000s and has only intensified during the 20 years since then. Following the events of the early 2000s—the failure of the Camp David conference and the outbreak of the violent second *intifada*—the Jewish population in Israel for the most part became rightwing. The peace camp gradually lost strength until it became a small minority in Israeli Jewish society.

In order to deeply understand the significance of this radical change, it is particularly important to take a close look at the changes taking place in the dovish public—that is, the leftwing camp.

The Change in Attitudes among the Left-wing Public

The change taking place in the beliefs and the attitudes of members of the peace camp during these years was of dramatic importance, as to a great extent, it determined the political map for the following years. In this context, it should be remembered that right-wingers during this period maintained their views and even held them more stridently, and thus, when discussing "the radicalization among the Jewish public in the 2000s"—this refers to a process taking place in the center and on the left of the political map, a community which swung substantially rightward and the dominance of the rightist political orientation was solidified.

In a survey I conducted in March 2002, 29% of Israeli Jews reported that before the Camp David summit, they had believed that the Palestinian leadership was making efforts to achieve peace with Israel, but now they no longer believed so. Fifty-six percent reported that they had never believed in the sincere intentions of the Palestinians and that they still didn't. And only 8% reported that they believed in the sincere intentions of the Palestinians to achieve peace with Israel and that they still did. **Among those who had voted for Barak in 2001, 43% reported that they had changed their opinions of the Palestinians for the worse, while 23%**

reported that they had never believed in Palestinian intentions, and 29% stated that they continued similarly to believe in Palestinian sincerity.

And how did those on the left explain this sharp shift in their attitudes? Let's return to our study of interviews conducted in 2002–2003: "*I come from a home where we were very open and very democratic but in my opinion, I am no longer democratic [...] I think that I am a rightist because of the all the experiences I have had, because of all the events I have experienced, because of all of the thought I devoted to it, and that have led me to this position [...] It was the intifada that made me change. My brother was killed in a terror attack in Jerusalem when he was leaving a Labor Party activity. In these elections, I went with the Likud,*" said one of the respondents. Another interviewee stated: "*I always thought they were human beings and that they deserved to live just like us and that we had to reach some kind of agreement with them (so that) we could continue to live together. That was also the accepted opinion on the kibbutz and I was influenced greatly by my adopted parents, and they were also very humane ... Recently, I have begun ... it seems that it has not only happened to me; it has happened to many more people recently—I am beginning to doubt that approach. I think that we won't be able to reach an agreement with them.*"

Accordingly, the data show that the Israeli public experienced a dramatic psychological change during the first year of the *intifada*. The failure of the Camp David summit and the violent terror attacks in its wake, along with the framing of these events by the leadership, caused a tremendous impact, involving all society members in what was taking place, arousing wide-ranging public debate, and in fact, deeply affecting the wellbeing of the Jews in Israel. The new circumstances that were created forced Israeli citizens, and particularly leftwing and center voters, to reevaluate their socio-psychological repertoire relating to the conflict and to their main opponent—the Palestinians. The result was loss of hope by some and a return to the fatalistic view that it was impossible to conduct a peace process with the Palestinians.

In sum, these two constitutive events and the way they were explained with constitutive information, led to significant changes in public attitudes that continued to grow even more intense as time passed: There was both a movement rightward and a change in the repertoire towards narratives of support for maintaining the conflict. As a result, deep revisions in the political structure began to appear, in addition to changes in social identity and guiding values of society. These trends have, in fact, continued up to the time these lines are being written in 2022. In order to deeply understand these dramatic changes in public opinion, we must examine the interpretation they received by the leadership, the army establishment, and the media.

An Explanation for the Dramatic Change

a. The effect of the violence. During the *intifada*, there were about 140 suicidal attacks causing extreme loss of life, in addition to shooting attacks (including lengthy shooting attacks on civilian settlements), stabbings, violent demonstrations, and more. The large number of deaths during the five years of the second intifada created a sense of threat leading to fear and insecurity. That is what made it such an extremely important factor in affecting the worldview of the public.

Did You Know?

Extensive research with a sample of 781 Jewish Israelis aged 17–93, conducted from March-May 2008, checked the connection between exposure to violent conflict-related events and feelings of emotional distress as a function of their ethos of conflict beliefs. The results of the research indicated that it was actually those who did not adhere to ethos of conflict beliefs (that is, those on the left) who, when exposed to violent conflict-related events, suffered increased distress caused by the sense of threat and pressure, and their hatred directed towards Palestinians was significantly increased. This was due to their surprise at the difficult reality created by the Palestinians. People on the right who held ethos of conflict beliefs were less affected by the threatening situation as they held a belief system which had inured them to change. In other words, ethos of conflict beliefs led them to permanently believe that the Palestinians were violent and that provided them with a defense because it gave them a clear explanation of what was happening. They did not change their negative feelings after exposure to the violence.[129]

In that sense, the second intifada was a watershed: The extreme violence that was taking place dramatically changed the agenda of Israeli society. The threats and dangers assailing Jewish Israelis, and the State of Israel in general, again advanced to the head of the list; and saliently. The public who had supported leftist positions were affected by them and reformulated their attitudes correspondingly. However, a violent reality cannot provide a full and satisfying explanation for such a dramatic change of public opinion, as we do not lack cases in which societies in conflict who were suffering from widespread violence, ultimately signed peace agreements. One example is Israeli society which, twenty odd years previously had signed a peace agreement with Egypt, despite the threat of violence that had preceded it. Accordingly, there must be another important factor that influenced the formulation of Israeli citizens' worldview.

b. The effects of the constitutive information interpretation. The interpretation and explanation of the outbreaks of violence by leaders and opinion makers—usually via the mass media—filled an important role throughout the years of the conflict, but in the case of the 2000 events, it represented a crucial factor, because of its final and hermetic conclusion which left no room for competing interpretations: "There is no partner..." Alternative information transmitted by academic channels, whether from abroad or from certain channels in Israel, were not passed on to the wider public. Nor were the various reports that have been mentioned above brought up for public discussion. The Israeli public was limited in its perception and evaluation of events to one-directional narratives disseminated by political leaders and most of the media.

Of course, the two constitutive events we have focused on greatly affected the public in their own right, and still do. However, it is important to understand the explanations and interpretation they received by leaders and media, and then, how they were interpreted by the great majority of society members. Thus, we will now trace how political and military leaders presented information via the media and how it was assimilated by the public. Specifically, we will present the effect that the leading figure, the prime minister at the time, Lieutenant General (res) Ehud Barak, had on the Jewish public.

c. The influence of Ehud Barak. Socio-psychological research indicates that if the source of information is perceived as reliable, as expert and as trustworthy, his/her ability to convince is high and has a decisive effect on the individual who is receiving the information.[130] Barak, without a doubt, fulfilled these three criteria. First, he was identified as someone with a high level of professional expertise. He had been the army commander-in-chief, known as "soldier number one" as he had been the most decorated soldier in the history of the IDF. Naturally, he was considered an expert on security issues—an area of knowledge considered most important for an individual called upon to lead the nation. In addition, he was an amateur pianist, a physicist in his spare time and an occasional watchmaker. Ehud Barak had always been presented to the public as exceptionally intelligent in every sense of the word. In line with these skills, he was perceived as an expert in political and security matters, and especially as devoted leader to peace making. This image was determinative to the acceptance of the constitutive information provided by him, in spite of the fact that he did not succeed in preventing the outbreak of the second *intifada* and defined the Camp David meeting as a failure.

But the most important element in determining the effect of new information on its recipients is the measure of trustworthiness attributed to the information source. Trustworthiness is derived primarily from the orientation of the information source as it is perceived by the listener, and especially the evaluation of the personal motivation and interest the source may have in transmitting the information. It appears that the information supplied by Barak was considered very reliable, precisely because it seemed to conflict with his own personal interest. Because Barak had been chosen as prime minister in 1999, in order to set peace negotiations in motion, it was accepted that the information he provided about Arafat's "real intentions" (that is, the destruction of Israel disguised as a peace initiative) did mortal harm to his own political interests and greatly reduced his chances of being reelected for an additional term. Moreover, it should be remembered that Barak presented the Palestinians in a most negative light, but shortly after he had just offered them what most Israelis considered extremely generous concessions. From that standpoint, Barak was perceived to be extremely trustworthy, considering that he was brave and honest enough to give the public information that would, in retrospect, present his own judgment capabilities in a negative light.

Lastly, concerning the third element—the measure of his credibility—it should be remembered that Barak was the leader of supporters of a peace process, and as such, his credibility among them was especially high at that moment in time. It is no wonder that a significant number of them changed their opinions in light of the constitutive information that he provided. If similar information had come from a rightist leader, for example, it would not have been accepted as reliable and valid in the same measure. A similar position was expressed by Professor Gadi Wolfsfeld in his important book, *Media and the Path to Peace*, published in 2004: "*The fact that the leader of the Labor Party was the one who led the attack against the Palestinians*," he wrote, "*ensured its great support in the development of anti-Palestinian public opinion.*"[131] In the short run, perhaps it is the due to the fact that a Labor party leader was in the driver's seat, along with a leftist government (which included ministers from the leftwing Meretz party), that was also an energizing factor—in retrospect, it appears that the existence of continuous contacts with the Palestinians aided in moderating the violence during the *intifada*. A month after the round of talks in Taba, Ariel Sharon won the elections for prime minister, and his statement that the government would not conduct negotiations under fire immediately led to a dynamic of escalation. The Palestinians increased the violence and the cycle of bloodshed worsened.

CHAPTER 4

Further Escalation

ARIEL SHARON ENTERS THE PICTURE

In March 2001, Ariel Sharon formed the twenty-ninth government of Israel. It was the first and, to date, the only time an election for Prime Minister had been held without parallel elections for the Knesset. But despite his large margin of victory over Ehud Barak, his party, the Likud, was not the largest in the Israeli parliament (Knesset). Thus, Sharon formed a national unity coalition with Labor-Meimad and other parties. Only after the clear victory of the Likud in the Knesset elections held in January 2003 could he form a stable coalition based on center-right parties. His first mission was to put down the Palestinian uprising that had claimed many casualties among Israeli citizens and had made life in Israel unbearably insecure. As noted, after Israel had been struck by a wave of suicide bombings in 2002; Sharon decided to launch Operation Defensive Shield to re-conquer the West Bank and he began the construction of a barrier around the West Bank, a few miles into the territories.

The failure of the Camp David Conference and the outbreak of the second *intifada* heralded a return to conflict supporting narratives after several years during which peace supporting narratives had predominated. Accordingly, the new government under Sharon initiated unilateral steps that clearly reflected his own assumptions, as identified by the researchers from the Jerusalem Institute, Yaacov Bar-Siman-Tov, Ephraim Lavie, Kobi Michael, and Daniel Bar-Tal:[132]

1. Even if Israel had not officially abandoned the Oslo agreements, the political peace process had, in practice, ended due to the military conflict and due to the absence of a partner on the other side.

2. Even if Israel had actively adhered to a solution of two states for two peoples, doubt was

3. expressed about the feasibility of such a solution in the short or medium term as the Palestinians had, in fact, rejected it.

4. Israel's proposals to the Palestinians in Camp David and in Taba or its agreement with Clinton's draft no longer obligated it, start-

ing from the moment the Palestinians had rejected these proposals and had chosen a violent struggle.

5. The Palestinian leadership had decided to achieve all its goals by violence and thus, it had returned to terrorism. The war was defensive and had been forced on Israel. It was an existential war which did not allow for compromise (a war to defend our homes), a continuation of the War of Independence and the most important of all Israeli wars up to that time.

6. The Palestinian violence was a clear violation of the Oslo process, and renewed political demands were dependent on a complete end to the violent struggle.

7. The Palestinian leadership (and primarily, Yasser Arafat) had not only ceased being a legitimate partner and not worthy of a political process, but the leadership was also an obstacle to peace, and without its disappearance, it would be impossible to conduct a political process.

8. Israel was willing to negotiate with a different Palestinian leadership, which would reject terrorism, fight against it, and institute democratic reforms in line with President Bush's speech of June 2002.

9. In the absence of any chance of settling the conflict, Israel would focus on managing the conflict with the aim of ending it or greatly reducing it by preventing any Palestinian military or political achievement.

The guiding fundamental assumptions of the new policies were different in their objectives to those which were at the basis of the Oslo negotiations. First, there was no chance of settling the Israel-Palestinian conflict in the foreseeable future and second, the only open option for Israel in order to bring a quick end to the violence was unilateral conflict management, while negating any military and political achievements by the Palestinians. In this respect, the direct link between the hegemonic political perspective and the country's military strategy was created, both of which were completely in line with the new (old) socio-psychological repertoire among Jewish Israelis that was already hegemonic in the past.

These fundamental assumptions rested upon the new interpretation that had been given in retrospect to Palestinian attitudes from the beginning of the Oslo process—the Palestinians were now perceived as rivals and enemies with evil intentions who, from the beginning, were not trustworthy in their resolve to achieve peace. In that sense, the new political viewpoint, whose proponents were Prime Minister Ariel Sharon, Minister of Defense Shaul Mofaz, and IDF Commander-in-Chief Moshe Yaalon, completely accepted the updated appraisal of the Palestinians formulated by Barak. Furthermore, this appraisal was also totally in line with the previously formulated views of Sharon, who had opposed the Oslo process from its start, and had even seen it as a real danger to the existence and security of Israel. It also conformed to the opinions of Mofaz who, as IDF chief-of-staff, had unequivocally rejected Barak's concessions at Camp David and at Taba; but Mofaz also disagreed with the "policy of containment" by the political echelon and refused to carry it out during the first days of the *intifada* both in language and in spirit. The change in these assumptions was not a result of a change in the evaluations of the intelligence branches regarding Palestinian aims or of appraisals by any other professional evaluation organization; it appears that Sharon, following Barak, determined his attitudes in accord with his personal beliefs, which were reinforced by the heads of the army (the commander-in-chief and his deputy) and not by any professional organizations in the security system.

DISENGAGEMENT FROM THE GAZA STRIP IN 2005—THE THIRD CONSTITUTIVE EVENT

From December 2003 until August 2005, the government of Israel under Prime Minister Ariel Sharon initiated a series of unilateral steps. The most prominent of these were the evacuation of the Jewish settlements in the Gaza Strip (in addition to a number of settlements in northern Samaria) and the transfer of Gaza to the Palestinians, termed the "Disengagement Plan"; and the construction of a separation wall built along a line east of the 1967 border and enclosing most of the Jewish settlement blocs on the West Bank. The unilateral policies that did not in any way consider the desires and needs of the Palestinians continued after the death of Yasser Arafat in November 2003, even though his successor, Mahmoud Abbas, firmly expressed his complete opposition to the use of violence and stated his readiness to open negotiations with Israel.

Although from the moment that it was proposed the disengagement from Gaza was perceived by most Israelis as an initiative that benefitted the Palestinians and fulfilled their demands for an end to the occupation, it was actually the implementation of the new political approach favoring unilateral steps, in complete negation of the dominant Israeli approach of the Oslo period.

The Disengagement Plan, first proposed by Sharon in 2003, was approved by the government in June 2004, and in October 2004 it was passed by the Knesset. It was intended, first of all, to decrease the number of Palestinians under full control of the occupation, as stated by Sharon at a Likud Party meeting on May 26, 2003. The actual disengagement was carried out in August 2005 and was completed on 12 September of that year. Approximately 8,600 Jewish settlers were evacuated from 21 settlements, as per the plan, including four settlements in the northern West Bank. In opposition to the position of the upper echelon of the security establishment, Sharon refused to coordinate the withdrawal with the Palestinian Authority and insisted that it would be unilateral. He also rejected a coordinated wide-ranging plan to be formulated by Israel and the Palestinian Authority to improve the conditions in the Gaza Strip and to connect it to the West Bank, as proposed by then United States Secretary of State Condoleezza Rice. Nevertheless, Dror Moreh, who directed the documentary film *Ariel Sharon* in 2008 and interviewed dozens of individuals working with him, found that Sharon had gone through a major psychological change, and had intended to withdraw from the greater part of the West Bank and to redraw new boundaries for the State of Israel. In his seminal speech at the meeting of the Likud faction in the Knesset on 26 May 2003, he not only objected to the occupation but also said, "*You want to stay forever in Jenin, Nablus, Ramallah and Bethlehem forever? I think that it is wrong.*" However, he did not trust the ability of Abu Mazen, the new Palestinian leader, to cooperate on such a move, and waited for his consolidation of power.

Returning to the withdrawal—the houses of the Israeli Gaza settlements were destroyed by Israel at the time of the evacuation. The greenhouses which remained intact aroused public interest in Israel: For many Israelis, they symbolized an example of goodwill towards the Palestinians. The facts, however, indicate that about half of the greenhouses had been dismantled two months before the evacuation by their owners, and the other half were looted by the Palestinians at a time when orderly self-rule did not yet exist. Mobs looted the pipes, pumps, and other materials. When the Palestinian Authority initially entered the picture and imposed order, it invested about $20 million dollars to repair the agricultural infrastructure and by October 2005, there was renewed agricultural activity. However, it became clear that export of produce was dependent on Israel—as it controlled the checkpoints out of the Gaza Strip, and these were opened only infrequently. The Palestinians, therefore, did not succeed in exporting their harvests and in the end, the produce was thrown away.[133] These facts did not prevent the Jewish public from believing that Israel had been generous in leaving the greenhouses intact, but that they had fallen victim to Palestinian barbarism.

It appears that this is a recurring pattern in the Jewish public's attitude towards the Palestinians in Gaza. In contradiction to the popular perception which still exists, a thoughtful view indicates that Israel did not "disengage" from the Gaza Strip in 2005 and did not end the occupation, but simply changed its character—over time, Israel created a new system of control and supervision over both the people and the territory.[134] At the beginning of 2006, due to the elections bringing Hamas (the ultimate enemy) into power in Gaza, Israel imposed severe sanctions on Gaza, and when Hamas gained ultimate control in June 2007, Israel officially proclaimed the Gaza Strip as "hostile territory." This meant instituting a total blockade of the entire area. From that point on, Israel controlled the air and sea space—and, *inter alia*, it narrowed the fishing area for Gaza inhabitants from 30 kilometers to 5.6 kilometers—and closed off the eastern and northern borders. Egypt, on the southern border, for various reasons closed the Rafiah crossing point both to people and to material. The Gaza Strip became a territory under complete siege and the IDF began to supervise all materials and people entering Gaza.[135] To that end, it made a list of materials and merchandise that were forbidden entry, among which were basic food supplies. In 2012, with the publication of new information, it became clear that in its attempt to prevent creating a humanitarian crisis in Gaza, over the years Israel had calculated the minimal number of calories needed to survive, and permitted entry only to the amount calculated, less the food produced within the territory.[136] Not only was quantity controlled, but quality was also regulated. Israel limited the amount of vegetables, meat, and dairy products that could enter, but in contrast, it increased the amount of sugar. In addition, a list of foods was arbitrarily prohibited, such as chocolate, pasta, margarine, jam, cookies, vinegar, and nuts, among others.[137] Furthermore, various other materials were forbidden for seemingly security considerations—for example, cement, which could ostensibly be used to build tunnels used for terrorism. These prohibitions included items necessary for normal life, such as wheelchairs for the disabled, children's paint, toys, paper, musical instruments, shoes, books, matches, shampoo, buttons, baby food, newspapers, cosmetics, industrial salt, pet foods, and more.[138] Exports from Gaza were prohibited and that, of course, held true for imports of machines required for work and for industry. As a result, the limited small-scale industry that had existed in Gaza collapsed and unemployment soared into relatively high double digits.[139]

The harm to the Strip's economy and health system, and actually to every other aspect of life, was enormous. Many states and international organizations viewed the blockade as illegal collective punishment.[140] Attempts to break the blockade by sending ships to Gaza were unsuccessful. For example, the ship, the Marmara, left Turkey for Gaza in 2010, and while taking control of the ship by the Israeli navy, nine of its passengers were killed. In an attempt to solve the chronic shortage of basic products, the Palestinians built tunnels, particularly in the direction of Egypt (at a certain stage, it was estimated that there were 3,000 of them), and a wide network of smuggling developed.[141] Israel made every effort to destroy the tunnels as these also enabled arms and ammunition to reach Gaza. The severe lack of essential materials and products continued for many years, and shortages still exist.[142] From 2009 onward, Israel took some steps to ease the blockade in response to pressure from the international community, but up until today, 2,000,000 Gazans are living under the strict supervision of Israel, and that supervision directs innumerable aspects of the inhabitants' lives. As an illustration, every infant born in Gaza must register with the Israeli authorities or s/he will not be able to leave the Strip anytime in the future; every farmer must gain permission from Israeli authorities to export agricultural produce; every merchant must receive approval to import merchandise for his/her store; anyone who visits Gaza must receive approval from Israel to enter; every inhabitant of Gaza must receive permission from Israel to leave.[143] The result is that Israel determines what can go out and what cannot be brought in and prevents any economic development. As evidence, Lieutenant Colonel (Res.) Michael Sirolnik, past coordinator of the Economic Office of the Gaza Coordination and Liaison Administration, responsible for the coordination of economic activity between the Gaza Strip and the State of Israel, stated in 2018: "*In the past, material for the textile and furniture industries of Israel were produced in the Gaza Strip, but after 2007, the state eliminated any possibility of economic development. Every government took very forceful steps to starve and harm the Gaza population in order to harm Hamas, but the reality has proven that this simply has not helped."*[144]

Through the years, the humanitarian situation in the Gaza Strip has greatly deteriorated, in no small measure due to the continuing blockade imposed by Israel. According to a report published by the United Nations Office for Coordination of Humanitarian Affairs in January 2018, out of two million inhabitants of the Gaza Strip, approximately one million were in need of humanitarian assistance. Unemployment in the Strip is about 43%, while 53% live in poverty, electricity is supplied between four and twelve hours per day, sewage is overflowing, the garbage remains uncollected, clean water is supplied to the pipelines only every four to five days, and even then only for a few hours (96% of the water is not potable). The health system is always in a state of crisis—there is a shortage of basic medication and Israel approves only about half of those in need of appropriate care outside of Gaza.[145] According to the UNWRA report in February 2021, *"economic indicators reflect the severity of the protracted crisis, aggravated by COVID-19 and the accompanying lockdowns and curfews. The unemployment rate stood at 49 per cent in the third quarter of 2020. The crisis has eroded coping mechanisms and the living conditions of Palestine refugees who remain highly dependent on the humanitarian assistance provided by UNRWA to meet basic needs. The volatile security situation, compounded by political instability, the chronic electricity crisis and lack of access to clean water deepen the extreme hardship that Gaza's people endure."*

What the Jewish Population Understood

All the information above strikingly contradicts the attitude of the Israeli public regarding Israeli involvement in the Gaza Strip. Most of the Jewish public believe that, after the Israeli withdrawal from Gaza, the Palestinians received full control of the area—that is, in their viewpoint, the occupation in Gaza had ended, exactly as the Palestinians had demanded. Thus, responsibility for building a sustainable future depended and still depends only on them.

In the view of most Jewish citizens, Israel paid a very heavy price for the disengagement, considering the difficulties involved in uprooting a population of thousands from the Strip, settling them within the borders of the State of Israel and rehabilitating them, not to mention the compromise in principle involved in this action, as they viewed it. As Prime Minister Sharon stated in his speech on the day of disengagement in 2005: "*Now the Palestinians bear the burden of proof. They must fight terror organizations, dismantle their infrastructure and show sincere intentions of peace in order to sit with us at the negotiating table.*"[146] This interpretation placed the responsibility for the crisis on the Palestinians. Instead of celebrating that they had achieved their goals and thanking Israel for ending the occupation, and instead of using the liberated area for agriculture as the Israelis had done before them, the Palestinian Authority, who had received the Strip on a silver platter, did not manage to hold on to it and its adversary, the Hamas organization—which has made destruction of Israel its motto—gained control after having won in relatively free elections that took place in January 2006. The victory of Hamas was understood by Israelis as proof of Palestinian preference for violence as a method to reach their national goals (usually identified as characterizing the Hamas organization) rather than the political approach (usually identified as characterizing the Fatah organization). The rightwing leadership instantly transmitted this constitutive interpretation of the elections in Gaza to the Jewish public in Israel. At an urgent meeting of the Likud Party, the then-head of the faction, Benjamin Netanyahu said: *Today a momentous event took place. Hamastan—an Iranian satellite—was established before our very eyes. And this is all happening one thousand meters from us. A touch away from our airport, Lod, from Jerusalem, from the cities of our central plain.*"[147] These perceptions deeply penetrated the consciousness of the Jewish public. It concluded that withdrawal from the territories was not a guarantee of an end to violence and did not predict a conflict solution, but that the opposite was true—every withdrawal from the occupied territories intensified the danger of harm to Israel and its citizens. The Peace Index of October 2015 found that about 74% of the Jewish public in Israel believed that even if Israel withdrew from all the territories up to the Green Line and the occupation ended, Palestinian violence would not stop and would perhaps even grow stronger.[148]

Under the new circumstances created in Gaza in which, according to Israelis, the Palestinians were responsible for their own fate, the dominant Israeli narrative further maintained that the occupation had ended, but that the Palestinians had begun to use the liberated area in order to initiate a violent struggle against Israel and its Jewish citizens. From this point of view, the violence was interpreted as proof that the occupation was not the reason for Palestinian violence, but the independent and timeless desire to harm Israel and even to destroy it. It was argued that Hamas, which had complete control of the Gaza Strip, cynically takes advantage of the local population in order to achieve these objectives. This view argues that the Palestinians have brought these troubles upon themselves by supporting Hamas, and Israel must defend itself against a violent adversary.

Thus, mediated by Israeli leaders and by most of the Israeli media, the great majority of the Israeli Jewish public were fixed on a number of beliefs regarding the end of the Gaza occupation, and although there was a very small grain of truth in them, they were very far from reality in their entirety and their scope. However, it should be noted that these beliefs were strengthened and became even more well established as a result of acts of violence against Israel by Hamas, including firing on civilian settlements, which has caused serious harm to cities, towns and villages in the south of the country, and by threatening rhetoric through the years by Hamas leaders. From 2001 on, rockets and mortar shells have been fired into Israel at settlements close to the border with Gaza. Since Hamas took control of Gaza, these attacks have made life intolerable for the inhabitants of areas close to the Strip. The range of these rockets has gradually increased, and they have also been fired at the cities of Beersheba, Ashkelon, and even Tel Aviv. It must be understood that the two realities—the first, that Gaza is living under a severe blockade and second, that rockets are being fired from Gaza—are not contradictory but are complementary. They constitute a vicious circle in which one complements the other.

Another aspect that must be added to this situation is the division of Palestinian territories between Hamas, which controls the Gaza Strip and Fatah, which controls the A area on the West Bank. For Jewish Israelis this is another reason that the conflict cannot be solved in a political process with the Palestinian Authority as there are actually two different political entities, and these are themselves involved in a dispute. This split among the Palestinians has served as a kind of warning signal cautioning that even if an agreement is signed with the Authority, led by Fatah, Hamas could win future elections on the West Bank or could gain control by force. On the other hand, in 2011, when the Palestinian political extremes were about to sign a reconciliation agreement, the official reaction by Israeli Prime Minister Benjamin Netanyahu was: *"The Palestinian Authority must choose either peace with Israel or peace with Hamas.*"[149] In other words, both a Palestinian split and Palestinian unification serve as support for the same belief that determined that it was impossible to make progress with them for a peace process and in general, Palestinians could not be trusted. The fact is that the split well serves Israel and is well encouraged by the Israeli government. According to the old principle of divide and rule, Israel is actively preventing unity and at the same time, is rewarding each of the entities to maintain the separation.[150]

THE WARS IN LEBANON AND GAZA

The four limited wars that took place between 2006 and 2014—in 2008, 2012 and 2014, following the withdrawal from Gaza, and the war in Lebanon in 2006 were viewed by most of the Jewish public as defensive wars, wars for which Israel had no choice but to fight, and resulted from violence on the part of the Hezbollah organization on the northern border and the violence of Hamas towards the settlements bordering Gaza in the south. In all these wars, an overwhelming majority of the Jewish public focused on the injustice caused by Hamas or Hezbollah and viewed itself as the sole victim of Arab aggression. However, an in-depth examination reveals that the factors leading to the outbreak of each of these violent conflicts are much more complex.

On 12 July 2006, Hezbollah ambushed an IDF patrol, during which three soldiers were killed and two were kidnapped, while they simultaneously shelled the area of Shlomi, a town near the northern border. Israel reacted with a bombardment and heavy shelling of Lebanon, attacking also civilian sites. Hezbollah then massively shelled the Israeli north with so many rocket attacks that a quarter of a million residents in the north felt no other alternative but to leave their homes for the center and south of the country. On 20 July, Israel launched a ground attack into southern Lebanon, and on 12 August, the Security Council announced a cease-fire. Forty-four Israeli civilians and 122 soldiers were killed during the war. On the Lebanese side, there are estimates between 800 and 1,200. The great majority of casualties were civilians and the UNICEF estimated that 30% of Lebanese killed were children under the age of 13. Following the war, due to criticism of how the war had been managed and the fact that its objectives were not achieved, a government committee was appointed under the headship of Justice Eliyahu Winograd, which reported on deficiencies in the way the war had been handled, and concluded that the war had been a severe missed opportunity as it had not resulted in a clear victory.

Two years later, on 4 November 2008, during a temporary lull (*tahdiya*—a cease fire) in activity of a half year between Hamas and Israel, which was meant to last until 19 December, and during which Hamas had stopped firing on the southern settlements, an IDF ground force penetrated into Gaza in order to destroy a tunnel that had been dug from Gaza towards Israel and was considered "a ticking time bomb." During the action, Israeli forces encircled a Palestinian house and in the resulting exchange of fire, a Hamas activist was killed. It didn't end there. On the following day, 5 November 2008, Israel, from the air, destroyed a vehicle with five people whom the army had determined were "Hamas fighters." In response, Hamas renewed their shelling of the southern towns. In a response to the response, Israel initiated "Operation Cast Lead," which began with an air attack on a training parade for graduating Palestinian traffic police. Then, in 2012, Israel targeted and killed the commander of the military branch of Hamas in Gaza, Ahmed Jabari. In reaction, Hamas again began to shell the southern towns, and in a reaction to the reaction—again—Israel began another operation, this time called "Pillar of Cloud." Sometime later, then-Minister of Defense Ehud Barak stated with pride that the killing of Jabari had been meant to serve as the surprise opening blow of the operation. Finally, in the summer of 2014, the kidnap and murder of three teenage boys by a Hamas activist led to a wave of arrests of Hamas members in the West Bank, including many who had been released in the Shalit agreement, signed three years earlier. In this agreement, in 2011, Israel freed 1,027 Palestinian security prisoners in exchange for one Israeli soldier, who had been abducted in 2006 by Palestinian fighters. Hamas viewed this as a harsh violation of the terms of the agreement and began massive shelling of the Israeli south and center: In response, Israel initiated "Operation Protective Edge"

In "Cast Lead" in 2008, over 1,160 Gaza Palestinians were killed—926 were unarmed and 345 of them, children. In the "Pillar of Cloud" operation, 174 Palestinians in total were killed—107 of them civilians. In "Protective Edge" in 2014, about 2,200 Gaza citizens were killed, of whom about 1,490 were civilians and at least 526 of them children.[151] In these three military operations Israel suffered the following losses: In "Cast Lead" three Israeli civilians and ten soldiers were killed (four by friendly fire); in "Pillar of Cloud" four Israeli civilians and two soldiers were killed; and in "Protective Edge" a total of 67 soldiers were killed, and six civilians were killed as a result of rocket and mortar fire. Since there are significant disagreements about the Palestinian casualties, the numbers cited are relatively low estimates.

Although there are differences between these four events, in each of them, Israel had to decide on an initiative or a reaction which evoked a response on the other side. You need "two to tango" when either the instigation or the reaction is violent. Violence leads to violence. Israeli leaders, the Israeli public, and most of the media almost always disregard the instigations carried out by Israel in the Gazan violent confrontations and focus on the Palestinian reaction, viewing it as the initiation of the hostile activity.

The factors involved are therefore clearly complex, but not according to Israeli public relations which always attempt to describe Palestinian violence as having no reason, as being arbitrary, and as an expression of pure hatred against Israel. And in terms of Israeli public opinion—their attempts are also successful. The great majority of the public supported the Israeli decision to initiate these wars. The Peace Index of July 2006 found that, during the Second War in Lebanon, about 93% of the Jewish public in Israel believed that the campaign in Lebanon was justified. The Peace Index of November 2012 indicated that about 84% thought that the Pillar of Cloud Operation was justified, and the Peace Index of July 2014 showed that about 95% considered Operation Protective Edge justified.[152]

In March 2018, Gaza inhabitants began weekly marches towards the separation fence between Israel and the Strip, terming them "the marches of return," and calling to allow Palestinian refugees and their descendants to return to the State of Israel. However, these immediately became a protest both against the blockade of the Gaza Strip and the announcement by U.S. President Donald Trump that he was moving the American Embassy from Tel Aviv to Jerusalem. During the demonstrations, thousands of Gaza inhabitants, both Hamas activists and those who were not, clashed with IDF forces at the fence encircling Gaza. Snipers positioned on the border fired at Palestinians. The numbers of dead and wounded in these events were higher than at any time in the conflict since the second *intifada*. According to the UN Committee for Humanitarian Affairs, by February 2020, more than 200 Palestinians (including young people under the age of 18) had been killed by IDF fire, using live ammunition, and 36,000 more had been injured, among whom were about 8,500 children. In return, in addition to firing rockets, Palestinians in Gaza began sending incendiary kites and balloons to ignite fires in the Israeli fields. At least one Israeli soldier was killed in this violence, and a few were injured. Israeli officials claimed that the demonstrations were used by Hamas as cover for launching attacks against Israel, and some of those killed were members of Palestinian military organizations.

The Peace Index of April 2018 showed that 83% of the Jewish public defined the policies of the IDF during these events as "correct," despite the high number of victims. In the same Index, it was also discovered that 67.8% of the Jewish public did not agree with the argument that the economic situation in Gaza had greatly declined in recent years or that Israel should alleviate the conditions of Gaza residents, for example, by showing greater flexibility regarding the transfer of materials in and out of Gaza.[153]

In May 2021, a new cycle of violence broke out. The first spark that lit the flame was the decision by the Israeli police to set up barricades at the Damascus Gate entrance to the old city toward the end of Ramadan in April, the Islamic holy month. This barricade was later removed. The immediate trigger was in Jerusalem, where Palestinians had been demonstrating for months against the possible eviction of six Palestinian families in a Palestinian neighborhood, Sheikh Jarrah, which had been annexed by Israel. The eviction, based on Israeli law, is viewed as extremely unfair because it permits Israelis to reclaim property in East Jerusalem that was held by Jews before 1948. Yet Palestinians are not allowed to do the same with property they once owned in West Jerusalem. In addition, violence erupted in the compound of the al-Aqsa Mosque on the Muslim holiday, Qadr Night (one of the holiest nights in Ramadan and the Islamic calendar). At the same time, ultra-rightist Jews declared their intention to march through the Muslim Quarter with Israeli flags on Jerusalem Day, marking the capture of the Old City and East Jerusalem in the 1967 Arab–Israeli War.

On 10 May, Hamas gave Israel an ultimatum to withdraw security forces from the Temple Mount complex and Sheikh Jarrah. When the ultimatum expired without a response, both Hamas and Palestinian Islamic Jihad launched rockets into Israel. In response, Israeli air force attacked the Gaza Strip and Hamas responded with rocket attacks that reached Tel Aviv. A cease fire came into force on May 21. During the hostilities, Palestinian armed organizations fired more than 4,300 rockets and other ammunition at Israel. Israeli forces carried out more than 1,500 air, land, and sea strikes throughout the Gaza Strip, demolishing 258 buildings and damaging 14,536 housing units. From May 10 to May 21, the Human Rights Commission verified the killing of 243 Palestinians including 66 children and 38 women (at least 129 of the fatalities were civilians). In the West Bank, at the same time, 27 Palestinians (22 were men) were killed by Israeli forces during demonstrations, clashes and attacks, and 6,794 people were injured. In Israel, there were a total of 12 fatalities (two children, five women, and five men), including one soldier and three foreign nationals, by Palestinian rocket fire or while they were rushing to find shelter during such attacks. A plea by the U.S. President Biden on May 19 and negotiations brokered by Egypt, Qatar, and the United Nations led to the cease fire. Of special interest is the fact that this mini war led to violent confrontations between Jews and Arabs citizens of Israel, especially in ethnically mixed cities. A number of Jews and Arabs were lynched and killed. More than 2,000 were arrested, the great majority of them Arabs (more than 90%). These events have shaken the fragile Jewish-Arab coexistence in the state. With regards to the Gaza war, a poll conducted by *The Times of Israel* on May 20 revealed that 72% of Israelis believed that Israel should not accept the ceasefire and continue the military operation in Gaza.

About a year later, on March 22, 2022, a new wave of terror attacks began within the borders of the Israeli state. An Israeli Arab murdered four Israelis by stabbing and vehicle ramming. Following this event, another attack occurred in Hadera carried by two Israeli Arabs who murdered two Israelis, and then in Bnei Brak (five Israelis were murdered) and even in the center of Tel Aviv (where three Israelis were murdered by Palestinians from the West Bank). Following these attacks, Israeli forces entered to search for collaborators and in the clashes that erupted, 18 Palestinians were killed. In April, a new round of violence began around the Al-Aqsa mosque when the police stormed the grounds of the mosque in response to stone-throwing Palestinians. This round, as other in the past, reflected a religious conflict between radical religious Jews and Muslims. Jewish extremist religious groups planned to perform a Passover sacrifice on the Temple Mount where two holy Muslim mosques stand. In turn, Palestinians hurried to defend their holy ground. In these violent confrontations, 48 Palestinians were killed, among them 16 children and four women.

In any event, the violent encounters did not change the shaky situation in the relationships between Israel, Hamas, and the Palestinian Authority.

The key problems remain unsolved and another round of violence is a real possibility.

As seems clear, the automatic Israeli interpretation is that every war is necessarily defensive and that every confrontation, in the north or in the south, is proof of the desire of Hezbollah or Hamas to harm Israel and even to attempt to destroy it. Moreover, as in all the wars and confrontations that have been discussed, the Arab civilian population has suffered greatly; many voices have been raised throughout the world in protest, and there have even been demands to investigate. This international reaction has automatically been perceived, both by the government and by a great majority of the Jewish public, as an expression of anti-Semitism and anti-Zionism. A document termed "Anti-Semitism in 2014" issued by the Ministry of Jerusalem and Diaspora Affairs under Naftali Bennet asserted that *"expressions against IDF actions during Operation Protective Edge were a smokescreen for anti-Semitism saturated in hatred that does not distinguish between an Israeli and a Jew."*[154] This type of reaction has three goals. One is to frame the events for the Israeli Jewish public, which has developed siege mentality. The second is to remind European governments and societies about their indirect responsibility for the Holocaust (for Germany, it is a reminder for its direct responsibility). The third goal is often achieved—it is to discourage Europeans and Americans from criticizing Israel for its immoral behavior.

The violence occurring during the first two decades of the 2000s and the interpretation it received, in addition to the withdrawal from Gaza and how that was interpreted in Israel, reinforced the rightward drift of the Israeli public and reestablished the ethos of conflict beliefs, and in general, all the conflict supporting narratives with their eight themes. However, to receive a complete picture of the situation, we must add the analysis of attempts to find a solution to the conflict, all of which failed.

THE FAILURES OF THE PEACE PROCESS

Through the years there have been a number of attempts to revive the peace process, despite the cycle of violence. In 2002, a roadmap framework proposal was issued by the United States, Russia, the European Union, and the United Nations as an outline for a solution to the Israeli-Palestinian dispute which was planned to end by 2005. The map obligated an end to building in the settlements and the dismantling of outposts that had been set up after March 2001, along with a demand for a serious and effective struggle by the Palestinian Authority against terror. Although the two sides accepted this plan in principle, in actuality both failed to fulfill their obligations. Thus, the plan disintegrated. On 28 March 2002, the Saudis presented an initiative, later known as the Arab initiative, to achieve a general peace between Israel and the Arab countries, and the foreign ministers of the Arab League approved it at their conference in Beirut. The Arab initiative proposed normalization of relations between Israel and the Arab states in return for full Israeli withdrawal from the Golan Heights, the Gaza Strip, Judea, and Samaria (including East Jerusalem), and the establishment of an independent Palestinian state with its capital in East Jerusalem. At the end of March 2007, the Arab League, with the participation of 22 heads of state, ratified the proposal. In reaction to the Arab initiative, Israel not only refused to accept the proposal, but also refused to officially respond to it.

Another attempt to restart the peace process took place in November 2007 at the Annapolis Conference in Maryland, in the United States, with the participation of both Israeli and Palestinian leadership, along with that of many other nations. The conference did not include negotiations, but rather was an attempt to motivate the two sides to renew the peace process. At the conference, for the first time, the two sides agreed that dividing the country into two states was a solution that would bring an end to the conflict. In addition, both promised immediately to fulfill their commitment to the roadmap of 2002, and to enter negotiations which were planned to be completed by the end of 2008 with the signing of a permanent agreement. The United States offered to supervise the process. And what happened in reality? The negotiations between the Israeli Prime Minister, Ehud Olmert, and the Head of Palestinian Authority, Abbas, indeed did continue for a few months and led to a number of very significant agreements, but these never reached completion for a variety of reasons, among which was the resignation of Olmert, who was under suspicion for crimes of corruption; thus, the negotiations ended.[155] These were probably the most significant negotiations that touched on all the issues of dispute between Palestinians and Israeli Jews. They also proceeded the farthest and almost were completed.

In the Israeli elections of 2009, after the resignation of Olmert, the rightwing bloc was victorious, and Benjamin Netanyahu began several terms as prime minister. American pressure and preliminary conditions demanded by the Palestinians led Netanyahu to announce a partial freezing of new construction in the occupied territories for ten months. However, after only nine months of construction suspension, in September 2010, the Palestinians agreed to return to direct negotiations. The peace talks, which opened with a festive ceremony at the White House, exploded after only three weeks due to Palestinian claims that Netanyahu was not conducting serious negotiations and was refusing to present clear positions regarding the borders of a Palestinian state. Thus, these negotiations broke down as well, and only after Barak Obama's reelection to the presidency in November 2012 did serious diplomatic efforts resume for the renewal of direct negotiations between the sides. At the end of an intensive round of preliminary talks, American Secretary of State John Kerry, who had facilitated the contacts, formulated understandings that would enable resumption of negotiations. The sides even agreed that negotiations would include all core issues for a permanent settlement, and that a signed agreement would put an end to the conflict and to mutual demands. As the talks approached, the Palestinians agreed to stop petitioning the United Nations to recognize Palestine as a state, while Israel agreed to free 104 Palestinian security prisoners in three stages. In July 2013, negotiations officially began in Washington and were scheduled to continue for nine months. During this period, Kerry met with the leaders of the two sides dozens of times, but finally, in April 2014, the talks collapsed with both sides hurling the blame on the other.

Unexpectedly, after the election of Donald Trump to the presidency in 2016, he announced the preparation of the ultimate peace plan that would be presented to both sides. The president appointed his son-in-law, Jared Kushner, and his lawyer, Jason Greenblatt, to be responsible for the negotiations, and the new ambassador representing the United States in Israel, David Friedman, joined them. The team, which was perceived as very biased towards Israel, began to prepare its proposals. The plan remained top secret, but during the negotiations, President Trump recognized Jerusalem as the capital of Israel and moved the United States Embassy to the capital. This act was seen by the Palestinians as contradictory to United Nations resolutions and they stopped cooperating in negotiations, announcing that the United States had lost its status as a fair mediator. Finally, on 29 January 2020, in Washington, with the attendance of the

Israeli prime minister Netanyahu, a peace plan was presented by President Trump's team. It was considered by the Palestinians and by many other countries as completely biased towards Israel. In addition, it was rejected by the European Union, Russia, the Arab League states, the Organization of Islamic Cooperation, and the entire Democratic party leadership, which expressed strong criticism of the plan. Although the plan talked about the establishment of the Palestinian state, it also mandated dividing the Palestinian Authority by transferring East Jerusalem to the State of Israel, allowing Palestinian autonomy under Israeli security control, and allowing Israel to annex large parts of the West Bank. Importantly, the State Department cancelled the use of the concept "occupation," which had been employed until 2019. Furthermore, on November 18, 2020, Secretary of State Mike Pompeo rejected the legal opinion of the State Department, issued in 1978, stating that the Jewish settlements in the West Bank were a violation of international law.

All of the initiatives that ended in failure were perceived by most of the Jewish public in Israel as supportive evidence that there was no partner for negotiations on the Palestinian side, and that they were not interested in reconciliation but rather in a struggle to conquer the entire country. This was also the way negotiations between Ehud Olmert and Abu Mazen were viewed, although they had advanced the farthest towards a solution to the conflict but had been cut short towards the end. This view of negotiations to end the conflict has been expressed politically through all seven of the elections that have taken place from 2001 onwards, and is still valid as these lines are being written in 2022. All the governments elected were either rightwing or center. In addition, except for a short two-year period between 2006–2008, serious and substantive negotiations between Israel and the Palestinians have not taken place. From 2009 and up to the present, Israel has conducted an extreme version of "conflict management," while the ethos of conflict narrative, with its eight themes, has become the leading ideology of the leadership and of most of the Jewish public in Israel. This is even the situation in 2022; Israel has been governed since 2021 by a coalition of parties coming from far right to Zionist left and even one Arab conservative party. The parties in the coalition agreed not to negotiate with the Palestinians and not to change their status because of the tremendous differences in their views and aspirations.

There is no doubt amongst these parties that the belief that the West Bank belongs exclusively to the Jewish nation and is not occupied territory, constitutes a significant obstacle to a solution to the conflict.[156] First of all, it contributes to the psychological difficulty of withdrawing from the area because it is considered part of the homeland. Secondly, it strengthens the feeling that talks involving withdrawal from the territory or parts of it represent negotiations that require significant compromise only on the Jewish side. Thus, willingness to conduct negotiation under these conditions is, naturally, almost nonexistent. The preferred option is continuing control over another nation. In the Peace Index of May 2019, about 45% expressed the belief that a continuation of the existing situation had the best chances of being realized in the foreseeable future, while about 20% believed that annexing the territories with limited rights for the Palestinians had the best chances of being realized.[157] But in November 2020, a year and half later, in a study carried out in cooperation between the Israeli Macro Center and the Palestinian Center for Policy and Survey Research among a national sample of Jews, who were asked about their preferred status of Israeli-Palestinian relations, 36.6% preferred to reach a peace agreement, 15.8% preferred to annex the territories or part of them, 15.53% preferred to wage a definitive war against the Palestinians, and 15.25% preferred to maintain the present status. Only about 28% of the respondents thought that the long-term aspiration of Israel was withdrawal from part of the occupied territories; and about 31% believed that Israeli aspirations were either to annex the territories without giving the Palestinian political rights or to extend the border of the state and expel them. The rest replied that they did not know what Israeli aspirations were or did not want to respond to the question. We may conclude that the vision of a two-state solution is gradually disappearing from the Jewish public as an achievable possibility. The concrete signs of its disappearance are the increasing talk, as well as realistic steps being taken towards annexation of Area C to Israel, and wide agreement among the rightwing and center parties, including Blue-White Party that was conceived as the center of the political spectrum, about annexing the Jordan Valley.

THE POLITICAL INTERNAL ARENA

To return to a description of events in Israel, the rightwing- extreme rightwing government, in power from 2015–2019, led to fundamental changes and these will be discussed in the coming chapters—there have been radical changes in the nature of the regime, in statehood, in the judicial system, in education, in the status of the media, in relations with other countries of the world, and more. The state has been moving in a more authoritarian direction, considering the laws it has enacted, the functioning of the democratic organs, the discourse among government leaders, their relations with the opposition, and the expansion of racism and extreme nationalism. In this period, the hegemonic ethos of conflict has not only deepened the conflict but has also critically harmed the democratic foundations of the state. **The latter point is of critical importance in the present analysis because, on the basis of observation of developments in Israel and in other states involved in intractable conflict, we suggest that the continuation of an intractable conflict with the hegemonic narratives supporting it, necessarily deteriorates democratic principles and increases the authoritarian practices of the regime. This premise will be discussed in Chapter 5.**

The elections of 2019 only further intensified the tendencies that had been seen in the preceding years. The personal victory of Benjamin Netanyahu in leading the Likud Party (which gained 35 Knesset seats), despite the indictments issued against him by the attorney general before the elections (which will be elaborated on later), indicated that he has a basis of very loyal supporters. In addition, the rightwing bloc, including all the rightwing and religious parties, gained 65 Knesset seats. Despite the victory of the rightwing bloc, Benjamin Netanyahu did not succeed in putting together a coalition due to political disagreements about ultra-Orthodox army service, as well as personal rivalry with the leader of the rightwing Yisrael Beitenu Party, Avigdor Lieberman. The Knesset adjourned and announced new elections on 17 September 2019. In these elections, another deadlock ensued as the head of the Yisrael Beitenu Party, which received eight Knesset seats, did not agree to join the rightwing bloc with its 55 Knesset seats (the Likud Party with the ultra-Orthodox and the ultra-rightwing Yemina Party). In the meanwhile, a retired Lieutenant-General (res.) Benny Ganz, ex-chief of the general staff, who had entered politics and founded a political party, Israel Resilience, established an alliance with a centrist party Yesh Atid (There Is a Future) and the new alliance was called Blue–White. Thus, neither Benjamin Netanyahu of the Likud nor Benny Ganz, the Blue–White Party candidate, were able to form a coalition; the Knesset again adjourned and new elections were scheduled for 2 March 2020.

In these elections, the rightwing bloc received 58 Knesset seats, but then the coronavirus pandemic broke out and Israel entered an emergency period and locked down due to the spread of the virus, which gravely affected all areas of existence, especially economic life. During this short period, there was a struggle between the prime minister, who headed the right-wing bloc, and the alternative Blue–White leader, Benny Ganz. It would have been possible to form a minority government with the support of the Arab party, but this was strongly opposed by several members of the Blue-White party. Finally, Ganz, who had already received a mandate from the president to form a government, decided to join the Netanyahu coalition with the party he headed. This caused a split in the Blue–White Party, and the larger faction headed by Yair Lapid (leader of Yesh Atid), decided not to join the coalition but to move to the opposition. In addition, three elected parliament members of the Labor Party also joined the coalition, and the leftist block was crushed. In the deal, Netanyahu served first as prime minister, while Blue–White leader Benny Gantz was to serve as prime minister starting October 2021.The new coalition had 36 ministers and was plagued by continual crises. However, the deal did not materialize because the Knesset was again dissolved in December 2020 after a continuous dispute over the budget for 2020–21 that actually should have been approved in the fall of 2020. In addition, the numerous manipulations carried out by Netanyahu finally led to a loss of Ganz's trust. Eventually the Knesset was dispersed and the fourth elections were set for March 23, 2021. In advance of these elections, Ganz's party lost its key members, who decided to leave politics. In sum, Netanyahu engineered a two-year stalemate that prevented Israel's government from functioning normally.

Towards the fourth in the series of elections, one of the past Likud leaders, Gideon Saar, left Likud and formed a new rightist party, New Hope, to compete with Netanyahu. In addition, after the leader of the Labor party left politics, a new leader (Merav Michaeli) tried to reestablish and renew the face of the party. The results of the fourth elections did not bring the hoped for clear solution to the stalemate. However, in these elections, several meaningful political developments took place.

1. The Arab alliance of parties broke up and a conservative religious party, the United Arab List (Ra'am), decided to run separately. Surprisingly, it won 5 seats and became a potential tie-breaking party that was even courted by Netanyahu to join his bloc. With this move, he legitimized an Arab party as worthy of participating in an Israeli coalition- an important political change.

2. For the first time in Israel, an openly nationalist-racist party ran for parliament with the support of Prime Minister Netanyahu. This party ideologically refused to accept the support of Raam, the previously mentioned Arab party, in a Netanyahu coalition. Eventually, two blocs confronted each other: on the one hand, the right-religious homogeneous bloc and on the other, a very heterogeneous bloc of parties from the right to the left that were united in one goal, to remove Netanyahu from office. Without entering into the details of the Byzantine negotiations that took place in the effort to replace Netanyahu's 12-year tenure as a prime minister, eventually Yair Lapid, who headed the opposition bloc, succeeded in forming a very strange coalition.

The coalition, formed in June 2021, included the progressive Zionist party Meretz, the revived Labor party, the centrist party Yesh Atid (There is a Future), the centrist party Blue–White, the center-rightist party, Yisrael Beiteinu (Israel Our Home), and two far right parties, Gideon Saar's New Hope party and Naftali Bennet's Yemina (To the Right) party—with the formal support of the conservative Arab party Ra'am as part of the coalition. Strangely, according to the coalition agreement, Naftali Bennett of the Yamina party, which received only 7 MK, was serving first as the prime minister, and then would be replaced by Lapid (with 17 MKs) in 2023. No doubt this coalition improved the performance in many domains and especially in guarding the principles of democracy. However, as noted, the parties in the coalition have decided to abstain from dealing with negotiations with the Palestinians or ending the occupation. These issues are divisive for the parties of the coalition—the Labor Party and Meretz are committed to the two-state solution and opposed to settlements and annexation, while Yemina and New Hope have exactly opposing views; they oppose the establishment of a Palestinian state and support wide scale Jewish settlement in the West Bank and at least partial annexation.

The new government focused mainly on internal problems of Israel with solidification of the relationships with the Arab states in the Arab peninsula that took part in Abraham Accords and took steps against Iran. But in the spring of 2022, the coalition of 61 Knesset members began to disintegrate with defections of Knesset members from the extreme right and the left. The government lost support and on June 22, Prime Minister Naftali Bennet and his successor Yair Lapid announced their desire to disperse Knesset and have new elections. On June 29, 2022, the Knesset was dispersed, Yair Lapid became the Prime Minster, and new elections were set for November 1, 2022. Naftali Bennet decided to take a break from political life.

The elections took place on time and were transforming. Thus, I will elaborate on their results and the implications. The outcomes of the elections showed that Netanyahu's bloc got 64 mandates and the alternative bloc got only 51 mandates. Therefore, Benjamin Netanyahu was the big winner of the elections. With 32 seats for his Likud party, 18 for ultra-Orthodox parties, and 14 for a far-right alliance he was the unequivocal victor. His bloc is a combination of a Zionist religious party that was combined of three political forces, and three ultra-orthodox parties. The new government combines messianic, extremely nationalistic, racist, and fundamentally religious political forces.

The Zionist Religious Party, which included Otzma Yehudit (Jewish strength), had unprecedented success, more than doubling its votes, thus becoming the 3rd largest party in the 25th Knesset. Otzma Yehudit is the ideological descendant of the outlawed Kach party (ultra nationalist religious-racist movement). The party advocates the deportation of those who they consider to be the "enemies of Israel", and the leader Itamar Ben-Gvir was associated with the original racist-nationalistic and religious Kach movement. Otzma Yehudit calls for a one-state solution, including the annexation of the West Bank and complete Israeli rule of the land between the Jordan River and the Mediterranean Sea. The party is against the formation of a Palestinian state, and advocates cancellation of the Oslo accords, as well as imposing Israeli sovereignty over the Temple Mount. Betzalel Smotrich, the leader of Zionist Religious, holds similar views regarding the annexation of the West Bank, Jewish settlements, and the formation of Palestinian state. He demands legalization of over 100 outposts that were built illegally throughout the West Bank. He also holds racist, extreme nationalist and anti-gay views. The three ultrareligious parties, Agudath Yisrael (Union of Israel) and Degel HaTora (Banner of the Torah) that ran together in the elections and Shas (party of Sephardic religious and traditional Jews) have an ethnocentric orientation, extreme religious and nationalistic views since Likud built settlements for ultrareligious population in the West Bank. One third of the Jewish settlers come from ultrareligious background and thus the three parties also adopted Greater Israel ideology. The Likud, after Netanyahu expelled the moderate personalities, the largest party in Israel, combines anti-democratic, religious and nationalistic views. Netanyahu's outlook about Palestinians, Greater Israel and the Jewish settlement are well known. He will have unlimited support from his religious partners. In addition, the new coalition is planning an overhaul of the judicial system by giving it to the hands of the politicians, control of the mass media, supervising the educational system and installing religious laws over different aspects of life in Israel.

The elections results show that majority of the Jewish population in Israel embraces apartheid and anti-democratic views. They confirm the trends that have been festering for many years of the different shades of right-wing politics from the soft version of the right and all the way to the hard right, then all the way to the religious messianic and ultra-right. Netanyahu did not invent this system, but he improved and exploited it to a maximum for his political and personal gains. It has left the tatters of Israeli democracy that even previously was hardly functioning. In addition, the Prime Minister, who has been on trial for corruption because of three counts of bribery, fraud and breach of trust will try to derail his trial without bearing consequences of his deeds. Corruption is not issue for his followers as the leader of Shas party and several members of the Likud party are involved in trials for corruption.

In contrast to the big success of the rightist-religious forces in Israel, Meretz, the only Jewish party that campaigned against the occupation and against discrimination of the Arab Israeli citizens did not pass the minimal quota of votes and will not be present in the elected Knesset. This is a great loss that indicates the apathy that characterizes the Jewish public with regard to the issues of occupation and its implications regarding violations of human rights and apartheid.

Before moving to the summary, it is important to say a few words about the Covid-19 pandemic that represents an important constitutive event in Israeli politics.

THE COVID-19 PANDEMIC

Covid-19 arrived in Israel, as to many states in the world, at the beginning of 2020. The pandemic has been a constitutive event that nobody in the world had expected. A new international era developed, as every state began to cope with the danger that brought death, illness, hardship and uncertainty. The pandemic met Israel unprepared medically, as it did in much of the world. The beginning was chaotic with much mismanagement, lack of information, misinformation, and lies. However, ultimately, the government announced a closure with various limitations in spring 2020. The schools were closed, along with many businesses and cultural institutions. The pandemic spread throughout Israel with vicious consequences and as a result, in September 2020, a new longer closure was declared that was perceived by many as a way to prevent demonstrations against Netanyahu, which had also spread throughout Israel.

The situation did not improve, and a new lockdown was declared in January 2021 that lasted until 6 March 2021. During this period, Israel experienced over 6,300 deaths and about 830,000 residents were infected. In late fall, Israel began to vaccinate its citizens and within the short period of a few months, about 5,000,000 people had been vaccinated at least once and about 4,000,000 had received the second inoculation. Netanyahu played an important part in the success of the vaccination project by pressuring the Pfizer company, which also recognized the specific benefit of vaccinating an entire society as a clinical experiment. But the crisis resulted in great harm to the trust of Israelis in their government and in democracy following the exposure of the political and personal interests that had guided many of the decisions made by the Prime Minister, who had already been charged by the state prosecutor with serious crimes on three counts. It soon became clear that certain sectors, especially the ultra-orthodox, did not follow the rules issued by the government, and the prime minister did not intend to enforce them because this population were his political allies. A similar phenomenon could be found in the Arab sector, which just did not trust the government. Netanyahu also violated the principles of democracy by limiting citizens' freedoms, leading to their control and supervision, and tried to limit the demonstrations that were spreading across the country, but especially in Jerusalem, demanding his resignation.

By May 2021, it looked as though Israel had succeeded in overcoming the pandemic, when the number of new cases had dropped below 50, but in August, a new wave struck the state and the number of newly sick people reached over 4,000 per day, with the threat of the new, more dangerous variant called Delta. Some restrictions were reinstated, but the government made every effort to avoid a fourth lockdown that could be devastating for the economy. Israel experienced a fifth wave with the new variant

Omicron, which caused massive infections. Daily over 60,000 individuals were infected, though deaths as a result of infection were very low. The government lost control over management of the pandemic: the educational system was paralyzed, the lines for the PCR test were very long, and different businesses were financially hurt. But of special importance were political and psychological consequences—all Israelis began to live in uncertainty and unpredictability, many of the Israelis lost trust in the new government, the opposition under the leadership of Netanyahu was active in trying to thwart the government in the media, social networks, and Knesset, and the supporters of Netanyahu started demonstrations in his favor. Eventually, at the end of April, the wave subsided, and the government allowed Israelis to return to live normal lives, even without masks in enclosed places. In June 2022, the sixth wave broke out, but the government did not impose any restrictions, and life continued with its normal routine. Israel decided to take a new road- just to ignore the dangers of Covid and allowed the Israelis to live normal life without closures and any restrictions.

SUMMARY: THE CIRCLE IS COMPLETE

At the beginning of the 2000s, the themes of conflict supporting narratives cited above again became central in the collective repertoire of Israeli society. For 12 years, the head of the political pyramid had been a prime minster whose worldview expressed the ethos of conflict, and the government formed in 2015 included parties that held a clearly rightwing perspective (Jewish Home, Likud, Shas, and Kulanu, with the addition of Yisrael Beiteinu that joined the coalition in May 2016). The elections of 2022 were even worse. They brought to power a radical religious-nationalistic coalition. During the 2000s, a widely based front of support for the basic principles of the ethos of conflict became established which, even if it did not accept all rightwing goals, blocked any progress in the peace process.

It is clear that Jews in Israel believe that the danger of another Holocaust still exists. They view the State of Israel as an island of sanity or as a refuge in the middle of a jungle, surrounded by hostile states, nations, ethnic groups and organizations. The difficult realities that have developed in the region in recent years serve as clear confirmation of the justice of these beliefs for the Jewish public. This reality lends support to the belief among Jews in Israel that the use of force is necessary when attempting to ensure the continued existence of the state, including specific military operations or even wars, and even more importantly, control, supervision, and even suppression of the Palestinian population in the occupied territories. These methods are considered "reasonable" or "realistic" and thus, they are also thought to be moral, while the public often demands an even greater use of force and complains from to time about the "leftism" of the army. For example, recurring opinion polls show that most of the Jewish-Israeli public agree with statements like "*Any means are acceptable in Israel's struggle against Palestinian terror*" (about 70%) or "*All military activity initiated by Israel is justified* (about 55%)." Clearly, these popular positions are likely to be considered support for the use of great force, as seen in Lebanon in 2006 and in Gaza since 2006.

In an attempt to deal with this reality, beliefs as to the very positive self-perception of the Jewish nation, the state of Israel, and even specifically of the army, have grown stronger. The statement that the "*IDF is the most moral army in the world*" has become a required mantra in speeches by ministers and army officers. For example, Prime Minister Netanyahu stated in 2010, "*There is no army more moral that the IDF and we have proved that time after time, when facing the most despicable enemies who sanctify death and barbarism while we sanctify life and enlightenment*." Research conducted by Ruthie Pliskin (a political psychologist at Tel Aviv University) and her colleagues in 2014 showed that a majority among the Jewish public in Israel believed that Jews are more morally principled than other nations (51%) and that, in general, Jews are more intelligent than other nations (77%).[158] Another long-standing belief, first expressed by Golda Meir (and one that flourished during the operations in Gaza), is that Hamas has "forced" Israel to kill innocent Palestinians. This was conveyed by Netanyahu in a speech given in 2011: "*We didn't seek those wars,*" he said, "*They were forced upon us. But when we were attacked, we knew that we could not lose even one battle.*" Even Tzipi Livni, one of the opposition leaders during "Protective Edge" stated in 2015: "*Accompanied by a sense of deep justice, they went out to fight the war of this nation. And this war is being carried out with the sense that there is no choice and this has given them the strength to go into battle.*" It is no wonder that beliefs of patriotism and the importance of national unity have become all the more important during these years. The Peace Index survey from April 2018 indicated that 91% of Israeli Jews are proud to be Israeli and about 76% would prefer to live in Israel even if they had the possibility of emigrating.

There is great compatibility of support for these basic principles between the center and rightwing parties and public opinion, even though, in each of the parties of the political center, there are Knesset members whose opinions are to the left on the political map. But the leaders of the Zionist Union list and Yesh Atid (later Kahol Lavan—Blue–White) chose a strategy of support for the new fundamental principles of the right, formulated by Ariel Sharon, including the arguments that Israel is in existential danger, that the Jews in Israel are the victims of the conflict; that the wars initiated by Israel in Lebanon and in Gaza were necessary; that the security forces are fighting sensibly, fairly, and necessarily against Palestinian terrorism; that the Israeli nation is moral and so is the army; that we must struggle against Israeli organizations and people who present information about Israeli violations of Palestinian human rights, especially when it is revealed to the rest of the world; that the nations of the world, even if they are not anti-Semitic, do not support the Jewish nation; and that an international coalition has coalesced, including the radical left and right, that is anti-Semitic and anti-Zionist and they have been joined by Jews. The political map of Jewish society in Israel has been moving even further rightward, after it had crystallized in the early 2000 with the clear dominance of the rightist camp. These opinions are expressed not only by party leaders but are also dominant in most Israeli media outlets. Information that contradicts these understandings whether coming from the outside world or from Israeli sources, is usually framed in a way that negates its veracity or sometimes even as attempting to do harm to Israel. Criticism of Israeli policy and action are rejected and seen to be anti-Israeli. The daily independent newspaper, *Haaretz*, as an exception, has in recent years adopted a clearly liberal and critical position, supporting democracy in the state of Israel and trying to advance the peace process. As such, it has "earned" delegitimization by the leaders of the right.

Israeli society has thus gone full circle: from the hegemony of beliefs, narratives, and attitudes supporting a continuation of the conflict during the 1950s, 1960s, and even the 1970s, to growing hope during the 1980s and 1990s, expressed in an increase in beliefs and attitudes supporting a political agreement with the Palestinians (at least among a sizable sector of society and some state institutions); and then, a dramatic retreat from these understandings and a return to the beliefs of the ethos of conflict. And as time passes, the conflict supporting narratives with the ethos of conflict are just growing stronger as it

has become a kind of "comfort zone" that grants the Jewish public in Israel a sense of security, while exiting this zone would lead to feeling that they were taking an unnecessary risk. In this sense, the conflict has become routine, and it is now perceived of as an inseparable part of the life of the nation—a large part of the public, as well as most of its leaders, feel that the nation is dealing with this situation successfully and in their opinion, the situation could continue for the next generations. Other possibilities, in contrast, arouse fear, uncertainty, insecurity, and discomfort.

Israel is not noticeably paying a high price for the continuation of the occupation and the conflict. Under these circumstances, the establishment of a foreign entity in the heart of the state that, according to general consensus, would, in all probability, eventually become hostile (an understanding which greatly intensified following the Arab spring, and not only as a result of the disengagement), is really a choice which cannot be taken for granted. So the idea of two states for two nations as a solution to the Jewish-Palestinian conflict that was dominant for decades clearly began to crack among both Palestinians and Jews.

Under the circumstances, maintaining the conflict supporting narratives has therefore become a pressing need in order to justify the fragile situation as it exists, in which "we will forever live by the sword." Again, these narratives supply the basic needs of society members— just as they did at the peak of the conflict, during the 1950s and 1960s, without awareness that they fuel the conflict and create cycles of violence and that there are other narratives that can satisfy the human needs. However, the radicalization of Jewish society that has occurred during the last two decades is not only expressed in opinions or abstract perceptions— but has penetrated the institutional system of the country and has become an inseparable part of political and national culture. It has changed the essence and character of the state of Israel and its institutions, its values, and even its identity. I would like to use the detailed analysis of Israel as a case study of a society that, under conditions of bloody and lasting conflict, has moved to conflict supporting views because of the flow of misinformation and indoctrination that has become systematic, continuous, and widespread. The government, necessary for maintaining the conflict, needs the support and readiness to participate in conflict activity in different capacities, including the use of security forces that not only kill, but whose members are also killed or injured. In some respects, it is a miracle that in this context, a peace camp, anti-racist, moral and involved in the defense of human rights, still exists in Israel, considering the difficult conditions it faces, of being mistreated and delegitimized, with active attempts to silence its voice.

In the next chapter we will further discuss these changes. And here, the second argument comes into play. The processes described in the next two chapters have been unavoidable—the construction of a new statehood, new political structures with institutions, and even a new identity with functionaries loyal to the leader. This deterioration of democracy cannot be separated from the continuing occupation and the Jewish settlement in the occupied territories. But most of the Jewish public in Israel are, at best, indifferent to these processes and no small number of society members support this direction. This will be discussed in the next chapters.

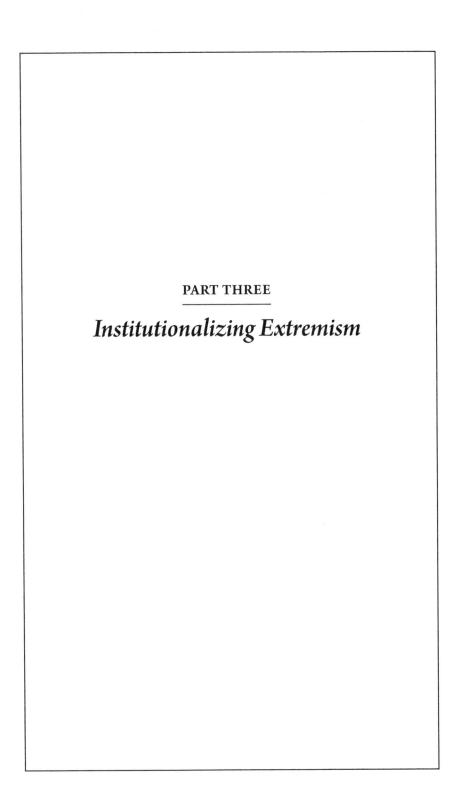

PART THREE

Institutionalizing Extremism

CHAPTER 5

Occupation and its Implications

The events of 2000 and the beliefs and attitudes that subsequently developed about the conflict led to a structural change in Jewish-Israeli society. This was unavoidable considering the escalation in the conflict and the intensification of the occupation with the increasing role of settlements in the occupied territories. That is the second argument appearing in the introduction to this book, which maintains that, in a society with a conflict supporting narrative that becomes hegemonic for a long period, changes take place in the shape of the conflict culture which affect the structure of society, all its institutions, and even its identity in the spirit of this culture. These processes are general, as other processes described in the first part of the book: development of narrative supporting the conflict and evolvement of the culture of conflict. The culture of conflict necessarily has major effects on all the institutions of societies involved in bloody and lasting conflict. As noted, we can detect these effects in Turkey, Rwanda, Morocco, and India at present, or in El Salvador or Guatemala and South Africa in the past.

The shift to the right in Israeli society that took place at the end of Prime Minister Barak's term and continued during Prime Minister Sharon's term accelerated in the following decade, expanding and solidifying over the next ten years. It thus contributed to the continuing Israeli-Palestinian conflict despite the heavy price that Israeli society had to pay. In this chapter, the political and institutional forces behind the turn to the right will be described—how they contributed to it and were simultaneously nourished by it, as well as what the results of this process were. The mutual relations between the violence in the field and the hegemonic worldview in society and its institutions will also be outlined. Both the violence and the worldview sustain one another. However, while the violence is clear for all to see, the worldview that constructs reality and the forces that promote a continuation of the violence are concealed and they must be summoned to the forefront and analyzed in detail. In contrast to the 1950s and the 1960s, at present there is no real uniformity in Jewish society about the conflict. The opposite is true—there is great polarization resulting in a political-social split among Jews. However, most of the Jewish public accepts the narrative supporting the hegemonic conflict and relies on the information and its interpretation regarding the conflict and the occupation provided by the leaders whose worldviews are similar to theirs, and by formal supporters in the media who justify the policies.

But first, in order to understand this process, let me analyze the significance of the long years of West Bank occupation and the continuous siege of the Gaza Strip, which is just another form of occupation—a continuing constitutive state of affairs, at the highest level, with crucial influence on all aspects of Israeli life.[159] The occupation is the factor around which Israeli society is organized, about which it shares opinions and makes decisions. And when society undergoes important changes, as it did in the 2000s, the key to understanding them is embedded in that game-changing event of the Six-Day War: the occupation. **And that is interesting since the word "occupation" has disappeared from the lexicon of most Israelis, its brutal daily reality is concealed and repressed. The formal Israeli institutions have crushed it under a steamroller, even though it is impossible to erase the deeper meaning of an occupation from the occupied nation or the occupier. The occupation exists not only 30 miles from Tel Aviv and a few yards from Jerusalem, with all consequences on the lives of the Palestinians, but also with all its might in every corner of the lives of Israeli society members, even if it is not discussed. First, I will elaborate on the meaning of occupation because many readers may not be familiar with its dynamics, as this type of subjugation has almost disappeared in the present world.**

THE MEANING OF THE OCCUPATION

Since the West Bank was conquered in 1967, its legal status has been in dispute: Is it an "occupied territory" or a "disputed territory?" Almost all states and international organizations, together with a minority in Jewish-Israeli society, support the first formulation. This position has clear significance, as occupation implies temporary control of territory against the will of its inhabitants by a state that does not claim permanent sovereignty over the territory.[160] Those who support the second claim indicate that the territory was not under the sovereignty of a political entity (as it had been meant to be part of the Arab state, in accord with the 1947 United Nations division). However, during the War for Israeli Independence in 1948, the West Bank had been conquered by Jordan, which annexed it in 1950 (only Pakistan and Great Britain recognized this annexation). Thus, according to a minority of legal experts, the Israeli conquest was allegedly not an occupation according to definition under international law. A similar question arises about the Gaza Strip which, until 1959, was hypothetically ruled by a Palestinian government, recognized by the six states of the Arab League, and then was under Egyptian occupation until its conquest by the Israelis in 1967. However, the latter approach does not consider the most important factor in the equation —the population living in the West Bank and the Gaza Strip. For them, the legal status of the territories doesn't really matter; it is a question that doesn't have any effect on their lives. Israeli military and civil control on the West Bank and the complete siege of the Gaza Strip, in contrast, leave their mark on every aspect of their lives.

Through the years, the Israeli occupation has had to develop methods of control and supervision over the Palestinians, using the army, the police, the General Security Services, the Mossad, and the legal system, with the support of the political system, institutions, and formal and informal organizations with enormous resources coming from many different sources. The solidification of the occupation has involved recruitment of tens of thousands of Palestinian collaborators and informers via deviant methods, demonstrating continual control by force (or as it is sometimes called in IDF orders: "creating a sense of persecution") and killing Palestinians considered dangerous to the lives of soldiers, policemen, or civilians. It has also entailed assassinating Palestinian leaders and the killing and arrest of children, the use of detention without trials, torture and court hearings, prevention of entry to the West Bank and refusal of residency permits, collective punishment, home demolition, displacement, roadblocks, and closures. The occupiers confiscate land and private properties, settle even private Palestinian land, demolish houses, expel civil population from their homes and living areas, create a stable sense of insecurity and supervision using a variety of methods, bureaucratize control, sometimes requiring more than one hundred permits for different requests, supervise population registration, and surveil many aspects of life for the occupied population.[161] Israel is systematically crushing the space in which the Palestinians live by coveting dunam after dunam and taking over territories that do not belong to it through violent means of the Jewish settlers.

Even A areas are not secure for Palestinians because the Palestinian Authority allows both regular units and Israeli undercover units (dressed as Arabs) to enter Palestinian designated regions to arrest suspects. Only in

2022 did the Israeli army arrest dozens of Palestinians in Area A with the quiet permission of the Palestinians security forces. As of August 2022, Israel is holding 712 Palestinian detainees without trial. This is the highest number in 14 years. They are held in Israeli prison facilities without an indictment being filed against them, and there is no judicial procedure in their case in courts. Until very recently, up to June 13, 2021, the army could enter any Palestinian home at any hour of the day or night for what is defined as "intelligence and security reasons," without any special permit.[162] Israel uses military checkpoints for control and supervision of the Palestinians. They are part of a larger system regulating the entry of Palestinians into Israeli areas and even some predominantly Palestinian areas like East Jerusalem. Palestinians need special military permits to pass.

Israel says checkpoints are needed to protect Israelis from potential attackers following a period of suicide bombings in the early 2000s, while Palestinians consider them a degrading infringement on their freedom of movement and a symbol of Israel's control over their lives. Numerous humiliating incidents occur in these checkpoints that not only violate human rights, but also cause injuries and death, as in the death of American-Palestinian Omar Abdalmajeed As'ad, 80 years old. Israel is upgrading its West Bank checkpoints with facial recognition technology to verify Palestinians' identities as they cross into Israel. The new system, which began rolling in 2021, eases their passage with shorter wait times—but is drawing criticism about the role the controversial technology plays in Israel's military control over Palestinians. In 2022, it was decided that an officer in the Defense Ministry's Coordinator of Government Activities in the Territories (COGAT) would decide whether a foreign professor would be allowed to teach in the Palestinian universities and foreign students could attend them. An "authorized official" in COGAT will also decide and define the "essential areas of activity" for Palestinian companies in which they may employ foreigners. The entry of businesspeople and investors will be permitted "in accordance with economic criteria that will be determined by the authorized person in COGAT."

And in such a reality, when every act that may be interpreted as opposing the occupation is considered "an act of terror" and the institutional viewpoint is in accord, there is a resulting proliferation of harm to human rights, along with a wide range of other forms of injustice. Almost every day, the Haaretz daily newspaper publishes information about harm done to the Palestinians in various forms described above. Every Friday it publishes a striking case of human rights violation in a weekly column. All of this does not move the great majority of Israeli Jews. They prefer to remain in the comfort zone and avoid knowing what their state, as an occupying force, is doing. A striking example of the relationships between the occupier and the occupied can be seen in the case of the village of Issawiya, near Jerusalem, which has become a Jerusalem suburb. In 2019, confrontations developed between Palestinians and the army which continued for many months. On the one hand, the Palestinians were expressing their opposition to the occupation by stone throwing, strikes, demonstrations, and violent confrontations during which police were injured; and on the other, the police were applying collective punishment by day and by night, making use of raids, blockades, stun grenades, home incursions, and shooting, leaving dozens wounded and one dead (as these lines are being written); hundreds incarcerated, including children, beatings, fines, the use of sirens sounding through the night, and more.[163] A report by United Nations Office for the Coordination of Humanitarian Affairs (OCHA) has stated that in 2019, about 15,500 Palestinians were injured: 2,468 from rubber coated metal bullets, 4,449 from real bullets, and the rest mostly from tear gas inhalation. In February 2021, the Israeli army held a military exercise simulating fighting in a threatened area inside Palestinian villages in the southern West Bank. As part of the exercise, which also included shell fire, army vehicles drove over fields, causing damage to crops, and destroyed a main road in one of the villages. In the view of the Mount Hebron Jewish Settlements Council: "*This is one of the ways to increase governance, hold on to the open spaces and impose rule of law and order.*"[164]

More recently (in August 2021), it was reported that, within three months, the army had killed 40 Palestinians in the West Bank, including non-combatants and even children. In total in 2021, 319 Palestinians were killed in Gaza and West Bank by Israeli forces, including dozens of children. Over the course of the same year, 11 Israelis were also killed—29 times less. By the end of October 2022 over 100 Palestinians were killed by Israeli soldiers in the West Bank from the beginning of the year, including at least ten children and two women. Between 1.1.2008 and 1.1.2022, more than 5985 Palestinians lost their lives to the conflict (an average of 427 annually). This number is about 20 times higher than the number of Israeli casualties in the same fourteen-year period. The number of Palestinians wounded in the same time span is even more staggering: 132,840 (an average of 26 people daily).

What is very troubling is the fact that Israeli forces arrest adolescents below 16 years old and even children—investigate them and even try them in line with the legal Israeli practices of the occupying forces in contradiction to the international law.[165] On May 11, 2022, Israeli forces shot dead a longtime TV correspondent for Arabic Al Jazeera, American-Palestinian Shireen Abu Akleh, in the occupied West Bank. This was the conclusion of the investigation carried out by the UN Human Rights office and later even confirmed by the Israeli forces. She was a symbol of the Palestinian resistance[166] by continuously reporting on the occupation.

This is not unusual or unprecedented. Far from it. **Every occupation which exists against the will of the occupied has necessarily aroused violent opposition.** If we focus only on the modern period, examples like Algeria, Kenya, Sri Lanka, and India come to mind, all in the framework of decolonization during the second half of the twentieth century, as well as Poland and Hungary, occupied until a hundred years ago, Ireland and Slovenia, occupied for hundreds of years, and even the United States and the countries of South America, 200 years ago. In all these states, the occupied rose up violently against their occupiers, and the occupiers in turn used every possible means to repress the uprisings. We can go back even earlier, to ancient times, when Jews rebelled in 167-160 BCE against the Greek Seleucid kingdom, or when Jews rebelled against the Romans in 63-73 AD during the reigns of emperors Nero and Vespasian, and then again in 132 AD against the emperor, Hadrian. Until today these rebellions are revered by the Israeli Jews, as justified resistance and as fighting against an occupation of foreign forces.

Opposition to occupation in contemporary life is considered legitimate, and that is one of the main reasons that, over time, almost all occupations have ended. In fact, while this book is being written, there is only one other case of long-term occupation against the will of the occupied population without their having received full rights (even if only hypothetically): the occupation of Western Sahara, freed from colonial Spanish occupation by Morocco, which took control of 80% of its area and also brought in settlers.[167] But we need to remember that Morocco does not claim to be a democracy, and Israel does. Therefore, Israel is the only state in the world to claim to be democratic while occupying a country against the will of its inhabitants, the Palestinians, who resist this occupation. Nevertheless, such an occupation, in Israel, as well as in Morocco, leads to intensive confrontations involving continuing violence between the two societies, the occupier and the occupied.

In the asymmetric conflict between Israelis and Palestinians,[168] Palestinians often use indiscriminate terror attacks against civilians, military actions against Israeli occupying forces, demonstrations, stone throwing, and shooting rockets at Israeli residential areas. Israeli Jews, especially after occupying the West Bank and the Gaza Strip, have many more options using different types of violence because of the state's military might, its surveillance capacity, its technological advantage, its economic power, and political strength and support.

In addition, there is also state terrorism. In 2004, the Security Council of the United Nations accepted Resolution 1566 which describes terrorism as *"criminal acts, including against civilians, committed with the intent to cause death or serious bodily injury, or taking of hostages, with the purpose to provoke a state of terror in the general public or in a group of persons or particular persons, intimidate a population or compel a government or an international organization to do or to abstain from doing any act, which constitute offences within the scope of and as defined in the international conventions and protocols relating to terrorism."* One key question is whether a state can perpetrate acts of terrorism. One of the recent inclusive definitions also includes state acts, suggesting that terrorism is a strategy rather than just actions of specific actors.

"'Terrorism' is the strategically indiscriminate harming or threat of harming members of the target group in order to induce the psychological states of an audience group in ways the perpetrator anticipates may be beneficial to the advancement of their agenda." [169] Israel thus in its action activates terror in order to induce psychological state of the Palestinians in ways it anticipates benefiting its agenda.

Viewing these confrontational activities universally, there is a circular process—all the occupations begin with control of the occupied society. Signs of opposition among the occupied population motivate the occupying forces to reinforce their control, and the process is repeated. No amount of explanation on the part of either side will help, as the occupier views the violence of the occupied as terrorism and its own violence as maintaining order and preventing terror, while the occupied view their own violence as legitimate opposition to the occupier, and that of the occupier as collective terror. Over time, this dynamic leads to changes in the society of the occupier, even if not all these changes are visible at first glance. Yehudit Karp, who served as deputy attorney general, noted:

> "*The Green Line has become lost to us not only as a territorial concept, but also as the line that separates government activities characteristic of the rule of the* military occupation *in the territories, and government activities in the presumably democratic State of Israel. The work methods of the occupation government seem to be slowly permeating, perhaps due to habit, ease and convenience, from the territories to Israel—as though they were a single governmental unit. One of the characteristics of the occupation regime in the territories is that its subjects have become transparent. Their humanity has been stolen from them and their human dignity taken from them, along with their basic individual rights. They are subject to decrees that cause severe harm to their routines and their livelihood—decrees that land on them from above without their participation, without the possibility of appeal, without any need to explain their logic and with indifference to their consequences. It's enough that the military governor has been persuaded that something is required in order to safeguard security. Some of the practices common in this government system are regular surveillance by the* Shin Bet *security service of the entire population, and the gathering of personal and intimate information, profoundly undermining privacy, without the need for oversight; a ban against demonstrations and protests and the silencing of freedom of expression; entering homes without a court order in order to carry out a search or with some other excuse, and arrests without a reason and without a review by the courts; arbitrary severance of farmers from their land and a malicious blow to the livelihood of others; closures, sieges and checkpoints that constitute a daily tool for enforcement and control.*"[170]

In October 2021, Defense Minister Benny Gantz outlawed six civil society organizations in the West Bank, designating them terrorist organizations, including ones that track Israeli violations of human rights (for example, Al-Haq, which documents violations of Palestinians' human rights in the West Bank and Gaza Strip; Defense for Children International-Palestine, which monitors the killing of children and the situation of children who have been arrested). The decision hurt the ability to get financial assistance from European countries. Eight months later, leading European diplomats examined the issue and found no evidence to confirm Israel's claims.

The more opposition grows, and the stronger the subsequent oppression becomes, these changes become more perceptible.[171] This occurs in every place in the world sooner or later in a society that is occupied against its will. But of special note is the way the leaders of the USA, Germany, and some other states act with regards to the violent confrontation between Israel and Palestinians. They continuously and constantly make statements about the security needs of Israel—disregarding the need for security for the Palestinians, who suffer daily insecurity because of the occupation.

Throughout the years of the brutally violent acts, in a very few cases, external forces have intervened to stop Israeli acts that contravened international law and were immoral by nature. The usual routine is condemnation and a call to the Israeli government to refrain from committing the act. In a very few cases, Israel has conformed to the demands. This routine has become a tango, in which each side performs its well-rehearsed part with a foreknown end. In addition, the U.S. government has served throughout the years as a defender of Israel. Over the past few decades, the United States has vetoed at least 53 UN Security Council resolutions critical of Israel. Even in this situation, Israel has violated **28 resolutions** of the United Nations Security Council (which are legally binding for UN member nations). Of special significance is the fact that Israel refuses to accept the *de jure* applicability of the 4th Geneva Convention that provides guidance for the protection of civilians in times of war, including military occupation of the Occupied Palestinian Territory, including Jerusalem, and has committed serious violations of every provision of the convention.

In Israel there is spatial contiguity between the state and the occupied territories, and the territories have been settled by citizens of the occupier, clearly violating Article 49 of the Fourth Geneva Convention of 1949 (ratified by Israel). Settlement by occupiers has taken place not only in contiguously occupied territories, as in Tibet or even in Algeria, which is separated by only 754 kilometers (469 miles) from Marseille, but also in occupied states that were separated by thousands of kilometers from the occupying state. In 1998, the Rome Convention, signed by more than 100 states, stated that severe violations of the 1949 Geneva Convention would be considered war crimes. Thus, they are subject to be tried and punished in the International Criminal Court. Indeed, on the basis of the Rome Statute, the International Criminal Court (ICC) prosecutor announced an investigation of alleged crimes performed in Palestine, after a preliminary examination that had lasted five years. Moreover, the Israeli occupation has continued for more than 55 years, and this protracted time period raises legal questions about the objectives of the occupier which may desire to change the status of the occupied area.

Borders and boundaries become less and less distinct in more ways than one—**various developments and manifestations which characterize every occupying society have, in the Israeli case, unavoidably penetrated from the occupied territory to within the Green Line (the line that was drawn in the 1949 cease fire agreement between the Arab states and Israel until the conquests in 1967), and over time, have caused long-term changes**. The best example of the penetrating practices can be found in relations with the Arab citizens of the State of Israel. Specifically, for instance, the dominant behaviors reflecting occupation have been recently observed in the Negev towards Bedouins in the framework of the conflict about land that has overshadowed them for decades. In this conflict, the police commit many of the violations that are carried out against Palestinians in the occupied territories—sudden arrests in the middle of the night, sometimes even without arrest warrants, use of violence against arrested citizens, shooting rubber bullets that cause injuries, the arrest of children, prevention of medical treatment to the injured, or use of checkpoints.[172]

An occupation has grave consequences which are unavoidable in every occupying society, and their characteristics are more or less stable. New dogmas and narratives tend to appear in order to justify the continuing occupation; new stakeholders emerge; new norms and practices develop; new laws are legislated; new language is created; new measures of morality are determined in order to legitimize the occupation; the desire to control resources, exploiting the occupied territory and its inhabitants, is aroused; differentiation between Jewish and Palestinian populations residing in the same occupied territories have to be built; security forces and budgets are directed towards the revised objective; a system of control and supervision is constructed; new diplomacy is developed to explain the struggle against opposition to the international community; a new political culture forms in order to maintain the occupation; revised security needs and new military strategies arise; groups appear which want to annex the occupied territories, and on the opposing side, there are groups who reject the occupation and conduct a political struggle; a fundamental political rift develops; and these are only a few of the effects. It all means that an occupation is dynamic for both the occupying and the occupied societies. But there is one major difference— while the great majority of the occupying society may continue to live their normal lives, all members of the occupied society are permanently affected by the occupation in their daily lives, and very frequently these effects are detrimental.

In time, these developments lead to changes in the occupying power, even if they are not all visible at first glance. The deeper the occupation and the greater the opposition, the more discernible the changes are. A society occupied against its will always expresses its opposition, and the occupying society necessarily tries to suppress it, even if the opposition is minor, such as issuing a declaration proclaiming opposition to the occupation or organizing a nonviolent demonstration. However, almost always, the opposition also involves violence. Violent reactions of the occupier automatically arouse a response from the occupied society, and thus the two societies initiate a system of reciprocal relations consisting of waves of infinite violence at different levels of severity, that quickly spread to other realms. Cycles like these are well known *vis-à-vis* the Israeli occupation. They are unending even if the level of violence weakens to the point where the basic needs of the occupied population are supplied, as has occurred in all the cases we have pointed out. These are blood-soaked conflicts and only genocide, as experienced by the native populations in Australia and the United States, or a peace agreement, such as the one between Egypt and Israel, can end it.[173] The former "solution" sounds unacceptable in human terms, but nations that have carried it out have solved the challenges of living with the occupied or the colonialized natives. However, what was possible in previous centuries is legally and morally forbidden today.

The detrimental process of occupation significantly intensifies when, as we have pointed out, leadership decides to settle a civilian population in the occupied territory. This creates the need to develop well justifying reasons for their settlement, to grant them security, to provide tax benefits to tempt citizens to move to the occupied areas,

and to construct a special legal status for them (as they are subject to Israeli law in a territorial space in which Israeli law does not apply). Thus, a judicial system and laws and regulations develop which, in actual fact, separate the two populations of different ethnicities living in close proximity. This necessarily involves a violation of the basic principles of justice, morality, and human rights, and as a result, the occupying society is condemned to a process of deterioration and degeneration, at least as far as their democratic, humane, and moral character is concerned. It becomes an apartheid state, at least fully in the occupied territories—that is a very demeaning status in the international community.

It is important to note, however, that not all of these violations are deliberate—many of them not only have not been deliberately chosen, but are also unwanted in social life,[174] and there are those who will say, also unwanted considering the Jewish character of society. The conflict and the continuing occupation have created violence, oppression, exploitation, control, and discrimination—and the settlement project in the occupied territories has only made all these situations worse. Thus, Israeli society, as an occupier, has been forced to adapt itself to a long-term occupation, to adjust to it, to contain it, to deal with it, and to live with it. Eventually, it has also had to frame the occupation in line with personal and collective needs and to present it in a positive light (or conceal it). Specifically, as noted, Israeli society has succeeded in blotting out the concept of occupation from its lexicon and from public discourse, psychologically distancing its character from the state of Israel, while concealing what goes on in the territories from Jewish interest and Jewish consciousness.[175] In addition, it has succeeded in fragmenting Palestinian society, which lives in non-contiguous areas, and in dividing the two main factions, Hamas and Fatah, in in accord with the principle of "divide and rule." Furthermore, it has managed to separate the Jewish and Palestinian populations in the territories, constructing bypass roads, separating living spaces, and closing off Jewish settlements. These have all required the deployment of a powerful military and security system in the territories in order to oversee and administer the Palestinian population, and to develop a civil control mechanism that has succeeded in supervising and controlling all areas of Palestinian life.[176]

In this reality, there are always groups of people (usually small groups) in whom the harm done to the occupied population arouses not only guilt, but also a motivation for them to act in order to reduce these harms as much as possible, and they take action in various ways. For example, there are groups who aid the occupied population by participating in its demonstrations and providing legal or medical help. There are also groups who document the vulnerabilities and the harm done to the occupied population and, in order to prevent them, disseminate the information in Israel and transmit the collected documentation to the international community on the assumption that its representatives can stop the harm. Active opposition to the occupation by these groups is always considered treasonous by the occupier and thus, such action is disparaged, blocked, suppressed, and even punished.

The Occupation as Perceived by the Jewish Population in Israel

When the West Bank of the Jordan River had just been conquered, a large portion of the Jewish public, and among them, almost all the national-religious public, viewed the territories as "liberated"—primarily because of religious, historical, national, and cultural reasons. Others viewed them as being "held" (*muhzakim*—that is, temporarily). There were also a very few who perceived them as "occupied." In time, the psychology supporting the concept of the territories as "liberated" became clear. Jews in Israel who related to the territories in this way exempted themselves from all the ramifications of the concept of "occupation," including harm to one's self image, and cognitive dissonance between self-perception as an enlightened nation and actual reality and collective guilt.[177]

This view had to be reinforced top-down. Thus, the leadership created a discourse presenting the occupied territories as an inseparable part of the homeland, from time immemorial. Prominent leaders, including leaders of the Labor Party, used rhetoric referring to *"a return to the land of our forefathers"* or *"the promised land,"* and asserted that *"we have returned in order to remain here forever."*

An additional aspect of the discourse initiated by leadership was the security factor. The territories, consisting of mountains and hills overlooking a plain which encircled them, were presented as essential to the defense of the state; these settlements were compared to the confrontation line settlements which had ensured defense of the state just after it had been established. Much was said about the need to control the Jordan Valley as a border to prevent entry of foreign forces to the West Bank and the possibility of shelling Ben Gurion Airport from the hills of Samaria.[178] This assumption was accepted by the government and security figures following the conquest of the West Bank. These explanations are unfounded but reflect the worldview of those who expressed them. There is no doubt that the possibility of violence nourishes them and that threats do exist, but it is perhaps also possible to understand that the perception of their intensity is different among Jewish groups in Israel. In addition, various solutions have been proposed to these defense problems and that proves, as already explained, that attitudes regarding insecurity or security are subjective and solutions are proposed in accord with these attitudes.

In general, the conception of the territories as "liberated" and as essential to the security of the state was powerful at the end of the 1960s and the beginning of the 1970s, then became weaker in the 1990s, and again gained popularity in the 2000s. This, of course, was in line with political events as they unfolded at the time. Moreover, leadership succeeded in almost completely denigrating and deleting the term "occupation" when referring to the territories, and, as noted, a large section of the public, as well as various organizations and institutions, eliminated the word from public discourses. Use of the word serves as an identification of leftists, who are consequently viewed as outcasts. This, of course, is known to have had a significant effect on attitudes towards a solution to the conflict and an end to the occupation. People who view the West Bank as "liberated" territory do not identify a problem in the circumstances of the occupation, and naturally are more greatly opposed to the possibility of transferring this territory, which they consider part of the homeland, to the Palestinians. However, even many of those who do define the situation in the territories as an occupation justify it and alternatively, do not support putting an end to it. These people activate psycho-dynamic defense mechanisms, usually unconscious, both on personal and collective levels. These include repression, denial, avoidance, and rationalization. For example, "Palestinians are violent from birth and we must prevent them from carrying out acts of terror." These mechanisms are activated in an attempt to deal with the unpleasant sense of dissonance, guilt, or shame, and they assist the individual to avoid facing the contradictions between behavior of the collective to which s/he belongs, and norms, morality, and accepted social beliefs in contemporary global society. The ethos of conflict is the collective expression of this behavior. It enables the construction of social beliefs justifying the circumstances of the occupation, while creating a positive social self-image, a deep sense of victimhood and delegitimization of the occupied population. **Thus, the way people deal with the occupation psychologically is one of the significant foundations of maintaining it and the lack of willingness to solve the conflict peacefully.**[179]

Did You Know?

Three studies conducted in Israel in 2004, 2007, and 2016—which included a representative sample of the Jewish population in Israel— unequivocally found that people who denied the reality of the occupation did not know about the costs of the occupation, did not feel guilt, were not open to new knowledge, had no trust in Palestinians, and did not believe in the possibility of solving the conflict peacefully. In addition, the research demonstrated that as time went by, fewer and fewer Jews defined the situation on the West Bank as an occupation. In 2004, 51% of Jewish Israelis defined the situation as an occupation; in 2007, only 27% defined it as an occupation; and in 2016, the number was similar at 30%. The conscious effort to avoid the use of the concept of occupation and the elimination of the Green Line from maps of Israel have had their effect.[180]

In order to draw a full picture of the situation as it exists today, we must consider that, for decades, two generations have grown up during the occupation and have had no awareness of the Green Line, which served as the internationally recognized eastern border of the state until 1967. Formally, the Green Line was made to disappear as early as 1972, when, on the instruction of the then-Minister of Education Yigal Alon (Labor Party), the Green Line was eliminated from official maps of Israel. In time, the fact of its existence gradually weakened in the cognitive map of these new generations, and ultimately it disappeared completely. Today, for most people in Israel, the territory stretching between the Jordan River and the Mediterranean Sea is one homeland space. Moreover, many of the younger generations have grown up in an atmosphere in which the rightwing view, its power and guiding principles congruent with those of the national-religious ideology, has become hegemonic. Most of the media have similarly come into line; they have reported cases of violence and failing attempts to solve the conflict as expressed by leadership, and they have also similarly interpreted these events. So in Jewish society, a strong link has been established between age and support for rightwing positions—the younger the people, the more they tend to support rightwing attitudes.

A survey of attitudes was conducted in 2016 by the Macro Center for Political Economics among teens between the ages of 15 and 18, and young adults between 21 and 24. It found that young people were becoming more rightwing and more religious in comparison to the data collected in 1998 and 2004. In 2016, 67% of Israeli Jewish youth defined themselves as "rightwing" (including right-center), while only 16% identified themselves as leftwing, in comparison to 2004, when 56% said they were rightwing, and 25% were leftwing. Furthermore, in comparison to 1998, when almost half of Israeli youth defined themselves as secular while only 9% were ultra-orthodox, in 2016, only 40% identified themselves as secular, while the proportion of ultra-orthodox had risen to 15%. (Others replied that they considered themselves religious or traditional).[181] Of course, part of the explanation for these results are the demographic changes that occurred during those years, when the religious and ultra-orthodox population expanded due to their naturally higher birth rate.

These findings were replicated in a very detailed study performed by the same research center in November 2020. On every index of political views, including delegitimization of Palestinians, trusting or distrusting them, ethos of conflict, negative emotions towards them and more, young Jews aged 18–29 were found to be more hawkish (rightist) than older generations (30 and above). A study performed in late spring 2020 by aChord (Research Institute of Social Psychology for Social Change of the Hebrew University) among a national sample of high school students aged 16-18 found that almost 50% of religious youngsters, including ultraorthodox, hold negative stereotypes of the Arabs, but among secular youngsters only 19% hold these stereotypes. The religious sample also felt much stronger fear of Arabs and hatred towards them than secular youngsters.[182]

The Ideology of the Greater Israel Movement and the Settlements

The ideology of Greater Israel was not formed with the occupation of 1967 but had been rooted deep in the hearts of various political movements for many years before the Six-Day War: these included the Ahdut Avoda Movement, the Revisionists, and the Religious Zionists. Their worldview dictates that the Jewish nation has the exclusive right to all the area west of the Jordan River, a right that cannot be transmitted to the Arabs under any condition.[183] But in spite of these views expressed by a minority, most of the Jews had lived contentedly within the Green Line up to 1967 and had accepted it as the final border of Israel. The revolutionary change took place immediately following the capture of territories in the Six-Day War. Already in July 1967, the Movement for a Greater Israel was established, and included central figures in Israeli society. However, this ideological-practical torch was actively held aloft by the members of the National-Religious Movement, an offshoot of Religious Zionism. Following the revolt of the youth movement, pressing for a hawkish turn, in 1974 the Gush Emunim (Bloc of the Faithful) movement was formed, spearheading Jewish settlement on the West Bank, in the Gaza Strip and on the Golan Heights. But some of these ideas had already appeared in the early 1950s with the foundation of the Religious Zionist group Gachelet (Ember) that propagated "the Torah regime," which demanded full observance of Torah rules in Israel with the commitment to nationalism and patriotism.[184]

Gush Emunim supporters believe that building Jewish settlement on land God has allotted to the Jewish people as outlined in the Hebrew Bible is an important step towards the redemption of the Jewish people. According to the perception of its spiritual leaders, above the authority of the state, there is a more binding religious authority. These beliefs were based on the vision of the founding father of the Gush, Rabbi Tzvi Yehuda Kook, who stated, "*The question has been asked, 'Is this the state that our prophets envisioned?' And I say: This is the state that the prophets envisioned. Of course, it has not yet attained perfection. But our prophets, our sages, and those who followed them, said: The seed of Abraham, Isaac, and Jacob will return and will reestablish settlement and independent political rule in the Land.*"[185] Under the leadership of Kook, with its center in the yeshiva founded by his father, Jerusalem's Mercaz HaRav Yeshiva, thousands of Orthodox Jews campaigned actively against territorial compromise, and established numerous settlements throughout the West Bank and the Gaza Strip.

The principal premise "Am Yisrael, Eretz Yisrael, Torat Yisrael" (People of Israel, Israel's Country, Torah of Israel) has served as the epistemic dogma of the Zionist movement. The results of the Six-Day War and the territorial achievements of the war shaped a new religious, political, and cultural consciousness, and called for this sector to have a renewed encounter with the land of the patriarchs and a sense of renewed Zionist fulfillment and history. The return to the holy places ignited a desire to build Jewish settlements in the Holy Land. Many of these settlements were subsequently granted official recognition by Israeli governments, both by the left and right governments. Later, the Judea and Samaria Regional Council took the place of Gush Emunim in continuing the settlement project.[186] The subversion of the political "rules of the game" and the understanding that violation of the law is permissible if it serves sacred purposes led to the initial establishment of settlements without a government permit, continued with the organization of a Jewish underground aimed at harming Palestinians, and culminated with demonstrations against the Rabin government. These manifestations grew in the fertile ground of de-legitimization and violations of governmental decisions.

In view of these beliefs and narratives, it is not surprising that already in his first term as Prime Minister in 1976, Yitzhak Rabin identified this movement as very dangerous to Israel, similarly to Levi Eshkol a few years before him. In his book, published in 1979, he wrote:

> *"In Gush Emunim, I saw a very severe phenomenon—a cancer in the body of Israeli democracy. Against their basic view, which contradicts Israel's democratic foundations, it was necessary to fight an ideological struggle that reveals the true meaning of the Gush positions and ways of operating ... There are few cases in the history of Judaism that such a disorderly group has taken a mandate in the name of heaven ... all under the foul disguise of love of the Land of Israel, that breaks into the streets rudely to inflict horror and terror ... I was ashamed of ourselves that we could deteriorate into such a slump."*[187]

Jewish settlement on the West Bank began before the creation of Gush Emunim—already in the summer of 1967 in Kfar Etzion, in opposition to the opinion of Theodore Meron, the legal advisor of the Ministry of Foreign Affairs, who viewed settlements over the Green Line as a breach of the Fourth Geneva Convention. Even earlier, on 28 June 1967, Israel annexed East Jerusalem, destroyed Arab houses in the Jewish quarter, and began to restore the Jewish neighborhood. However, the government hesitated and was in a dilemma, even confusion, about what to do with the territories. This left a vacuum for various groups to move in. In April 1968, a group of religious Zionists entered Hebron to celebrate the Passover Seder. The army helped and they also had the support of Yigal Allon, who even paid them a visit. In time, the government decided to settle Jews in proximity to Hebron, and the Jewish town of Kiryat Arba was established. In 1979, Jews also settled within the city of Hebron.[188] Prime Minister Levi Eshkol understood their methods and said in prophecy, *"The settlers entered the city as visitors and then created facts on the ground. That wasn't a good thing, but that's what happened. Using a method like that about everything—small things as well as large ones—will undermine the authority of the government, if not something more serious."*[189] And so it was to be. The devoted religious group with their messianic dogma became the frontrunners and the activists of Jewish society in Israel. They exploited every opportunity; they were ready to suffer considerable discomfort in settling the first sites in the occupied areas. They successfully aroused enthusiasm in various spheres of Jewish society in Israel and among conservative segments of Jews throughout the world, and they wisely succeeded in mobilizing the political and military echelons for their cause. They considered themselves pioneers of the new epoch who continued to build the state by settling the homeland, as their predecessors had done decades before.

During the Labor Party governments after the 1967 war as well, there were enthusiastic supporters of this group among its members, who favored settling Jews in the occupied territories (for example, Yigal Allon, Shimon Peres, Yisrael Galili and Moshe Dayan). With regards to the West Bank, already in June 1967 Prime Minister Levi Eshkol, in his status as chair of the Ministerial Committee for Security, proposed that the defensive border of Israel should be the Jordan River. In July 1967, an unofficial plan was prepared by Yigal Allon, which had a salient effect on settlement policy on the West Bank and the Gaza Strip.[190] According to the plan, the eastern border of Israel would be the line of the Jordan River, and therefore, all the Jordan Valley would have to be in Israeli territory. In addition, the plan stated that Jews would be settled in an area in the shape of a triangle around Jerusalem: The Etzion Bloc, Maale Adumim, and Modiin Illit. In addition, in this period, the government began to build the neighborhoods (for example, Ramot Eshkol) in East Jerusalem as a link to Mount Scopus, and a ring of neighborhoods was planned to surround East Jerusalem with Jewish areas (for example, Gilo).[191]

All of these plans and their execution provided a clear indication that Israeli leadership from the beginning of the occupation did not intend just to hold on to the territories as a deposit for a time of peace-

ful resolution of the conflict but saw the occupation as an opportunity to extend the borders of the state. In fact, recently revealed historical documents in the state and IDF archives show that detailed preparations were being made in the military system in the years before the 1967 war to organize in advance the control of the territories that the defense establishment estimated—with high certainty—would be conquered in the next war. The Sinai Peninsula and Gaza from Egypt and the Golan Heights from Syria were not a side effect of the fighting but were an expression of strategic perception and preliminary preparations.[192]

With the establishment of the Likud government in 1977, a sharp rise in settlement activity began. Prime Minister Menachem Begin, the leader of the Likud Movement, was a clear ideological supporter of Jewish settlement in the occupied territories and provided assistance to the settlement project, both officially and unofficially. Especially powerful support was advanced by the Minister of Agriculture, and later, Minister of Defense, Ariel Sharon. He was the central "mover" in the government. His plan added Jewish settlement in the "security strip" on the western slopes of Samaria and along the Green Line. In addition, with his support, Gush Emunim initiated settlements on the mountain ridge around and among Palestinian cities and villages in order to prevent Palestinian territorial contiguity, so that the Palestinian areas looked like holes in a Swiss cheese on the map. This later dictated the division of the map into areas A, B, and C at the Oslo second agreement in 1995. Palestinian settlements which were defined as Area A or B were surrounded by Area C, which was under full Israeli control. This prevented their possible development: The West Bank was split up as Ariel Sharon and his Gush Emunim supporters had planned, and Israel was given freedom of action in 60% of the West Bank. Building bypass roads and roads to the length and breadth of the territory simplified the expansion of the settlement project. They shortened the trip into the center of the country and relatively increased the Jewish travelers' sense of security, enabling travel for the Jewish population without having to see Palestinians. The 1997 master plan of the Settlement Division of the World Zionist Organization reinforced the existing settlements and expanded them. Dozens of additional settlements were built illegally with the assistance of the Israeli cabinet, the Settlement Division, and the security forces.[193]

In sum, there is need to see the Jewish settlement project in the West Bank as having a general goal to expand the territory of the state of Israel, as its borders were never defined, and to prevent the establishment of the Palestinian state. The project began immediately after ending the war in 1967 in East Jerusalem and expanded with time over the West Bank.

Despite differences between the various stages in the settlement enterprise, it is possible to reveal a consistent process with internal logic.[194] In this process, each of the stages relied on the reality built in the previous stages. This is regardless of the political composition of the Israeli governments, either led by Labor or by Likud. In the first stage, the state took over 25% of the West Bank land owned by the Jordanian state and established Jewish settlemement in the Jordan Valley, the surroundings of Jerusalem, and a number of outposts in the West Bank. At this stage, two wide roads were paved to connect the Jordan valley and the center of the country as the main arteries of the future road network. In the second stage, a takeover of land that amounted to half of the West Bank through massive expropriation occurred, using the Ottoman law requiring Palestinians to prove ownership of their land—knowing they would have difficulty proving it. At this stage, an effort was made to spread the settlement throughout the West Bank, with an emphasis on building a local infrastructure along the latitudinal axes. After the process of expansion of settlements in the Jerusalem area and the coastal plain, it moved throughout the West Bank. This plan succeeded in transporting Jews to the western slopes of the mountain ranges in the West Bank and in fact prevents the viability of the Palestinian state. In the third stage since Oslo, the settlement rate has increased with the formation of strips of Jewish settlements in the east and west of the ridge, and the creation of a network of Jewish settlements along a network of latitudes and longitudes that bypass Palestinian cities and isolate them into separate and besieged territories. The illegal outposts were intended to widen the corridors along the roads, splitting the bank mainly in the east-west axis. At this stage, the transit routes to the settlements were expanded on the one hand, and on the other the Palestinian cantons were isolated. Thus, the State of Israel, even if it did not openly declare it, added more space to the Jewish population, began to control natural resources of the West Bank, including water, began to control main roads and accessibility between the territories and the center of the country, created security borders in the eyes of the Israeli leadership, and of course established economic benefits in cheap labor of the Palestinians and in the dependence of the Palestinian economy on the Israeli economy.[195] All this was at the cost of continuing the bloody conflict and the brutal occupation.

All Israeli governments since 1967 have contributed in one way or another to expanding the settlements on the West Bank, in the absence of any clear and detailed plan for the solution of the Israeli-Palestinian conflict by the Israeli government. It is obvious that rightwing party governments that have been in power almost continually since 1977 have supported the project of Jewish settlement in the occupied territories and have done everything possible to implement it, even with illegal actions. In this endeavor, religious Zionism was the catalyst, leading the settlement project. **The movement was also a primary force in the massive objection of the rightist parties and organizations to the Oslo agreement because it implied withdrawal even partly from the occupied territories.** The "Union of Rabbis for the People of Israel and the Land of Israel," which was founded in 1993, included principle Rabbis of religious Zionism, and declared that handing over territories under Israeli control to foreigners, even in exchange for a peace agreement, was contrary to Halacha (the collective body of Jewish religious laws). They also called on the soldiers not to obey the commands instructing them to hand over territories to foreigners, which they saw as a command that contradicts the Torah.[196]

Imbued with religious fervor, enthusiasm and a pioneering spirit, this group initiated, led, implemented and acted with the greatest effort while applying unending pressure on the government, on leaders, on institutions and on society as a whole.[197] On the other hand, all of this exuberance would not have been effective if not for the public and implicit support of the government, the army, the police, the justice system, the settlement institutions, and wealthy Jewish individuals abroad enthused with the ideology of Greater Israel. These supporters provided resources, created conditions, aided in building, constructed infrastructure and primarily, covered up for the settlers even if they had broken the laws of the State of Israel, as, for example, the acts listed in the reports about the illegal outposts written by Talia Sasson and Edmond Levy.[198]

In order to understand the success of the settlement project, it is important to recognize that the army had to have helped to advance this effort. Without the cooperation of the army, it would have been impossible to construct the network of settlements, legal and illegal, with infrastructure, roads, institutions, and industrial areas.[199] No group could have moved a truck with a house or cabin loaded onto it without the army seeing what was going on and reporting on it.[200] Even today, the army may frequently turn a blind eye, helping and even protecting the project by allocating forces and supervision, with control over the Palestinian population, which it continually "brings to order."[201] The army often even stands aside without intervening when settlers harm Palestinians by shooting at them, beating them, throwing stones at them, or preventing cultivation of their private land.[202] Such violence has been extended towards Jewish volunteers who come to protect Palestinian farmers.[203] The report of Yesh Din–Volunteers for Human Rights claims that only area A, supposedly in full control of the Palestinian Authority, 63 incidents were committed against Palestinians between 2017 and 2020 involving violence, property damage, and desecration of mosques. Police complaints were filed in 60 of the 63 offenses by Israeli civilians inside Palestinian villages documented by Yesh Din-Volunteers for Human Rights. The police have concluded 38 of the investigations.[204] Not a single indictment has been filed. Furthermore, figures collected by Yesh Din from 2005 to 2021 show that 92 percent of all complaints never resulted in charges being pressed, and in 65 percent of those cases, the reason given was "unknown perpetrator." "*Over the years, the law enforcement system has allowed the settlers to run wild,*" said Yesh Din in a statement. "*The police's failure to address settler violence against Palestinians is consistent—failed investigations, closure of cases under curious circumstances, and very negligent policing.*" The newspaper *Haaretz* inquired and found that only 3.8 percent of criminal cases pertaining to violence against Palestinians were actually filed. In absolute numbers, 221 of 263 cases that were opened were closed without any action taken. Only ten of those cases resulted in an indictment. The rest are still under investigation.[205] In 2022, the attacks by Jews increased dramatically. In October, within 10 days, over 100 attacks by Jews were reported on Palestinians, and no action was taken against the perpetrators.

Moreover, it has been documented that soldiers helped to construct an illegal outpost and attacked Israeli Jews who had come to help Palestinians who had suffered hardship.[206] In a few cases, the settlers also attacked army officers who dared to intervene to stop their attacks on Palestinians. At the same time, any act by the Palestinians that does not conform to "law and order" as it is defined by the military government is immediately met with a resolute reaction. In this context, three important points should be noted: a. In the opinion of quite a few senior officers, safeguarding the settlements poses a heavy burden on the army and large sums of money are set aside for this purpose; b. Many senior officers believe that there is no security value in the West Bank territories thanks to the modern advanced weapons possessed by both Israel and its enemies[207]; c. A very significant and large group of more than 300 retired generals, security and intelligence officials delivered a letter in November 2021 to members of the Knesset, Israel's parliament, decrying settler violence against Palestinians as a threat to the rule of law and the country's international standing. *"Groups of settlers have been perpetrating deadly acts of violence against Palestinians —for the most part helpless villagers—in areas under our control,"* they said. *"This is completely unacceptable from an ethical and humanitarian perspective, and it stands in contradiction to Israel's Jewish values."*[208]

Another state institution that has contributed to the success of the settler project is the Settlement Division of the World Zionist Organization. This division operates independently and, representing the Israeli government and with its full funding, operates to establish rural settlements, care for them, and strengthen them. According to the contract signed by the government and the World Zionist Organization in 2000, the division has operated in the Golan, in Samaria, in the Binyamin hills and Judea, in the Jordan Valley, and in Gush Katif (until it was evacuated in 2005). All these territories were conquered in 1967. As the Settlement Division has not been defined as a public authority, it is not subject to the law guaranteeing freedom of information, which makes it easier to use it as a pipeline for the transmission of money to construct the settlements, as well as setting up seed groups in the center of the country, without being subject to any supervision or control.[209]

In addition, Keren Hakyemeth LeIsrael–Jewish National Fund (KKL-JNF), a 120-year old organization controlled by the World Zionist Organization, is dedicated to "redeeming" land in Israel for Jewish settlement. It is a powerful organization with resources that acts as a state within the State owning 13% of the land in Israel with revenues of over 400 million dollars. It extended its activities of land redemption in the occupied territories. Its board is dominated by rightist groups and as a result the organization has been involved in building infrastructures in existing Jewish settlements in the West Bank and purchasing land for building new settlements. It is also involved in suits to evict Palestinian families from their homes (for example in Silwan, Hebron, and Susya).[210]

For large sectors of religious Zionism, settling the West Bank and Gaza

Strip with Jews is an expression of a deep-rooted and holistic religious outlook about redemption and the sanctity of the land. This outlook has been completely congruent with the ideology of the ethos of conflict. The belief in Greater Israel has supplied its goals and justification. In addition, the religious Zionist public is characterized, on the one hand, by the glorification of the Jewish collective as "the chosen people," and on the other hand, by prejudice against Arabs who are considered the biblical enemy, "Amalek." Finally, deeply ingrained among the Jewish religious public is the self-perception of victimhood, which is an inseparable part of Jewish tradition.[211] These elements perfectly match the ethos of conflict that represents a cultural foundation among most of the religious public, the ultra-orthodox and even those defining themselves as traditional. So religious Zionist leaders have given settlement activity the highest priority, and have not hesitated to place it in opposition to and above values such as the authority of the state, the rule of law, and even the Jewish principle of the sanctity of life.[212] Illegal activities that have challenged the state authority have included building in settlements without state approval—and even against Israeli law—in an attempt to force authorities to accept responsibility for these communities and to prevent any attempt to reach a territorial compromise. In the framework of their illegal activities, ordinary settlers, who have even fulfilled roles in the Israeli establishment, openly and secretly assist the "hilltop youth."[213] The nickname "hilltop youth" refers to young people who, for the most part, live in illegal outposts on the West Bank, based on their ideology that settling the land is of crucial importance, even if achieved illegally. They aim to determine facts on the ground and even to ultimately establish the "Kingdom of Israel." Quite a few of them participate in "price tag acts" of retribution carried out against Palestinians and their possessions as well as against leftwing activists who have come to defend Palestinians.[214] "Price tag acts" are usually carried out in response to harm done to Jews by Palestinians, including terror attacks on Jewish settlers or throwing stones at Jewish cars in the occupied territories. The price tag acts include stone throwing, damaging mosques, burning fields and orchards, destroying property, and even causing physical harm to people, including murder.

It is important to remember that the idea of Greater Israel has never achieved broad consensus among religious Zionists. There have been leaders and intellectuals (such as Rabbi Yehuda Amital, Rabbi Aharon Lichtenstein, Uriel Simon, Professor Avi Ravitzky, and Rabbi Michael

Melchior) who have expressed opinions in opposition to the ideology of Greater Israel in the spirit of compromise and moderation.[215] **However, a comprehensive doctoral dissertation examining religious Zionism, by Hanan Moses, supervised by Asher Cohen and Moshe Hellinger, found that more than 80% of those defining themselves as religious Zionists place themselves on the political right, 15% in the center, and only 5% consider themselves on the left of the political spectrum.**[216] Considering these findings, the use of the religious Zionist label refers to supporters of the rightwing which represents the great majority of this population sector.

In sum, the continuation of the occupation with the settlement of Jews in the West Bank is a purely political project, the largest in scope since 1967. It has numerous, very severe effects. It violated the Fourth Geneva Convention, the Declaration of Human Rights, and the Rome Statute of 2002. It causes ongoing violence, in which Palestinian and Jewish human beings have lost their lives. It absorbs tremendous political, economic, and societal costs. It has led to enormous security investments. It puts Israel into conflict with different states, international organizations, and populations in the world, including segments of Jews in Israel and in the world. It has escalated the conflict and brought it to the level that a significant portion of the leaders and public in Israel and the world think that it is impossible to solve with the paradigm of two states. It has deteriorated the democratic foundations of the State of Israel. Last but not least, it has turned the regime in the West Bank into apartheid. All these consequences will be analyzed in more detail in the following chapters. It is clear to me that all the observed consequences of the occupation and Jewish settlements in the occupied territories will be denied by the Israeli government, the army, formal institutions, various organizations, and most Israeli Jews. Moreover, there will be attempts to delegitimize the information provided in the book. Will it be surprising? Absolutely not! All societies in the world exert effort and resources to maintain a positive self-collective image with positive social identity and to justify the chosen goals and policies, even if they lead to immoral acts. They avoid looking in the mirror and sometimes severely censor those who break the norms of censorship and self-censorship by bringing to light information that contradicts moral self-collective perception.

Looking around, it is possible to see how Turkey still struggles to deny the Armenian genocide carried out over 100 years ago; how France refused for dozens of years to apologize for war crimes carried during the Algerian war; how Belgium and Holland have tried to hide atrocities undertaken in their past colonies (Indonesia and Congo); how China refuses to acknowledge its crimes against the Muslim minority Uyghurs; and how Russia disallows attention to the atrocities carried out in Chechnya and invents imagined narratives to justified its attempt to occupy Ukraine. Similarly, many citizens and institutions of the United States have great difficulty, even today, accepting the genocide of Indians and the enslavement of Africans, or the involvement of the state in various anti-democratic acts in different parts of the world (like Chile, Argentina, Iran, or Guatemala), and Japan has had great difficulty apologizing for war crimes carried out in War World Two. Even in the first agreement between German and Israel in 1952 regarding the reparations paid to Israel with goods and services for the loss of the six million Jews in the Holocaust, Germany did not apologize during the historical meeting between West German Chancellor Konrad Adenauer and Israeli Prime Minister David Ben Gurion on March 14, 1960, in New York. Adenauer avoided all expression of genuine remorse and admissions of responsibility demanded by Ben Gurion in return for Israel establishing relations with Germany after the Holocaust. Are these practices moral? Of course not! But the world keeps on turning. It acts on the basis of interests and needs and mostly disregards moral directives.

CHAPTER 6

Religious Zionism as a Leading Force

THE EXPANSION AND INSTITUTIONALIZATION OF THE INFLUENCE OF RELIGIOUS ZIONISM

As described above, the dogma of religious Zionism has played a crucial role in the significant changes that have taken place in the country and its society, and it still does. It gradually made its way from the margins to the political center.[217] Beyond the fact that it has supplied the religious epistemological basis for the idea of Greater Israel and the construction of settlements in the occupied territories, it has also served as the leading source of strength in their ideological realization on the ground and has spearheaded far-reaching changes in Israel social life, as we will detail.[218] This presence everywhere makes this movement prominent and central in many areas of society: a key presence in the army, in the legal system, in the educational system, in the media, and in government. And thus, it has become a focal point of influence in public and political discourse much more than its relative size in the general population. This does not mean that the individuals and groups in these systems have become religious. No! It means that religious Zionism succeeded in constructing a new identity, a political culture, political policies and decisions and public discourse—all around the core interests and values in the permanent incorporation of the West Bank under Israeli sovereignty. It is expressed in the de facto creeping annexation, full control of the Palestinians, carrying out the project of Jewish settlement in the West Bank, eliminating the discussion of the occupation, disappearance of the term peace and conflict resolution from the public discourse, and delegitimization of the societal forces in Israel and the world who demand an account for the misdeeds in the occupied.[219]

Let me begin with the army.

In the Army

Religious Zionism understood that, after years of only relatively marginal status in Israeli society, in order to achieve their goals, they would have to play a central role in the army—a hegemonic Israeli organization with wide-scope public consensual support. This primarily resulted from unification around the recognition that the time had come to challenge the Ashkenazi-secular sector of society, the founders of the state and nation, who were identified with the Labor movement. More or less simultaneously, Ashkenazi-secular youth had begun to suffer from a crisis of identity and motivation, and the combination of these developments enabled the "knitted kippah"[220] religious youth to stand out in the army and gradually to take a dominant place.[221] The majority of the Ashkenazi-secular Jews began to search for units that helped to satisfy their aspirations for self-fulfillment in intelligence or in computer branches of the army.

It goes without saying that the attitude of the religious-nationalists to the army was totally different than that of the Ashkenazi-secular population. In the eyes of religious Zionism, drawing from a religious theological outlook, Israel's modern wars were deliberately directed by God's will. They were meant to advance the redemption by freeing the territory of the Land of Israel. The attitude towards army service was in accord with this approach. Thus, the mobilization of *yeshiva* students was, for the army, a reservoir of quality soldiers, faithful to army behavior as empowered by the ethno-national ethos. A central tenet in the ethno-national ethos is expressed by the myth of the "settler," well anchored in both Jewish and Zionist symbolism. At the basis of the myth is the combination of several characteristics—the new religious Jew playing an active role in the redemption of the land, is not satisfied only with studying the Torah but is imbued with a sense of patriotism, a sense of military mission for his homeland, his nation, and his God. In this way, new candidates for "the salt of the earth" were created, as an alternative to the "great guys" of the Labor Movement. These were young people who aspired to actively participate in building the nation and defend their country and who considered themselves the future leadership of the Jewish people.[222]

One of the main expressions of this process was the increased representation of soldiers and officers wearing the "knitted kippah" in elite military units in contrast to their proportion in the population. As an example, while in 1990 the overland officers course included only 2.5% religious participants, in June 2017, about 40% of the participants defined themselves as religious and this trend continues.[223] Thus, a substantial number of the low and middle level officers in the battle units are religious. This development has definitely affected the army, as rabbis are attached to military units, women soldiers are sometimes excluded, study days of a religious character are scheduled, synagogues are constructed at bases, and more. This process, called "religionization," has accelerated since the beginning of the twenty-first century. It developed top-down, in an attempt by army officers to strengthen army motivation in dealing with the second *intifada*. Thus, for the first time, the identity of the army as a Jewish army was stressed, a move that greatly empowered the military rabbinate and impacted the Education Corps to employ Jewish messages. Religionization also developed from the bottom up to the top, in the form of pressure from religious soldiers whose numbers were growing, and in the demand for orthodox Zionist rabbis—the heads of Hesder Yeshivas (a program combining Torah studies with military service), religious pre-army courses, and higher *yeshivas* that supplied soldiers to the army—to redesign army culture.[224] It should be noted that while religious Zionists serve in army like secular Jews, most ultra-Orthodox Jews do not. They are exempted because of their continuous religious studies. This practice was already established by Prime Minister David Ben Gurion in 1948.

On a concrete level, in a Knesset discussion, on 17 July 2018, it became clear that two-thirds of the "educational Shabbat'" programs in the army[225] were taught by representatives of orthodox organizations, and almost 80% of external lecturers invited by the Jewish Identity Branch of the Israeli army to lecture to soldiers were from this stream of Judaism. From the data, it appears that in 2017, 115 military rabbis were active in the standing army, as well as 485 in the reserves,[226] and these numbers are higher than the service lists funded by the Department of Religious Services for local councils throughout the country. In addition, it appears that the budgets of religious rightwing organizations allocated by the army have gone up by dozens of percentage points, and thus they have succeeded in reaching many more military units. On 23 August 2018, it was publicized that the army had transferred—only to orthodox organizations—training sessions and activities on forming Jewish identity among the IDF junior command.[227] It also became known that the IDF has contributed to the socialization of its soldiers in the national-religious spirit. The effect of the religious Zionist spirit can be demonstrated by a Command Page issued by Givati Brigade Col. Ofer Winter, publicized during Operation Protective Edge (the 2014 Israeli operation in Gaza): "*I lift up my eyes to the heavens and call with you: Hear O Israel, the Lord our God the Lord is one.*" Winter wrote to those under his command: "*The Lord, the God of Israel, make our path on which we go successful, as we are poised to fight for your people Israel against an enemy that abuses your name.*"[228]

Growing Beyond

The implementation of the Zionist religious ethos was not limited solely to the years of military service. Religious Zionism also initiated a project of sectoral pre-army preparation in a one-year program with the aim of strengthening the national-religious worldview among graduates of religious high schools and integrating them into the IDF in command positions. Another of their goals is to inoculate religious Zionist youngsters against potential influence resulting from the meeting with secular soldiers in the army, and even to influence them to encourage secular soldiers to support the Zionist-religious dogma. To date, 24 religious preparation program centers have been established, alongside about 30 secular or mixed centers. The religious programs share a certain similarity to another religious-national project: the establishment of more than seventy Torah seed groups (groups of families from within the ranks of religious Zionism) in secular residential neighborhoods throughout the country. Their formal goal is creating a social bridge between religious Zionism and the local population and strengthening the link between the secular residents and Jewish heritage by community and explanatory activities. But in reality—as a political-religious force being financed almost without limitation by the state and other resources—they aim at changing views of secular Jews about religion, about the project of settling occupied territories, and about the religious-Zionist dogma that underlies this political-religious force. Of special note is the penetration of religious Jewish settlers from the occupied territories into the secular space (a kind of opposite movement to settling the occupied territories, in order to fulfill a religious mission) and the establishment of local religious settlements in the middle of Arab neighborhoods to demonstrate Jewish dominance in cities of mixed Jewish-Arab population, such as Yaffa, Lod, Ramla, or Acre.

The significance of this process of broadening the religious space should be understood considering the unequivocal findings that have shown that there is a clear connection between level of religiosity and rightwing opinions. A survey by Peace Index conducted in July 2013 showed that about 87% of the ultra-orthodox and the orthodox, as well as 70% of traditional respondents, classified themselves as belonging to the rightwing camp. Only about 39% of secular respondents classify themselves as rightwing.[229] In research by Ben Meir and Bagno-Moldavsky, under the aegis of the Institute for National Security Studies, in 2013 the same firm link was

Daniel Bar-Tal

found between level of religiosity and political attitudes with reference to the conflict. Sixty-seven percent of the ultra-orthodox and 65% of the orthodox, for example, are not interested in any solution to the conflict, compared to 43% of traditional religious respondents, and 33% of traditional non-religious respondents, and 28% among the non-religious. Only 11% of the ultra-orthodox and 28% of the religious respondents expressed support for a plan based on two states for two peoples, in comparison to 65% of the non-religious and about half of the traditional respondents. Ben Meir and Bagno-Moldavsky summarized their research, saying: "*The level of religiosity remains the element that most defines political climate in Israel*" (p. 45).[230] In the elections of 2015, the two elections in 2019, the election in 2020, and the election of 2021, the ultra-orthodox and the orthodox parties presented themselves unequivocally as a rightwing bloc, and as supporting Binyamin Netanyahu, as their choice for prime minister.

Returning to religious Zionists—they, together with the rightwing of society, have understood that, in order to influence the direction the state should take, they would have to be integrated within social institutions. Thus, they established media outlets, research institutions, a communications school, and Ariel College (eventually recognized as a university by the Council for Higher Education in Judea and Samaria), which was founded by the army command despite the opposition of the Committee for Planning and Funding and state university heads. Eventually they yielded to political pressure. In addition, they set up the Jewish Statesmanship Center to educate rightwing intellectual leadership.

With almost unlimited resources, mostly acquired from governmental ministries, institutions, organizations, and supporters living abroad, the religious Zionist movement has acted to change the shape of Israeli society in directions that they support, and in time, they have become societal leaders. This is in spite of their proportion of the Israeli population being relatively small. For example, in the 2015 elections, about nine percent of the electorate voted for the religious Zionist party—the Jewish Home. But with the formation of the extreme rightwing government, their representatives received key positions in the cabinet: The Ministry of Justice and the Ministry of Education, in addition to responsibility for contacts with the Jewish diaspora, and the Ministry of Agriculture. Controlling these departments as ministers enabled them not only to be an energizing force in the government, but also gave them the practical ability to influence the directions taken by the state of Israel. The Ministry of Justice determines the legal directions of the state and the Ministry of Education deals with the socialization of the younger generation (and no small number from the ultra-orthodox stream) in Israel.

In this way, religious Zionism has become a very important leading force in disseminating the ideology and ideas that today lead the state in enacting legislation, appointing judges, determining social behavioral norms, preparing educational curricula and determining budget distribution to schools, controlling extra-curricular activity, developing relations between groups in Israeli society, establishing settlements, and determining relations with diaspora Jews. In addition to these specific areas, religious Zionist ministers also influence domestic and foreign policy.[231] The Regional Councils of Judea and Samaria, which represent the settlers in the occupied territories, have become political bodies with great influence, and with a strong lobby whose representatives can enter any government office, present political demands and insist on resources to expand settlements, to which the reply is often positive. It is no wonder, then, that at the end of 2018, the Ministerial Committee for Legislation approved a bill to advance the recognition of more than 60 outposts and neighborhoods in settlements that had been built illegally in the last 20 years (including settlers on private lands taken from Palestinians). Thus, through the years, offices, branches, departments and organizations have been established on all government levels in order to serve settlement objectives, from planning to implementation. This system, administered and activated primarily by settlers, continues to operate by inertia and as such, it deepens the occupation. The senior officials in these organizations and departments are chosen for their support of rightwing ideology or their acceptance of it just in order to remain in office. In short, they simply give in. In this way, over the years, the government has coerced various institutions—the Ministry of Agriculture, Israel Land Administration, the Ministry of Justice, the police, the Antiquities Authority, Jewish National Fund, the Land Authority, the Settlement Division, and others—into implementing its desired policies in the occupied territories.[232]

In 2022 the Zionist Religious party returned to the government with 14 mandates, strengthened by its unification with the extreme Otzma Yehudit party. It doubled its power, now the third strongest party in Israel and thus playing a determinative role in the new coalition of Netanyahu.

The long road to power taken by religious Zionism could not have been successful without the assistance of parties, organizations and people who identified with its worldview and its methods, beginning with the main sources of power in political parties and state institutions including the Likud, Shas, Yahadut Hatorah; the Zionist Agency, organizations supporting Israel, Zionist organizations abroad, and wealthy individuals living outside of Israel. First, it should be understood that many supporters of religious Zionism are in a variety of rightwing parties. Second, many traditional and secular rightwing supporters have very similar views to those of religious Zionism regarding the conflict with the Palestinians, Israeli democracy, relations with Arabs, relations with Jews around the world, and relations with the international community. **In sum, the Zionist religious sector of society served as the ideological incubator, the motivating force and especially as an executive body that has become a pioneer of the rightwing camp, with tremendous influence on the supporters of these ideas and the governmental institutions.**

In order to understand the institutionalization of rightwing attitudes in addition to the activities of religious Zionism, we must also consider the civil institutions operating to disseminate conflict supporting narratives and to obstruct and eliminate those in opposition. For example, in the last two decades, several research centers have been established, such as Mercaz Shalem (the Shalem Center), the Institute for Zionist Strategies, the Israel Institute for Strategic Studies, the Jerusalem Center for Public Affairs, the Begin-Sadat Center for Strategic Studies, and the Kohelet Policy Forum. These integrate economic and political conservatism and publish opinion papers as a basis for legislation and setting policy. National and religious organizations have also been initiated with the goal of openly propagating rightwing-religious ideology and preventing the creation and spread of counter-narratives. Through the years, quite a few rightist NGOs in various areas of activity have been established and expanded; these include Elad (The Ir David Foundation), Im Tirtzu ("If You Will It…"), Regavim (Protecting our National Lands), Zechuyot Adam Kacholavan (Blue and White Human Rights), Ihud Harabanim L'ma'an Yisrael (The Union of Rabbis for the Land of Israel), Ne'emanei Har HaBayit (Temple Mount Faithful), Amutat Ateret Kohanim (Crown of the Priests Faithful), Yisrael Sheli (My Israel), Lehava (The Flame- Prevention of Assimilation in the Holy Land), and Ad Kan (Up to Here). Im Tirtzu, for example, characterized by Judge Raphael Yaacobi in 2013 as having certain similarities to fascist organizations, for many years enjoyed great influence in government ministries. In 2010, Minister of Education Gideon Saar, was an honored guest at its conference. Most of its energies are devoted to tracking discussions among individuals and organizations identified with alternative worldviews in order to denunciate and censure them. At the beginning of 2019, Im Tirtzu publicized a list of 80 university lecturers who, in their opinion, were transmitting messages contradictory to government narratives. A long list of organizations and associations set up during the years under discussion shared the same objectives as Im Tirtzu as tracking organizations, such as INM (Israel NGO Monitor), IAM (Israeli Academia Monitor, Ad Kan, and Isracamp. All these organizations work with the government in one way or another. In this context, the Ministry of Public Security, Strategic Affairs and Information, headed by Minister Gilad Erdan in the 34th Knesset, aided rightwing organizations to disseminate the government narrative about the conflict, and at the same time, battled against organizations and associations propagating opposing narratives, both in Israel and abroad. Those organizations do not only receive help from government ministries, but also gain financial resources from Israeli donors and from supporters abroad. Of course, in opposition to these rightwing organizations, organizations and communications channels have been established which express messages of support for a peace process, opposition to settlements in the occupied territories and to the occupation, and support for human rights and democratic values: The New Israel Fund based in USA with an objective to establish social justice and equality, Association for Civil Rights, B'Tselem (The Israeli Information Center for Human Rights in the Occupied Territories), HaMoked (Center for the Defense of the Individual), Molad (The Center for the Renewal of Israeli Democracy), Yesh Din, Breaking the Silence, The Adam Institute for Democracy & Peace, Sikha Mekomit (Local Discourse), and Hamachon L'Democratia Yisraelit (Israel Democracy Institute) among others. However, these organizations do not receive financial support from the government, lack resources, have difficulty accessing schools, and some are delegitimized.

CONSTRUCTING A NEW COLLECTIVE IDENTITY

One of the results of the process of radicalization is the reconstruction of the Jewish-Israeli identity, which has changed and radicalized.

The conquest of the "land of the forefathers," the birthplace of Jewish heritage and identity, aroused deep feelings in many Israelis, which gradually developed through the years, until a real change took place in contemporary Israeli identity. Of course, this did not occur on its own. **The moves initiated by supporters of Greater Israel, with the settlers leading the way along with their enthusiasts in the government, posed the territories at the heart of the new collective identity**, as territory may often be considered the important resource in constructing national identity.[233] The secular, traditional, and especially the religious rightwing thus conducted a systematic propaganda campaign, placing the West Bank at the very center of the homeland. The heart of the propaganda campaign stressed the "value" of Greater Israel, including a belief in the sole Jewish ownership of the land, the link to the Bible and Jewish tradition, ancient history of the Jewish nation and its mitzvot (precepts). In addition, there is a sense that "the people of Israel will dwell alone" (Bible, Numbers 23:9) as a victim of the nations of the world, a permanent sense of existential threat that the Holocaust might be repeated, and a rejection of the other and the stranger—and especially Arabs. In addition, with the new identity, emphasis was placed on Zionist narratives, symbols, and myths, especially, of course, on the narrow and extreme meaning of nationalism, which has taken the place of the fundamental values of democracy, and human and civil rights. In essence, the newly developed identity has unequivocally professed that the Jewish pillar, in its narrow orthodox definition (excluding the wide scope of conservative and reform Jewish movements) receives more weight than the democratic one. This skewed character of statehood and identity has been expressed in budgets allocated, educational curricula, ceremonies, legislation, leaders' speeches, and more.

At the same time, activity in the field was demanded in order to achieve control of the land. So, as the years have passed, more than 60% of West Bank land (area C), called the "heart of the homeland," has been appropriated by the settlers. Moreover, a variety of means have been used to mobilize support for the ideology of Greater Israel, along with the elimination of the Green Line from maps, the renaming of the West Bank as Judea and Samaria, the use of Hebrew names for the settlements and points of interest, the establishment of national parks, identifying archeological sites in an attempt to create a connection between the territories and tradition, history and Jewish patriotism, and developing religious myths about the various sites as representing figures from the Bible and from Jewish tradition. The occupied territories have been presented as the place where roots were planted and grew into Jewish identity, so that, for that reason exactly, it is claimed, the Jews have a right to the territories. **This ideology perfectly fit the narratives supporting a continuation of the conflict as presented in the conflict ethos and collective memory: the themes of the land of Israel belonging solely to the Jewish nation; Zionism, not in the sense of being inclusive and open, but rather in the narrow exclusionary, limited sense, closing off channels to the rest of the world and to other nations. Emphasizing the existential danger facing the Jewish nation through the generations, the exclusion of the Jewish nation throughout history, the heroes who defended the land, the dehumanization of enemies who tried to harm the Jewish nation, the victimization which characterizes Jewish history, the patriotic spirit that beats in the heart of the nation, and the wish to live in peace (but only ideally)—all of these have been absorbed as the foundations of collective identity.**

Children, whose political consciousness is in the process of developing, have learned all of this in kindergartens and elementary schools. Holidays and commemoration days are marked in the educational system: Hanukah, Purim, Holocaust Memorial Day, Passover, Memorial Day and Independence Day, Lag B'Omer, and Jerusalem Day. All these commemorations are permeated with contents that correspond to the themes of conflict supporting narratives, such as justness of the goals, delegitimization of the enemies who wish to annihilate the Jewish nation, the eternal threat under which Jewish people live, the sense of self collective victimhood, the self-glorification with patriotic feelings, and the importance of military service as the ultimate defense of the Jewish people.

Furthermore, students are also taken on trips to Jewish sites in Israel and in the West Bank, so that they can see them with their own eyes. Various rightwing national-religious associations, such as Ateret Kohanim or Elad, have taken possession of national parks and archeological sites in the West Bank and Jerusalem in order to embed Jewish content throughout the occupied territories, and IDF soldiers have also participated in this educational process, during study days and field trips. In addition, a public relations campaign was initiated, called "To Settle in Their Hearts," devoted to bringing the public closer to the settlers and the settlement project. The settlers were presented as acting in the tradition of the pioneers of the

1920s, and the settlements themselves have been compared to the "wall and stockade" settlements of the 1930s. The word "occupation" has been eliminated, and instead, the educational system uses only Hebrew names of places, including the term Judea and Samaria, in place of identifying the West Bank as occupied territory. Various organizations present the importance of the settlements, organize tours for adult groups and enter schools to speak to students. In short, the nation has experienced and is still experiencing an educational project focused on creating a new identity. In the framework of building the new identity, we must also take note of the journeys to Poland undertaken by almost all Jewish youngsters in the eleventh and twelfth grades. The Ministry of Education has defined the goals of the journeys as *"strengthening national inclusion and the connection to history and heritage."* Every year, about 30 thousand students go on a "journey of death." This term is used because most of the journeys are very similar and include visits to the death camps of Auschwitz-Birkenau, Majdanek, Treblinka, with stops at cemeteries, sites of past ghettos and locations of mass murder, all with the aim of illustrating the horrors of the Holocaust without setting foot in Germany. This journey can be viewed as an **initiation ceremony** for young people to enter Israeli Jewish society. **Initiation** is defined as a rite of passage marking entrance or acceptance into a society. It can thus be seen as a formal or informal admission to adulthood in the Jewish community, adopting the identity of the eternal victim and believing that the threat is constant and continuous. However, the strong Israeli army is a savior and therefore, fulfilling the patriotic duty of service is of prime importance, even to the point of the young soldier being ready to sacrifice his/her life for the state.[234] These journeys stopped recently because of disagreements with Polish government.

This new identity has penetrated deep into the soul of Jewish society in Israel. At its center is one narrow and very specific perspective of nationalism (Zionism), Jewish orthodox exclusion, xenophobia, with the addition of traditionalism, all of which diminish the importance of democracy. It is an ethnic Jewish identity that excludes 20% of Israeli citizens (the Arabs) as well as another 5% of citizens from the former Soviet Union who, according to halacha (Jewish law), are not Jewish. At a time when there is general agreement about the narrow ethnic-national component, society members are divided about the religious component. There are those who accept the traditional-cultural level as identification of the Jewish nation and others who accept the religious interpretation of the Jewish nation. Of course, the religious component ranges on a scale from ultra-orthodox at one extreme to secular Judaism on the other. But even the secular sector marks most of the Jewish religious holidays and traditions which, through the years, have become imbued with more religious content.

This new identity, designed under national-religious leadership, has become an obstruction to any political solution which would demand compromises regarding the division of the land, and would require a perception of Arabs as human beings and as partners to a peace agreement. It has also excluded the Arab minority of Israeli citizens from the political space, as Arabs are not considered to be legitimate decision makers in the country, nor can they be accepted as coalition partners in the government. The legislation of the basic law: Israel as the Nation-State of the Jewish People hammered in the definition of Israel in a discriminatory way. Moreover, Israel has closed its doors to the world dreamed about by many of the Zionist founders—a nation like all other nations: open, involved, and integrated in the international community. And in many senses, it has abandoned the identity nurtured when the state was first established, an identity emphasizing the establishment of a new Israeli culture in the spirit of Jewish-universal values, which would link with the nation's ancient identity based upon age-old Jewish culture, and a culture would develop with the aspiration for normal national life and membership in the family of nations.[235] In spite of the fact that we understand today that these were mainly slogans that came from mouths of the leaders—but were not reflected in their actions—they still delineated an aspirational direction for Israeli society.

How the Institutionalization of Extremism Looks – Case Studies

Earlier in this book, I have described the broad social processes that have aided in the formulation of attitudes about the conflict, the settlements, the concept of Greater Israel and democracy by Israeli Jews. Now I will try to illustrate how this takes place in reality by focusing on an analysis of two foci of socialization: the educational system and the media.

The Educational System

The field of education often serves as one of the main socialization tools in conflict areas. In most years of the state's existence, it

has served as an agent dedicated to inculcating conflict supporting beliefs and narratives, such as justification of collective aims in absolute terms, delegitimization of the opponent, self-glorification, self-victimization, and patriotism. These beliefs are instilled in students from their kindergarten years up to high school graduation. The messages grant meaning to the violent reality in which students live. For example, beliefs that undermine the legitimacy of the other should explain the reason for the violence taking place from the outset ("The other side wants only to destroy us"), while alternatively, beliefs that cultivate a collective positive self-image supply hope and optimism ("Our nation is strong enough and it will overcome the enemy").[236] It is not for naught that Mark Sommers of Boston University maintained in his report to the World Bank: "*Many who conduct modern wars are expert at using educational settings to indoctrinate and control children.*"[237]

The Ministry of Education, which directs the educational system in Israel, to a great extent determines the curriculum and up until recently, approved all its textbooks. It still allocates resources, encourages the appearance of certain organizations in schools, controls the Pedagogical Council, oversees the subject supervisors, and issues directives to set out educational guidelines. In addition, the ministry instructs school principals and teachers about what they should be emphasizing in various content areas. Nevertheless, it would appear that behind classroom doors, teachers have the freedom to transmit content they choose; however, in actual fact, the ministry also greatly affects what goes on in the individual classrooms by unofficially inculcating the prevailing spirit of the minister, who continually expresses his/her opinions in the media. With short breaks, since 1996, the Ministry of Education has been controlled by rightwing ministers, and primarily by national-religious figures. These ministers set out a national-religious agenda throughout the entire system. This is expressed in various ways, such as publishing books that narrow the civics knowledge presented to the student; limiting the critical approach and preventing openness, values which form the basis of education; they eliminate books that are not in line with their worldview and appoint senior professionals to the ministry who support their opinions. We must also remember that, among the many dozens of thousands of teachers, there are many who support the dominant propagated nationalistic-traditional orientation of Jewish Israeli society.

In addition, the public school system is discriminated against in comparison with the public-religious system, in both budgets and resources. This development is especially serious when the public-religious school system (representing religious Zionism) has full and complete autonomy, as determined in the Compulsory Education Law of 1953. The public school system has no such autonomy, and it is open to coercive demands by Ministers of Education coming from religious Zionism, all of whom have a very specific worldview which may sometimes contradict the views of parents sending their children to the mainstream public school. This is especially serious as the ministers who have headed the Education Ministry have generally come from the extremist branch of religious Zionism, like Naftali Bennett or even Rabbi Rafi Peretz, who was the leader of the extreme nationalistic and religious Jewish Home Party.

During the first decade of the 2000s, with the retreat from the peace process and the escalation of conflict, the educational system adjusted itself to the new leadership. There was a return to the ethos of conflict as a hegemonic narrative—simultaneously, education for peace, which had begun during the term of Education Minister Yitzhak Navon and accelerated during Amnon Rubinstein's term, almost disappeared from the educational system. In line with this change of direction, there was a significant decline in education for cooperative living with the Arab citizens of Israel, and education for democracy, which is imperative for a democratic lifestyle. In contrast, during these years, the ministers of education chose to emphasize Jewish religious values in order to strengthen a narrow Jewish and nationalistic identity, in line with government policy and the spirit of the period.

A series of initiatives issued by the Ministry of Education under Gideon Saar (2009-2013) demonstrate the focus on these goals, as for example the program "Going up to Hebron," in which thousands of school children visited the Cave of the Forefathers. Moreover, during Saar's term as minister, many organizations and associations identified as rightwing, began to freely enter public schools, while, on certain occasions, Saar himself expressed narrow perceptions of identity and anti-Palestinian attitudes, including opposition to discussion of the Palestinian narrative in the educational system. He also buried a policy report on "Education for Jewish-Arab Coexistence," which was submitted to Education Minister Yuli Tamir in January 2009, and which summarized the recommendations of a public committee charged with implementing wide-ranging steps in an attempt to educate for coexistence between the Jewish majority and the Arab minority. Saar also forbid the use of a book which presented, side by side, the Jewish narrative and the Palestinian narrative. These actions are not surprising, considering the fact that Gideon Saar identified with the attitudes of the organization Im Tirtsu (If You Will It…), which, as we have already pointed out, was determined by a district court judge in Jerusalem to have certain characteristics similar to fascist organizations. While still serving as education minister, he spoke at the annual meeting of the organization in March 2010, and reinforced attempts to "advance Zionist values in Israel."[238]

Naftali Bennett, the head of the Jewish Home Party, who assumed the post of Minister of Education after the elections of 2015, continued Saar's policies, and his term was even marked by an escalation of ministry closure and prohibition of broadminded information about the conflict. This was accomplished by practices like the elimination of budgets, the removal from the curriculum of materials deemed as "loaded," firing people whose opinions did not suit the hawkish ideology of the minster, appointing like-minded people to positions in the Ministry of Education, setting new criteria for funding, rewriting existing textbooks, adding a new required core subject to be taught only in public education (and not in the religious schools) under the title "Jewish-Israeli Culture," the essence of which was setting religious Jewish beliefs as a cornerstone for public school students, and making a significant change in the Bible curriculum.[239] Even though this was not an official system of censorship, the limitations, enclosure and the reduction in Israeli students' exposure to other narratives achieved similar results in reality.

In the summer of 2018, Bennett replaced the inspector of civics studies, Yael Goron, who had been marked as a leftist, with Aynat Ohayon, from the realm of religious Zionism, whose opinions well suited those of the minister. In 2016, he fired Professor Ami Volansky who served as a chief scientist in the ministry because Volansky advanced a project of a struggle against racism in cooperation between the ministry and the Israeli army. Thus, while the religious public education system, because it is autonomous, does not permit any interference by a secular minster of education, the secular public education system has been losing its secular character because of the heavy-handed intervention in its content, its appointments, its division of resources, and its curricula, by ministers who come from the religious Zionist sector. The minister may also subsidize the entry of religious organizations and seed-groups into the public schools. This is an anomaly and a distortion that leads to grave discrimination in the division of resources and to deviation from the goals of openness, pluralism, and critical thinking, all of which are minimum demands which should characterize the public school system.[240]

During Bennett's term there was another important development. On 17 July 2018, the Knesset approved an amendment to the State Education Law,[241] granting far-reaching authorities to the minister of education, and among them, the authority to prevent entry into schools by organization or lecturers whose activities stand "in serious and significant contradiction" to one of the twelve objectives of the public school system—intentionally vague wording actually intended to authorize exclusion of organizations challenging the official narrative. The law also enables the minister of education to block entry to schools by organizations operating abroad to advance political steps against the state of Israel due to actions by IDF soldiers. Thus, during Bennett's term, a blacklist was assembled of organizations and lecturers whose entry into schools was prohibited. Within the framework of this legislation, another item was added to the objectives of the educational system, stating that students should be educated to "*do significant service in the Israeli army or in the national service program.*" Thus, Bennett succeeded in eliminating any willingness to deal with controversial issues in the classroom, and as reinforcement, a further reform was enacted during his term to change the "culture basket" program which now included a list of cultural products that students were not permitted to see.

In 2015, budgetary support for external organizations disseminating Jewish culture totaled about 177 million shekels while organizations dedicated to coexistence or democracy received about 1.5 million shekels. In the 2018 budget, schools received 119 times more money for Jewish education than for democracy and coexistence with Arab citizens. From the allocation for Jewish culture, about 94% was given to rightwing settlement organizations while only 6% went to pluralistic Judaism. Leading up to the school year beginning in September 2019, the Ministry of Education employed 477 new Judaism teachers and only seven new physics teachers. The budget for Jewish subjects in 2019 was enlarged by dozens of percentage points in comparison to the budget for 2015. Research has also shown that bulletins from the ministry with content on democracy were very few in comparison to those on Judaism.

In June 2019 (during a transition government), the prime minister fired Education Minister Naftali Bennett and appointed Rabbi Rafi Peretz in his place. Peretz, whose opinions are even more extreme than those who served before him, is liable to completely destroy the educational system: He came out against homosexuals and then retracted his statement; he has come out against seculars; he has come out against the Enlightenment, and he thinks that "universities of prophesy" are the wave of the future. He is also in favor of annexing the occupied territories without giving Palestinians equal rights. The minister of education of the State of Israel, who should serve as a personal example and a leader for Israeli students, publicly expresses racist beliefs, extreme nationalism, and chauvinism, with a religious tinge, and thus directs the educational system down an improper path, one that is unacceptable in a state claiming to be democratic and Jewish.[242] In May 2020, ex-general Yoav Galant was appointed as Minister of Education. Galant also represented a narrow nationalistic orientation and during his term, the Ministry of Education called for hearings against a high school headmaster who had "dared" to invite a spokesman for a human rights NGO to appear before the student body. He also objected to the most prestigious award of the Israel Prize in Mathematics to Weizmann Institute Professor Oded Goldreich, because he signed a petition calling for the halt of EU funding for the Israeli Ariel University on the occupied West Bank. Eventually, although the new Minister of Education Sasha Biton also refused to grant him the Israel Prize, a Supreme Court ruling forced the state to recognize his academic achievement and grant him the prize.

In the new government, after the Netanyahu era, the portfolio of education was delivered in 2021 to Dr Yifat Shasha-Biton, a member of nationalist rightist New Hope party, led by Gideon Saar. It is hard to know how she will pursue education against racism or education for democracy. Meanwhile she also blocked Professor Oded Goldreich from receiving the Israel prize because of his political views. It was a short term of Sasha-Biton because in the elections of 2022 she was removed from her office because her party was in the anti-Netanyahu block. Instead, Netanyahu gave the portfolio to an extremist who will direct the educational system to religious and nationalistic terrains, omitting the deep discussion of human rights and democracy,

In summary, the policies adopted by the Ministry of Education, under the leadership of Saar, Bennett, Peretz, and Galant, distanced the educational system at every level from humanist values like pluralism, tolerance, freedom of expression, acceptance of the other and maintaining his/her dignity, human rights, education for coexistence, and education for democracy. Instead, it represents conflict supporting narratives, but even more importantly, it harms the two significant values of every education system and the goals of educational activity in general: openness and critical thinking. Under the leadership of the Ministers of Education coming to their office with rightist political orientation, the system censors books, punishes educators who raise narratives contradicting the official Zionist narrative, prevents meetings in schools with NGOs which accuse Israel of violation of human rights and prevents studying *Nakba* by law (the Palestinian disaster of 1948). In the context of the present interest, an extensive study of the educational curricula and the schoolbooks found that the presentation of the occupation appears in most textbooks for several decades in the form of denial based on disregard or normalization. The researcher explained his findings with the preference to practice self-censorship on the divisive and sensitive issue of the occupation.[243] However, in spite of the described climate in the Ministry of Education, various local authorities, as for example, in Tel Aviv, specific schools, and even classes conduct educational activities to struggle against racism and to strengthen democracy.

The Media

The media are meant to provide an important pillar of support in every democratic system. They serve as the most vital agents of knowledge and information transmission; this knowledge and information functions as the raw material for delineating beliefs and attitudes. But as the "fourth estate" of a democratic political system, it should function as a "watchdog for democracy," with the objective of casting a supervisory eye on the government, exposing corruption and revealing omissions, lies, manipulations and failures. Thus, the media are meant to supply the basis for democratic values in the state and to defend individual freedoms and minority rights, such as freedom of expression, freedom of information, pluralism and tolerance. But we are witness to the fact that, in most countries of the world, the realities are far from these ideals. In many countries, the media are biased and selective in their reports, as most serve the powerful and those with vested interests. I, of course, am cognizant of the great influence of the many social media channels that have developed in the past decade. They play a very important positive and negative role in the social-political-educational arenas and their role is expanding. But in this book, I have decided to focus only on the mass media, which have clear structures and leadership, and are identified with and still serve to communicate information and knowledge. There have been many studies examining media functioning in the world and this research has brought the many negative aspects to the surface.

The Israeli media do not hold a very respected place in the gallery of safeguards for democratic values. Of course, we should not accept this as a wide sweeping generalization, as there are, no doubt, many media figures and media channels that fulfill their roles faithfully and maintain a free flow of information. However, many media agents (most newspapers, TV channels and radio stations) played the role of "mobilized media" during the first decades of the state, subservient to the demands of state leaders who applied censorship and encouraged self-censorship.[244] As time passed, with privatization and the appearance of many more networks, the media became more open and changed completely, both in quantity and in quality. However, very quickly, economic changes created new power centers with new stakeholders, intending to use the media to advance their own economic and political interests. Thus, new unacceptable norms of dependence on wealthy tycoons were created, along with business dealings between these tycoons, media figures and politicians.[245] These machinations were entirely exposed during the second decade of this century, with the indictments issued against Prime Minister Benjamin Netanyahu in intrigues also involving owners of media channels, politicians, editors and media figures.

Thus, in contrast to the image held by most of the public, and as opposed to the way the rightwing leadership, and particularly Benjamin Netanyahu as prime minister has presented them, the Hebrew speaking media for the most part advance the conflict supporting culture, and do it with zeal.[246] Through the years, there were no significant differences among the three leading newspapers—*Yedioth Aharonoth*, *Maariv*, and *Haaretz*—in subjects related to security, to the conflict and to the way Arabs are presented.[247] Only in the past decade has independent newspaper *Haaretz* taken a unique line, supporting the peace process, presenting the other, and defending democracy. In addition, several websites in Hebrew and English have been established, bringing alternative information to the hegemonic narratives regarding the occupation, the conflict and the Palestinian opponent (for example, Sicha Mekomit [Local Discussion], 972–Independent Journalism from Israel). The same claim may also certainly be made about the news programs and documentary films on television.[248] That does not mean that there are reporters and commentators who are not right-wing—of course there are, but I am referring to the way the **on-the-spot news** information about security, occupation, violent encounters with Arabs, violations of Palestinians human rights and the conflict in general is framed, especially when real events occur. Media news presentations with regards to events related to the conflict are perceived by most of the public as objective truth in contrast to reports on other issues, op-ed articles and commentaries which are considered expressions of the subjective opinion of the writer or the speaker. In this context, however, there are some mass media journalists who present alternative views to the dominant conflict supporting narratives.

First of all, for many years, the media have been tools for directing public opinion to support wars and military operations, as well as doing the same for security or political crises in the context of the conflict.[249] For example, almost all television and radio channels, and newspapers supported the military confrontations in Gaza and expressed a hardline approach to dealing with the Palestinians in the West Bank and even with the Arab citizens of Israel. Second, there have always been quite a few rightwing journalists in media, but in recent years their number has grown dramatically. This trend accelerated during Benjamin Netanyahu's long term as prime minister, with his attempts to appropriate the media and to direct the news to serve his personal interests. In recent years, this tendency has become obvious with reporters who openly serve Netanyahu. Third, the right has received powerful reinforcement in the form of a daily newspaper, *Yisrael Hayom (Israel Today)*, distributed at no charge throughout the country since July 2007, and it has the widest newspaper circulation among the Israeli public. It is not only given out methodically and systematically at no cost in the streets, but it is also placed at sites where people must wait their turns, such as banks or medical clinics. This newspaper, whose clear objective is to aid the rightwing and particularly Binyamin Netanyahu, to mobilize support by presenting his narrative, is financed by the Adelson family—American supporters of rightwing causes and friends of Netanyahu. Fourth, it has been discovered that several media channels and media personalities have given positive coverage to the Netanyahu family and to the rightwing in general due to external pressure, and that this coverage has also brought them benefits.

Ultimately, on 21 November 2019, Attorney General Avichai Mandelblit submitted a bill of indictment against Prime Minister Binyamin Netanyahu, accusing him of bribery, fraud, and breach of trust. In the indictment, called Case 4000, the prime minister is charged with being in a "give and take" relationship (that is, bribery, fraud and breach of trust) as he used his authority and power to advance the interests of the head of the Bezek telecommunications company, Shaul Elovitz (a tycoon who holds the Israeli telecommunications giant and mass media channels) in return for positive coverage of Netanyahu and his wife on the Walla website. In Case 2000, Netanyahu is charged with fraud and breach of trust for making a deal with *Yedioth Aharonoth* daily newspaper owner, Noni Mozes, in which *Yedioth Aharonoth* would cover him positively in return for legislation that would harm the newspaper's main competitor, *Yisrael Hayom*, as described above. These charges and later testimony in the trial shed negative light on the general functioning of some of the media outlets in Israel, which are open to manipulation and direction by their owners. The strange thing is that, throughout these investigations, which involved publishers, managers, and editors, these individuals have remained in their powerful positions in the media.

A wide-ranging study by Sagi Elbaz in 2014 analyzed the contents of the dominant written and broadcast media in Israel using the content analysis method.[250] First, Elbaz found that, most of the time the great majority of media outlets echo the attitudes of the political and security system elites, who view the use of military force as a legitimate and desirable way to deal with the Israeli-Arab conflict. Second, a great majority of media outlets tend to accept the reality of an intractable military struggle and even support it. Third, most media do not cast doubt on the information transmitted by the political and security leadership regarding the existing threats and dangers. Fourth, most media minimize exposure to other opinions and emphasize the official narrative, including those items referring to Jewish self-glorification, on the one hand, and perceptions of sole Jewish victimhood, on the other. Fifth, most of the media tend to disregard the suffering of the Palestinians and the harm inflicted on them by Israeli forces. Finally, the media almost never grant a platform to alternative information publicized by Palestinian and Arab sources, or by other sources in the international media; this establishes an obstructive barrier to the flow of information which might illuminate the conflict in another light and might supply the public with a wider and more reliable angle of vision. Finally, the media repeat the motives of "a nation in uniform," "the entire nation is the army," and "the soldiers are our children," which prevent serious discussion as to how the army functions—its roles, budget, morality, and more.

In almost every security crisis, especially those accompanied by violence, the media is almost entirely present and supports the narrative supplied by the government and the army without criticism. Elbaz' conclusion in his analyses of Israeli journalism is striking. He notes that, through the years, Israeli media have shown qualitative changes in their coverage of different economic, social, and other issues, but their treatment of Israeli security, the conflict and the occupation has basically remained unchanged through the decades in almost all media.[251] One of the latest examples was the case of assassination of a high ranking figure in the Jihad Ha-Islami organization in Gaza, Abu al-Ata, on 11 November 2019. The media, which reacted automatically, as in emergency situations, did not ask key questions about the purpose of the assassination, the cost to the state, whether the decision was made considering the costs involved, the timing of the action in the existing political context of attempts to establish a government coalition by Gantz, and the distinctions between political, security and military reasons for the assassination. Almost all Jewish politicians supported the assassination, even leadership of the Blue-White party, which was politically harmed by the act and its results. In the political atmosphere of Israel, they had no choice. An expression of criticism against the assassination could have ended their careers.

Leading Israeli journalist Amira Hass of *Haaretz*, who covers the Palestinian, issues wrote on February 8, 2021:

> *The Hebrew-language media remains silent because it willingly accepts the official lie, that operations such as that in Khirbet Humsa are legitimate enforcement activities.*[252]
> *By its silence it is normalizing the slow and ongoing expulsion that the Israel Defense Forces, the Civil Administration, the Jerusalem Municipality and the Interior Ministry are carrying out against the Palestinians. In these cases, the media serves the basic master plan of Israel's governments: crowding*

the Palestinians into Bantustans, so that most of the West
Bank will be annexed to Israel and so that the Jews will benefit from the cheap real estate there. This silence moves between
cowardice and deliberate collaboration with the crimes and
the material gains that they yield.[253]

The doctoral dissertation of Lara Ingram at the University of London in
2016 gives an additional look into the ways the media operates.[254] The
researcher examined a number of media outlets (*Yisrael Hayom, ynet,
Haaretz, Yedioth Aharonoth, The Jerusalem Post, The Times of Israel,* Channel 7, *Matzav*) in three different cases. Findings indicate that the newspaper *Haaretz* is different from all others in bringing comprehensive and
critical reports to the public. The other media channels downplay Israeli
violence, use terms like "defense" and "security" when reporting any harm
done to Palestinians, understate information from Palestinian sources, use
delegitimization labels when describing Palestinians, do not supply wide
background information about Israeli or Palestinian violence, and present
Jews as victims of Palestinian violence.

The interesting thing is that even though most of the Israeli media are far
from being open, unprejudiced, and free, they receive countless accusations and much mudslinging for not giving sweeping support to the prime
minister, despite the criminal acts he is accused of by the police and the
justice system. Through the years, Netanyahu has also taken political
steps, some of them illegal, in order to subdue the media to his authority.

On 30 January 2017, in one of Netanyahu's attacks on the media, he
claimed: "*The leftist media is organizing a Bolshevik hunting expedition, a
brainwashing and character assassination project against me and my family.
This is occurring every day and every evening. They are creating a flood of fake
news about us …There has never been such a thing in the history of the state
or in democratic states. Why? Because the left undemocratically dominates the
media.*"[255]

**In summary, the media do not function in a vacuum. In societies in-
volved in intractable conflicts for dozens of years, they are an integral
part of the societal mobilization agents by disseminating a national
ideology, of which an inseparable element is conflict supporting narratives. These narratives are primarily imparted in times of violent
confrontations, but also in relatively calm periods, during which po-**

tential threats and preparations for the next round of violence are continually expressed. Thus, most of the fourth-estate channels serve as important agents of maintaining the conflict culture and its basic assumptions. Although the media are not completely homogeneous in terms of the power of their employees, when viewing the accumulation of various media reports, a clear and uniform picture emerges supporting the ethos of conflict, excluding a small number of isolated voices. This is of crucial importance as the Israeli public is almost never exposed to alternative information from other sources. This orientation was becoming more and more intense as Binyamin Netanyahu exerted his influence on media channels: his attempts to lessen the independence of the public broadcasting authority; the information about his involvement in directing reports by the Walla news website; his efforts to influence the publication of information in the daily *Yedioth Aharonoth*; his intervention in the reportage of *Yisrael Hayom*; his attempts to close down Channel 10; turning Channel 20 into a mouthpiece for news supporting Netanyahu and turning it eventually into news Channel 14, competing with other channels; his intervention in the coverage by Maariv; nominating his supporters to key functions in The Second Authority for Television and Radio;, the attacks of mudslinging on Channel 12 and on media channels in general; the division of the public broadcasting corporation into a general corporation and a news corporation; and the appearance of a new type of journalism that professes to be neutral in the present climate —all of these are indisputable testimony to Prime Minister Netanyahu's desire, during his long years as head of the government, to control the media in order to influence Israeli public consciousness.

Considering these political actions, it has become clear that part of the Israel media is directed to no small extent by the owners, politicians and editors of Israeli newspapers, which report as these communications figures see fit. In other words, an analysis of media messages and the way they operate illustrates how media information is created, managed and dictated. And we haven't yet mentioned social media, which today represent an inseparable part of how the public is influenced. Leaders, parties and organizations transmit messages on Facebook, Internet, Twitter, and Instagram, which are completely unsupervised, and there too, messages are circulated which are completely untrue. It is well known that in addition to volunteers, wealthy people and politicians employ workers who operate these open media channels for payment.

Binyamin Netanyahu, who served as prime minister consecutively for longer than 12 years, played an extremely important role in determining the direction of the state of Israel and its society. Therefore, it is important to say something about his orientation and the road along which he led the state. Even though he descended from the government arena for a short period, his legacy cannot be easily changed. Norms that have been instituted for a long time do not disappear in one night, especially in view of the fact that the Likud party has remained a large and well-organized party in Israel. Moreover, the ideas and the programs have been internalized by his supporters that formed a loyal and obedient sector holding a system of beliefs called "Bibism."

BINYAMIN NETANYAHU AS A CENTRAL IMAGE IN CONFLICT CULTURE

A central figure in Israeli radicalization has been Binyamin Netanyahu, who served as Prime Minister between 1996 and 1999, then again from 2009 until 2021 and returned to power in 2022. In his long second term, he succeeded in organizing a relatively stable block that included the Likud party together with the ultraorthodox parties, the Zionist-religious party, and ephemeral parties when they ran in the elections. He also succeeded in building the very large and stable Likud party, which has gained at least 30 seats in the parliament in all elections since 2009. Finally, he succeeded in assembling a very loyal base in the Israeli electorate, including both mainstream and social media, as well as political and social arenas. This broad base blindly supports him in spite of his being indicted for bribery, fraud, and breach of trust by the Israeli attorney general. From 2009 and for the next 12 years, Netanyahu led Israel, leaving his stamp on the political culture of the state, the consciousness of a large segment of Israeli Jewish society and on the culture of the conflict. In 2022, he succeeded in forming a coalition-based on ultra-religious parties and a Zionist Religious party that had moved extremely rightward. This influence penetrated deeply into the layers of society and could still be observed in the last elections and even in the time that he was out of office. In 2021-2022, when Netanyahu was in the opposition and the government of change was leading the country, the policies towards the Palestinians were the same regarding Jewish settlement, violence of settlers, the refusal to negotiate with the Palestinian leadership, and in general towards the occupation as during his years in power. The alternative government consisted of a broad coalition spanning from extreme right to left and thus decided not to change policies towards Palestinians.

Binyamin Netanyahu as the undisputed leader of the Likud Movement and thus of the Israeli rightwing, is the dominant figure in Israeli politics, and for years there has been no competition for leadership. Much of the Israeli public consider him an outstanding leader and support him and his opinions. For years, at least until 2019, he had been thought of as the best possible leader by the Jewish public, with no competitors. His speeches are well thought out and touch the emotional and symbolic core of the Jewish collective, increasing support for his policies. Admiration of him has continued even after the charges against him were publicized and the trial began.

His aides, ministers, and other Likud party Knesset members and rightist media figures have gathered around him in support and accept his every word as sacred and binding, with no criticism. They are also sent out to defend him and to construct a supportive basis among the public. Anyone who dared to criticize him or to express an autonomous opinion in his party or was not liked by his wife was moved downward or forced to quit the party. It may be assumed that without the criminal charges, Benjamin Netanyahu could have governed Israel for a long time, but the charges diminished his broad support.

He has a well-structured belief-system regarding the past, present, and future of the Jewish nation and the state of Israel.[256] Thus, it is important to analyze his views about the conflict and especially, about the narrative he imparts to the Jewish public.

In a study in 2020, Rosler, Hagage-Baikovich, and Bar-Tal analyzed Binyamin Netanyahu's speeches throughout his long political career, beginning from the time he was appointed Deputy Chief of Mission at the Israeli embassy in Washington D.C. in 1982.[257] The analysis reveals his political world and testifies to the consistency of his beliefs through the years. It indicates that the themes of the ethos of conflict have always been reflected in them, while beliefs dealing with security (and primarily lack of security) appear with the greatest frequency and most dominantly, alongside all the other ethos of conflict societal beliefs. He has ignored a series of major events that took place from the 1980s until 2000, adhering to his ideological views, and resisting numerous opportunities to embark on the road of peace with the Palestinians.

In the context of security, Netanyahu often emphasizes the security-existential threats which, in his opinion, constitute a danger to the continuing existence of the State of Israel. In addition, he frequently outlines the necessary conditions to ensure security of the state vis-à-vis these threats, such as Israel's right to deal with security threats using military forces and maintaining the present state borders, which attribute strategic importance to ensuring the security of the state and its citizens. Finally, he emphasizes the need for a strong army and for the support of the United States. In order to demonstrate the dangers, he makes great use of symbolic threats, such as the Holocaust, to stress the severity of the perils facing Israel and to arouse fear in the public. He speaks of dangers like the Iranian threat, primarily their atomic potential, terror from the Gaza Strip, Hamas, ISIS, and a Palestinian state in the making, while as a backdrop, he returns time after time to the terrible events of the Holocaust, warning against its possible return. For example, on 7 April 2013, on Holocaust Remembrance Day, he spoke at Yad Vashem and said, "*This hatred (against the Jews) has not disappeared from the world. It has simply been replaced by murderous hatred of the state of the Jews. What has changed since the Holocaust is our determination and our abilities to defend ourselves with our own power.*"

In a recent interview, Shai Piron, who was Minister of Education during 2011-2012, he told the following story, which reflects a very meaningful worldview of Netanyahu: "I once guided Netanyahu in Auschwitz. We were all alone. We talked about the meaning of the Holocaust and he explained antisemitism to me and said that the whole world is against us. And therefore, a peace agreement is a strategic threat to the Jewish people, because if there is peace we will not have a single thing that unites or bonds us."[258] I believe that this revelation at least explains the political steps taken by Netanyahu through the years he led Israel and negotiated with the Palestinians.

It is not surprising that he does not mention the word "occupation" and at the General Assembly of the United Nations in 2014, he stated: "*The nation of Israel does not occupy the land of Israel.*" Accordingly, Netanyahu does not see any connection between the occupation and the Israeli settlements and violence from the Palestinian side. In addition, he keeps repeating the belief that the Palestinians, including their leader, Abu Mazen, are not legitimate partners for negotiations and in his opinion, this is indicated by their refusal to recognize the State of Israel as a Jewish state. He considers that they are also responsible for all the wars that have broken out during the 2000s.

He believes that the Jewish nation is the only victim of the conflict, and he is strongly opposed to the idea that Palestinians may also be its victims. In contrast to these beliefs, when he speaks publicly, he again and again repeats Israel's desire for peace, and defines Israel as the only democracy in the Middle East, a country which safeguards equal rights and freedom of speech, and he views the state as moral and the Israeli army as the most moral army in the world. In addition, he relates to ancient Jewish history and reminds his listeners of the myth of the Jews as the "chosen people"—a unique nation. In this way, he satisfies the needs of his audience for identity and belonging.

Another societal belief receiving numerous references in Netanyahu's speeches through the years relates to the theme of *peace*. Interestingly, in the vast majority of his speeches, Netanyahu has referred to peace as an abstract and utopian wish, exactly as this theme is defined in the ethos of conflict. He depicts Israeli Jews as peace-loving people, who reluctantly have had to take part in a violent conflict due to circumstances beyond their control.

Together with the expression that Israel is *"stretching out a hand to reach peace,"* Netanyahu supports the Greater Israel movement and believes that the occupied territories belong solely to the Jewish nation and that the settlements are a realization of the right of the Jewish people to settle in their homeland. These views show that, under his leadership there is no possibility to advance meaningful peace-making. In his book, *A Durable Peace*, published in English in 2000, he writes that the *"idea that the Palestinians are a separate nation, entitled to self-determination, is borrowed directly from the Nazis."*[259] The research indicates that, nevertheless, Netanyahu has slightly changed his political positions through the years *vis-à-vis* the creation of a Palestinian state and the return of occupied land. This change was expressed in the famous Bar Ilan speech in 2009, when he announced for the first time that he recognized and supported the idea of "two states for two peoples." This was the first time the prime minister had stated his agreement to a land division as a general principle, without detailing the division. However, in the next election campaign in 2015, just before

Election Day, Netanyahu promised his supporters: "*Under the conditions that they demand at present, a Palestinian state is out of the question [...] The speech at Bar Ilan is not invalid, but the Palestinians have simply extracted its content. They have chosen conflict instead of negotiations*[260]... *Anyone who is going to create a Palestinian state, is giving territory to extremist Islam....*" When he was asked: *If you are elected prime minister, a Palestinian state will not come into existence?* he replied, "*Yes, that is true.*"[261] Since 2017, Netanyahu publicly and openly does not obligate himself to the two-state solution and has raised the possibility of a "Palestinian state minus." In addition, Netanyahu has promised not to dismantle any settlement in a solution to the conflict (both in 2009 and in 2019), and during his term of office, there was a return to building outposts without the confirmation of the government and in clear opposition to Israeli law. In the two election campaigns of 2019 and the one in 2020, ideas were raised about annexation, at least in area C, and particularly, in the Jordan Valley. Proposals have also come up about expanding the settlements, non-removal of settlements (even isolated ones), building bypass roads, legalization of illegal outposts, and even Jewish building on private Palestinian property. Leading up to 1 July 2020, Netanyahu promised to annex a part of the West Bank that had been intended for Israel in the Trump peace plan. But eventually this move was canceled due to international pressure and ultimately, the terms of the peace agreement with the United Arab Emirates ensured that Israel would not take this step.

In summary, it can be said that Israeli Prime Minister Binyamin Netanyahu is a pragmatic ideologue. He is an ideologue since he has a firm well-organized plan for the realities he desires to achieve for the Jewish people in the land of Israel. He has not changed his basic outlook for decades, despite the dramatic changes that have taken place in the area, in the world and in the local context of the State of Israel. He is pragmatic because he knows how to moderate his views in response to outside pressure (such as the pressure from U.S. President Barak Obama) or internal constraints (such as the wish to win the elections in 1996), and to accept the Oslo Accords or the idea of two states. However, each time that the pressure recedes or disappears, he immediately returns to his original opinions. His personality and his ideological outlook sharpen the disagreements characterizing the Israeli-Palestinian conflict, and through the years, he has set conditions that reinforce the conflict or even inflame it. In his political conduct, he does not indicate readiness to carry out significant concessions or to advance a political process with the Palestinians. He objects completely to the establishment of Palestinian state and to relinquishing full control of East Jerusalem. He encourages Jewish settlement in the entire West Bank, even the illegal outposts, that make the two-state solution almost impossible. He supports annexation of large parts of the West Bank and refuses to negotiate with the Palestinian leadership. He advocates "peace for peace" instead of "peace for land," believing that it is possible to build relationships with Arab states without solving Israeli-Palestinian conflict. Indeed, four Arab states—UAE, Bahrein, Sudan, and Morocco—have "come out of the closet" after having, for years, had an informal relationship with Israel, and they formalized this relationship by signing a peace agreement with Israel.

As an ideological leader, he is inaccessible to information contrary to his beliefs, and rejects appraisals that do not suit his opinions. No small number of security figures in the present and past have expressed different assessments that are antitheses to his views, but as Israeli prime minister, he gathered around himself people whose worldviews and opinions were very similar to his own and he seeks advice only from them. Those among his advisors or other members of the Likud who have dared to express positions that are incompatible with his own, or Likud politicians who are perceived as a threat to his status, have found themselves on the outside (for example, Dan Meridor, Gideon Saar, or Limor Livnat), and instead he has preferred individuals whose main characteristic is absolute loyalty. He began to appoint only people who were dependent on him as ministers and other office holders, so that they would be unequivocally loyal to him. The appointees were usually sent out to the media with supporting and justifying arguments for Netanyahu statements, policies and acts. Their role was to glorify him and cultivate worship as well as implementing policies and performing acts to secure his role as a prime minister. Thus, in Netanyahu's close circle, group thinking became the order of the day in expressions of conformism and deference by the members of the group, while accepting decisions in accord with the expectations of the leader. Even when indictments were issued against Netanyahu, all of the Likud ministers and almost all of the party's Knesset members remained loyal to their leader and have continued to defend him.

In addition, during 2018-2020, he increased his mudslinging of law enforcement institutions to the point of accusing them of conducting a putsch against him. This was how he chose to defend himself from the charges and indictments brought against him by the police and prosecutors. He has also excoriated the media which, in his opinion, have been part of the plot to bring him down. On the day his trial opened, 23 May 2020, while the leadership of the Likud crowded around him, he stated: *"They are trying to bring me down, along with all of the rightwing camp. For more than a decade the left has not succeeded in doing it at the polls, so in recent years they've found a new method. People in the police and in the state attorney's office have gotten together with the leftist newspapers. I call them: 'Just not Bibi.' They've tacked together imaginary criminal files against me."*[262]

He expanded his mudslinging when demonstrations broke out against his continued rule in the wake of the charges against him and his persistent harm to democracy. He called the demonstrators, who had come from every stratum of the nation, *"leftist anarchists who want to destroy democracy."*

One of the most important characteristics of Netanyahu's term as prime minister is his authoritarian style of leadership that moved the Israeli regime away from democracy and towards authoritarianism. He did not hesitate to cross the red lines of democratic rules and principles by using populist tactics in attacking mass media, the legal system, the police, and the state prosecutors, and by lying to the public and inciting against the Arab minority when it served his interests. At the same time, he initiated the authoritarian steps of limiting the functioning of the legislative branch, and even violating Israeli laws and breaking agreements. In line with his authoritarian leadership pattern, he turned against legal opposition coming from the left and branded them as a delegitimizing element in the political system. He represented the opposition not only as unable to govern Israel, but even as endangering the existence of Israel, and presented himself as super leader. As the possibility of losing office increased, Netanyahu became ready to use all of the tactics he could to stay in his office Returning to office as head of an extreme collation may break the previous red lines that prevented him to move to the authoritarian end of leadership.

This has had an enormous effect on his supporters who accept what he says as reflecting Israeli realities. Accordingly, his supporters have used both acceptable and unacceptable means to pressure politicians and judges, including threats on their lives. This shows that Binyamin Netanyahu is willing to destroy the basis of Israel democracy. He presents erroneous and false ideas about the function of democracy and its institutions and harms his supporters' faith in democratic processes, especially *vis-à-vis* the legal system. For example, he stated on December 29, 2019, that *immunity* (for the prime minister) *is the cornerstone of democracy*. In this way, a populistic, ego-centered, and oversimplified worldview has been created which has pushed Israel towards an authoritarian regime. Thus, **Binyamin Netanyahu's conduct raises three distinct characterizations: The first refers to a leader who has lost inhibitions and red lines in leading the nation, and in his readiness to ignore laws and norms of the basic foundations of democracy; the second refers to members of the leader's close circle (ministers, Knesset members, and other leaders) who certainly (or at least some of them) have perceived of the damage done by their leader to a state which was meant to function as a well-managed democracy. Nevertheless, they still give unrestrained support to his methods and all his actions; and the third is the unconditional support of his political base, who are willing to accept his conduct without objection.**

These characterizations are not unique. They could be seen in the past in different countries and they can be seen in the present as well, throughout the world, and even in the United States during the leadership of ex-President Trump. But the point that I would like to make is that states involved in protracted and bloody conflict often descend into authoritarianism with an authoritarian leader. Particular contexts that limit democratic principles, i.e., free flow of information in order to maintain hegemonic, conflict-supporting narratives, necessarily increases authoritarianism. This can be observed in India, Pakistan, Turkey and Russia, Rwanda and Sri Lanka, as well as in Israel. However, it is also possible to raise serious questions about the nature of human beings and their ability to function in a democratic regime which, by its very essence, demands openness, upholding the law and thinking critically. **Based on their research, two well-known political scientists in the United States, Charles Taber and Milton Lodge, have concluded that *homo politicus*, the voting citizen, does not have the cognitive abilities or motivations to fulfill the demands for rational behavior in a democratic regime.**[263] **Human beings are absorbed in narratives that they learn and that are maintained by their leaders and agents of socialization which construct their world views.**

CHAPTER 7

Conflict Supporting Narratives

It is time to more extensively explore the conflict supporting narratives: how they are constructed and maintained. This chapter fulfills this role.

In any case, it should be understood that conflict supporting narratives are not created ex nihilo. They are transmitted by leaders, the media, textbooks, and other transmitting agents to the general public and are internalized and enrooted. Their direction is determined even by the way they are created. Thus, I will now go into detail regarding these methods.

METHODS TO CREATE CONFLICT SUPPORTING NARRATIVES

How, then, is a worldview constructed that reinforces a hegemonic narrative in a variety of channels? The following are some of the main methods being used on a daily basis. The provided examples are from a recent period. In time, they have become second nature in media reports, and they are almost completely concealed from the eyes of the average media consumer.[264]

Relying on Supportive Sources

Reports in which conflict supporting narratives are transmitted are constructed on the basis of sources—speeches, reports, testimony, documentation, discussion, lectures, and interviews—that from the outset, are supportive of the central themes of the conflict. For example, most of the media channels in Israel rely on formal Israeli sources when security-related events occur. These, in all cases, relay the government narrative, with no serious attempt to seek information that could illuminate the events in another way. Media researcher Dan Caspi, calls these bodies "guardians of the walls," that is, those who supervise the flow of information regarding the Israeli-Arab conflict.[265]

The continuous and systematic attempts to construct Israeli citizens' consciousness have continued since the establishment of the state. The government and the security forces try not only to hide any information about wrong and immoral actions of the governmental and military systems, but also to actively construct the worldview of the citizens in line with what they think the citizens should know. This is done by various methods and through different agents, such as governmental offices, the army or security agencies and a range of organizations—all in order to impart information that supports the hegemonic narratives propagated by the government and security forces, and block information that contradicts these narratives.

Some time ago, an Information Ministry was established, and later, a Ministry for Strategic Affairs, which was budgeted hundreds of millions of shekels to fight against organizations that have expressed criticism towards the state of Israel. In 2018, the "Consciousness Department" was established within the Operations Branch of the General Command of the army, in order to deal with the question of Israel's international legitimacy as well as legal aspects of army activity. It operates in conjunction with foreign armies, diplomats, foreign media and international public opinion. There have also been many campaigns, official and unofficial, against "subversive" bodies that object actively to the occupation and its implications. In their attempt to fight against the spread of alternative narratives that the establishment wishes to hide, almost all of the authorities that have been mentioned above have activated more or less permanent systems of action. As one minor recent example, in August 2021, it was revealed that the Israeli Army has been employing the operator of a popular Telegram news channel as a consultant for psychological operations on social media. The Telegram news channel has become one of the most influential Hebrew-language channels on Arab affairs and security issues in general. The channel supplies information provided by the army—and at the same time insists that it does not come from any military source. The channel also frequently attacks prominent Israeli journalists who criticize the IDF's policies, sometimes even trying to undermine their credibility and question their professionalism.[266] In January 2022, the new government decided to invest through foreign ministry about 64 million dollars for three years to strengthen positive perception of the country and combat delegitimization discourses on social networks and in global media.[267]

In order to diagnose the way relying on certain materials supports the hegemonic narrative in Israel, we can easily compare Wikipedia entries touching upon the Israeli-Arab conflict in Hebrew to those in English. The difference is tremendous. Wikipedia entries in Hebrew generally rely upon Israeli sources and ignore an abundance of other information, thus presenting a selective, erroneous and distorted picture of conflict topics.

In comparison, Wikipedia entries in English present many of these subjects in detail, relying on other sources, including those which are critical to Israeli policies and actions. In addition, during violent events and wars, Israeli TV channels and radio stations customarily bring reserve Israeli generals and security experts as commentators, who mostly agree with the hawkish frame corresponding with narratives supporting the conflict. Recently appeared journalists whose main task is to defend Netanyahu based on information supplied by him.

Magnification of Supportive Information

In general, events concerning the conflict which are in line with the conflict supporting narrative gain greater and more salient coverage. For example, from time to time, one of the media outlets brings up the doctoral dissertation written by the Chairperson of the Palestinian Authority, Mahmoud Abbas, in 1982, dealing with the links between Zionism and the Nazi regime, leaving the impression that the Palestinian Authority is infected by anti-Semitism. In contrast, Abbas's statement some 30 years later, in 2012, that he would return only to the city where he was born, Tsfat, as a tourist—meaning that he has actively given up the right of return—has almost never been mentioned in relevant discussions. In addition, any information about harm sustained by Jews in terror attacks, violent encounters, or wars is given prominence for a long period in all media channels through repeated individual reports. At the same time, reports about the harmful intentions of Palestinians are augmented and emphasized.

Marginalization of the Importance of Contradictory Information

Agents of conflict supporting narratives grant diminished importance to information that contradicts their themes, particularly by emphasizing its lack of importance, avoiding its discussion or locating it in peripheral places in the report. For example, reports of harm done to Palestinians in the West Bank receive little coverage in the Israeli media. In 2018, the Israeli army killed 290 Palestinians: 254 in the Gaza Strip, including two women and 47 under 18 years of age. B'tselem, the Israeli Center for Human Rights in the Occupied Territories, investigated and found that 149 of those killed had not taken part in any hostile activities and only 90 had clearly participated in hostile acts. In that year, injuries to Palestinians by settlers also increased. There were 265 cases during which Palestinians were killed or injured or suffered harm to their possessions or property

(7,900 olive trees had been cut down and five vehicles had been destroyed) by settlers—an increase of 60% in comparison to 2017. In addition, 459 structures had been destroyed or taken over, leaving hundreds of Palestinians, including women and children, homeless. This enormous number did not evoke public discussion in Israeli society due to the way the victims were described (or not described). Israel's legislative and administrative regime in the West Bank, coupled with its institutional unwillingness to prosecute offending settlers, shields settlers from the consequences set out in law and has allowed such violence against the Palestinian civilian population to continue and intensify. Settlers involved in the planning and perpetration of such acts have remained largely immune from the enforcement of the law.[268]

The daily newspaper *Haaretz* encountered vicious attacks for daring to publish, on the front page, photos of 67 children killed by Israelis in the 2021 war in Gaza, copied from *The New York Times*, on May 27, 2021. All the other major sources of mass communication would avoid such a graphic presentation. We may only imagine what would have happened if dozens of Israeli Jewish children had been harmed.

Falsification of Information

Conflict supporting narratives may also include information that does not contain even a grain of truth. At the 37th Zionist Congress, in October 2015, when relating to the famous meeting in November 1941 between the Mufti Haj Amin al-Husseini and Adolf Hitler, Prime Minister Netanyahu stated: "*Hitler did not want to destroy the Jews at the time; he just wanted to exile them ... Haj Amin al-Husseini came to Hitler and told him, "If you exile them, they will all come here ... Hitler asked him, "So what should I do with them? The mufti answered, "Burn them.*"[269] In his speech, Netanyahu seemed to have presented new details about that historic meeting, but this information has never been confirmed by any historian or Holocaust researcher. In other words, this was a falsification of the historical facts in order to manipulatively connect the memory of the Holocaust to Palestinian terror, and to present the image of the Palestinians as a real existential threat to Israel from time immemorial. This did not prevent the important media outlets from quoting Netanyahu's words in detail, without giving any appropriate historical context. Only later did criticism appear about this falsification of history.

Omission of Contradictory Information

In contrast to the previous methods cited, in which the information is erroneous or distorted, in this case, there is total omission of information—especially when referring to evidence that presents the moral image of Israel or the justness of its goals in a negative light. Since the 1980s, new information published through academic research, documentary films, and investigating journalism has revealed an almost completely new picture of reality regarding the events of the conflict. But this information does not change the views of the great majority of citizens who prefer to adhere to the hegemonic narrative provided by the government. Take, for example, one recent omission during the escalation that took place in September 2015 *vis-à-vis* the violent events at the Temple Mount compound. The Israeli leadership adopted a propaganda line that argued that the violence broke out because of planned incitement by Palestinian Authority's Chairman Abbas and others in the Palestinian leadership. However, the contribution of the Israelis involved in escalating the climate of violence was completely ignored in the dominant narrative. Official versions did not mention several factors to the public, including the arrival of Agriculture Minister Uri Ariel from the religious Zionist party at Temple Mount in a demonstration of confrontation and defiance, as well as demands that suddenly appeared one fine day to expand the rights of Jews for religious practice at the Temple Mount compound and support for these demands by senior ministers. In addition, there was a surprising change in the regulations for Muslim prayer and an Israeli decision to freeze the transfer of a half billion shekels of tax revenues from the Palestinian Authority in reaction to Abbas's decision to join the Rome Statute and the International Court in The Hague, and of course, the Palestinian despair at the absence of any political horizon.

In general, in the Israeli media, there is a clear tendency to present Palestinian violence as arbitrary and without reason, expressing a violent character and evil intensions (mostly inborn), while Israeli violence is presented as almost always focused, as it is meant to defend a civilian population which has been harmed. During the 1936 Arab revolt and beyond, the military Zionist group, Irgun, carried out dozens terror attacks against Palestinians in which were killed at least 250 innocent men, women and children. These practices are omitted from school textbooks, while Arabs attacks appear prominently in them.

Changing Language

The analysis of this method is based on the assumption that the language of a text and its choice of words affect the readers' perception of the reality it describes. As early as 1987, the author, David Grossman, recognized this in the context of the conflict in his book, *The Yellow Wind*. He examined expressions generally used by the Israeli media when describing the reality of the conflict. For example, the expression, "met his death" (an exact translation of the Hebrew), was almost always used referring to Palestinian youth who have been killed, or "disrupting order" (again, a literal translation of the Hebrew), always used when describing Palestinian protests, and Grossman coined the term "a laundry list of words." Since then, many more Hebrew expressions have been "laundered" in order to normalize the conflict, such as "moderate physical pressure" (torture), "closure" (blockade), a "targeted strike" (a targeted killing or assassination) or "a ticking bomb" (a person planning an immediate terror attack), and more and more.[270] Even more important, in recent years, rightwing leaders and their supporters have also succeeded in removing a series of expressions and concepts from the realm of legitimate discourse, including "occupation," "peace," "leftwing," or "human rights struggle," which have all become marks of non-belonging to the Jewish community in Israel.

Framing

A unique achievement of the right in the battle to construct reality is the automatic framing of violent acts on both sides. Every act by Palestinians expressing opposition to the occupation is immediately labeled "an act of terror." Even when it is done in the realm of diplomacy, it is tagged "political terror" and it is related to as such. Needless to say, referring to all of these acts as "terror" —ranging from non-violent assemblies, and economic protests to throwing stones and other expressions of spontaneous opposition—is not in line with the accepted definition of terror in research literature and international institutions. But that is only one side of the coin. The second side is the reference to all acts of collective punishment such as destroying homes, blockading a city or wholesale harm to civilians, as "restoring order" or "preventing terror," while according to all accepted definitions in international law and academic discourse, these are, for all intents and purposes, acts of terror. An additional example of framing is the attempt to prove that the West Bank is Jewish. This is expressed not only in the permanent use of the term, Judea and Samaria, but also in the use of Hebrew names for settlement sites, historical locations, and tourist and geographical spots.[271]

The use made of the two methods relating to discourse that have been described above—changing language and framing—is even sharpened when comparing between the language used at present, in the twenty-first century, to report on the conflict or its framing, and descriptions of violent protest, including terror in the past, used against the British and the Arabs during the British Mandate at the beginning and middle of the twentieth century. Jews who carried out acts of terror, such as throwing hand grenades into crowded Arab markets, killing politicians (Lord Moyne, who was the British Minister of State for the Middle East, and later, Swedish Count Bernadotte, who was mediating between Israel and its neighbors), murdering British soldiers or harming the Arab village population—were considered "freedom fighters" in the newspapers of the period, and even today, they are related to with titles that glorify them. It has already been said by others that terrorists can become very respected statesmen with the passage of time. The history of the state of Israel can also claim to recognize some of these people with respect.

The attempt to create public consciousness in Israel does not only focus on information supporting the hegemonic narratives supplied by the government, as described, but also continues by obstructing information opposing this narrative.[272]

THE STRUGGLE AGAINST ALTERNATIVE NARRATIVES

Together with everything that has been said above about establishing the rightwing extremism, it must be noted that, during those years, there were also alternative narratives. Beyond the fact that they supported different programs for an end to the conflict, including far-reaching compromises, they also presented the Palestinians and their leaders—at least on the West Bank—as partners for a peace process, as human beings and as victims of the conflict. These narratives were expressed by individuals, mostly from academia and from cultural life, working with human rights organizations, civil society organizations, research institutes, and opposition political organizations.

And yes, this is a time when the government of Israel, its institutions and much of its media, private as well as public, have made every attempt to hide the injustice, the harm to human rights, and the violations of international law, and even of Israeli law. But simultaneously, different people and various organizations, primarily from the leftwing (such as Breaking the Silence, B'Tselem, Checkpoint Watch, Yesh Din–Volunteers for Civil Rights, Gisha, Peace Now, HaMoked: Center for the Defense of the Individual, The Public Committee against Torture, Doctors for Human Rights, and the Association for Civil Rights in Israel), have transmitted information that has also presented the ugly immoral face of Israeli society and the state. This, of course, has had ramifications. State authorities, the army, official and unofficial institutions, as well as various organizations, and even individuals have more and more frequently begun to try to block alternative information, and to fight against those who distribute it. **The great majority of the Jewish public, as well as other publics throughout the world, cannot bear accusations of unjust deeds that have been done by their national compatriots. These accusations have significance *vis-à-vis* the public welfare and personal and collective identities.**

In Israel several of the following methods are used to block alternative information.

Delegitimization of Counter Information and/or of its Source(s)

This method includes all actions aimed at presenting information indicating that alternate narratives were unreliable, and alternatively, to undermine the legitimacy of the source of information and to present it as given by someone who wanted to harm the interests of society and the state. The system is widely used in Israel by state institutions, by the army, by political parties and even by some of the media. Each of these bodies—and sometimes all of them together—use silencing and delegitimizing methods directed at people and organizations which have undertaken to bring to light actions that negate human rights or are immoral or illegal, taking place in the occupied territories. The leadership and their supporters firmly oppose the work of these organizations and even present it as "treason."

Delegitimization labels have expanded to include the concept of "leftism" which is used by the rightwing and centrist leaders to neutralize sources of information that contradict the hegemonic narrative supporting the conflict. The chair of the Yisrael Beitenu party, Avigdor Lieberman, stated in this context, that *"these are organizations that are collaborators with terror, and their only aim is to weaken the Israeli army and its determination to defend Israeli citizens.*"[273] In October 2014, then Prime Minister Benjamin Netanyahu termed the activity of the Peace Now movement *"national ir-responsibility"* and accused the organization of publicizing the government approval to build a neighborhood on Givat Hamatos, in the West Bank, in order to sabotage his meeting with U.S. President Barack Obama.[274] And when this is the climate, it is no wonder that a survey taken by the Israel Democracy Institute in 2017 found that about 60% of the Jews in Israel greatly agree or relatively agree with the determination that human rights organizations, like the Association for Civil Rights in Israel and B'tselem, cause harm to the state.[275]

For years, any information that criticizes the policies of the State of Israel, especially from abroad, by Jews and even by Israelis, has been termed "antisemitism." Indeed, a definition of anti-Semitism by the International Holocaust Remembrance Alliance (IHRA) in 2016 was adopted by many states.[276] But it was unclear and widely open to different interpretations. The IHRA definition includes eleven "examples" of anti Semitism, seven of which focus on the State of Israel. This caused confusion and generated controversy, with accusation that it allows Israel to blame critiques of wrongdoings by Israel as anti-Semitism. As a result, the Jerusalem Declaration on Antisemitism was prepared and published by internationally renowned scholars who attempted to resolve this problem by offering a working definition that successfully solved the objections raised.[277]

The accusation of being anti-Semitic greatly frightens non-Jews, as the Holocaust was fed by ant-Semitism, and no one wants to be associated with the Holocaust. : For example, in October 2022, even Prime Minister Yair Lapid slammed a United Nations report accusing Israel of violating international law as being *"written by antisemites"*. So, people and organizations are afraid to be called anti-Semitic, while in various countries, criticism of Israeli government policies has even received official legislative classification as a type of anti-Semitism. Thus, with the support of the government of Israel, possibilities for providing critical information about immoral conduct on the part of Israel and even about acts which are in opposition to international law, are narrowed. This is particularly striking in Germany, where the memory of the Holocaust still resonates, and Germans fear being labelled anti-Semitic for any criticism of the Israeli government.

During the demonstrations in 2020, Binyamin Netanyahu attempted to slander the many demonstrators who were lawfully demonstrating opposite his home in Jerusalem, in Tel Aviv, in Caesarea, and at bridges and intersections throughout the country, demanding his resignation. He and his supporters argued that the demonstrators are radical leftists, anarchists, and that they are harming democracy, are violent, and that they desire to harm him and his family and are sowing destruction. This delegitimization, of course, is intended to disparage them, especially in the eyes of his supporters.

Monitoring and Control

This mechanism relates to the permanent tracking system conducted by government and non-government institutions to access information disseminated in the public space—schools, reports of non-government organizations, the media and research studies—with the aim of identifying statements contradicting the conflict supporting narrative—which leads to "condemnation" of those who are responsible. As we detailed earlier in the chapter, during the 2000s, a number of non-governmental organizations have been established to carry out this identification and the denunciation of these "subversive" organizations in academia, while in 2019, it became clear that Gilad Erdan, in his capacity as Minister of Internal Security, acted to establish a database of Israelis involved in the boycott movement BDS or those only supporting it, along with Israelis supporting a boycott of products coming from settlements in the occupied territories. In 2022 it was revealed that the Shin Bet (General Security Service) has long been tracking a database collected from the journalists' cellphones to monitor their activity[278].

Punishment

This system is also used to prevent monetary remunerations to institutions expressing narratives contradicting the hegemonic one and even sometimes, to impose punishment. In 2011, the Knesset enacted the Nakba Law, according to which, a body receiving a budget from the state will be economically sanctioned if it has approved any financial expenditure on a message that would negate the existence of the State of Israel as a Jewish democratic state, or present Independence Day or the day the state was established as a day of mourning, or participate in an act of destruction or physical debasement, harming the honor afforded to the state flag or state symbol. This wording was ultimately intended to prevent funding for events marking Nakba Day in the Arab sector. Its goal is to block any mention of the Palestinian Nakba (catastrophe in Arabic) that took place in 1948, when about 700,000 Palestinians were uprooted and about 450 localities were destroyed.

In 2018, in a similar fashion, the attorney general, Avichai Mandelblit, approved the passage of the "Culture Loyalty Law," advanced by then-Culture Minister Miri Regev. The law mandates a change in the criteria required for a Ministry of Culture grant to support institutions, and the negation of public grants to those which have broken the following laws: rejection of the existence of the State of Israel as a Jewish democratic state; incitement to racism, violence, or terror; support for armed struggle or an act of terror by an enemy state; terming Independence Day or the day the state was established as a day of mourning; or an act of destruction or physical debasement of the Israeli flag or state symbol. The singularity of this law lies in the fact that, for the first time, it ties artistic content to monetary support granted to creators and state cultural institutions. For example, former Minister of Culture Miri Regev froze funding to the al-Midan Theater after they produced the play, *Parallel Time*, which was then taken out of the "culture basket" of the Ministry of Education. She conditioned funding for the Elmina Theater on its manager, the actor Norman Issa, appearing in the Jordan Valley.[279]

This total war has taken place in particular against the organization Breaking the Silence, which has collected soldiers' testimonies about immoral acts that they have carried out during their army service. This testimony strikes at the heart of the national and army narrative which advances the view that the IDF is "the most moral army in the world." The activities of Breaking the Silence are considered as undermining the army which defends and protects the Israeli nation. In addition, the wider public relates to soldiers as "the sons of everyone" and cannot bear to hear reports that they are committing immoral acts. It is no wonder, then, that the political elite has completely mobilized against this organization, using rhetoric presenting it as treasonous, and they have prohibited its entry into schools and public institutions. They have even legislated to limit the organization's activity.[280]

Another type of punishment—less ceremonial, more practical—was imposed by the army Coordinator of Activities in the occupied territories. It has recently begun to demand that leftist organizations conducting meetings between Israelis and Palestinians inform the office of their activities, the sources of their funding, their work and media activities, as a condition for receiving approval for Palestinians' entry to Israel. As this demand, in any case, is an addition to the security check conducted by the General Security Services, it can only be concluded that it is just meant to make things more difficult for leftwing organizations in their attempt to hold meetings between Israelis and Palestinians. In addition, in the past two years, the army has prevented the Palestinians from reaching the alternative Memorial Day ceremony held in Tel Aviv, after many years of Palestinian participation.

The GSS itself has also not hesitated to get involved. After Netanyahu's victory in the 2015 elections, it became customary to informally delay Israeli citizens and foreigners when entering the country, asking them about their political opinions and possible links between them and human rights organizations. This approach, adopted towards people known for their (lawful) activities against government policies, arouses the suspicion that the government has decided on a policy of fear and terrorization against opposition organizations.

It should be noted that the Israeli government rewards people and organizations who, by word or deed, support the hegemonic narrative disseminated by the establishment. For example, the ex-Culture Minister determined that cultural institutions which appear at settlements in the occupied territories will receive an extra incentive of ten percent of additional financial support, and those which refuse to appear in the territories will have their support reduced by a third.[281] This practice was eventually abolished by the Supreme Court. In addition, in 2017, it was decided to award the important Israel Prize for life accomplishments to David Be'eri, the chairperson of Elad, an organization dedicated to establishing a Jewish presence in the Palestinian village of Silwan by building The City of David. The Judaization of the village has often been accomplished by violent means including land expulsion and deeds which fly in the face of international law, frequently with the help of Israeli authorities.

Censorship

The censorship apparatus to prevent information which might harm the hegemonic narrative is complex. "Censorship in the newspapers and media," better known by its former term, "military censorship," operates in Israel by virtue of a regulation in the Defense Emergency Regulations enacted by the British Mandate in 1945. Regulation 87 determines that the censor has the power to prohibit the publication of material which, in his/her opinion, could harm "the security of Israel or the wellbeing of the public or public order." Regulation 97 determines that the censor can demand that any person submit any material for his/her examination, before its publication. So the Israel censor often prevents the publication of various materials—especially material which might present public figures in a negative light, sometimes even when there are no security ramifications. For example, in 2002, the censor ruled against allowing the screening of the film Jenin Jenin, but the Supreme Court invalidated this decision. In 2017, Israel closed down the office of *Al Jazeera* following an internal Arab crisis with Qatar, which actually had no connection to Israel. In addition to the use of censorship, it should be remembered that Israeli society conducts widespread self-censorship regarding moral wrongdoings in wars, violent encounters, or even about routines in occupied territories. People and institutions themselves censor relevant information about the conflict for a variety of reasons, including the desire not to disseminate information that might affect the image of the State of Israel, even if there is no requirement to do so.[282]

Limiting Access to Archives

Imposing closure on archival documents is a method of implementing censorship. The objective is to prevent exposure of sensitive documents, usually those which might include information contradicting the conflict supporting narrative. Israel insists on censoring war crimes carried out by military forces. For example, Israel makes every effort to hide the list of historical documents revealing suspicions that Haganah soldiers committed murder, torture, theft, and looting during the War of Independence.[283] The report by Akevot Institute for Israeli-Palestinian Conflict Research stated: "*The continued censorship is not meant to protect the state's external interest, but is directed internally … The concealment does not only make it difficult for historians; it has a concrete influence on the internal Israeli academic, public and political debate in our times. It is intended to preserve a neutered and distorted state narrative about the foundations of the Israeli-Palestinian conflict, and from there—it has a concrete and decisive interest to maintain it, and on the horizon to end it.*"

In 2010, the confidentiality law on many archival documents was even extended by law for another 20 years, and now totals up to 70 years.[284]

Materials from the Shin Bet security service and Mossad are inaccessible for 90 years from the date of their creation. In addition, in February 2016, the state archives decided to close its study room, making it very difficult for researchers to get to the material they are requesting to see. At present, they must order material by internet and wait for weeks or even months to be able to scan it, to obtain approval from the military censor and to put it up on a website.[285]

At the beginning of 2018, in a report that he prepared, Israeli Chief State Archivist Yaacov Lozowick sharply criticized the conduct of the state which had extended confidentiality to 50 years and in certain cases, also used censorship to hide failures of the past, including war crimes and injuries to Arab citizens. The excuse used was "safeguarding the security of the state."[286] At the beginning of 2019, Prime Minister Binyamin Netanyahu increased confidentiality on General Security Service and Mossad intelligence organization documents for twenty additional years (for a total 90 years) in contradiction to the opinion of the Supreme Archive Council.

In summary, these methods, which have long become established, have led (along with other factors) to the decline of Israel on the scale of freedom of the press, conducted by the Reporters without Borders organization, falling from 46th place in 2008 to 96th place in 2009. In 2013, Israel had fallen to the most negative classification on this measure; it was ranked 112 out of the 179 countries measured. On the 2016 scale, it was ranked 101, while among the examples of harm to freedom of expression in Israel cited by this organization were the refusal of the Broadcasting Authority to broadcast a segment issued by human rights organization, B'tselem, which included the names of Palestinian children who had been killed in the Protective Edge operation in Gaza, as well as an event in which an Israeli army force fired in the direction of Palestinian journalists in the West Bank. In the latest ranking, just as this is being written in 2021, Israel appeared in 86th place, after Albania, Mongolia, and Malawi, out of 180 countries evaluated each year.[287]

SUMMARY: A NEW REALITY

Using all the strategies mentioned above, the Israeli rightwing, with views determined by the settlers and their supporters, has understood that in order to prevent the division of the country and an end

to the occupation, they have had to reconstruct the Israeli state, revising its statehood and identity and especially building a new consciousness among Jewish society members. My central claim is that they have succeeded! Success has come due to the domination by the rightwing in the political space and in the Israeli state apparatus, and the enormous influence that the rightwing has gained over all facets of Israeli life. In addition, from the standpoint of the Jewish faith, religious Zionism, with the help of other forces, has succeeded in inculcating and expanding the traditional-religious element into Israeli nationalism (Zionism), and a tight link has been established between the rightwing and religion, from the ultra-orthodox to the traditional. Moreover, it has managed to create an organizational system through which it affects public opinion, and in parallel, has achieved dominant access to the public and political structure.

On this journey, religious Zionism, which developed into its present format starting from the end of the 1960s and the beginning of the 1970s, has designed its ideology around the Greater Land of Israel movement. It has been the locomotive, which, with the help of its supporters, began to draw Israeli society as a whole towards the place it occupies today. This form of Zionism has been enormously successful and has carried out a dramatic change in the minds of millions of Jews, both in Israel and in the diaspora. Today, the views of the rightwing about Israel, the physical land itself, its existential threats, the settlements, the conflict, the occupation, the Palestinians, the annexation, anti-Semitism, patriotism or virulent nationalism, anti-Jewish racism, the leftwing, the minority of Arab citizens of Israel, and even democracy and human rights—constitute the bread and butter of the supporters of religious Zionist political parties, the ultra-orthodox, the Likud, Yisrael Beitenu, and even some supporters of the Blue-White party. A great majority of the public, despite its heterogeneity in socio-economic status, country of origin, and even including people with a great number of disagreements about various social, economic and religious subjects, have formulated a comprehensive consensual worldview (consciousness) regarding subjects that are still at the focus of Israeli Jewish life and that determine Israeli voting decisions. These views to a great extent reflect the opinions of Binyamin Netanyahu who, if he was not involved in criminal charges, would have received massive support from the rightwing and religious pop-

ulation and would be able to govern the state for many years to come on the basis of his security-political-agenda.

Even during the political-health-economic crisis of summer and fall 2020, the extreme right, under the leadership of Naftali Bennett has been gaining very significant support as an alternative to the Likud and indeed in the very strange coalition resulting from the last elections, he was nominated to be a prime minister. As prime minister, before meeting US President Biden at the end of August 2021, in an interview for *The New York Times*, he said that he would expand West Bank settlements, that he objects to the creation of a Palestinian state, and ruled out reaching a peace agreement with the Palestinians during this term.[288] In fact, he simply reiterated the views of the right that dominate Israeli politics, despite the existence of the broad coalition at present. The Jewish left is a negligible minority and the center is also a minority. Considering the new reality for Arab citizens of the state, with the participation of one Arab party in the coalition, it is not clear whether the new situation will last and what kind of effect it will have on the Israeli politics.

It is important to point out, as will presently be detailed, that these views express the different value systems characterizing rightists in contrast with leftists. Jonathan Haidt, an American social-psychologist, along with his colleagues, has supplied an important theory explaining the difference between rightists and leftists.[289] Their theory of moral foundations has received research validation for its proposals according to which, human beings have five different moral foundations used to evaluate and judge actions, people and events. These are: 1. Basic caring for the "other" in general; 2. Caring about unfairness, inequality and universal justice; 3. Focusing on obligations to the in-group, loyalty to it, and readiness to sacrifice, with rejection of betrayal; 4. Respect for social order, authority and hierarchical relations, including obedience; 5. The desire to avoid physical and spiritual corruption and the aspiration to rectitude and supervision over intentions. In Haidt's opinion, people of the liberal left are characterized primarily by moral values that stress basic consideration of the other, and caring about unfairness and justice, and on the other hand, they are less motivated by obligation to their in-group and authority. In contrast, conservative rightists are characterized by concern for their ingroup and its security, their identity and loyalty to it, as well as their response to authority. They are less open in general, and also less sensitive to general unfairness and injustice. These differences clearly indicate the dissimilar emphases in the characters of rightists and leftists internationally and including Jewish society in Israel.

If we return to an analysis of society, it becomes clear that the public, the media, the educational system, and even the Israeli army have, in recent years, become institutions employed by the rightwing to frame the Israeli mainstream. They have simultaneously delegitimized the leftwing who have proposed an alternative ethos to the conflict, in order to exclude it from the legitimate Jewish community and from public discourse. To that end, the rightwing have instituted a continual process of mudslinging, which, inter alia, even expresses doubt about the Jewish identity of the left. There is no question that this campaign has succeeded. People, leaders, organizations and political movements from the center and left have begun to take precautions in order not to be considered "leftists," which has become a mark of disgrace, now identified with disloyalty, treason, hatred of Israel, rejection of Judaism, loving Arabs and more. Another tactic has been attaching the concept of "left" with "extremism" so that all leftists are extremists by their very nature. The rightwing organization Im Tirtsu has surpassed itself by publishing a list of leftists under the title "Stool Pigeons" —a list which includes leading artists and professors. The rightwing has also succeeded in instilling the perception that everything it does and all activity of the government is patriotic and for the good of the nation, while any criticism or protest on the part of the opposition is "political," that is, illegitimate. The protests of 2011 died off because they were submitted to this definition. Teachers avoid discussing questions in dispute lest they be accused of being "political." Ethiopian demonstrators for equal rights take care never to say that their demands are political, and social workers, when they were striking, did not consider their strike as a political action. There is no doubt that a leader who succeeds in designing public consciousness by imprinting his ideas on the citizenry, constructs reality for the nation, defines it, determines the public's evaluation of good and evil and directs its behavior. If the nation accepts the leader's definition of reality, it is under his control.

In research by the Israel Democracy Institute in 2019, respondents in a representative sample were asked what images of "rightwing" and "leftwing" were in their minds. It was found that among those that identified themselves as rightwing, 55% said that people on the left hated Jewish groups and that they were traitors; 35% attributed negative qualities, like stupidity, to them; 25% spoke of their desire to give up territory; and 18% attributed love of Arabs to them. On the other hand, people on the left negatively perceived rightists: 43% said that they were corrupt; 30% spoke of power and aggression by rightists; 30% accused rightists of extremism and fanaticism; and 26% attributed negative qualities to them, like ignorance.[290] These findings indicate polarization between the two groups. In addition, the rightist Likud party exerts special efforts to inflame the polarized relations between Jews coming from Asian–African states (among whom the Likud has a firm base) and Jews coming from European–American states.

Following the events as they have been described above, the left has been greatly weakened. In the 1980s, about 40% identified themselves as being on the left, and in 2019, according to the same research conducted by the same institute, only 15% identified themselves as such. The right has significantly increased its strength through the years, and in 2020, more than 60% of Jews in Israel supported the rightwing.[291]

In a similar way, the right has continued its smear campaign against Arab citizens of Israel. The leaders of the right have persisted in viewing this minority, 20% of the Israeli population, as a fifth column who are not loyal to the state of Israel. In every election campaign, Binyamin Netanyahu has attacked Arab citizens, painting them as illegitimate in the eyes of the Jewish public and thus, preventing any type of political connections between Jewish parties and Arab parties, and especially against any relationship with the Joint List, which has unified Arab parties under one umbrella. The right makes a special effort to connect the parties on the left to the Arab public in order to deepen their delegitimization. On the day of elections, 17 March 2015, the prime minister encouraged his voters to hurry to the polls to vote by warning them that *"the rightist government is in danger. Arab voters are hurrying to the polls in great numbers. Leftist organizations are bringing them in by bus ... With your help and with God's, we will set up a national government that will safeguard the State of Israel."*[292] Just before the elections of September 2019, Binyamin Netanyahu turned to those who follow his Facebook page and asked them to insist that *"there must on no account be a leftwing government that relies on Arabs who want to destroy all of us."*

Following the September elections, the chair of Yisrael Beitenu, Avigdor Lieberman, rejected the formation of a government on the basis of support by the Arab party and said that *"it is clear that the Joint List is a fifth column,"* not in quotation marks but rather with double meaning. In this way, the rightwing Jewish leadership rejects an entire sector of the political spectrum of the State of Israel. A similar picture emerged in the elections of March 2020, when the Likud presented an alternative: The electorate must choose between Bibi (Benjamin Netanyahu) or Tibi (a leader of one Arab party). Then, even when Yisrael Beitenu was finally willing to cooperate with the Arab Joint List, a number of elected representatives from the Blue-White party and Orly Levy from the Avoda-Gesher party were strongly opposed, and the proposal fell by the wayside. Interestingly, even the Joint List itself found it difficult to make the recommendation to the president that the former Army Chief of Staff, Benny Ganz, who headed the Blue-White party, be appointed prime minister. Ultimately, despite their great hesitation, they did take this step, which indicated their readiness to cooperate with opposition parties from the center and from the moderate rightwing. But only in the spring of 2021 did Benjamin Netanyahu begin to court the conservative Arab party, Ra'am, aspiring to form a rightist government. Eventually, however, the Arab party joined the alternative coalition and made history as the first Arab party to be part of the established government.

In any case, all the events played an important role in the weakening support for parties which had made a point of supporting the advance of the peace process, and the increasing strength of rightwing parties pressing for the continued settlement movement, reinforcing the occupation and even advocating annexation of the occupied territories and adopting an aggressive stance towards the Palestinians. A position of honor in creating this situation for most of this period must go to the prime minister of Israel, Binyamin Netanyahu. Netanyahu deepened the rift with the Palestinians and escalated the conflict by using aggressive rhetoric with expressions of the conflict supporting narrative which, in turn, also appeared on the Palestinian side. He also intensified the internal-social gaps in Israel by continual incitement against the left, against Arab citizens of Israel and against asylum seekers who had arrived in Israel illegally. This state of affairs continued during the term of the alternative government in 2021-2022. The best expression of this policy was delivered in Netanyahu's speech on 26 November 2015 at a special session of the Knesset to mark ironically the twentieth year since the assassination of Prime Minister Yitzhak Rabin:

> *We succeeded in making peace with two of our neighbors:*
> *Under the leadership of the late Menachem Begin, with*

Egypt; and under the leadership of the late Yitzhak Rabin, with Jordan. However, despite all the efforts of the six prime ministers since the Oslo Accords, peace has not been reached with the Palestinians.

There is a profound reason for this: The Palestinians are not prepared to recognize the nation-state of the Jewish people; they are not prepared to end the conflict once and for all and to genuinely relinquish the dream of returning to Acre, to Haifa, to Jaffa. They are not prepared to relinquish the dream of establishing a Palestinian state not alongside the State of Israel, but rather in its place. They still teach their children to hate Jews, to see Israel as a colonialist, imperialist entity, the source of all evil.

Most of us know a simple truth: Peace must be anchored in security because security is the foundation for peace. The Palestinians' hope, and that of all our enemies—that one day they will defeat us through the power of the sword—must be denounced. Must the sword devour forever? If we lower our sword, their sword will consume us. Only when they understand that they will not succeed can we return our sword to its scabbard.

As prime minister, he planned policy, and as leader of the right, he is the most significant figure in designing the political discourse of the rightwing camp, and even more broadly in the general Jewish population. There is much evidence that his interpretations regarding policy connected to conflict events is accepted time after time by much of the Jewish public. His influence is most considerable when interpreting events about which the public has no direct knowledge. Only then is Netanyahu the one who supplies the narrative, that is, he explains exactly what happened and how the event should be understood. For example, findings of a public opinion poll among a representative sample of the Jewish population taken by Mitvim—The Israeli Institute for Regional Foreign Policies—in September 2019, revealed that the Jewish public accepts the narrative presented by Netanyahu regarding foreign policy.[293] Most of the public believes that the Palestinian president, Abu Mazen, is not a partner for peace negotiations with Israel (67%), that a peace treaty could be signed with the Gulf States even without progress in the peace process with the Palestinians (51%), which has actually occurred, that the European Union is more of an opponent than a friend to Israel (51%), that relations with the United States, and not just with Trump, are very good (67%); 43% of the public think that the type of government in a state does not have to be a consideration when determining relations between it and Israel, and only 40% think that preference should be given to relations with democratic states. In a poll published by the Peace Index in November 2015, a sample of the Jewish public was asked, "Did the present wave of terror occur spontaneously in the Palestinian public itself or is it a wave which had been planned and guided by the Palestinian leadership?" About 61% repeated Netanyahu's argument that the terror had been planned by the Palestinian leadership.[294] Even after the new government was formed and Netanyahu moved to head the opposition, in the survey taken on January 30, 2022 by Channel 12, 31% of the Jews in Israel would have liked to see him as the prime minister, and only 4% preferred Naftali Bennet, the then-Prime Minister.

When summarizing the years of rightwing government, and especially the cooperation between the Likud, the rightwing religious Zionists and the ultra-orthodox, we can distinguish new basic principles characterizing this coalition that are different in essence from those formulated during the term of Arik Sharon as prime minister, at the beginning of twenty-first century, which were themselves already very different from the principles posed by Yitzhak Rabin during the Oslo process. In fact, these new principles represent a complete discontinuity not only from the attempt to solve the conflict in a peaceful way but also, a complete reversal in managing the conflict, using methods that were designed during the second intifada. The major enveloping principle among them is the creation of a new reality in the occupied territories that will prevent the establishment of a Palestinian state and will transmit the sense of a victory based on strength over the Palestinians. The following are new fundamental assumptions which have developed by the coalition in power during the second decade of the twenty-first century:

a. The international and regional context enables acts of creeping annexation on the ground which, on the one hand, enables considerable expansion of the Jewish settlements in the occupied territories, and on the other hand, prevents the establishment of a Palestinian state.

b. In the end, the realities on the ground will determine the future of the occupied territories, and this makes what the Jews do unilaterally during the coming years vitally important.

c. There should be no serious negotiations with the Palestinians for a solution to the conflict and if international pressure is created to negotiate, efforts must be made to prevent this from happening.

d. The status quo of control and supervision must be maintained over the West Bank territories and also over the Gaza Strip, with the help of the Israeli Defense Forces and with the assistance of the Palestinian Authority, which must continue to function in its limited framework, maintaining security cooperation with Israel.

e. It is necessary to maintain the separation between the West Bank and Gaza Strip.

f. The number of Palestinians living in Jerusalem and in Area C should be reduced.

g. Laws and regulations should be advanced that enable the expansion of the Jewish settlement project in the occupied territories and the transfer of the settlements to the civil authority of the State of Israel.

h. Palestinians living in the occupied territories should not receive full civil rights in the State of Israel.

i. All necessary means should be used against opponents in Israel and abroad, of reconstructing a new Jewish reality in the occupied territories in the spirit of Greater Israel.

j. In the international arena Israel should defend its policies regarding the Palestinians, accusing any criticism as an expression of anti-Semitism

Finally, during the years of rightwing government, planned and systematic actions have been taken to implement the worldview of the leadership on a practical basis. These actions include appointing people with rightwing views to key positions, establishing institutions to put these views into practice and the creation of supportive organizations. The process has primarily involved the mass media and the educational system, but has also found expression in the police, the Mossad, the state attorney general's office, the legal system, the civil service commission and the state comptroller's office.

Netanyahu as prime minister made every effort to divert the media to serve his world outlook. Education Ministers redirected the educational system in order to instill principles and beliefs that are in line with right-wing political ideology. Ministers have been trying to change the legal system to support this worldview or at least to minimize its involvement in what is going on in the occupied territories. The ex-Culture Minister did her best to prevent exposure of any works of culture which are not in line with the national-religious perspective.

As a result, a new generation in Israel has been growing up, who have received only the hegemonic narrative as absolute truth, and, at the same time, this has enabled the development of an intellectual echelon that supplies an ideological basis for the government, and even deepens and broadens the narrative by providing supportive arguments. These ideologies can be found in public service, in academia, and in the media. Social networks which support the new public order are also very active, and they continually disseminate messages supportive of rightwing orientation. It may be said that, utilizing the methods and institutions described above, the hegemony of conflict supporting narratives has been strengthened. Thus, opinions supporting the conflict have become "imperial doctrine" expressing the real and only Zionism, and this is in conjunction with persecution of those with alternative opinions, in an attempt to eliminate their beliefs from public discourse in Jewish society in Israel. Zionism, as a national movement, has been defined in its very narrow meaning of nationalism that subscribes only to its rightist definition.

In parallel, the Israeli government has also begun to adopt authoritarian characteristics, such as appointing "our people" to "gatekeeper" positions. For example, the state comptroller between 2012 and 2019, Yosef Shapira, had to undergo an "audition" at the prime minister's residence on Balfour St. before he could be appointed, apparently in an attempt to make sure that he was "loyal." Netanyahu has chosen a number of people for sensitive positions from his own ideological environment: Roni Alshech was selected as police commissioner; loyalist Avichai Mandelblit, who had been his cabinet secretary, was appointed attorney general; and Daniel Hershkowitz was chosen to be civil service commissioner. In 2017, Netanyahu appointed Yulia Shamalov-Berkovich as Chair of the Second Authority for Radio and Television, a body which is supposed to safeguard the media from political interference. Recently, in 2019, Netanyahu chose Matanyahu Englman to replace Shapira in the central position of state comptroller, responsible for maintaining the integrity of the government. Englman has already issued instructions which do harm to the performance of tasks that should be undertaken to fight corruption—in December 2019, it was announced that the new state comptroller had altered a report on deficit data issued by the Finance Ministry to make it less critical, and after a few days, it was publicized that he had softened a critical report about attempts by the political echelon to dominate the media. However, it should be clarified that not everyone chosen by Netanyahu has made him happy. The police commissioner and the state attorney general preferred justice to bias in dealing with Netanyahu, and it must be assumed that they have disappointed the prime minister, who has personally attacked them.

This combination of activities of a political nature has led to a change in the spirit of Israeli society. By their very nature, people tend to support a strong political power with resources, which supplies them with a sense of security and belonging. Moreover, Binyamin Netanyahu regularly places his personal interests at the head of his priorities. For example, the 2015 elections were called because Netanyahu wanted to retain the circulation and status of his very supportive newspaper, *Yisrael Hayom* (*Israel Today*). In addition, the first elections of 2019 were called on the assumption that he would be able to put together a new government before his criminal hearings, in which he was accused of breach of trust and bribery. Furthermore, he terrorized state institutions in order to avoid punishment for his deeds, which were apparently illegal, and he attacked the police, the state attorneys, the legal system and the attorney general. Even after the elections on March 23, 2021, Netanyahu found himself with the largest party (Likud with 30 MK members) in the opposition with 59 parliament members (the coalition has 61 members).

In the delicate balance between "Judaism" and "democracy," the State of Israel has become more Jewish and less democratic. Jewish identity is defined as a system of nationalistic and religious expressions advancing an identity which is particularistic, and this, always at the expense of universal and humanistic values. By defining the occupied territories as the heart of the state and of Jewish identity, by settling them, and by delegitimization of the other, and especially the Palestinians—the new Israel evokes feelings of bitterness among the Palestinians, in the Arab world, and indirectly, in Western countries. This approach also strengthens separatist aspects of the Israeli identity and revives biblical slogans like "a people dwelling apart, not reckoning themselves among the nations" and increases siege mentality. This has left Israel even more closed in, closed off, and isolated in its social beliefs, which, in turn, limits additional democratic values —pluralism, and freedom of expression and of assembly. This is unavoidable when a leadership who wishes to retain the hegemonic narrative uses a variety of methods in order to prevent the flow of alternative knowledge about the harm to human rights in the territories and breaches of international law, as well as Israeli law. In this way, a full authoritarian governmental culture has been created, directed towards advancing one political worldview and invalidating a competing one. Usually, such a culture establishes a political climate which not only prevents the dissemination of information contradicting the conflict supporting collective narrative, but also creates fear of expressing it, conformism, obedience and self-censorship. And that is what is happening in the case of Israel. We will further discuss this in the next chapter.

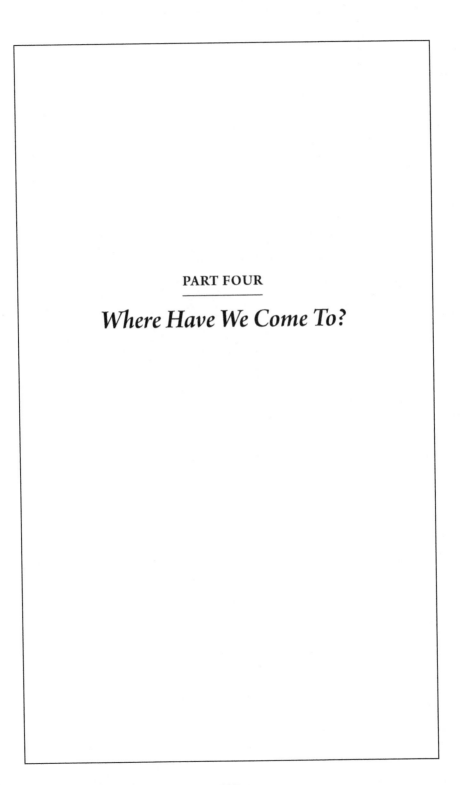

PART FOUR

Where Have We Come To?

CHAPTER 8

The Obstructive Factors

Israel is the scene of a strange paradox: The country's leadership argues that the State of Israel is the safest place for Jews in the world and that the real danger lies in living in the diaspora. But everyone knows that Israel is caught up in constant violence and continuous threats of incipient war or bloody encounters which leave their mark on every aspect of life, including interpersonal relations and public spaces. So how is it that the leadership still encourages Jews to immigrate to Israel, even though no one can foresee how the violent conflict will continue to develop? This mindset is clearly and powerfully connected to a perpetual awareness of the Holocaust which is still intensely present in collective Jewish consciousness as a timeless event, continuing to exist and to recur, but with other and frequently changing enemies (Palestinians, Iranians, extreme Muslims, the European left, and more). Antisemitism has always existed, still does, and is even increasing.

However, that argument alone, even if it is correct, explains only one side of the paradox—it refers to the danger lurking for those who live outside of Israel. What about the other side—seeing life in Israel as secure, not to mention peaceful, despite the realities on the ground? How is it that most members of Jewish society feel comfortable with the existing situation even though they are aware of the possibility that they may live out their entire lives in conflict? Clearly the Covid-19 pandemic with its effects and the economic crisis may change these feelings and thoughts. But up until 2020 most of them felt that the economy was flourishing, life seemed good, military might appeared protective, and thus, according to research by the Israel Democracy Institute in 2019, 84% of Jews living in Israel would choose to live in Israel even if they were offered American citizenship or citizenship in any other Western country.[295] Therefore, there is almost no public discourse regarding the costs of the conflict, costs which are multi-systemic and do harm to every aspect of societal life. **Yishayahu Leibowitz's prophecy, presented at the beginning of the book, has come to pass. Israeli society is losing its democratic, humane, and moral character. It has been unavoidable, but very few were able to foresee that Jewish society in the State of Israel would develop in this way, and few have even cared.** It appears that Israeli Jews are completely unaware of the prices they pay—the ones cited above and others which are more substantive, such as the extensive economic costs. Some Israelis are even unaware of the changes their society has undergone and continues to undergo. In several recent studies we found that Israeli Jews are not moved by costs such as loss of life, mental health, and economic costs. Moreover, it is even difficult for them to imagine how much they and the country would benefit by achieving peace. **And so the conflict continues and even escalates, and simultaneously, the occupation has become entrenched. At present, there is no light at the end of the tunnel, signaling a proximate solution.** And why? In this chapter we will try to answer that question, while summarizing what has been presented up to now. The chapter focuses on the barriers which nourish the continuation of the conflict.[296]

BARRIERS TO PEACEFUL CONFLICT RESOLUTION

The Violent Context

The most striking characteristic of the reality in which Israeli society exists is the violence of the conflict, which leaves its mark on every aspect of life. This violence dictates the needs and aims of society and the challenges with which it must deal. It has also created psychological conditions, the main feature of which is the sense of threat leading to fear and insecurity. This state of affairs is a very important factor in sustaining the continuation of the conflict. The violence supplies the adhesive for the conflict supporting narrative presented in the book and strengthens it, while substantially contributing to the violent reactions of Jewish society, which, in turn, lead to violence on the other side, and thus, the circle of violence becomes a permanent part of Israeli life. This circle ultimately leads to mutual mistrust and feelings of hopelessness about resolving the conflict peacefully.

Summarizing what has already been said, the violence has continued for more than one hundred years. It began as the Jews were returning to their ancient homeland, when it became clear to them that hundreds of thousands of Arabs also viewed this as their homeland and opposed Jewish settlement. The violent conflict between Jews and Palestinians has changed its form through the years, but in the 1990s, many considered it to be finally moderating and moving towards a solution. However, certain sectors in both societies still viewed the agreement in progress as harming their national aims and did everything in their power to make sure that a solution would not be realized. What is important from the Jewish perspective is that those forces on the Palestinian side initiated a violent reaction and thus, the peace process, which was meant to bring security to the Jews, instead brought acts of terror and loss of life. The second *intifada* became a watershed. The violent Palestinian revolt included numerous acts of terror and during a five-year period, more than a thousand Israelis were killed, most of them civilians. And the numbers increased following the violent Second Lebanon War, and terrorizing events in Gaza and in other places.

During the second decade of the twenty-first century, violence has continued with frequent rocket attacks on Israeli settlements, which ultimately have also reached the larger cities of Ashkelon, Beersheba, and even Tel Aviv. The settlements near the Gaza border have been turned into a battlefront, suffering from constant threat and, they too are victims of the cycle of violence. In 2015 the "*individual intifada*" broke out, during which the Palestinians primarily made use of knives and car-ramming attacks, but also used other types of violence, causing many deaths. From September 2015 to October 2016, 39 Israeli civilians were killed and more than 440 were wounded. In 2017, hostile acts killed 20 Israeli civilians, near the number killed in 2016. In 2018, 12 Israeli civilians were killed in terror attacks and in 2019, there were 26 acts of terror in which five Israelis (one soldier and four civilians) were killed and dozens more were injured. In the short war of May 2021, several thousand rockets were fired on Israel and for the first time after many years, alarm sirens were activated in Tel Aviv and civilians moved to shelters. From August 2020 until September 2022, there were 125 significant terrorist attacks in the West Bank according to the Meir Amit Intelligence and Terrorism Information Center. Of special significance were the violent events of spring 2021 in which Arab citizens of Israel also participated in mixed Jewish-Arab cities. They engaged in lynching, violence and vandalism. Jews were also involved in this violence on the same level. In short, since 2000 Israeli society has experienced constant violence at various levels, not only causing loss of life, but also strengthening the sense of threat, the lack of security, and the fear, which are all deeply ingrained in the Jewish spirit. The ongoing violence is an important reminder about the lasting bloody conflict, contributing to a sense of threat and, in turn, to fear and insecurity.

Did You Know?

Research by Israeli scholars conducted in 2007 unequivocally found that direct individual exposure to terror and to other types of violent behavior linked to the conflict lowers readiness to support efforts to achieve peace. The research also showed that psychological distress and a sense of threat created by exposure to the violence are factors which encourage hawkish attitudes towards the conflict over time. The research was conducted among a national sample of Jewish citizens in Israel and a national sample of Palestinians on the West Bank and in the Gaza Strip and findings were similar. The researchers concluded that loss of life due to the conflict is a barrier to attempts to break the cycle of constant violence as they increase opposition to a peace process. Breaking the cycle of violence is the challenge facing leaders and society members both in Israel and in Palestinian society.[297]

The threats and dangers facing Israel actually exist, and are valid. The public is aware of them, and their outlook and worldview are affected by them. However, the violent reality cannot serve as a full explanation for the deadlock in the peace process, as other places in the world which have suffered from extreme violence have managed to conduct peace talks and have even ultimately signed peace agreements. Even before the Oslo Accords, and before Egyptian President Anwar Sadat arrived in Israel, there was violence in the conflict—yet there were also agreements. In addition, the State of Israel is a military superpower, armed with the best and newest weaponry, and with the support of the United States. Russia, China, and India have also become friendly to Israel. Some of the Arab countries, like Syria and Iraq, are in disarray, while others feel threatened by Iran. Some Arab countries are involved in their own wars or have signed peace treaties with Israel that are stable and permanent. In 2020, a number of Arab states that had long had informal relationships with Israel made them public after the Trump administration in the U.S. promised them significant military and/or political rewards (United Arab Emirates, Bahrain, Sudan, and Morocco).

The threat of Iran not only concerns Israel, but the whole European community and the United States as well. Each country in its way tries to deal with this threat, so Israel is not alone in its struggle. In addition, Iran too is dealing with difficult crises, including a serious attack of Covid-19. Moreover, in contrast to Netanyahu, who brought up the Iranian nuclear threat at every opportunity and called for the cancellation of the nuclear agreement with Iran by the nations who signed it, some professionals in the Israeli defense system including the Israeli army, the army intelligence branch (which evaluates national threats) and the Atomic Energy Commission, responsible for nuclear issues, support maintaining this agreement and see it as a positive contribution to national security. Despite its disadvantages, the treaty has closed off the trajectory of nuclear weapons development in Iran and has removed the only threat considered existential against Israel. In any case, events in the Iranian context occur very quickly and are dynamic and constantly changing.[298] The rise of new hawkish president Ebrahim Raisi has created a new context that preoccupies all of the negotiating partners with Iran. It is a concern that crosses boundaries and is global. Thus, we return to the internal threats affecting the development of Israeli citizens' worldview, which cause the sense of fear and insecurity.

The sense of fear and insecurity are not just a result of real and concrete threats, but also of the way these are mediated by various agents of authority. This mediation is one of the major producers of fear and insecurity in Israel. As we have already noted, like in many other places, due to the ambiguousness of most situations evoking fear, and the fact that most of the public are not exposed to non-institutional sources of information, society members depend on information coming from official and unofficial sources—these sources mold their beliefs about insecurity and their sense of fear. However, the information that these sources disseminate is saturated with selective interpretation and bias from the start. The type of threat and its level are predefined, and so are the steps that must be taken to improve security conditions.[299] Feelings of fear and insecurity are conditions for conformity and obedience, reverence towards the security forces, internalization of narratives supporting the conflict and the occupation, and eventually submissive acceptance of decisions taken by the government and the security leaders regarding the ongoing violence. To paraphrase the very diagnostic words of George Orwell, I could say that bloody conflict *"is not meant to be won, it is meant to be continuous."* Occupation is only possible on the basis of ignorance. *"This new version is the past and no different past can ever have existed."* In principle, the violent effort is always planned to keep society on the brink of ignorance. The bloody conflict and brutal occupation are waged by the ruling group against its own society as well, and they pay a tremendous price, *"and its* *object is not the victory, but to keep the very structure of society intact."* Israelis heard this from Shai Piron, who was describing Netanyahu's vision.

Feeling of Fear and Insecurity

In times of conflict, like the Israeli-Palestinian one, society members develop a collective emotional orientation towards fear that has, in our opinion, a crucial effect on the development of the conflict. And that is just what has happened in Jewish society in Israel. This orientation is expressed on both individual and collective levels through public discourse and social texts, like leaders' speeches and messages in the media, national texts, learning content in kindergartens and schools, and cultural products.[300]

Feelings of fear, as set out in the first chapter, are considered one of the main factors in the outbreak of violent intractable conflicts. Fear may be aroused by direct or indirect exposure to violence, following threats or dangers which take place in the present (for example, rocket firings) or deduced from past experience (for example, having participated in a war), as well as learning from a variety of sources such as parents, teachers, leaders, or educational and cultural products (for example, fear of another Holocaust). The result is the development and fixation of deep chronic generalized fear among the collective as a whole—in psychological language, termed angst.[301] But it doesn't end there. Angst is accompanied by insecurity—a different psychological manifestation than a sense of fear, despite their close connection. Insecurity is, in essence, a cognitive reaction created following a process in which the individual identifies a danger and considers that it will be difficult for him to defend him/herself. Like fear, insecurity is subjective, and also like fear—it can be learned but, like fear, it can also be changed by persuasion.

It must be understood that this is all about subjective knowledge. As evidence, even in the present, members of the security apparatus at the highest levels differ in their evaluations of these issues. (There are significant differences in the evaluations of major-generals and lieutenant-generals like Yoav Galant, Amiram Levine, Benny Gantz, Gadi Eizenkot, Moshe Yaalon, and Yair Golan. These differences have existed continually since the 1970s, as we have already seen.) These issues usually have no objective "professional" answers. Leaders and political, military, and social analysts have their own principles and ideologies and different political interests, and they evaluate security situations according to these subjective factors. In presenting these evaluations, they are interested in persuading the public to accept their positions and outlooks. In the context of a discussion of fear and insecurity, it must be remembered that, in January 2020, the international pandemic, Covid-19, caused by the coronavirus, broke out. Corona reached Israel as well. It became a constitutive event due to the victims it claimed, its devastation to the economy, which was almost completely paralyzed, and its harm to every aspect of life. Most Israeli residents entered full lockdowns without knowing when it would be over and what would happen at the end of the crisis. This reality also had a decisive effect on the political situation that was developing. This atmosphere only reinforced the insecurity, uncertainty, and fear.

In any case, it is only between the lines that we can understand or guess that there are other opinions among those in the security services who do not agree with the opinions of the political establishment. This has even occurred during the Covid-19 crisis. However, the security establishment cannot publicly and clearly speak out against the political establishment as it is subordinate to it. Only after retirement have former members of the military establishment made their views known in public and spoken out against continuation of the conflict, with warnings about the future. For example, in the documentary film by Dror Moreh, *The Gatekeepers*, six former heads of the General Security Service, the *Shabak*, expressed their oppositional views. In addition, Meir Dagan, who had been an IDF general and the head of Mossad, also expressed his criticism, and another six Mossad heads of the past sounded their warnings in an interview with the daily newspaper *Yedioth Aharonoth* on Passover eve in 2018.[302] Moreover, 300 colonels and generals of the IDF joined the movement Commanders for Israel's Security, supporting initiatives to resolve the Israeli-Palestinian conflict, and many other officers expressed their opposition to government policy regarding conflict and security in the framework of the Council for Peace and Security. But those who have been critical have been delegitimized by the government and their influence has been negligible. It should also be remembered that the libraries of academic institutions and even the internet are full of alternative up-to-date information about the realities of the conflict. But a very small minority take the trouble to look for this information and many are satisfied with the information that flows from Israeli political leaders and from the Israeli media.

The results of the dominance of fear and insecurity is destructive. They prevent logical thinking, as Edmond Burke, an Irish statesman and philosopher of the eighteenth century, argued: "No power so effectually robs the mind of all its powers of acting and reasoning as fear." When people are afraid, it is easier to lead and direct them. Therefore, leaders often use threats in order to arouse obedience and conformism.[303] The continual experience of fear and insecurity also narrows the worldview of the Jewish public because of the link between the present and experiences of the past connected to the conflict. Similarly, expectations for the future are defined only by what is known from the past. These diversions make it very difficult to separate the present from the past—a necessary condition for creative thinking and for raising new and courageous alternatives to resolve the conflict. In addition, Jewish society, which has suffered from an overabundance of sensitivity to hints of fear and insecurity, often tends to interpret information incorrectly as signs of threat and danger, even in situations indicating good intentions. Insecurity has become a major characteristic of Jewish society that is inculcated from an early age and is maintained and reinforced through the years by different methods and contents. It has been internalized by the great majority of the Israeli Jews and it is presented to the national and international community as the real context in which the state exists, used as a major argument in internal and foreign policies and state activities. Therefore, the statement that Israel has the right to "exist in security" or "has the right to defend itself" has been repeated constantly in many national, bilateral and international forums.

This has all the characteristics of a vicious circle. Jewish society in Israel, deeply affected by its perception of permanent existential danger, tends to react violently whenever there seems to be even vaguely threatening circumstances, whether real or imagined. And as violence is a habit based on past experience, Israeli society does little to adopt new behaviors that would extricate it from the circle of violence. It chooses the military alternative time and time again. Especially salient in preparing the nation for life by the sword are the following assumptions: a. It is impossible to believe Palestinians because of their essential negative qualities (especially violence and untrustworthiness). These are inborn qualities and cannot be changed; b. An independent Palestinian state presents a fundamental strategic threat to the existence of the State of Israel, so it is impossible to resolve the conflict; c. The state of war will continue forever and therefore, we must live by the sword.[304]

Distrust

In addition to the emotional factor of fear and the cognitive factor of insecurity, distrust—as another cognitive reaction—plays a major role as a barrier to the peace building process and therefore, demands special reference. It is a relatively complex cognitive element involving thoughts that characterize advanced human beings. First of all, it requires expectations, prediction of a situation, impression formation, calculation of risks, planning one's own behavior, reliance or lack of reliance, and perhaps other thoughts as well. The definition of trust/distrust suggests: "*Lasting expectations about future behaviors of the other (a person or a group) that affect one's own welfare (of one person or of one's own group) and allow for a readiness to take risks in relation to the other.*"[305] In the case of distrust, society members expect evil behavior from the rival group that will affect their welfare, and this expectation does not allow them to take risks in the relationship. Specifically, in the case of the Israeli-Palestinian conflict, both societies have lost the trust in each other that prevailed for a short time during the Oslo process. Lack of trust underlies the view that there is no partner for peace on the Palestinian side, that no risk can be taken in the peace process, that Palestinians will not respect any signed peace agreement and eventually will try to harm the State of Israel and the Jewish people.

Distrust between Israeli Jews and Palestinians develops somewhat differently. While Palestinians are subjected to occupation that affects every aspect of their daily lives on a behavioral level, most Israelis do not experience daily violence. Thus, Palestinians develop their distrust mostly because of their daily experiences derived from the practices of the occupation. Israeli Jews, on the other hand, develop their distrust mainly based on the negative stereotyping including delegitimization of the Palestinians.[306] Obviously use of violence by both sides increases distrust greatly. In fact, violence continuously validates the distrust because of the intentional harm inflicted on the group. Distrust has several consequences. Society members who distrust the rival also have negative feelings about him, live under continuous threat that the rival may cause harm, and therefore they must be continually primed and ready to absorb information about that potentiality. Distrust leads to chronic suspicion, persistent expectations of negative acts from the rival, unwillingness to have intimate/equal/civil contact with members of the rival group, sensitivity to confirmatory information, and selective information processing that confirms expectations. And most importantly, lack of trust considerably diminishes readiness to support a peace process.

Minimal trust must be developed in the initial phases of the peace-making process at least by a segment of the society because readiness to conduct negotiations towards peaceful resolution of the conflict is risky by nature. It is trust that allows society members to take the risk of being vulnerable and to make conciliatory initiatives to the other party with some degree of confidence that these will not be exploited. Thus, distrust must be overcome if Israelis and Palestinians are to begin serious negotiations towards resolving the ongoing conflict. Until then, distrust prevents serious steps towards peace building.

Culture of Conflict as a Barrier

Feelings and thoughts of fear, insecurity, and distrust are not the only factors posing barriers to a peaceful resolution of the conflict. Together with additional feelings, like hatred and anger, they are an inseparable part of conflict culture, which also includes conflict supporting narratives (the ethos of conflict and the collective memory). All the elements of the conflict culture serve as the most significant obstacle preventing renewal of a peace process.[307] It should be remembered that the conflict culture in its most extreme form already dominated Jewish society in Israel hegemonically and completely during the 1950s and the 1960s. However, through the years, it had weakened and become more moderate so that, in the 1980s, a culture of peace developed and became established with the development of alternative narratives. Thus, for two decades, the two narratives competed with similar levels of social support. However, during the 2000s, the conflict culture with its supporting narratives grew stronger, until it again became hegemonic. The significant difference between the narratives of the two conflict cultures in Israel, that of the early years of the state and that of the present, is primarily in their goals and their infrastructures. At the time the state was established, it had to ensure its very existence and set its borders in accord with the ceasefire agreement of 1949—the Green Line. Israel also desired to take its place among the nations of the world as a Jewish democratic state, accepting various universal principles, even if only for appearance's sake.

Today, the aims of the conflict from the standpoint of the present leadership are to enlarge the State of Israel to the borders of Greater Israel, as demanded by religious-national commandments, and to prevent the establishment of an independent Palestinian state between the Mediterranean Sea and the Jordan River. In addition, the leadership aspires to institute a narrow ethnic identity while weakening democracy as an equal basis to the pillar of Judaism. One of the bases of the conflict supporting narratives is collective memory of the conflict, imparted to society members through the channels of socialization and communication. It is selective, biased and distorted, and is meant to serve the goals of the leaders and needs of society members rather than to tell the history of the conflict in an objective way. Collective memory fuels the continuation of the conflict as does the other narrative, ethos of conflict—both provide fundamental narratives underlying the culture of conflict.

Did You Know?

In research conducted by Rafi Netz and the writer of this book, in August 2008, a representative sample of Jews living in the State of Israel were asked questions about the facts of conflict events as they are remembered. Some of the findings that touch upon the information that we will present forthwith indicated that about 22% of the respondents thought that Arabs had been a minority in the country before the beginning of Jewish immigration, motivated by the Zionist Movement in 1882; 37% thought that they were a majority; and only 23% said that they were a large majority (In reality, 95% of the population were Arabs); 69% did not know that the division of the country according to the United Nations resolution in 1947 gave the Jews, who were a minority, a larger expanse of territory than that given to the Arabs (About 1.2 million Arabs received 43% of the country while about 600,000 Jews received 56% of the territory.); 41% of the Jewish respondents stated that Palestinian refugees left the country due to their fear and the call of their leadership to leave, in contrast to 39% who added that there were also expulsions of Arabs, and 8% who only cited the expulsion (In actuality, a significant portion of the Palestinians were expelled by the Israeli army); 41% maintained that the first *intifada* broke out due to the natural hatred of Arabs for Israel; 37% felt that at least half of the Arabs who are Israeli citizens have been involved in acts of terror against Israel (Actually, only a minis-

cule percentage of Arab citizens of Israel have been involved in acts of terror). This research also found that support for a selective narrative of collective memory predicts hawkish attitudes and lack of desire to be open to additional information.[308]

In the context of collective memory as it serves the conflict culture, society also preserves past traumas—both from far and recent past: from pogroms, expulsions, punishment, and hardship in the past while living the diaspora, along with the peak of Jewish suffering in the Holocaust, and to the struggle for independence against Arab violence, conflicts presented by formal institutions as all having been wars of no-choice, and finally, the incessant terror of Palestinians harming Jews. In every harm-causing event, the establishment and the media make a special point to give detailed and graphic descriptions of personal and collective distress among the victims in a one-sided way and thus, to sustain and reinforce the sense of victimhood which has lingered for so many generations among Jews. Maintaining the national consciousness that constantly compares the present to the past and what could happen in the future on the basis of experiences of the past, bolsters the awareness that the conflict is a way of life, and the fate of the nation cannot be changed. It is, in any case, the most convenient and best alternative in comparison to other possibilities. In the opinion of the Jews in Israel, including all past prime ministers, the Holocaust could happen again despite the existence of the state and the strong, capable, and well-armed military.[309] Thus, it is not by chance that even Defense Minister Yitzhak Rabin stated during the ceremony for Holocaust Remembrance Day in 1987: *"In every generation they rise up to destroy us and we must remember that this could happen to us in the future. We must therefore as a state be prepared for this."*[310] So, when relying primarily on the very negative memory of the past, the present becomes submerged, and society members are unable to think about a future which could bring a new and better reality of security and prosperity.

Did You Know?

A study conducted by Daphna Canetti and Gilad Hirschberger and their colleagues empirically demonstrates the effect of the Holocaust on judgement of the Israeli-Palestinian conflict. The research conclusively found that mentioning the Holocaust to Jews in Israel increases their support for aggressive steps and decreases their readiness for compromise, especially among those who identify with Zi-

onism. However, it became clear that this reaction exists only when the Holocaust is defined as a crime against Jews. When the Holocaust is defined as a crime against humanity, this reaction disappears. Another study found that Holocaust survivors and their offspring adopt the same attitudes when the Holocaust is mentioned to them. The researchers call their findings Holocaustization of Jewish consciousness in Israel.[311] In other words, persistence of Holocaust memory—with its particular lessons—ensures the persistence of the conflict.

The conflict culture functions as a system of social beliefs and feelings which direct the judgment and behavior of society members, constitutes a basis for their socialization, motivates their actions, serves as a source of a variety of different types of convictions, and sustains collective identity.[312] In all these functions, the conflict culture represents a psychological barrier. The blind fixation on conflict culture ensures a continuation of the "blood and sweat." Leadership, and most of the public, following their example, view reality through the prism of conflict culture, absorbing and evaluating new information through its lens, and drawing conclusions which strengthen its worldview. The circular process which has been created operates in this way: Information is presented selectively, biased and distorted, in order to validate the conflict worldview. The conflict supporting narratives are imparted and maintained. The violence continues both in word and deed, providing proof of this worldview and that leads to our violent behavior, and so it goes on and on. At the same time, alternative information which could shed light on the situation in another way is neglected and rejected and changing the path of violence to one more moderate is unthinkable. A cycle has been created which unceasingly revolves around us, the Jews and the Palestinians, maintaining this perspective and retaining the violence, and the challenge is to break this cycle either from the attitude-narrative side or the behavioral side, or both at the same time, as Yitzhak Rabin attempted to achieve. This is the most difficult challenge, as we learn from other cases of conflict, but there are nations which have succeeded in meeting this challenge (as in the achievement of a solution to the conflict in Algeria or in the Basque region in Spain).

Moreover, a hegemonic culture of conflict, like the one that has developed in Israeli society, clearly leaves its mark not only on the leadership and the public but also penetrates social institutions, changes their structure and constructs new identity. These changes alter the character of the state as the new forces design a new form of statehood based on the dominant conflict supporting narratives. This is a very significant development as a change in social consciousness demands a change in the social-political structure that has put down roots and has been described in detail in the previous chapter. In summary, it may be said that the barriers to a peace process begin with a change in the social-psychological repertoire of society members and continue with social-sociological changes in the character of social institutions and an accompanying change in the nature of the state.

These barriers play a central role in the fact that we find ourselves at a dead end today. Furthermore, they have become an inseparable part of the compass and the prism directing the leadership of the state. Anyone who studies very bloody conflicts that continue interminably knows that accompanying the physical confrontation, there is a sharp confrontation of narratives. Every side in the conflict tries, first and foremost, to inculcate its narrative among the members of its nation, and to convince the international community of the truth and justice of its goals.[313] On the other hand, it aspires to present the opposing society as unjust in its goals, as violent and immoral. As in the Israeli-Palestinian conflict, each side tries to present itself in a positive light, as humane, moral and advanced, and as the only victim of the struggle. Each society tries to refute the justifications, the descriptions, the explanations, and the excuses presented by the other about the conflict, and to demonstrate that these are baseless and untrue. The struggle is total and brutal, just like the physical one. In this struggle, no prisoners are taken, and each side tries to establish its kernel of truth in the most convincing way, in order to explain the conflict in its entirety. It was not by chance that one of the heroes of the series, Game of Thrones, Tyrione Lannister, said, *"What unites people? Armies? Gold? Flags? Stories. There is nothing in the world more powerful than a good story. Nothing can stop it."* Leaders understand this and make every effort to tell a persuasive story and impart it to society members through every channel and means that they can. Israelis have developed and have used a propaganda system that systematically, continuously and efficiently propagates the hegemonic narratives that fuel the conflict. That does not mean that stories are not told on the Palestinian side. These stories also play a very significant part in the tragic situation that has been created. But we always need to remember that the conflict is asymmetrical: The Jews achieved their national goal and established their state, while Palestinians have been under occupation for decades and see how the Jews have been settling expansively on occupied land, making the two-state solution almost impossible.

Political Socialization

A full analysis must include an additional important factor: the political socialization that all Israeli Jews experience from the moment they are born, while living in a reality of violence and conflict culture. Their earliest socialization includes echoes of the conflict during their first life experiences (Think about what babies or toddlers feel when the sirens begin, and they must go down into the shelter, and how they experience the fears and tensions of their parents). Afterwards, in kindergartens, the children are exposed to political education, during which they hear the hegemonic-official narrative of collective memory with all of its themes, including the stories of Hanukah, Purim, Passover, Holocaust Remembrance Day, Memorial Day, Independence Day, and Lag B'Omer.[314] Little children learn about the victimization of the Jewish people, that various nations have wanted to obliterate the Jews in every generation, and they hear about the threats facing the nation at present. Simultaneously, Jewish patriotism is inculcated, and children are told about those ready to lay down their lives for the nation during struggles with the enemy. In many cases, the Arabs are mentioned as the enemies of Israel and as those who are continuing to hate Jews at present. (The use of these themes in kindergartens was demonstrated in research by Meytal Nasie and the author of this book).

Did You Know?

In research carried out by Meytal Nasie and the author of this book, 17 compulsory kindergartens were observed (nine state kindergartens and eight in the religious stream) during the spring and summer of 2014, at ceremonies for Holocaust Remembrance Day, Passover, Memorial Day, Independence Day, and Jerusalem Day. The findings of the observations and an analysis of how the kindergarten teachers were explaining these events indicated that in most kindergartens, the message transmitted was one of continuing victimization and a heroic struggle for survival, while pointing out the relevance of events in the past for the present. In the present, the Arabs fulfill the role of the Egyptians and Nazis (and apparently also the Greeks on Hanukah and the Persians on Purim) who wanted to destroy the Israeli nation. But the nation was saved from all of these threatening dangers, and this continues in the present thanks to the strong army

that can defend the state from possible destruction. This research shows how early Israeli children begin their socialization in which they acquire the ethos of conflict, which stays with most of them, engraved in their memories as they grow up and become adults, as can be seen in a variety of other studies conducted in Israel.[315]

Political education continues even more intensively in the schools, where the educational system systematically transmits this narrative via textbooks, curricula, educational trips, ceremonies, teachers' explanations, and preparation for IDF service. So from an early age, a worldview is developed in which the themes of the conflict supporting narratives of collective memory and the ethos of conflict are internalized.[316] By the end of high school, most young people are inducted into the army, where there is institutionalized indoctrination (educational programs, commanders' talks, participation in operations in the occupied territories, educational handouts, the military rabbinate). The army, of course, continues the messages of the ethos of conflict. In fact, army service is one of the most important factors in the Israeli experience on personal, familial, and formal levels while growing up in Israel, both in the secular and the Zionist-religious sectors. It remains so during later years when men must do reserve service every year, and later their children continue to fulfill the unquestioned requirement of army service.

Most media outlets transmit the news based on messages that suit the narrative, and at times of crisis, they even mobilize to support the government and the army. Through all of this, an important factor is that the government has succeeded in creating an awareness that all alternative information incongruent with its own narratives is "political" while its own messages reflect reality. Opinion polls through the years have shown that a sizable number of society members really do continue to maintain this repertoire and it reflects their worldview at maturity. The repertoire is very accessible and when it is repeated very many times, it has obvious implicit effects.

Did You Know?

Research carried out by Keren Sharvit, a political psychologist, found that when students with an admitted dovish worldview saw a bus damaged in a terror attack, they tended to return to the beliefs of the ethos of conflict, those beliefs that every individual in Israel

learns in his/her socialization process. However, the interesting finding was that even when the members of this group saw an image of a bus that had been damaged in a serious road accident, this reminded them of the buses damaged in terror attacks, and they returned to the ethos of conflict beliefs even though they knew what the reason for the destruction was. This occurs because people do not have control over their fears and under stress, their fear overcomes rational considerations and leads to automatic and stereotypical thinking which has been learned at a very early age. This research illustrates the effects of socialization in Jewish society on its members' attitudes.[317]

Investment in the Conflict

An additional factor that has contributed to prolonging the conflict is the investments made by individuals and groups taking an active part in it. In this context, it is important to understand that after the investment has been made and is justified by the system of conflict supporting beliefs, any retreat from these beliefs becomes even more difficult. There are already no small numbers of gambling chips in the game. For nations, it is difficult to relinquish investments that have already been made, and like casino games, the more you invest, the stronger the impetus to keep on investing.

The ultimate example of such investment is, of course, loss of life. Israeli society, like others involved in conflict, has suffered through the years from great loss of life, both soldiers and civilians. Each such loss is a universe, an unimaginable tragedy, but nevertheless, it should be noted that it is only in the context of the conflict that the loss of one person is perceived as the loss of a complete group, in contrast, for example, to someone who is killed in a road accident. That in and of itself increases the emotional involvement of society as a whole in the conflict.

Loss of life also leads to ceremonies, rituals, and monuments honoring collective memories. They glorify battles and wars, the bravery of the fallen, and stress the evil of the enemy and the need to continue to struggle in order to realize the patriotic "last will and testament" of those who have "paid" the ultimate price. One such example can be found in the words of a young Israeli who described his opposition to withdrawal from the occupied territories captured by Israel in 1967, quoted in research by Shai Fuxman in 2011, when he interviewed dozens of young Jews in Israel about their attitudes towards the Israeli-Palestinian conflict: "*I am not in favor of giving up this territory ... for peace. It hurts me since people fought, people died for this territory, so why should we return it? Do you know how much Jewish blood is still there?*"[318] In other words, people have died to achieve "sacred" national goals and thus, we cannot compromise and withdraw from even a part of our homeland and transfer it to the Palestinians. Armed with these "insights," the hawkish non-governmental organization, Almagor, established by relatives of victims of Palestinian terrorism, operates in the field. The organization conducts wide ranging activities against the Palestinians, such as demonstrations, lobbying in the Israeli Knesset, and abroad, and giving lectures, all devoted to the delegitimization of the Palestinians and to the attempt to prevent any humane gestures and acts that may moderate the hatred and eventually lead to a peaceful resolution of the conflict. It should be noted that, parallel to powerful Almagor, an opposing organization was established, The Forum for Israeli and Palestinian Bereaved Families, whose members are Israelis and Palestinians who have lost a family member in the violence of the conflict. Their goal is to advance reconciliation between the two nations. The government operates against this organization and against its message of opposition to the narratives that the political leaders promote.

Another type of investment, this time taking place on the collective level, but directly affecting the status of individuals in society, is the huge material investment in aspects relating to the conflict. In every intractable conflict there are sectors of society that profit by maintaining it. For example, people who earn money from industries that produce military weapons and equipment, ex-security officers who are employed as consultants in different military firms, developers of surveillance, cybernetics and cyber-security systems, owners of businesses benefitting from resources in the disputed territory, and more. There is no doubt that the great profiteers from the situation are army officers and security personnel who gain status and prestige in the bloody conflict that they manage. They benefit from the highest status in Israeli society and the political echelon yields to their financial demands. For example, in August 2021, the government agreed without any objection to raise the pension rights of professional officers, adding about $300,000,000 to the budget during the pandemic. The current annual pension payments for retired officers are among the highest in Israel and total about $2.8 billion dollars each year.

Over time, these sectors, benefitting from the vast resources and the accompanying influence and status, have become powerful barriers to any possibility of advancing the peace process. During the period of the violent conflict, Israel has developed the most advanced weapons and surveillance systems and has then tried them out in confrontations. The various start-ups in defense and military areas are prospering; exporters of weapons and security knowledge are flourishing, and Israel has become one of the highest-level international arms exporters. Even though these enormous economic powers do not publicly express their opinions about the conflict, their great profits are an additional covert motivation for its continuation. U.S. President Dwight D. Eisenhower, who had served as Supreme Commander of the Allied Expeditionary Forces in Europe during World War II, actually warned of the influence of the military-industrial complex during his term of office (1953–1961) at the time of the Korean War. In Israel, the military industries owe their excellent reputation to the fact that their products have been tried out in the field, in action, and it is not by chance that they are among the leading arms and security systems exporters in the world.

The ones who most publicly benefit from the conflict are the Jewish settlers who, by 2021, numbered 475,000—less than 5% of the Israeli population (living in about 127 settlements and in more than a hundred outposts), not counting the Jewish population (about 220,000) who settled in East Jerusalem. First, ideological settlers lobbied the government for many years, continually and methodically, applying immense political pressure to settle the West Bank, the Gaza Strip, and even the Golan Heights. These first settlers made a significant psychological investment. For some of them, settlement was a supreme aim, stemming from religious-national aspirations. There were also settlers who chose to live in the occupied territories for economic reasons. Settlement in these territories was for them, the realization of the dream to improve their living conditions and their economic status. In addition, to solve a severe housing shortage, thousands of the ultra-orthodox moved to the West Bank, into two cities built for them by the government—Beitar Illit and Modiin Illit, as well as in smaller settlements like Maale Amos and Immanuel, where more than a third of the settlers are now living. In general, realizing the national project of settling the West Bank, Israel has invested many dozens of dollars in building infrastructures, settlements, roads, and providing continuous security to the settlers.

In addition, in order to encourage Israeli citizens to move to the settlements, Israel has created a system of benefits and incentives accorded to settlements and settlers, with no connection to their economic status. Settlers receive a subsidy of the price of the land, enabling them to build inexpensive homes and allowing for the development of settlement infrastructure, including access roads. In addition, most of the settlements on the West Bank have received comprehensive benefits in education, such as transportation to and from school, improvements in teachers' salaries, small classes and improved psychological and consultation services. In addition, they receive additional benefits in medical and welfare services, grants and subsidies to industries and agriculture, including compensation for the taxes imposed on their products by the European Community, and significantly lower taxation rates in comparison to Israeli settlements within the Green Line (the international border). In addition, the government grants surplus budgets in the framework of balancing grants, as positive discrimination. Any peace agreement in the conflict will obligate the dismantling of many of these settlements and will lead to losses. Therefore, most of the settlers participate in a pre-planned campaign to prevent such a solution.[319]

Through the years, leaders have also used justifications for the continuation of the conflict and have invested great effort in convincing the public that it is an existential need; they would find it difficult to retreat from their positions, and have actually become even more entrenched. During the election campaign of autumn 2019 to March 2020, all of the rightwing and center parties spoke specifically of their desire to annex the Jordan Valley. In that sense, their devotion to continuing the conflict expresses a political commitment which would be very difficult to breach, as they would be open to strong criticism for being inconsistent. A change in opinion, or a zigzag, could be considered the admission of a tremendous error if not shameful deceit. In societies involved in long-lasting conflict, a change in viewpoints to which leaders have publicly committed might lead to a loss of support by the public, or worse, to a loss of their legitimacy. At times—and we know this well from experience—such a change could mean an accusation of treason. There are very few leaders on the level of French President Charles de Gaulle, who, in 1958 ran for office with the slogan, "Algeria is French," but having been elected, understood the heavy costs that his country was paying for the continuation of the bloody conflict, and decided to advance a negotiated end to the dispute. De Gaulle was called "a traitor" for this, and between 1958 and 1965, he survived no less than thirty assassination attempts. In addition, a number of army units rebelled, and even began to march towards Paris, aiming at leading a coup.

Entrenchment in a position and remaining closed to alternative information are two of the main reasons that, in most cases, leaders stubbornly and blindly stick to their hegemonic positions without proposing any alternative which might lead to change. Furthermore, they use the themes of conflict culture in their election propaganda ("He will fight terrorism"; "He will divide Jerusalem"; "He will be firm against the Arabs"; and "They will return parts of the homeland"), while implicitly they are promising to continue the conflict and, in that sense, they contribute to the stagnation in public opinion. This too leads to a vicious circle. The leader strengthens the worldview supporting the continuation of the conflict and at the next stage, the support for this worldview limits the ability of the leader to advance a peace process, much less to initiate one.

This appears time after time in the methods of Prime Minister Binyamin Netanyahu, who made sure to satisfy his supporters by taking an uncompromising line towards the Palestinians and supporting expansion of the settlements. Obviously, his unreadiness to compromise also reflects his desire to retain the support of his followers who all are on the right of the political spectrum. The changes in his policies sometimes express the competition between Netanyahu and the leaders of the extreme right-wing for the support of the setters and other hawks. This usually takes the forms of discriminating against the Arab citizens of Israel, causing harm to Palestinians, encouraging settlement construction, expressing support for possible annexation, threatening to go to war against Gaza, attacking the Israeli left, or defending Jews who do harm to Palestinians or to Arab citizens of Israel. He often uses two particular methods: arousing fear and mudslinging. With the first method, he frequently brings up existing threats facing the state of Israel and the Jews who live in it, and with the second, he incites against the Palestinians in the territories, the Arab citizens of Israel, and people with leftwing opinions.

Routinization of the Conflict

And now there is an in-depth discussion about the important points that do not come up in public discourse: an analysis of the reasons that the conflict and the occupation continue. Living continually in the shadow of a violent conflict means that people become accustomed to living with it in daily life (routinization).[320] After the conflict becomes an inseparable part of our daily routines, always present in our physical and social spaces, interspersed in our expressions and symbols, this all becomes normal. It is perceived as natural, and thus it contributes directly and indirectly to the continuation of the conflict.

There is significant evidence of this in the research literature. In a study by the author of the book with Soli Vered, we interviewed eleven non-Jewish visitors to Israel in 2012, aged 20-33. This was their first visit to Israel and for all of them, their visit had lasted less than eight weeks. None of them had any family in Israel. Simultaneously, we interviewed six Jewish-Israeli students who had been born in Israel. The interviews with the two groups demonstrated that, while the Jewish-Israelis did not see anything strange about their lives in Israel, those who came from abroad perceived life in the state as very strange. Kira, 20 years old, from the United States stated, for example: *"The first thing that I noticed was that in Israel there are many soldiers my age. I told my mother that there were many children with rifles."* For most of the other interviewees, the fact that so many soldiers with weapons were circulating in public places seemed peculiar to them. Most also noted the large number of warplanes in the skies, the many memorial monuments, the daily media reports about the conflict and the great interest the news aroused among Israelis, and of course, the security checks everywhere. One of the interesting findings that came up was that the visitors did not feel a sense of increased security considering the quantities of weaponry and the number of soldiers in the streets.[321]

We may add the visual expressions of conflict cited by the interviewees, and specifically, the public shelters in parks or playgrounds; the large number of army camps, the heavy tank transporters on the intercity roads, the many shops selling army equipment, like the Ricochet chain, decorated with symbols of the army, and more. It should also be noted that there are no small number of public areas devoted to the memory of soldiers or to memorialize events connected to the conflict, in addition to the many museums connected to significant events of the conflict, the monuments and statues in memory of people who lost their lives during the conflict, positioned in the streets, parks, educational institutions, government offices, and other public areas. To be more specific, the victims of the War of Independence alone are memorialized in 150 monuments throughout the country, and from the first settlement in the country until the 1990s, there have been more than 900 monuments erected in memory of those who lost their lives in Israeli wars and conflicts.[322] In many social institutions, there are memorial corners for the victims, and of course, in most cities, towns and villages there are structures called Memorial[s] to our Sons (Yad Lebanim), in memory of the victims from that particular place.

However, the ultimate visual expression of the conflict, even in the category of general routinization, is the immense number of areas in Israel defined as "military areas": They encompass no less than 40 percent of state land (within the borders of the Green Line). They include training areas, army camps, army facilities and those of the Ministry of Defense, and military industries.[323] Some might say that the daily exposure to special expressions of the conflict does not end at the doorway of one's home—following the Gulf War in 1991, it was decided to construct "protected spaces" in every new building put up in Israel. Each new residential apartment being built must have a "security room." It might be said that the conflict has entered every home.

The conflict is not only seen in daily life, but also heard—it plays a central role in the public agenda. The media deals with it intensively, and it is ubiquitous in other cultural channels and discourse, a factor that we have already discussed. But it is also present in the building blocks of the language itself. Hebrew words and expressions which are in some way linked to the conflict often become part of the daily language when they are borrowed for events which are not connected to the conflict at all, like *hamshsush* (a soldier's weekend at home which has become slang for any weekend) and *pakal* (meaning military equipment but is now slang for a habit). In this context, the army is a fruitful source of slang words and expressions. In the field of compliments, there are many expressions with violent connotations: "a cannon" (describing someone who is outstanding), "a shell" (terrific, "a blast"), "an explosion" (fantastic), a "bomb" (a very attractive woman, "a bombshell"), and more. This perhaps sounds a bit ridiculous or petty, but it is one more important strategy for Israelis to normalize the conflict by getting used to a life saturated in unceasing violence.

An interesting fact is that millions of Israelis travel abroad each year, some living in other countries for long periods. Tens of thousands of young people, after completing their army service, spend a full year in far-away countries in South America, India or even Australia and New Zealand and African countries, to "clear their heads." They return to Israel and it doesn't even occur to them that it is different than other places, that life here goes on in another way—with chronic tension, uncertainty, a sense of insecurity and fear, aggressiveness, impatience, scenes of soldiers carrying weapons, exclusion of non-Jews, and other such phenomena. All of these seem normal to them and an inseparable part of routine life in the country. Perhaps they remain unaware because the thousands of young people who go abroad tend to spend their time primarily with their Israeli friends and are not open to the social environment of other societies. They have gone through a process of acclimation to the situation—routinization—and they go out on their journeys and return to their own society without question.

Why is there acclimation to the conflict? Becoming accustomed to signs of the conflict in daily life serves several important social functions. First, as we have seen from the linguistic examples above, it normalizes the complex and demanding living conditions created by an intractable conflict. In the end, flooding physical and social spaces with routines linked to the conflict leads to acclimation. The daily routines, by their very existence, become built-in and no longer attract attention. As routine becomes normal, the conflict as a whole becomes normalized.

In addition, routinization strengthens support for the ethos of conflict. In this way, the totality of beliefs, attitudes, values, norms, perceptions, and worldviews, accumulated knowledge and behaviors linked to the conflict all become normal, taken for granted, banal, or natural, and they are absorbed into the fabric of social life. Routinization also prepares society members to cope with a life of threat and danger—real or imagined. Daily signs of the conflict remind them that they must be ready for the outbreak of violence at any moment, such as a terror attack or some other act of violence and even war. They thus remain forever vigilant.

On the positive side, routinization also strengthens the sense of solidarity and cooperation among group members (although, in Israel, this solidarity does not include the Arab population, and sometimes even excludes groups in the Jewish population, like the ultra-orthodox or the Ethiopians). The signs of conflict the population is exposed to, the sights that they share, and the daily actions experienced by all, remind Israelis that they share a common past, a common interest in security in the present and a common hope for the future. However, at the bottom line, routinization leads to frozen thinking, which in turn creates difficulty in opening up to new situations and to stagnation—for example, the possibility of making peace.

Both individuals and the collective learn through the years how to cope with situations and conditions of violent confrontation and how to get used to them, and this leads to a perception that a state of conflict is understandable, customary and significant. Otherwise, why invest so many resources in it? The constant threat also causes dependence on leaders with military experience, of whom, their great advantage is in their ability to deal with the dangers that are already familiar, and not to create a new reality, a different future—for example, peace. Political parties in Israel commonly search for generals and especially ex-chiefs of staff who are extremely well respected by the public as experts in security problems. They provide a sense of security, one of the most important human needs.

Making peace, in contrast, demands a change in the well-known modes of action, the accepted approaches, based on coping and routinization. Moreover, a peace process, groping into the unknown and unfamiliar, demands, by its very nature, taking risks and using creative thinking. But the Jewish public in Israel prefers to suffer with the well-known, the familiar, the expected, as in the Irish proverb "Better the devil you know..." rather than to take risks which might lead to significant relief. This need is achieved by aiming at the comfortable routine, permanent and consistent, and well-known to all. As such, the establishment closes its doors to information which may conflict with what is accepted in the dominant narrative supporting the conflict, that is, imprisoning the public behind the walls that "defend" it from alternative information, building a distressing collective consciousness, and maintaining it with the help of basic needs, like the desire for security, for certainty, for cohesion, for unity of identity and a sense of superiority. This all occurs while struggling against openness, independent and reflective thinking, a critical approach, innovation, empathy towards the Palestinians, compassion for them, guilt, shame, and responsibility towards the stranger. The gaze is directed towards the past and the present, without delving into the future.

Jews in Israel have difficulty in imagining a situation of peace after so many long years of living in conflict, during which patterns of thought and behavior, considered to ensure Israeli existence and survival, are deeply enshrined. Israelis are acquainted with the dangers of the past, know them all too well and believe that they can successfully deal with them. Their thinking is based on what-is-already-known, without the ability to consider what the possibilities of the future will bring, and more than that—what benefits it could bring if the vision of peace was realized.

The Conflict as a Need

Here we get to one of the central messages of the book—actually, its basic premise. If we delve deeply into this adaptation, we find that, at the time of intractable conflict, the ethos of conflict and the collective memory, together with fear and insecurity—fulfill deep inner basic needs: This begins with the need to live in an understandable world that can be predicted, continues with the need to live in a secure world and ends with the need for a positive collective identity, a positive self-image and the sense of being right. The support for the psychological-social repertoire thus becomes both a personal and a collective need. As a result, a rather strange inversion is created: While the repertoire is functional—that is, it is meant to serve individuals and society as a whole only in times of conflict—the society members take another step and turn the very existence of the conflict into a need in itself, enabling them to remain in the reality of a bloody intractable conflict as their comfort zone. In other words, they have succeeded in fulfilling their primary and secondary needs while the conflict is present and active so they prefer the status quo over any change whose effects would be unknown. Conflict over peace. This, of course, on the condition that the violence of the conflict does not flare up over time and Israel succeeds in keeping it satisfactorily on a low flame.

The last point is very important and therefore needs more clarification. The smoldering conflict (with rare flare ups) and the threats that are heard from the opponent, supply real evidence of the dangers and provide reinforcements for the development of society members' attitudes and their narratives. However, what is central in constructing the narratives is the intensification of the existing fear and anxiety. The narratives told by the leaders, together with their control over them, and the distancing of alternative narratives, are the means to strengthen them via all social institutions, including the educational system, the mass media and the social media, governmental ministries, various organizations and more. Almost all prime ministers

have used these tactics, from Ben Gurion to Netanyahu and Bennett, and only a small minority have responded to the challenges of peace, have taken up the gauntlet, and have actively tried to reduce the threats and the dangers by reaching a peace agreement.

A new reality would involve uncertainty and great anxiety about what is to come. Public discourse would be bombarded with questions, like "What if a peace agreement actually leads to an increase in violence or opens us up to new dangers, for example, shelling the airport from the hills of the West Bank, Hamas gaining control of the West Bank, hostile armies entering the West Bank?" The reason such questions are asked so often by right-wingers is that they are an inseparable part of the account offered by those leaders who formulate the conflict supporting narrative. They reflect the belief that, up to now, Israel has dealt very successfully with the challenges of the conflict, and under those circumstances, any change brings with it a potential disaster. This approach has long characterized Israeli leadership, as expressed by Moshe Dayan in response to the peace proposals of Egyptian President Sadat, before the Yom Kippur War: "*Better Sharm-el-Sheikh without peace than peace without Sharm-el-Sheikh.*" And the rest is written in the history books.

It is important also to relate to the other side of the equation: Israelis are not just anxious about some unknown future—they also prefer a happy present. As a rule, Israelis are among the nations that are relatively satisfied with their lives. In research by the Central Bureau of Statistics, conducted in 2018, it was found that 89% of Israelis are "generally satisfied with their lives;"[324] and in an OECD survey taken in 2016, Israel was ranked in sixth place on the scale of satisfaction with their lives, especially thanks to replies by young respondents. In that sense, Israelis testify that they definitely have something to lose.[325]

In summary, as can be seen from this analysis, Jews in Israel feel comfortable with the conflict situation as it is and do not feel the need to change it. The opposite is true; they actually want to maintain it as it supplies some of their basic and primary needs. They are even ready to attest that a newborn male in both secular and religious Zionist circles is a future addition to the Israeli army, with the subtext that he may be a fighting soldier, with the possibility of becoming an army casualty. But the reality is much more complex. **They prefer to sink into the honey trap.** Israeli society as a whole pays a heavy price for the continuation of the conflict and the occupation, without any public discussion of its character. The establishment is not interested in this debate and the media avoids any such discussion. There is plenty of evidence of these heavy costs: some obvious, some implicit. They have become just a part of the everyday routine, and society members have become accustomed to them over many decades. The next chapter will detail them.

CHAPTER 9

The Costs of Continuing the Conflict and the Occupation

B loody and protracted conflicts are not free of extremely high costs. They are inherent in intractable conflict. Every society involved in them pays the costs—so it is in Israel, too. But those who lead the state are ready to pay these costs and they hide them successfully from public eyes. Thus, the costs to society members resulting from the continuation of the conflict are perceived as part of normal life and not all of them are even visible, in comparison to life in other countries that they visit. Over 600,000 Jews (about 10 percent of the present Jewish citizens of Israel) who have emigrated from Israel, some of them as a result of these costs, can testify as to what is happening in society. This chapter attempts to clearly present the great costs to Israeli society and the outcomes of its policies that must be borne due to the ongoing conflict, as well as illuminating issues that are the very essence of the occupation, fundamentally and by nature oppressive, exploitative and discriminatory. The chapter begins with the discussion of the highest of the costs —the cost in human lives.

Loss of Human Lives

Death is, by nature, the ultimate price to be paid by a society immersed in conflict. That is true in Israel, as well. According to Ministry of Defense statistics, the number of dead in Israel's wars from the start of the Israeli-Arab conflict in 1860, up until April 2022, was 24,068 people. In addition, between 1860 and April 2022, acts of terror took another 4,156 lives (according to the Institute for National Security Studies). During this period, there have also been over 36,500 wounded; some have even remained disabled with different levels of impairment for the rest of their lives. In these cases, the price cannot be expressed only in the cost of medical treatment and rehabilitation. They also must live with their physical disability and sometimes, with permanent emotional harm. **Although Jewish society is very sensitive to every Jewish death in the conflict, it does not develop a critical discourse about the need for the use of violence in achieving national goals, beginning with initiating wars, clashes and operations of various kinds, and ending with management of the occupation. The public sees the loss of human lives as a necessary** cost for ensuring security and even for survival. In two studies, one performed in a laboratory with a national sample of Jews, the results showed that information about Israeli human losses in the conflict did not change their views of the conflict. It must be clear to everyone that any act of violence by Israel will usually evoke a violent reaction by the other side, in which human lives, including those of civilians, may be lost.[326] But society has internalized the mantra that living in the shadow of the conflict requires loss of life.

Mental Health Costs

Involvement in violent events—whatever they may be—by its very nature, entails an emotional cost, affecting daily functioning on many levels. In the case of a conflict, those involved in the violence are primarily soldiers who have had difficult and perhaps even traumatic experiences during their service (even if they are not always aware of them), alongside civilians who have experienced violence that has left its scars on them—sometimes for the rest of their lives. However, this is not limited to those who have experienced direct violence or those whose family members have been harmed, but also to the many who have been exposed to violence virtually, by watching television, seeing graphic images or reading descriptions in the written media. Research conducted in 2003 during the second Palestinian *intifada* (uprising), by mental health researchers Avi Bleich, Mark Gelkopf, and Zehava Solomon, found that 16% of the respondents reported that they had been exposed directly to an act of terror, and about 37% reported that they knew of a family member or friend who had been exposed to a terror attack. However, no less than 77% of the respondents showed at least one symptom of emotional stress—both among those who had been exposed to terror directly and those who had not.[327] In this study, they found that no less than 9% of Israeli citizens showed symptoms of PTSD (post-traumatic stress disorder, which is considered one of the most difficult and most persistent of anxiety disorders). A study by NATAL - Israel Trauma and Resiliency Center (for Israeli victims of war and terror related trauma), conducted in September 2017, indicated that about 20% of Israeli citizens suffer trauma due to the continuing security tension in their lives.[328] Other studies have found that, during periods of conflict, tension and violent events, the rate of PTSD increases among the general population.[329]

For many years, the state leadership and the army ignored the mental health costs of the conflict, but in recent decades, awareness of the problem has increased, and most treatment is funded by the state. In 2001, the Ministry of Defense announced that they were treating about 1,800 former soldiers who were suffering from PTSD due to conflict violence.[330] However, it is accepted among researchers that the actual number is higher, due to the many cases which go unreported.[331] In any case, according to the same report from 2001, about 65% of those who have suffered from battle fatigue and who have been treated up to the date of the report, had served in combat units, and about 40% had seen combat during the Yom Kippur War in 1973. It is important to note that, despite the increasing recognition of battle fatigue and its harmful effects, identifying emotional distress among combat soldiers is still difficult and complex, and as, in many cases, soldiers remain undiagnosed, and thus, untreated, the costs are even higher.[332]

In addition, the specific character of the Israeli-Palestinian conflict creates unique emotional effects on participants in the security system—primarily soldiers and policemen who, during their service, carry out policing missions connected to the occupation, as for example, guarding at the roadblocks or arresting Palestinians in their homes.[333] In 2007, daily newspaper *Yedioth Aharononth* published the results of research conducted among thousands of IDF combat soldiers, which claimed that at least one quarter of the soldiers who had served in the occupied territories had abused Palestinians during their service, or were witness to such abuse. One soldier who was interviewed for the article explained why, in his opinion, this was so common: *"When you prevent free movement of thousands of people each day, it's impossible to do it nicely."*[334] Israeli society is not interested in a public debate about the actions of soldiers in the occupied territories, where there are, of necessity, acts of injustice.[335] The subject has been concealed and repressed, especially when the everlasting mantra is repeated that "the IDF is the most moral army in the world." Nevertheless, IDF soldiers do kill Palestinians, among whom are civilians, including children. This necessarily creates emotional distress at least among some people involved in the security system.

Did You Know?

The doctoral dissertation by Reut Zarkovitz, completed in 2020, investigated the reactions of soldiers to their killing of Palestinians

during army operations, interviewing ninety soldiers. They were divided into three categories: soldiers who took personal responsibility for the act of killing, soldiers who attributed responsibility for the killing to the military group, and soldiers who were not sure that their firing had caused the death of the victim. In addition, there was a control group who had not killed Palestinians. The killings had taken place during the second *intifada*, during the Cast Lead operation, and during ongoing activity in the West Bank and the Gaza Strip. It was found that soldiers who had taken personal responsibility for the killing expressed higher rates of PTSD in the past and the present and expressed higher levels of shame and guilt than other groups of soldiers who had killed Palestinians. In addition, soldiers who had carried out a killing did not find it possible to share thoughts and feelings that had been aroused. Regarding the military environment, the discussion of the killing was characterized by the focus on technical and operational elements, and it was not acceptable to share feelings about the deed. In addition, it was found that turning to the mental health officer was not a realistic possibility—even for those who were interested in sharing and were aware of the need to get help—and this was due to the stigma attached to such a move. Regarding the family environment, it was found that there were obstacles—both on the part of the family and on the part of the soldiers themselves—to deal with the issue; in some of the cases, the interviewees said that they wanted to share the experience of the killing with their families, but they met with refusal by their parents who tried to deny the involvement of their son in killing Palestinians. In other cases, the interviewees testified that they preferred not to share what they had been through with their families in order not to worry them and even more importantly, out of shame and anxiety at what they would think if they knew that the soldiers had taken part in the killing of Palestinians. It appears that, in time, an approach developed in which parents do not really want to know about these incidents and the sons prefer not to talk about them. Thus, in the end, those who kill remain alone with their feelings. In addition, the interviewees felt that Israeli society wanted to ignore the fact that acts of killing may lead to emotional distress and that those who experience such distress, suffer with it in isolation.[336]

Of interest is the fact that, through the years, much testimony (both fictional and documentary) has appeared in cultural products, books, films, theatrical plays and TV, as well as in the newspapers, about the heavy costs in terms of mental health, paid by Israelis due to the violence. Nevertheless, a recent study carried out by the author of this book found that these costs do not have any effect on the evaluation of the conflict or the willingness to end it.

If we return to the general public, Jewish society as a whole feels continual chronic fear as an outcome of the ongoing violent conflict. A series of studies conducted by Asher Arian and his colleagues for the Institute for National Security Studies found that, in 1993, 84% of Israelis expressed great anxiety or very great anxiety about the possibility that they or a member of their family would be harmed in a terror attack. A similar rate was found in later surveys: 76% in 1994, 85% in 1995, and 77% in 1997. With the outbreak of the second *intifada* in 2000, the level of personal fear among Israeli citizens dramatically increased. If in 1999, with the election of Prime Minister Ehud Barak, who had promised to lead Israel to a peace agreement, only 58% of Israelis reported that they were fearful or very fearful that they or a member of their family might be harmed in an attack by terrorists, in 2002, during the second *intifada*, almost everyone reported this fear—92%![337] It is not difficult to imagine what people living in the settlements near the Gaza Strip border must be feeling, as they have spent years under the threat of sudden rockets fired from the Strip since 2006. The inhabitants of this area, including children, are paying a heavy price by continuing to live under conditions of violent conflict.[338] The targeted areas have changed through the years: the Kiryat Shmona area and the Jordan Valley have been areas of confrontation in the past, and their residents lived with continual anxiety for months and even years under the shadow of the conflict. Jerusalem has remained under the constant possibility of violence since 1967.

Considering these statistics, it is no wonder that many define Israeli society as "a society living in constant trauma," and its behavior in many life areas should be judged accordingly.[339] Researchers associate life under the pressures of the conflict with negative daily behaviors, such as dangerous driving, interpersonal violence and more.

Direct Economic Costs

In contrast to the preceding costs, this category may be deceptive as, along with the costs —in this case, material—the occupation also brings considerable profit. That is a result of, *inter alia*, the expansion of the Israeli economy into the West Bank, the control of its natural resources including water, the flow of West Bank Palestinians aa a cheap labor force into Israel, and of course, the development of military industries producing the means to maintain the conflict and occupation. However, Economics Professor Yosef Zeira of Hebrew University, in his book *The Israeli Economy*, argues that these profits are of little value when contrasted to the costs paid by Israeli society for the continuation of the conflict, and when considering the potential profits which could be gained if the conflict was solved by peaceful means.[340] According to his calculations, until 1967, Israel's defense expenditures were less than 10 percent of the GDP on average (except during 1956—the Sinai War). After 1967, with the escalation of the conflict and the demands for spending in the occupied territories, expenditures doubled to more than 20 percent of the GDP. They remained at such levels in 1973–1976. After the Yom Kippur War, they ultimately reached 30 percent of the GDP. This was the period during which the wide Israeli-Arab conflict posed a significant threat to Israel and the costs of dealing with the violence placed a very heavy burden on Israeli citizens for almost 20 years. Only after the peace agreement with Egypt, which *de facto* ended the broad Israeli-Arab conflict, did they decrease in the early 1980s, and by 1987, they had been reduced to 14.5%. By the end of the decade, these costs had dropped to 12.1% of the GDP, and then, by 1994 they fell to below 10% and in 2018, were reduced to about 5.5%.

In the present period, the approved defense budget in 2019 reached a gross total (that is, with money supplementary to the governmental allocation of 55.3 billion shekels, such as, for example, U.S. assistance) of about 72.9 billion Israeli shekels—about $19.7 billion dollars (14% of the state budget). The defense budget in 2019 was increased by about 38% in comparison to that of 2014.[341] Together with expenditures through the prime minister's office for security organizations as well as additions received by the army during cycles of violence, the defense budget is the highest in Israel, higher than education and health. The first budget that was approved by the government in August 2021, after a stalemate in the

Netanyahu government preventing budget approval, will be about 73 billion shekels for 2021 and about 73.5 billion for 2022.[342]

By comparison with other countries, defense expenditures in Israel (5.5%) are very high, even at their low levels, when the conflict is waning. Additional direct expenditures that are spent through the Prime Minister's office (security organizations) and indirect expenditures (like the cost of conscription to the economy, security guards, military facilities, among others) must also be added; these add up to 14.1% in additional expenditures. In comparison, the average defense expenditures across the OECD is only 2.1 percent of the GDP. Among the other OECD countries, the U.S. has the highest defense spending, 3.2 percent of the GDP, but other countries pay much less.

Overall, Israel's defense spending is one of the highest in the world. According to the International Peace Research Institute in Stockholm, Israel was ranked in 14th place in 2017 for defense spending in terms of the total sum, but considering its territorial size, it is ranked higher- in 154th place, and considering population size, it is in 98th place. Another statistic bridges these enormous costs in everyday terms—a comprehensive study by an international institute to assess the costs of violence throughout the world, the Institute for Economics and Peace, dealt with the cost of the conflict in Israel in 2016 **alone** and found that it totaled $25.9 billion dollars, which represented about 9.7% of the Israeli gross national product—in other words, $3,152 dollars per year for every Israeli citizen.[343]

These numbers teach us that management of the conflict forces Israel to direct a great amount of monetary resources in order to maintain conflict challenges. The money is required in a great many areas including health, education, welfare, and transportation. Without a change in the path taken by the present leadership, defense spending will only increase, and other needs will become more acute. But again, as with other costs previously noted, the Israeli Jewish public is not affected by them and almost no public debate develops about them. Israeli Jews do not care about the costs they pay for the continuation of the conflict, the occupation, and expenses of Jewish settlement in the West Bank.

Indirect Economic Costs

The most significant indirect cost to the Israeli economy from the continuing conflict is the loss of potential growth which would be achieved by the arrival of peace. Stanley Fisher, the American economist who served as Governor of the Bank of Israel from 2005 to 2013, expressed sharp criticism of the accepted assumption according to which there is no connection between the geopolitical situation and economic growth. *"If the security situation changes and we move towards a real peace, as I hope we will do, it will raise the economy by 5-6% in the long term,"* Fisher stated in 2010.[344] That was not a meaningless statement—his point was supported by various economic models which attempted to evaluate the future economic implications of the conflict. The American research institute RAND, advising governments and international bodies on designing public policy, published a comprehensive study in 2015 investigating the possible ramifications of five different future Israeli scenarios.[345] The main finding determined that the scenario of two states for two peoples would supply the greatest economic potential both for the Israelis and for the Palestinians. According to the model, the Israeli economy would gain $125 billion dollars in the first ten years from the time a peace agreement was signed, in comparison to $50 billion dollars earned by the Palestinian economy. Alternatively, the research also estimated that an outbreak of a third *intifada* would lead to a loss of 10% of the Israeli gross domestic product and a 46% (!) loss on the Palestinian side.

In the context of the continuing defense costs, the question that should be asked is whether the presence of the Jewish settlements scattered throughout the West Bank contributes to maintaining Israeli security or is it a burden on the security system. As noted earlier, the answer accepted by most retired senior members of the security system is that the settlements burden the security system. They require considerable resources, lengthen the defensive lines of the state, and create innumerable points of friction with the Palestinians. The number of army troops required to hold onto the West Bank stands at more than half of the IDF combat strength, and during certain periods, that number may rise to two-thirds. And in contrast to the accepted assumption, the great majority of these forces do not deal with preventing acts of terror towards citizens within the Green Line, but rather, are engaged in defending the settlements. According to estimates, about 80% of IDF forces in the territories guard the settlements, while the other 20% focus on defending the state in its 1967 borders. The main reason is that most of the settlements were established in areas adjacent to Palestinian towns rather than at points of strategic military importance, which means that they require more protection. Moreover, settlements were built inside the West Bank on the mountains with the goal to prevent the establishment of the Palestinian state. Thus, the number of forces necessary to effectively defend the settlements is especially high considering the unique character of the task: protecting civilian settlements situated in the heart of hostile territory.[346] But interestingly, an ex-Israeli, Alex Stein, a judge of the Israeli Supreme Court who was imported from the USA by the right wing, rejected a petition filed by Palestinians against the renewal of military seizure orders, which allow the army to continue to hold a building in Hebron that was built mostly on private Palestinian land, in February 2022. He justified his ruling by claiming: "*The presence of the Jewish civilians constitutes part of the IDF's concept of spatial defense in the region. This is because the presence of the citizens of the state that owns the occupied land makes a significant contribution to the security situation in that area and makes it easier for the army to fulfill its role.*"[347]

When referring to a Jewish settlement in occupied territory, the price of creating the settlement project must also be included. It is almost impossible to ascertain the cost of this project in contrast to what it would cost to construct and populate settlements within the Green Line, that is, within Israel. Various government ministries, the Zionist Organization, private donors, organizations, the army, and other institutions participate in funding the project which is also highly subsidized in order to draw more settlers. There are those who estimate that the settlements cost at least a billion dollars a year, and there are years when much more must be invested.[348]

Did You Know?

In research entitled "The economic cost of the occupation for Israel," Shir Hever tried to estimate the cost of controlling and settling the West Bank from 1970 to 2008.[349] His calculations corresponded with the changes in prices and interest rate but did not include the profits accruing to the Israeli economy from international aid to the Palestinians and American aid to Israel. Hever's calculations found the following: About 104 billion shekels were spent on subsidies to the settlements, about 316 billion shekels went towards defending the settlements, and about 39 billion shekels came in as profits from the occupation. Thus, according to these figures, 381 billion shekels in total were spent on the Israeli presence on the West Bank from 1970 to 2008, including both military and civil expenses.

A Nation Torn Apart

Israeli society also pays a heavy price in terms of the absence of cohesion. In recent decades a group of citizens came to the conclusion that the conflict could be solved by peaceful means, and that aggression and occupation are immoral. This leftwing camp received the support of hundreds of thousands of Jewish Israelis. That led to a sharp polarization in the nation, even culminating in the murder of Israeli Prime Minister Yitzhak Rabin, who was leading a peace process with the Palestinians.

Today, the Israeli public is very deeply divided regarding the conflict and the occupation, to the extent of a serious rift involving the most negative implications for society in many areas of life, primarily because the lack of agreement also affects additional central issues, such as the nature of the state, the essence of Zionism, the character of the government, the structure of the legal system and especially the composition and the space of activity of the Supreme Court, treatment of minorities in Israel, human rights, the attitude towards the other, and even relations between religion and state. In the past two decades, support for the right has been increasing and the peace camp has significantly dwindled. But still, even as a minority, it has many supporters, and this includes Arab citizens of Israel. The rift has developed into extreme polarization while leftist opinions have become illegitimate for many on the right and thus, no small number of leftists feel alienated. A survey investigating the state of democracy in Israel indicated that 40% of the public feel that the tension between the left and the right is the most serious of the other five alternative sources of tension presented in the poll. This is particularly striking among people on the left (52%).[350] This rift has wide-ranging social significance. It has become a salient characteristic of interpersonal relations, in addition to the religious issue. Society members create relationships and social circles in terms of the right-left split, and this may often create a clash in the family or between friends. A recent study conducted in September 2021 indicated that 85% of the respondents thought that the polarization between left and right was increasing. But of special interest is the finding that about 41% of the rightist respondents felt that they would be disappointed if a family member married a person with leftwing views (37% of the leftists had the same feeling if a family member married a rightist). Finally, among rightists, about 39% reported that they boycotted businesses that were identified as belonging to a leftist and 32% of the leftists did the same with the rightist businesses.[351]

International Costs

Since the establishment of the state, and in many senses, even before that, the subject of Israel's international status has deeply occupied the agenda of the state and its institutions. In the past decades, the greatest efforts invested by Israel have been dedicated towards rejecting attempts to isolate the country, by the Palestinians, and by a number of Arab states and pro-Palestinian bodies throughout the world. Far beyond what is known about other scenes of conflict in the world, the persistence of the Israeli occupation has had its consequences and has aroused international opposition to Israel in many realms.

First, the European Union has leveled severe and continuing criticism against Israel for its policy towards the Palestinians, and the construction and expansion of settlements. Moreover, the ongoing conflict has prevented the implementation of the European proposal of 2013 to significantly upgrade its relations with Israel and with the Palestinian state of the future.[352] In 2009, after the Cast Lead Operation, the European Union also retreated from its intentions to upgrade Israel's status independently.[353] In 2012, the activity of the Council for Dialogue between the European Union and the State of Israel was frozen.[354] In July 2013, the institutions of the European Community even adopted a resolution that any agreements signed with Israel would not be valid in the occupied territories, and later, the Community even demanded that products coming from the settlements in the territories would be marked to distinguish them from products coming from within the Green Line. On 12 November 2019, the European Community court ruled that its member countries must mark food products coming from the settlements. Furthermore, in 2014, the parliaments of France, Italy, Ireland, Portugal, Spain, Sweden, and Great Britain, as well as the European parliament, decided to support recognition of the Palestinian state, a decision which was primarily declarative in nature. Up to now, only Sweden has actually put this decision into practice by officially recognizing a Palestinian state in 2014. **Without a doubt, continuation of the conflict and the occupation harms the entirety of Israeli relations with Europe, which has great political, economic, scientific, cultural importance, including questions of identification.**

If the European front is chilly, the Arab front is reserved. There is no doubt that the Israeli-Palestinian conflict is the central factor obstructing the development of relations and cooperation between Is-

rael, Jordan, and Egypt, which is, *inter alia*, the power motivating the strident opposition of the anti-normalization bodies in those states, acting vigorously against normalizing relations with Israel. To simplify, for as long as the conflict with the Palestinians is not solved, the relations between Israel and Jordan, and Israel and Egypt will remain those of a cold peace. Egypt and Jordan have avoided developing a warm peace with Israel because of the strong opposition of various social bodies to normalization until the conflict with the Palestinians is settled.

During the second half of 2020, a number of Arab states formalized their informal relationship with Israel that had existed for years, after U.S. President Donald Trump promised each of them considerable tangible incentives, either in terms of weapons to be sold to them and/or political gains that they badly wanted. The United Arab Emirates (UAE), Bahrain, Sudan, and Morocco announced normalization agreements with Israel. This added four additional Arab states to Egypt and Jordan that have formal and open relationships with the Jewish state. In return, Israel suspended plans to annex large parts of the occupied West Bank that had been announced by then Prime Minister Benjamin Netanyahu in 2020. And indeed, the opened relations with Morocco and United Arab Emirates cannot be underestimated. They added a very important value to construction of relationship with Arab countries. Especially the touristic open sky relationship that has flown many thousands of Israelis to Abu Dhabi is a remarkable achievement.

Most other states are precluded from officially recognizing Israel and from maintaining full commercial relations for as long as the conflict continues, even though, as mentioned above, some of them actually maintain relations of one form or another, especially in informal areas (and recently, as mentioned above, more and more states fall into this category). However, obstructions to official recognition of Israel prevent the possibility of general Mideast peace which will bring about wide-ranging trade benefits, economic development, tourism, and various other types of agreement.

But the heaviest price Israel has paid on a political level—as well as on the internal, Jewish level—is the relative deterioration of relations with Israel's greatest friend and sponsor, the United States, during the Obama terms in office. During the period in which Netanyahu and Obama were serving parallelly (starting from 2009), relations between the two countries deteriorated to an unprecedented low point, stemming primarily from disagreements about dealing with the Israeli-Palestinian conflict and facing the Iranian threat. The strong opposition by the Obama administration to the continued expansion in the settlements clashed with the Israeli program of massive construction across the Green Line; and on the other hand, the attempts by the American administration to bring about a return to negotiations with the Palestinians failed. The disagreements between the two sides also developed into a strained personal relationship between the two leaders, resulting in an extraordinary exchange of accusations, unparalleled in their severity, which were publicly leaked.

Towards the end of the Obama terms, the United States, for the first time, decided not to use its veto power in the Security Council on a vote critical to Israel, thus enabling the passage of Resolution 2334. This resolution determines the Israeli settlements in the West Bank and in East Jerusalem, captured in 1967, are illegal, and furthermore emphasized that any changes of borders, including in Jerusalem, would not be recognized except for those that would propose a framework of negotiations between the sides.

With the swearing in of Donald Trump as president in 2017, there was a dramatic change of atmosphere towards Israel in the White House. The new president expressed unmitigated public support for Israel and for Prime Minister Netanyahu. He advanced steps that strengthened the sovereignty of Israel over Jerusalem and the Golan Heights and made many symbolic gestures testifying to the personal friendship between the two leaders. At the same time, the American administration set about preparing a proposed program which would lead to a peace process; its details were published in January 2020 and have been described in Chapter 3. Nevertheless, the very recent book by Barak Ravid revealed in a personal interview a great disdain of Trump from Netanyahu.[355]

However, it was during Trump's term of office that figures in the Democratic Party began to voice positions which had never been heard previously in U.S.-Israeli relations. For example, in 2017, ten senators issued a letter to Netanyahu demanding that he refrain from destroying the Palestinian town of Susya, located in close proximity to Hebron. In May 2018, 76 members of Congress sent an additional letter to the Israeli prime minister, calling on him to stop destroying houses on the West Bank. And there have been other examples. In more general terms, the left wing of the Democratic Party, under the leadership of Bernie Sanders and Elizabeth Warren, has adopted a line sharply opposing the policies of the Israeli government and has expressed this policy line stridently. In the autumn of 2019, the two senators announced that aid to Israel should be conditioned on its policy towards the Palestinians. When Trump's peace plan was publicized, the main Democratic candidates for the presidency, Joe Biden, Bernie Sanders, and Elizabeth Warren strongly criticized it and warned against the annexation plan included in it. This clash of political positions, which took place, *inter alia*, against the backdrop of Trump's behavior and his polarizing statements (for example, his declaration in August 2019 that *"any Jewish person who votes for a Democrat is guilty of ignorance or great disloyalty"*) fractured the bi-partisan support that Israel had enjoyed in the United States. In October 2019, at a first-ever conference called by J Street, the large Jewish American organization, which supports the two-state solution by enlisting members of Congress (primarily Democrats), the idea was publicly raised to condition continuing aid to Israel on stopping the settlement project. In addition, the continuing occupation resonated strongly with a demand to stop the persistent abuse of human rights. Finally, during the May 2021 war in Gaza, even the consistently loyal supporters of Israel like Democratic Senator Bob Menendez and Democratic U.S. Representative Jerrold Nadler criticized Israel for its indiscriminate bombing of civilians in Gaza. These are all developments which indicate a dramatic change in the viewpoints of the Democrats and the Jews who support them. This is the beginning of a political process, and it is difficult to predict what its outcome will be now that the Democrats have regained political power in the elections of 2021, which brought a Democratic president to the White House, along with Democratic control of both houses of Congress.

But during the presidency of Donald Trump, from the Israeli perspective, Israel gained a number of achievements in addition to those presented in Chapter 3—the U.S. president recognized Israeli sovereignty over the Golan Heights, a Syrian range of hills that had been conquered by Israel and then annexed. Furthermore, Secretary of State Mike Pompeo stated in November 2019 that the U.S. no longer viewed Israeli settlements in the occupied West Bank as a violation of international law. He was also the first top American diplomat to make an unprecedented visit to an Israeli settlement in the occupied territories in November 2020. In addition, during a visit to the occupied territories, he announced that goods made in Israeli-controlled areas of the West Bank would be labeled "Made in Israel." Finally, Pompeo announced that the U.S. would designate the boycott, divestment, and sanctions (BDS) campaign seeking to isolate Israel over its treatment of the Palestinians as anti-Semitic.

Biden's Democratic administration, inaugurated in 2021, is not expected to initiate a new attempt to resolve the conflict or to take major steps to end the occupation, but while Biden has expressed the traditional statement of *"unwavering support for Israel's security and for Israel's legitimate right to defend itself and its people while protecting civilians,"* he also said something about Palestinians, stressing that Israelis and Palestinians deserve *"equal measures of freedom, prosperity, and democracy."* On the practical level, he decided to reestablish the U.S. consulate in East Jerusalem, restore diplomatic relations with the Palestinian Authority, resume American aid to the Palestinians, and reaffirm support for the two-state solution of the conflict. All these are Trump-era policy reversals.

More or less simultaneously, the political positions of the American public have been changing regarding Israel, whether due to the developments cited above or whether these developments have been the result of a previous change in attitude. In any event, a survey taken by the Pew Research Center in January 2018 indicated that while 79% of Republicans stated that they identify with Israel more than with the Palestinians, only 27% of the Democrats felt this way. However, the most important finding of the survey was the unequivocal picture it presented of young voters— among respondents aged 18-29, Republicans and Democrats alike, only 22% supported Israel.[356] Quite similarly, a survey conducted by the Gallup Poll in August 2018, found that Netanyahu was perceived among Republican voters as the most admired world leader (64% thought so), while among supporters of the Democratic Party, he was chosen the third worst leader in the world (at 17%)—the only two considered even worse were North Korea's Kim Jong-Un and Russia's Vladimir Putin.[357] A Gallup Poll conducted in February 2021 identified a new trend among the American public who support the Democratic Party—53% of them opted for more pressure on the Israelis. This percentage is up from 43% in 2018 and no more than 38% in the decade before that, marking a substantive change in Democrats' perspective on U.S. policy towards Israel.[358]

Finally, it is important to mention that, despite the Trump administration policy of inclusion regarding settlements, on 6 December 2019, the House of Representatives voted unequivocally (226 representatives against 188) for a decision stating that *"only a two-state solution … can ensure the exis-*

tence of Israel as a Jewish and democratic state, and at the same time, to realize the legitimate aspirations of the Palestinian nation for a state of its own." The decision even mentioned the long-term American opposition to *"the expansion of the settlements, the unilateral annexation of territories and efforts to establish a Palestinian state outside of the framework of a negotiated settlement with Israel."* This was criticism of steps taken by the Trump administration to grant legitimization to Israeli moves tightening its hold on the West Bank and the Golan Heights.

Thus, the alliance with the Republican Party initiated by Netanyahu, which began during the Obama presidency—reaching its peak in the nationalistic speech given by Netanyahu to the two houses of Congress in 2015 against the U.S. policy towards Iran—weakened the support for Israel in parts of the Democratic Party. The new Israeli government is trying to reestablish relations with the Democratic Party, and this has been received favorably by the Biden Administration. The president accepted the new Israeli Prime Minister Naftali Bennett warmly on Bennett's visit to Washington in August 2021. But some powerful U.S. senators, like Bernie Sanders, have still expressed public criticism of Israel because of its continuing harmful policies towards the Palestinians. In his visit, in July 2022, in Bethlehem, Joe Biden, president of USA, repeated his support for two-state solution to solve the Israeli-Palestinian conflict.

But relations with the U.S. have turned support for the State of Israel into a partisan issue. As such, the alliance has trapped American Jews—three-quarters of them, Democratic Party supporters—who have been asked to choose between their loyalties, which have become contradictory. In their case, it was only one aspect out of many that sharpened the gaps between their liberal viewpoints, and the conservative and isolationist viewpoints of Israeli Jews. Another controversial aspect of mutual relations was American Jews' comprehensive support for the Reform and Conservative movements, which in official Israel, are considered as outcasts. **Although national conditions now favor a rightwing government in Israel, it stands to reason that this will not always be the case. And when political change does take place in the United States, it may harm Israel at its most vulnerable point, the continuation of its rule in the occupied territories, unwaveringly violating the human rights of the Palestinians.**

Looking at the Jewish community in the United States—71% of Jewish Americans voted for the Democratic candidate, Hillary Clinton, while 24% voted for Republican Donald Trump. During Trump's presidential term, a majority of Jews objected to a range of policies and actual steps taken by the Trump administration, including his actions related to the Israeli-Palestinian conflict. Most American Jews disapproved of the way Trump conducted his job and above half even thought that Trump favored Israel too much. It is not surprising that Trump stated in 2019: *"In my opinion, if you vote for a Democrat, you're being very disloyal to Jewish people and you're being very disloyal to Israel. And only weak people would say anything other than that."*[359] In 2020, just 22% of American Jews voted for Trump, while 76% voted for the elected president, Joe Biden.[360] A recent study by Wright, Saxe, and Wald (2020) reveals an interesting finding. Drawing on two 2019 surveys of Jews in the United States, the researchers found that Jewish conservatives tend to oppose criticism of Israel and America for any reason, while Jewish liberals, who care about Israel, view criticism of the Jewish state as a legitimate expression of their emotional connection.[361]

Not only in the United States is the Jewish community divided on the question of its relations with Israel. Research in recent years indicates an increasing erosion of support for Israel among Jewish communities throughout the world, and an intensification of discord about the legitimacy of its actions. A survey taken in 2015 among British Jews found strongly negative attitudes—about 75% of respondents stated that the expansion of construction in the settlements was the central obstruction to peace, and about 45% felt that the Israeli government *"systematically creates obstacles in order to avoid a peace process,"* while about 58% agreed with the statement that Israel "would be an apartheid state if it tries to maintain its control within borders where there are more Arabs than Jews."[362]

And if support for Israel by Jewish communities is diminishing, the same is true among the general world population. An annual survey carried out by the British BBC among a general world sample ranked Israel permanently among the lowest-admired states internationally. In the last survey, conducted in 2014, Israel was graded the fourth most unadmired state in the world, while only Iran, Pakistan, and North Korea ranked lower on this scale.[363]

On a practical level, one of the greatest blows to Israel may take place in the International Criminal Court in The Hague. In 2015, court representatives began to conduct a preliminary investigation into the possibility that war crimes had been committed in the occupied territories. Two main issues which were examined were the establishment of settlements, and war crimes which were allegedly committed during the Protective Edge Operation (both by Israel and by Hamas) in Gaza. The investigation was enabled by the approval for membership of the Palestinian State by The Hague court in 2015. Of the two subjects under review—which could take years—the issue of the settlements was considered as having the greatest probability of reaching the stage of indictment. On 20 December 2019, the prosecution of the International Criminal Court determined that there was a basis for investigation against Israel due to its activities in the West Bank, the Gaza Strip, and East Jerusalem, for war crimes against the Palestinians. The next stage was transmitted to the court, which would have to decide about the question of its judicial authority in the West Bank and the Gaza Strip.

An additional front on which pressure has been applied and which constitutes another sign of the diminishing status of Israel in the international arena is boycott movements. These constitute a decentralized system of movements operating to institute economic, cultural, and academic boycotts against Israel. For many years, these movements had only a marginal effect, but their influence has been growing as a result of Israel army action to put down the second *intifada*, and most importantly, the Protective Shield operation in the Gaza Strip, which had a great international impact and provided fertile soil for the increase in anti-Israeli feeling. The leading and most well-known of these movements is Boycott, Divestment, and Sanctions, created in 2005. The activities of these groups penetrated the political agenda in 2010, when the Palestinian Authority led a campaign in the international media calling for a boycott on goods produced in the settlements. This succeeded in harming several large Israeli companies located over the Green Line, and most strikingly, Soda Stream, which shut down its production line in Mishor Adumim and moved to the Negev.[364] In summer 2021, Ben & Jerry decided to stop selling ice cream in 'Occupied Palestinian Territory.' The brand noted that they had made the decision because they felt it was **inconsistent** with their values to continue their ice cream sales in these areas.

These economic costs, which have been increasing recently, join the additional costs Israel has been paying during this period, primarily in the cultural and academic realms. From about 2005, there has been a considerable increase in the number of censures of Israel by researchers and academic institutions regarding Israeli occupation in the territories, along with calls for a real academic boycott of Israel. One salient example is the 2007 decision by British universities to apply an academic boycott, prohibiting cooperation with Israeli lecturers and researchers.[365] Then, in 2015, more than 300 academics from dozens of universities pledged to boycott Israeli academic institutions in protest of what they called intolerable human rights violations against the Palestinian people.[366] In 2013, members of the American Studies Association had voted to join the boycott of all Israeli educational institutions. In 2018, Israel's Strategic Affairs Ministry published a list of 20 organizations which support BDS, announcing that activists from these organizations would be barred from entering Israel. Among them are the American Friends Service Committee, a Quaker organization honored with the 1947 Nobel Peace Prize for assisting and rescuing victims of the Nazis, and the Jewish Voice for Peace.

Culturally, the main feature of the boycott has been the loudly proclaimed refusal of many artists and intellectuals to appear in Israel. This trend has also expanded in recent years. In 2015, British newspaper *The Guardian* published a letter submitted by about 700 international artists, stating they would boycott Israel *"until it honors international law and ends the colonial repression of the Palestinians."*[367] Prominent among the signers were the director, Ken Loach, the musician Brian Eno, and Jewish actress Miriam Margolyes. In 2021, a very well-known Irish author, Sally Rooney, decided to forbid the translation of her new book Beautiful World into Hebrew. This act was supported by 70 British writers and publishers. In 2022, actress Emma Watson publicly supported the Palestinian cause. Israel accused her of anti-Semitism, but the actress was supported by about 40 figures from the film industry. During Operation Protective Edge in 2014, a letter accusing Israel of violation of human rights was signed by dozens of Spanish artists, including actors Javier Bardem and Penelope Cruz, and director Pedro Aldomovar.[368] In September 2016, about 70 leading American intellectuals also called for a boycott of the settlements and their products.

When referring to the costs Israel must bear for the continuation of the conflict and occupation, we Israelis must look within and evaluate what the persistent conflict is doing to one of the two foundations of the state— its status as a democracy. The democratic understructure of the country is being eroded, and we will now discuss the problem more deeply.

The Deterioration of Democracy

The conflict and occupation continue with no solutions on the horizon. Moreover, as we have shown, there are enormous forces that are making an extreme effort to maintain the conflict and the occupation, and there are even those who profit from the situation—not necessarily cynically, but sometimes due to complex and deeply rooted social structures and processes, some of which have been described.

One factor that works to support the continuing occupation is that scant importance is actually accorded to maintaining a democratic regime. Occupation against the wishes of the occupied population and democracy do not go together. This is a universal rule that has been found in almost every occupying state. The occupied territory is always governed in undemocratic ways, and these eventually penetrate the occupying state as well. The very same premise can be held about a situation in which there is a protracted and bloody conflict that is conducted without the will to end it, at least by the stronger side. This situation requires maintaining conflict-supporting narratives within the culture of conflict and specifically, suppressing narratives and information that contradict them, in order to retain mobilization of society members to participate in it. Then, by the nature of this situation, at least the free flow of information and freedom of expression are limited. Formal institutions discredit and limit individuals and organizations that oppose governmental policies in the conflict context.

In addition, societies engaged in violent and vicious conflict become accustomed to mistreating the oppressed population. They violate its human rights, discriminate, persecute, and conduct acts of violence, along with many other transgressions. Each of the states—whether Israel, Russia, Turkey, or India, initiate these practices. On every indicator it is possible to find disparity between the majority group and the minority group. In Turkey, there is persistent discrimination of Kurds. For example, the Kurdish language cannot be used in private or public schools. In India the ruling Hindu nationalist government under the leadership of Narendra Modi conducts policies and enacts legislation ensuring Hindu supremacy, especially against the Muslim minority, who are viewed as the enemy. In the case of Russia, Putin has installed a pro-Russian dictatorial regime in Chechnya that, with Russian help, has conducted abductions and arbitrary detentions and arrests. Human rights are violated systematically, with allegations of torture and executions. These practices necessarily limit the democratic pillars of freedom, equality, and human rights—and thus decrease democracy.

A look at ongoing intractable conflicts easily indicates that Russia, fighting in Chechnya and Ukraine, Turkey, involved in the Kurdish conflict, India, in its Kashmir conflict, the Sri Lankan conflict between Tamils and Singhalese, or Rwanda with its conflict between Hutu and Tutsi, have all moved in the same direction of authoritarianism. All these conflicts involve bloody engagement over sacred goals, have lasted for over 40 years, require great investment, and no peace-making process is in sight. One of the major explanations for the development of authoritarian regimes is based on their context of intractable conflict that dictates governing directions.

It is therefore no wonder that, in Israel, in recent years, a disturbing trend has been the gradual reduction in democratic space. That is one of the most distressing side effects of the continuing occupation, which was predicted only by a few, notable among them Professor Yishayahu Leibowitz, who perceived the unavoidable consequences of continuing occupation as early as 1967. This year, one of the important intellectual experts in the study of Israeli democracy, Professor Benyamin Neuberger, wrote: "*At the present time, the greatest threat to the integrity of Israeli democracy is the continuing control of the West Bank.*"[369]

Developing Authoritarian Statehood

Of special focus should be the structural and valuative change of the state after a process of liberalization that followed the authoritarian regime established by Ben Gurion. Israel began to move towards authoritarian rule with the escalation of the conflict in the early 2000. The signs of authoritarianism increased with the ascendance to power of Benjamin Netanyahu in 2009 and accelerated with his establishment of the extreme rightist government in 2015. Rightist governments refrain from serious peace negotiation that may bring peaceful resolution requiring meaningful withdrawal from the occupied territories. Such withdrawal is seen as giving up promised land—the homeland. Continuation of the conflict is the only alternative for the right. In such cases, there is need to maintain continuous mobilization of society members for participation in the conflict through construction of a culture of conflict with conflict-supporting narratives and obstruction of contradictory information. The stronger and more hegemonic the culture of conflict with its supporting narratives, the more the signs of an authoritarian regime appear. This premise is valid because the culture of conflict necessarily leads to authoritarianism that has a major effect on statehood—that is, the way the state functions with its institutions and organizations. Specifically, the government and its organs try to block the free flow of information, interfere in the rule of law, impair and weaken the legal system, disempower institutions that serve as guardians of democracy, harm the system of checks and balances, violate human rights, use force, delegitimize opposition, instigate racism, spread discourse of fear, use xenophobic messages, and encourage ethnocentrism and self-glorification—to note the most distinguished authoritarian features.[370] All these characteristics have appeared due to practices that are carried out within the framework of the occupation. The attempt to block alternative information about the Palestinians, the conflict and the peace process; the efforts to stop societal forces that conduct activities opposing governmental policies, and occupation practices, the conflict, and Jewish settlement in the occupied territories—all neutralize the state institutions that prevent or stand in the way of the government in its conflict and settlement goals. Thus, it can be stated unequivocally that ongoing occupation and intractable conflict harm the foundations of the democratic system as will be explained at length.

There are many expressions of increasing harm to democracy. In recent years, at least until spring 2021, members of the Netanyahu government and the Knesset began to intensively advance initiatives harmful to the fundamental democratic character of the regime: abuse of minority rights, persecution of foreign workers, harm to freedom of expression and to activities of civil society organizations, delegitimization of the leftwing opposition, creation of a social rift by monopolization of patriotism, and then, the beginnings of an attack on the system of checks and balances between the branches of government. In addition, the government advanced legislation directed towards blurring the legal boundary between sovereign Israel and the occupied territories. And finally, under the claim of "harm to governability" and "deep state," there was a frontal attack on the various "gatekeepers": the Supreme Court, which "dared" to criticize government policy that was damaging to human rights (even if this criticism occurred much too rarely, as we shall soon see); the police, who "dared" to investigate or to recommend prosecuting elected officials; the state comptroller's office; the attorney general's office and the attorney general himself, when he did not automatically defend government policy, and especially when he did not defend the prime minister against whom he had issued an indictment; the officials of the state attorney's office, the Justice Ministry, and the legal advisors in other government offices, who refused to serve as ministers' lawyers and instead, insisted on fulfilling their roles as gatekeepers; government officials who acted as professionals and did not automatically support and advance every initiative of the prime minister or other ministers, and more. Thus, after firing or getting rid of those who did not agree with the prime minister's policies and practices, Netanyahu assembled a hive of loyal yea-sayers, who disseminated messages prepared by his office. This was the way he ruled as prime minister—especially over the last five years. Much harm was done in the name of safeguarding democracy and improving governance. In this fraudulent framework, the prime minister, ministers, and Knesset members propagated a series of diversions and fallacies about the essence of democracy and encouraged ignorance on the part of their supporters, in the spirit of George Orwell's novel, *1984*. Take, for instance, one obvious example: On 28 December 2019, Netanyahu strikingly stated, as was already noted, that *"legal immunity* (of the prime minister) *is one of the cornerstones of democracy."*[371] Recently in February 2022, one of the key leaders of Likud party, Miri Regev, who was the Minister of Culture and Transportation and is a candidate for the office of prime minister once Benjamin Netanyahu will be out, stated in Knesset: *"There are enough democratic countries. Another democratic country is not what is needed. What we need here is the only Jewish state in the world, which must be protected."*[372]

A democratic regime is the least of political evils as it enables free elections and equality, but in contrast to other regimes, the citizens must be very well acquainted with its rules, understand its nature, be involved in its development, and safeguard it against forces which aim to minimize it. Evaluating a democracy is based on two types of components: the administrative-structural component, including primarily free elections taking place at fixed time intervals, the principle of rule of the majority, government change in line with the voting results in the election, separation of powers (the executive, legislative, and judicial branches), the existence of an independent and fair judicial system, obedience to the law, transparency and acceptance of responsibility of the government for its citizens, and the absence of state corruption. The valuative components primarily include freedom of speech and assembly, a flow of free information, equality before the law, safeguarding human, civic and minority rights, and plu-ralism.[373]

The Declaration of Independence of 1948, as the canonic document, en-sured that "*[t]he State of Israel will be open for Jewish immigration and for the Ingathering of the Exiles; it will foster the development of the country for the benefit of all its inhabitants; it will be based on freedom, justice and peace as envisaged by the prophets of Israel; it will ensure complete equality of social and political rights to all its inhabitants irrespective of religion, race or sex; it will guarantee freedom of religion, conscience, language, education and culture; it will safeguard the Holy Places of all religions; and it will be faithful to the principles of the Charter of the United Nations.*"

Even though the realities of the first years of the state were different than the promises included in the declaration, the document gave direction to the political course. This was not easy as the State of Israel always remained in the category of young democracies, not fully established and still vul-nerable due to the threatening context in which the state existed—and because of the mixture of political traditions, some of them democratic and some that weren't, and some even anti-democratic. Despite the col-lective image fostered by Israeli leaders through the years, that Israel is an exemplary democracy, in reality it has always been deficient in important democratic elements, such as full equality, freedom or upholding the law.

According to international measures, the State of Israel deviates from being a democracy. It is deficient in the administrative-structural com-ponent, but it is primarily flawed in the realm of democratic values, and is moving consistently towards becoming an authoritarian regime. In re-cent years, the separation of powers has been dissolving. The legislative branch acts only as directed by the executive and the opposition is not successful, even when it wants to enact laws meant to contribute to citi-zens' welfare. In March 2020, even the Chair of the Knesset (the legislative branch), appointed by the Likud Party, refused to implement a Supreme Court (the judicial branch) ruling in order to prevent the establishment of Knesset committees which might harm the rightwing bloc, with Bin-yamin Netanyahu as its head. In general, there is widespread refusal by the government to uphold rulings of the Supreme Court time after time. The new government is committed to overriding the decisions of the Supreme Court. This would enable the Knesset to overturn the laws that contradict Israel's Basic Laws. One of the proposals that gains a majority of the new coalition voices suggests that just 61 votes can overturn Supreme Court decisions and it gives the coalition a free hand to do whatever it pleases, This will destroy the freedom of the judicial branch, leaving only the power of the executive branch.

The judicial branch is also affected by hidden agreements led by the executive and its coalition in the appointment of new judges. The executive and many members of the legislature have often tried to reduce the independence of the judiciary. In 1994, Yitzchak Rabin pointed out with a bit of envy that the Palestinians could operate *"without the Supreme Court and without B'tselem (a human rights NGO)"* and that they had a free hand in suppressing opposition, unlike in Israel. In the past decade, the castigation and mudslinging directed towards the Supreme Court by the prime minister, other ministers, and Knesset members reached peaks that had never before been seen. In addition, the idea was raised of adding an overriding clause, or even legislation to amend basic laws, in order to enable the legislature to override rulings of the Supreme Court, by a simple majority vote. This led the President of the Supreme Court, Esther Hayut, to make a rare announcement on 30 October 2019, after having suffered unmitigated slander from the then-Justice Minister and the Minister for Internal Security: *"These days, unprecedented in our political history, require all of us to stand firm and to do our work without fear, with responsibility and discretion, as those entrusted with the rule of law, with safeguarding it and reinforcing its position."*[374] Finally, as another sign attesting to the sad state of Israeli democracy, we may add the appointment to positions of the greatest importance that should be filled by those who can be independent and provide checks and constraints on members of the government. But these have often been filled by yea-sayers who are obedient and dependent on the appointer. Thus, in Israel, bodies that should be supervising and counterbalancing government powers have gradually been disappearing. Under Netanyahu, the government, that is, the executive, had become authoritarian, and was directed by an omnipotent leader. When serious indictments for corruption were drawn up against Prime Minister Binyamin Netanyahu, he organized retaliatory attacks against the investigative and enforcement authorities and even organized citizens' protests against them with the unfounded argument that democracy was being harmed. It is no wonder that the report of the Democracy Index of 2019 states that

> *"in comparison with Israel's relative place from the standpoint of its democracy with the states of the OECD, it is usu-*

ally placed at the bottom of the list. Only in one measure—political participation—is Israel placed in the upper median among members of this organization; in contrast, in eight other measures (such as civil rights, democratic rights, freedoms, civil participation, freedom of the press, and democratic equality), it is placed at the bottom, in the bottom quartile ... According to this organization, Israel is defined as a state where only electoral democracy exists. In other words, Israel is a state in which there are democratic elections, but full commitment to the basic values of liberal democracy do not exist."[375]

In the last few decades, an approach has been developed in social sciences—when evaluating whether a state is democratic, we need to evaluate it according to two criteria: a.) to what extent is it democratic, and b.) to what extent is it authoritarian. This is because social scientists have realized that most states exist within a hybrid system with democratic and authoritarian elements. Moreover, it is very difficult to find an ideal democratic regime, and thus it is necessary to talk about hybrid regimes that contain both democratic and authoritarian elements. Obviously, states differ regarding the ratio between their democratic and authoritarian elements. Some states possess mostly authoritarian elements, like Chad, Saudi Arabia, and Turkmenistan, and others possess mostly democratic elements like Iceland, New Zealand, and Denmark. Since independence in 1948, Israel has moved from an authoritarian regime to a relatively democratic one and then, at the beginning of the 2000s, it moved backwards, adopting the many authoritarian elements described above. The new government of extreme right is preparing new laws and policies that will move the regime further to the authoritarian end.

Fully authoritarian regimes that are totalitarian and dictatorial are characterized by the following elements: *Anti-democratic structural elements*—interfering with the rule of law and democratic norms; disrespecting rules and regulations; weakening and controlling the legal system and law enforcement agencies; disempowering institutions that serve as guardians of democracy; harming the system of checks and balances, limiting and controlling the opposition. *Anti-democratic value elements*—limiting freedom of expression and organization; violating human rights; favoring use of force. *Anti-pluralistic elements*—inciting and delegitimizing the opposition; monopolizing patriotism; obliterating criticism, trying to control free media and flow of information. *Discriminatory elements*—instigating racism, prejudice and discrimination of minorities; encouraging ethnocentrism, sexism and chauvinism; opposing immigration. *Populistic elements*—spreading discourse of fear; using xenophobic messages, focusing on external threats and enemies, characterizing the society in glorifying terms, appealing to personal and collective basic needs, *Self-interest elements*—appointing functionaries predominantly based on loyalty to the leader, encouraging adoration of a strong leader with omnipotent rights, and cultivating personal adoration. And finally occupying a conquered territory against the wishes of the indigenous population, violating their human rights, using control and violence. As described, some of these characteristics can be found in the Israeli regime, many of them, since the establishment of the state.[376] In the following sections, some of the noted features will be further described.

Did You Know?

An in-depth survey conducted by the Israel Democracy Institute enabled researchers to investigate citizens' opinions about the state of Israeli democracy.[377] The survey from 2019 shows that, in general, the appraisal of the state of democracy in Israel was extremely low. The Jewish-Israeli public can be divided into three sectors, almost equal in size: those who consider that the level of democracy is good, those who think it is fair, and those who think it is poor. But a deeper look indicates that there is a great gulf between most of the Jewish public who identify with the right, and the minority who identify with the left. On the right, only 20% of the respondents answered that Israeli democracy is in a relatively poor state or in a poor state, while 29% considered that Israeli democracy was in grave danger. On the left, 56% felt that the state of Israeli democracy was relatively poor or poor, and 84% thought that democracy was in great danger. In addition, on the right, 50% replied that the state of Israeli democracy was good or excellent, while on the left, only 13% agreed. These findings indicate that even in the appraisal of Israeli democracy, great polarization exists between the left and the right.

However, in order to deeply comprehend what the Israeli public understands about the essence of democracy, we must look at the results of surveys that investigated it during 2017–2018: Surveys by the Israel Democracy Institute showed, for example, that 77% of the Jewish public in Israel think that human rights organizations like the Association for Civil Rights in Israel and B'tselem (The Israeli Information Center for Human Rights in the Occupied Territories) cause harm to the state; 54% think that, in order to deal with the special problems Israel faces, a strong leader is needed who will not take the Knesset, the media, or public opinion into consideration. Surveys of the Index of Arab-Jewish Relations in Israel, conducted by Professor Sammy Smooha showed for example that 75% of Jews think that critical decisions by the state regarding peace and security should be made by a majority of Jews; 67% think that there ought to be a law stipulating that democracy should exist in Israel only if it does not harm the Jewish state. And most relevant for the elections that took place in March 2020, in a survey taken in 2019 for this index, about 58% of Jews opposed the addition of Arab parties to the coalition. All these perceptions contradict democratic principles. The findings also show that there is a strong link between rightwing perceptions and anti-democratic opinions. The more rightwing the citizen's opinions, the more anti-democratic s/he is.

We haven't invented anything. This reality is well known from Russia, Turkey, Rwanda, and Sri-Lanka—all states in which there have been long-standing conflicts. It is also true of Poland, Hungary, the Czech Republic, and even, in some ways, the United States during the Trump era—all states that have begun to slide into authoritarian regimes during the past decade.[378] But while political science researchers have been watching in despair at the changes taking place in these states, and have been arguing about the reasons for them, in Israel, it is very easy to discern one of the main sources at its deepest roots. Control over two-and-a half million people on the West Bank who do not have citizenship challenges the democratic character of the state more than anything else. Another 300,000 Palestinians living in Jerusalem should be added to this number along with almost 2,000,000 inhabitants of the Gaza Strip who are also under Israeli control. The occupation necessarily leads to a deterioration of democracy in Israel and the rise of an authoritarian regime. In the meanwhile, the Prime Minister Naftali Bennett, who got this role in 2021 announced that the present status of the West Bank and Gaza Strip would continue, meaning that the occupation is also preferred by the present leadership. The return of Netanyahu with the extreme right will worsen even the situation of occupation and conflict.

The native Palestinian population on the West Bank has lacked basic human rights and freedoms for many years, discriminated against and oppressed—this is in basic conflict with a democratic regime. And similar to what happens in all international states, the non-democratic nature of the occupied territories necessarily drifts over the border and into Israel proper. At this point in the chapter, we will discuss the fundamental harm to democracy stemming from the interminable conflict and especially, from the continuing occupation.

Occupartheid

An apt concept describing the unique realities of inequality is the principle that we call *occupartheid*, a portmanteau of "occupation" and "apartheid," because the occupation has moved Israel to a state of apartheid. In this system, there are no fewer than five categories of political status. The Israeli regime maintains this extreme inequality of status and negates freedoms, and as such, does not deserve to be called democratic.

At the head of the pyramid, in the first category, are the settlers in the occupied territories, receiving privileges and material benefits that are denied to most citizens of Israel, who can only dream about them. For example, until 2003, almost all the settlements enjoyed tax allowances, according to Article 11 of the Income Tax Ordinance. From 2012, 88 of 131 settlements enjoyed benefits that were granted to national priority areas. In addition, most of the settlements in the West Bank are recognized as Development Areas A, so they are eligible for a series of benefits, including accommodation and mortgages. At the bottom line, all these advantages grant them exclusivity and favor them in comparison to most citizens living within the Green Line borders.

The second category are Jewish citizens of Israel, who enjoy all the rights the state provides to its citizens according to the Israeli laws. The third category are Arab citizens of Israel who make up about 17.2% of the population. As a minority, and also because many of them consider themselves as belonging to the Palestinian nation (and the great majority of them would agree with this characterization), with whom the Jews have been in conflict for more than 100 years, they suffer from inequality, including cultural, institutional, and even legal discrimination.[379] This inequality has existed since the establishment of the state, when Arabs were living under military governance which ended only in 1966, and much of their land was expropriated. In 2021 almost half of the Arab population lived below the line of poverty. Although their economic situation has improved significantly through the years and their integration has intensified (for example, they constitute 19% of the students in Israel, 21% of the physicians, 50% of the pharmacists and 24% of all nurses), they are discriminated against culturally by racist practices instituted by Jews. One striking example of discrimination is that since the establishment of the state in 1948, about 700 new Jewish settlements have been established in Israel, and none for Arabs except seven small towns where Bedouins were concentrated after being expelled from their living areas in the Negev desert. Many of the new Jewish settlements were built on confiscated Arab land of about 4 to 16 million dunams (1 dunam =1000 square meters=0.25 acre).[380] The confiscations continued until the late 1970s.

They are also still discriminated against institutionally, in budgets and in development, and they attain fewer opportunities to advance, although even the Netanyahu government had directed allocations to improve their economic standing. For example, even in 2019, the government was allocating 40% less for Arabs high school students than for the religious Zionist educational sector, and 20% less than for the general-secular Jewish educational system.[381] Additionally, in recent years quite a few bills have been passed incorporating deliberate discrimination against this minority (for example, the Nakba Law, the Acceptance to Communities Law, the Citizenship Law, and the Nation State Law). For example, the Citizenship and Entry into Israel Law, enacted in 2003, was ostensibly intended to prevent Palestinians who had married Israeli citizens—*de facto* Israeli Arab-Palestinian citizens—from gaining access to Israel and committing terror attacks. In reality, the sweeping legislation collectively banned married couples, if they included an Israeli married to a Palestinian, from living together inside Israel. Either they had to leave Israel or be forcibly separated, except for limited provisions for temporary exceptions. Even when the law, which was extended every year, did not get enough votes in 2021 to be approved because of Likud party games, the Interior Minister Ayelet Shaked, coming from an extreme rightwing party, prevented unification of married couples using bureaucratic tactics. Eventually in March 2022, a new law was approved effectively barring Palestinians from the West Bank or Gaza married to Israeli citizens from gaining citizenship or residency.

This process of discrimination and exclusion is backed by the leadership of Jewish society, especially on the right. Rightwing leaders consider Arab citizens as disloyal to the state and have succeeded in so effectively delegitimizing them that most Jewish political parties in Israel, excluding Meretz, do not consider Arab political parties as legitimate partners for cooperation or for participation in the coalition. Only in 2021, did an Arab party for the first time as an independent party, join the new government coalition because without it, it would have been impossible to form a new government replacing Netanyahu. Nevertheless, the incitement against Arabs by the rightwing leadership, including the prime minister, has been going on for many years, and has become a permanent and persistent norm in some circles.

The fourth category consists of the Palestinian inhabitants of East Jerusalem, who, after the Israeli annexation of the area in 1967, received the status of permanent residents, which formally entitles them to services and to the same rights granted to citizens of Israel, except for the right to vote for the Knesset. In 2022 there were 362,000 of them. However, they too suffer from institutional discrimination and from neglect that can easily be observed in their neighborhoods in every aspect of life.

At the bottom of the ladder are the Palestinian inhabitants of the occupied territories outside of Jerusalem, with none of the civil and human rights granted to Israeli citizens. This means that on the West Bank, under the control of the very same Israeli government, living side by side, there are two groups, Jewish settlers and Palestinians, living under different judicial and legal systems, a situation solely dependent upon their national origin. The Palestinian population that constitutes a solid majority in the occupied area lives under military rule and every aspect of their lives has been regulated by directives of the military commander since 6 June 1967 (for example, work permits, administrative detention, reuniting or separating families, curfews, courts, preventing entry into Israel, home demolition, and more). In the same area, at a distance of a few kilometers, and sometimes just a few hundred meters, live people in the first category—Israeli Jews, residents of the settlements in the occupied territory, who live under Israeli civil law. This population is a definite minority which entertains an ethnically exclusive and privileged supremacy in order to maintain the occupation and enable ongoing settlement expansion. The Palestinians in contrast have no civil rights and lack many human rights as well, while the settlers have full rights in line with Israeli law and beyond. The system of the occupation enforces a myriad of discriminatory administrative regulations and restrictions on freedom of movement and carries out intrusive and at times brutal military activities in the guise of security operations. It conducts expulsions and arrests and often applies excessive force leading to the death of innocent civilians. Furthermore, Israel engages in the confiscation of lands and diversion of water resources for the exclusive use of the settlers.

A report by the Association for Civil Rights in Israel refers, in its conclusion, to "One rule, two legal systems":

> *"The review presented in this report reveals an official and comprehensive regime of separation between the laws applying to settlers and those applying to Palestinians in the West Bank, based on an ethnic-national distinction .... The separation between the laws that apply to the two populations is accompanied by clear discrimination against Palestinians in all aspects of life: They are subject to much stricter criminal procedures, which violate their basic rights; they are not entitled to participate in planning and building procedures that pertain to them and the enforcement in this area is stricter with regard to them; they are dispossessed of their land by means of the permit regime; their freedom of movement is violated; and their freedom of expression is restricted. This discrimination before the law contravenes the basic norms of the modern justice system, the laws of belligerent occupation and international human rights law."*[382]

For example, a Palestinian may be held for 96 hours before being accused of a crime and before being seen by a judge, while the Israeli must see a judge within 24 hours. Judges may also lengthen the detention of a Palestinian for 90 days without issuing an indictment, while an Israeli can only be held for 30 days. This state of affairs contradicts the Fourth Geneva Convention of 1949, which was signed by the State of Israel, prohibiting transfer of a conquering population to the occupied territory, inter alia, to prevent an inferior status for the conquered population.

Both in Israel and in the territories, law enforcement bodies are responsible for arresting those who break the law. However, if the lawbreaker is not caught while carrying out the act but apprehended only later—in Israel the suspect will usually be summoned for investigation and will be interrogated, while in the territories, the suspect will immediately be arrested. The usual method employed against Palestinians is as follows—the army breaks into the house in the middle of the night, and soldiers are equipped with list of names of the residents but without search or arrest warrants, of course; they are looking for men, sometimes boys, and in certain instances, even minors; the soldiers take them out of bed, arrest them, and transfer them to a detention camp or to the police station. As most civil, cultural, and political activities are considered crimes when they are carried out by Palestinians, including student council activities, teaching according to the Palestinian curricula in East Jerusalem, managing Islamic orphanages and charity organizations, Koran reading groups, and summer camp organizations—the procedure described is extremely common. It takes place daily, even with the cooperation of the Palestinian security forces under the auspices of the Palestinian Authority.

The reality of occupartheid has prevailed for more than 50 of the 70 years the State of Israel has been in existence, and considering its proportions, **it cannot be called "temporary."** The harm done to the principles of equality and freedom—the basis of every democratic regime—is devastating. Most of the Palestinians—1.3 million people who are living in Area A (18% of the West Bank) and 1.1 million people living in Area B (22% of the West Bank) —live in segregated *bantustans*, in which the Israeli security forces enter and leave as they please in order to arrest inhabitants, to keep them under supervision, and as described, to "enforce their sense of isolation." In Area C, constituting 60% of the territory of the West Bank and home to about 300,000 Palestinians (depending on who is counting them), along with several hundred thousand Jewish residents, there is a very high level of discrimination between the two populations. Since equality is one of the fundamental principles of democracy, its absence signals a very serious flaw in the system that may even question the basic existence of democracy.[383]

Did You Know?

Even now, according to the estimates of the Israeli Bureau of Statistics and that of Palestinian organizations in the West Bank, at the end of 2018, about 6.66 million Palestinians were living in the West Bank, and in September, 2019, there were 6.75 million Jews,

living between the Mediterranean Sea and the Jordan River, 6.5% of them living in the West Bank.[384] In March 2018, the daily newspaper *Haaretz* reported that the Deputy Head of the Civil Administration of the IDF, Col. Chaim Mendes, submitted statistics to the Foreign Affairs and Security Committee of the Knesset indicating that there were more Arabs than Jews living between the Jordan and the Mediterranean.[385]

The rightwing has a solution for the drift, in which Jews are gradually becoming a minority in the area. In recent years, rightists have begun to press for annexation of the West Bank, either partially or completely, with the aim of "strengthening the Jewish character of the state." This raises the question of giving rights to those living in the annexed territory. If full civil rights are given to the entire population—including the right to vote—the Jewish majority in the state will disappear. If not, apartheid will be clear to all, rather than just implicit, as it appears at present. In this case, the state will have citizens with rights, on the one hand, and inhabitants who will legally have no rights, on the other—as a permanent status that cannot be appealed. One of the supporters of this alternative is the ex-Minister of Education, Rafi Peretz, past chairperson of the Union of Rightwing Parties. He is not the only one—there are quite a large number who view open discrimination, in the spirt of apartheid, as a logical possibility for governing the State of Israel.

There are important voices declaring that Israel is already an apartheid state. At present, the prevailing legal system in the West Bank is constructed by two separate and unequal systems of law that discriminate between the two population groups living in the one territory—Israeli Jews and Palestinians and touches upon every aspect of daily life. According to the report the Association for Civil Rights in Israel:

> *A series of military decrees, legal rulings and legislative amendments have resulted in a situation whereby Israeli citizens living in the Occupied Territories remain under the jurisdiction of Israeli law and the Israeli court system, with all the benefits that this confers. The High Court of Justice has ruled that the rights enshrined in Israel's Basic Laws (equivalent to constitutional provisions) apply equally to these citizens, despite the fact that they do not reside in sovereign Israeli territory. A substantial portion of Israeli Law is also applied*

within the Occupied Territories to "Jews according to the Law of Return" and yet are not Israeli citizens.

By contrast, Palestinians in the West Bank are subject to much stricter military legal law —military orders that have been issued by IDF Generals since 1967. This is in addition to Jordanian Laws that preceded the region's occupation. Unlike Israeli citizens, Palestinians are tried in military tribunals for every crime from traffic violations to the theft of a carton of milk from the grocery store.[386]

The regulations that extend the application of Israeli law to its Jewish citizens in the West Bank have been in effect since 1967, and since then ratified every five years. When in June 2021 because of political turmoil the Knesset failed to extend the regulation, Justice Minister Gideon Sa'ar said that extending the regulation, *"concerns the beating heart of the national interest of the State of Israel and Israeli society,"* and that *"destroying the legal association between Israel and Judea and Samaria and turning them de facto into two separate entities is a legal and national nightmare. And these things are right without reference to one political position or another."*[387]

In June 2020, a leading human rights lawyer, Michael Sfard issued a legal opinion stating that *"the crime against humanity of apartheid is being committed in the West Bank. The perpetrators are Israelis, and the victims are Palestinians."*[388] Later, the leading human rights NGO in Israel, B'tselem, after examining the situation, declared in January 2021 that:

"[a] regime that uses laws, practices and organized violence to cement the supremacy of one group over another is an apartheid regime."[389] It explained: *"More than 14 million people, roughly half of them Jews and the other half Palestinians, live between the Jordan River and the Mediterranean Sea under a single rule. The common perception in public, political, legal and media discourse is that two separate regimes operate side by side in this area, separated by the Green Line. One regime, inside the borders of the sovereign State of Israel, is a permanent democracy with a population of about nine million, all Israeli citizens. The other regime, in the territories Israel took over in 1967, whose final status is supposed to be determined in future negotiations, is a temporary military occupation imposed on some five million Palestinian subjects.*

> *Over time, the distinction between the two regimes has grown
> divorced from reality. This state of affairs has existed for more
> than 50 years—twice as long as the State of Israel existed
> without it. Hundreds of thousands of Jewish settlers now re-
> side in permanent settlements east of the Green Line, living
> as though they were west of it. East Jerusalem has been of-
> ficially annexed to Israel's sovereign territory, and the West
> Bank has been annexed in practice. Most importantly, the
> distinction obfuscates the fact that the entire area between the
> Mediterranean Sea and the Jordan River is organized under
> a single principle: advancing and cementing the supremacy
> of one group—Jews—over another—Palestinians. All this
> leads to the conclusion that these are not two parallel regimes
> that simply happen to uphold the same principle. There is one
> regime governing the entire area and the people living in it,
> based on a single organizing principle."*

In April 2021, the widely respected Human Right Watch based in the U.S. released a 213-page report titled, "A Threshold Crossed," which found that Israeli authorities are committing the crimes against humanity of apartheid and persecution. It claims that the Israeli government perpetuates structural oppression to *"maintain the domination of Jewish Israelis over Palestinians in both Israel and the Palestinian territories, where today both groups of people are about equal in size."*[390] On September 27, 2021, the second largest party in UK, the British Labour Party, passed a motion at its conference that demands sanctions against Israel for its "apartheid" policy towards Palestinians and ends *"the building of settlements, reverses any annexation, ends the occupation of the West Bank, and the blockade of Gaza."*[391] On February 1, 2022, Amnesty International issued a report of over 270 pages accusing Israel of committing the crime of apartheid against Palestinians. The investigation details how Israel enforces a cruel system of oppression and domination against the Palestinian people wherever it has control over their rights.[392] One month after the report of the Amnesty International, the UN Special rapporteur, as **an independent human rights expert,** submitted to the UN Human Rights Council a report accusing Israel of practicing apartheid **in the occupied Palestinian territory.** He wrote:

> *"There is today in the Palestinian territory occupied by Isra-
> el since 1967 a deeply discriminatory dual legal and political*

system, that privileges the 700,000 Israeli Jewish settlers living in the 300 illegal Israeli settlements in East Jerusalem and the West Bank [...] there are more than three million Palestinians living under an oppressive rule of institutional discrimination and without a path to a genuine Palestinian state that the world has long promised, is their right ... Another two million Palestinians live in Gaza, described regularly as an 'open-air prison,' without adequate access to power, water or health, with a collapsing economy and with no ability to freely travel to the rest of Palestine or the outside world.[393]

All these reports differ regarding the accusations. While some claim that apartheid exists in the area between the Mediterranean Sea and the Jordan River, others assert that it exists fully only in the occupied area in the West Bank. I support the latter claim. Israel obviously unequivocally rejects all the reports and most of the Jews in Israel clearly support this rejection. As usual, any criticism of Israel is immediately attributed to anti-Semitism or to anti-Israeli views or both. Let's look at two polls that are relevant to these reports. In August–September 2021, *The Washington Post* deployed a questionnaire about the Middle East to expert scholars on the Middle East, drawn from members of the American Political Science Association's Middle East and North Africa Politics Section and the Middle East Studies Association; 557 of the experts responded. Some of the questions pertained to how to describe the Israel/Palestine territories. Fifty-seven percent of them said that a two-state Israel-Palestine solution was no longer possible, and 65% described the current situation as "a one state reality akin to apartheid."[394]

In spring 2021, a wide-ranging survey was carried out among Israelis and Palestinians. Of specific interest for the present analysis is the finding in response to the following question: *A regime in which one group controls and perpetuates its control over another, through laws, practices and coercive means is considered an apartheid regime. In your opinion, does this description fit or not fit Israel?* Seventy-seven percent of Palestinians say the description fits, but just 28 percent of Israelis agreed with this description—this includes 25 percent among Jews and 41 percent among Arabs citizens of Israel. Among Palestinians under occupation, the finding mirrors the trends regarding Palestinians' experience that Israel in fact controls many aspects of their lives. In contrast, 74 percent of Israeli Jews rejected the word "apartheid," despite significant agreement that Israel dominates and governs the lives of the Palestinians in reality. In sum, the researchers concluded that *"Israelis and Palestinians may disagree on whether the term apartheid applies, but the study shows that they are largely or completely aware, respectively, of realities on the ground."*[395]

It should be noted that at the same time that this dilemma is becoming clearer and clearer in all of its complexity, implementation of the alternative two-state solution, which could have ensured a significant Jewish majority in the new borders of Israel, has been eroding. The main reason for this is the Jewish settlement policy in the West Bank, stemming from the desire to expand the Jewish population into all the territory of "Greater Israel." In any case, the erosion of support for two states, empowering a movement towards annexation, is growing stronger. And this comes after years during which the rightwing political leadership "chose not to choose" on this issue and was inclined to continue to accept the occupation as a fact, repressing its future ramifications, as was noted. Just before the elections of 21 April 2019, Binyamin Netanyahu announced that following the vote, movement towards annexation of some of the West Bank territory could be expected. This was a declaration which had not previously been heard, and it was greatly aided (or perhaps created) by the support granted by U.S. President Trump to Netanyahu's political aspirations. Following the presentation of Trump's peace plan annexation became possible, and the prime minister pressed for its implementation before the 2020 elections in the U.S., considering that this was a window of opportunity which might close if the Democratic candidate won the election, as did occur. At present the annexation plan has been put aside following the normalized relationship that was established between Israel and the United Arab Emirates in August 2020. In reality, Israel does not need acts of formal legal annexation. It has informally been carried out continuously and systematically over the years. Just recently, in June 2022, as a next small step towards de facto annexation of the West Bank, Israel decided to place anti-theft inspection, under the control of the Israel Antiquities Authority. Like most Israeli government agencies, the antiquities authority is not authorized to act in the West Bank. It negates the international law.[396]

Did You Know?

On the question of the future of the occupied territories, just like on the issues that relate to what goes on daily in the territories, most of the Israeli public is apathetic to the fate of the Palestinians. The Peace Index of September 2015 showed that in a scenario in which full annexation would take place, 60% of Jews would oppose giving Palestinians full civil rights.[397] The Peace Index slightly more than a year later, in November 2016, indicated that 44% of Jews in Israel supported Israeli annexation of all of the area of Judea and Samaria.[398] According to the Peace Index of June 2016, 51% of Jews in Israel considered that the situation in the territories would remain the same, or alternatively, Israel would annex the territories—and whichever alternative would be chosen, equal rights would not be given to the Palestinians.[399] Annexation has become not only the acceptable solution for the right wing and centrist parties, but also for the two leftist parties—a poll conducted by the newspaper Haaretz in March 2019 found that 80 percent of Labor voters who answered the poll supported a two-state solution, but only 41 percent opposed any annexation of the West Bank; another 46 percent said that they supported annexing Area C. Among respondents who voted for Meretz, the most leftwing of the Zionist parties in Israel, 14 percent were in favor of annexing Area C. Another 14 percent supported annexing the entire West Bank if Palestinians were granted political rights.[400] A look at the future generation appears even more gloomy. A survey carried out in November 2020 found that while 42.63% of the older Israeli Jewish respondents (30 years old and above) preferred to "reach a peace agreement with the Palestinians," the younger Israeli Jewish respondents (aged 18-29) held a different opinion: 23.3% preferred to maintain the status quo; 20.88% preferred to "wage a definitive war against the Palestinians in which Israel destroys their military capabilities"; 18.68% preferred to "reach a peace agreement with the Palestinians"; and 14.07% preferred to "annex the territories or parts of the territories."[401]

The results make it clear that Israeli Jews have repressed the challenge that they are facing. They would like to hold the stick at both ends—to keep the territories and to maintain the Jewish character of the state—and they do not take into account that if they do not grant full civil rights to the Palestinians over time, that may lead to clashes with the international community or with liberal world Judaism, and alternatively, may erode the democratic character of Israel almost entirely—until it no longer exists. An analysis of the situation indicates that the Jewish state has already become less democratic, and simultaneously, has lost the wide support it has traditionally received from public opinion in the Western democracies.

The Nation-State Law, adopted in the summer of 2018, is particularly important in the context of the erosion of Israeli democracy.[402] It is a Basic Law, that is, a law with constitutional status, clarifying that the state belongs solely to Jews and therefore, it breaches the delicate balance between Israel as a Jewish state and Israel as a democratic state, in its open preference for the Jewish nation over minorities, who are also citizens of the state. The law is ethno-nationalistic, without civic inclusion or fundamental democratic values, expressing a narrow democratic worldview resting on the will of the ethnic majority. It is incompatible with, and even contradictory in spirit to the Declaration of Independence, as it does not in any way relate to values such as equality, liberty, and minority inclusion, which are pillars of a democratic regime. Moreover, the law determines preference for the Jewish population over the Arabs in the realm of settlement and accommodation, discriminating based on ethnic identification. It also diminishes the status of Arabic as an official language and places it in an inferior position. An important fact in evaluation is that by 21 July 2019, the law was already being used in 12 cases being heard in various legal proceedings of the court system. In the early days of the state, the democratic regime was limited, but the Declaration of Independence was a beam of light that at least lit the way into the future. These days Israeli democracy is broader than it was in the 1950s and 1960s, but the democratic beam of light has been extinguished. In July 2021, the Supreme Court upheld the law as legitimate legislation by the Knesset by a 10-to-1 ruling.

The Nation-State Law determines the Jewish character of the state in terms of extreme nationalism, rising arrogantly above minorities living in Israel and ignoring the needs of the native populations who have lived in the country long before the establishment of the state. It is meant to establish Jewish superiority in Israel, like laws instituted by a variety of countries in the years between the two world wars, enacted in order to establish the inferiority of Jewish citizenship. These laws recognized citizens, and Jewish citizens—two different categories with a clear hierarchy between them. Ardent supporters of the Nation-State Law, who represent the rightwing and religious Zionism, apparently did not recognize the difference between nationhood and extreme nationalism. Nationhood is based on the idea of national self-determination, the right of every nation to liberty, and cultural and national self-expression, even if it does not have a state. Thus, nationhood can be humanitarian, liberal, democratic, moderate, and positive. Extreme nationalism necessarily focuses only on one nation, usually the dominant one, and ignores the needs of other nations living among the dominant population, who are condescending and discriminatory, and often even racist. It views state institutions as tools to serve the dominant nation only, enacts discriminatory laws and often uses aggression against minorities. Nevertheless, the Peace Index of July 2018 found that 51% of Jews in Israel think that there is a need to officially determine that the State of Israel is the state of the Jewish nation, and **exclusively of the Jewish nation.**[403] In addition, 51% feel that a change in the status of the Arabic language is advisable. But there is still a ray of light—about 60% of the Jewish public also replied that they think that the law should also have referred to equality among all citizens, no matter their religion or nationality. The Nation-State Law is a concrete example of the political-social climate which has developed in Israel as part of the change in national perception. The ethos of conflict along with the aggrandization of Jews and delegitimization of Arabs are expressed in this law in all their glory.

The Damage Caused to the Courts

One of the central areas in which Israeli democracy has been damaged is related to the judicial system. Israeli judges are often demanded to legalize state practices carried out in the occupied territories—from the construction of settlements on private land owned by Palestinians, to torture and home destruction, and finally, cases of killing and injury. Through the years, the Supreme Court has had the reputation of being a leftist bastion, advancing universal values over the security of Jewish citizens. However, when examining the decisions of the Supreme Court since the occupation, it becomes clear that this image is very far from reflecting reality. So, for example, the court has avoided judging the legality (or illegality) of the settlements, in accord with Article 49(6) of the Geneva Convention.[404] The court has ignored 49(1) of the Geneva Convention and upheld deportation from the occupied territories; it has approved punitive house demolition and allowed wide scale changes in local laws for the benefit of the Jewish settlers.[405] It also chooses not to defend the human rights of Palestinians residing in the territories, in accord with international law.[406] The result is authorization of the occupation from every relevant legal standpoint. Time after time, the Supreme Court has ruled in favor of the state and, almost always, has supported the actions of the government and the army, even when these have contradicted international law.[407] The court has almost always given in to arguments based on the need for security, provided by the government, which are frequently political arguments in disguise, and the justices have not been ready to make any deep effort to ascertain what goes on across the Green Line.[408] Ofer Shinar's doctoral dissertation demonstrated that the Supreme Court even frequently makes use of ethos of conflict arguments in order to support their rulings.[409] Indeed, during the peace process of the 1990s, the Supreme Court began to show greater consideration for Palestinian rights, for both those that live in the occupied territories and those that are citizens of Israel. But, as a rule, since 1967, it has aided in reinforcing the occupation while disregarding international law and liberal values.[410] In addition, with regard to Supreme Court activity within the state, the wide-ranging dissertation of Reut Finger Dasberg has found another area of prejudice by the Court in its dealings with the Arab citizens of Israel. In this study, 181 rulings from 1948 to 2019 were examined to find out how Supreme Court judges anchor their rulings *vis-à-vis* petitions by Arab citizens of Israel. The study found that the court preserves the construction of foreignness that has existed through the years between Jewish and Arab citizens in the public and political spheres and associates itself with the Jewish people in whose name it speaks. It is clear that, throughout the years of its existence, the court, more than once, has used the pattern of "we" versus "they" in various contexts when evaluating the petitions of Arab citizens of Israel. It also identifies the Arab citizen as "the other," thus enabling "us," the Jewish people, to look at the Arab as an outsider and then claim that the rights of the Jew are superior to those of the Arab.[411]

As evidence, one of the significant injustices enabled by the Supreme Court has applied to Area C, consisting of about 60% of the entire West Bank territory and home to about 300,000. After a series of directives issued by an army commander, the Israeli Civil Administration became solely responsible for planning and development in the West Bank—both for Palestinian towns and villages, and for Jewish settlements. The administration grants almost no building permits to the Palestinians (who have received permits for less than 4% of their building requests), and they are forced to build with no authorization due to problems of population density and crowding. In fact, since 1967, the state has granted Palestinians less than 0.25% of West Bank land for building. In simple math, for every acre received by the Palestinians, the Jewish settlements have received 370 acres. This is in clear contradiction to The Hague Convention, Article 55, as follows:

> *The occupying State shall be regarded only as administrator ... of public buildings, real estate, forests, and agricultural estates belonging to the hostile State, and situated in the occupied territory. It must safeguard the capital of these properties and administer them in accordance with the rules of usufruct.*

Israeli administrative bodies have thus ignored their legal responsibility to provide the Palestinians with possibilities to obtain reasonable living conditions, but they do uphold the law—and with great severity—regarding all construction without permit, which is considered a criminal offense, sometimes to the point of completely destroying houses that have been built. From 2006 to 2018, more than 1,400 houses were destroyed, in which more than 6,000 people had been living, half of them children. And this brings us to the role of the Supreme Court: On various occasions, when this issue has been raised in the Supreme Court, the judges have completely accepted the state framework regarding "criminal" construction, and even determined on one occasion that the state planning policy in Area C is *"proper and reflects the needs of the residents."* As such, the Supreme Court has, for years, rejected hundreds of petitions against home destructions—in fact, only one or two were accepted. In February 2018, the Supreme Court partially rejected the request by residents of the Palestinian village of Susiya, in the South Hebron region for an interim order to prevent destruction of structures on the spot. In addition, in May 2018, the Supreme Court approved demolition orders for houses in the Palestinian village Khan al-Ahmar which had been built without permits. This was a Bedouin community with a population of 173—92 of them children who had lived in the village for dozens of years. It was also the site of a mosque and a school serving more than 150 children from six to 15 years old, half of whom were from the neighboring villages. The community had settled at that spot after they had been ejected from the area of Tel Arad in the Negev and then, subsequently, also from the area where the Jewish settlement of Kfar Adumim is situated. In the verdict, Justice Noam

Sohlberg, a resident of the Jewish settlement Alon Shvut, wrote that the point of departure *"which was indisputable"* was that *"the construction in Khan al-Ahmar—both the school and the houses of residents—was illegal."* Thus, the judges ruled that the state was authorized to issue a demolition order against them. It is true that the structures were built without a permit, but this followed years of vain efforts to receive building permits from the Israeli authorities, which hold the sole responsibility for the welfare of residents of Area C.

In order to "encourage" Palestinian residents to leave their homes, the state avoids connecting residents to electricity, water, sewage and road infrastructures. The Civil Administration prevents building homes and public buildings and reduces their grazing areas. This takes place while illegal outposts, some built on private Palestinian land, within days, or at most weeks, receive security services, water supplies, and education and health services. In place of the village, which will be demolished, a new neighborhood expansion of the settlement, Kfar Adumim is planned, and will be called Nofei Breshit (Genesis Views), with 322 residences.

Another example, this time in a different realm, can be seen in the following case—in 2015, the Supreme Court gave its approval for Israeli government to apply the Absentee Property Law on East Jerusalem, and actually enabled expropriation of Palestinian property while the owners were actually present on the West Bank. Expropriation mostly serves the aim of Judaizing Jerusalem. So the court has given authorization for the violation of Palestinians' proprietary rights and violation of international humanitarian law, which determines that this is territory under military occupation. Similarly, in December 2018, the Supreme Court rejected a petition brought by residents of Palestinian village Silwan and enabled the rightwing organization Ateret Cohanim ("Crown of the Priests") an Israeli Jewish organization that works for the creation of a Jewish majority in the Old City and in Arab neighborhoods in East Jerusalem) to continue evicting 700 Palestinians from their village, based on Jewish ownership of the houses before 1948. This decision came despite the judges determined that there were flaws in the legal process and expressed surprise at the procedure of transferring land to the organization. It is important to note that Arabs have no right to demand land or buildings which were privately owned by them in 1948 in Israel.

In April 2019 the Supreme Court permitted the destruction of dozens of houses in East Jerusalem in the neighborhood of Wadi Yasul in Silwan, where hundreds of Palestinians were living. The destruction would enable the rightwing organization Elad to build in the area. This decision seconded the decision of the district court of Jerusalem. The houses actually had been built illegally, but in Jerusalem there is no chance for an Arab to receive a building permit. In the same locality, the Jerusalem municipality requested to change the designation of a part of the area to prevent the rightist organization from having to destroy illegal structures that it itself had built. Again, in June 2019, in a precedential ruling, the Supreme Court enabled the destruction of thirteen buildings, among them living quarters, in a neighborhood under the control of the Palestinian Authority in East Jerusalem, with the argument that they were too close to the separation wall. Finally, on 1 September 2021, the Supreme Court rejected the appeal of six Palestinian families and the Israeli NGO of Physicians for Human Rights to limit the free entrance of Israeli security forces to Palestinian homes except when there are judiciary permits. As a result, an officer can decide when and why to enter a Palestinian home at any time while entering the home of a Jewish settler in the same region can be only carried out by order of a judge who has evaluated the reason, in line with the Israeli law.[412] On May 4, 2022 the High Court of Justice permitted the expulsion from their homes of about 1,000 Palestinian residents, including 500 children of Masafer Yatta in the southeast West Bank, for the benefit of Israel Defense Forces training. The justices, David Mintz, Ofer Grosskopf, and Isaac Amit, rejected the petitioners' argument that they had lived there before it was declared a firing zone in 1981. They rejected the claim that turning the area into a closed military zone was contrary to international law, and said that when international law contradicts Israeli law, the latter prevails. As a result, eight Palestinian villages whose residents have lived in them for generations will be destroyed. Interestingly, none of the hundreds of Jewish settlers living in the area (most of whom came later) has been asked to leave his home or his settlement for the army's firing zone.[413]

These examples show that the rulings of the Supreme Court clearly serve the political project of the Israeli government, whose aim is to gain control of as much as possible of Palestinian territory and to limit Palestinian construction in any way possible, while explicitly ignoring international law, which prohibits transferring occupying populations to the territory of the occupied. And these are only a few examples of the way the court acts in line with the policies of occupation. Additional decisions, for example, the ruling that a call to boycott the West Bank settlements and their products is "political terrorism," and is thus prohibited, or a court decision to prevent security prisoners from gaining higher education, reflects a similar tendency, and there are many more relevant examples.

Nevertheless, when the judicial branch rules in favor of Palestinian rights which are not in line with rightist preferences, something that occurs very infrequently, the courts become subject to a wild and unrestrained frontal attack by the rightwing. In 2013, for example, Knesset member Yariv Levin, who was then serving as the Head of the Knesset Committee, stated in an interview with the rightwing newspaper *Eretz Yisrael Shelanu* (Our Israel) that *"the Supreme Court is motivated by a leftist agenda, and in particular, poses a danger to our ability to safeguard our existence. It is no secret that a minority group of extreme leftists has taken control of the judicial system and especially, the Supreme Court, and they are trying to dictate their values to the entire society."* Knesset member Motti Yogev, from the Jewish Home Party, while his party was a member of the coalition, stated, *"that the government should use a D-9 (giant) shovel against the Supreme Court,"* in a reaction to the ruling that illegally built houses in the Beit El settlement should be demolished. The ex-Justice Minister, Amir Ohana, stated immediately after he had been appointed to the position in 2019 that, in certain cases, we do not have to carry out the rulings of the Supreme Court.

In sum, the seminal 2021 book by Kretzmer and Ronen, *The Occupation and Justice: The Supreme Court of Israel and the Occupied Territories* concluded 500 pages of analysis with many examples in the following way:

> *"In its decisions relating to the Occupied Territories, the Supreme Court has legitimized all controversial policies and practices of the Israeli authorities, including those incompatible with international law [...] With few exceptions the court has not intervened in policies and practices of the authorities in the Occupied Territories. Rather than subjecting the legality of such policies and practices to strict judicial scrutiny, the Court has generally placed the emphasis on issues of procedural fairness and whether the implementation of the policy or practices in specific cases meets the demands of reasonableness and proportionality. This has meant that, in practice, the most problematic policies and practices in the*

Occupied Territories have received explicit or implicit judicial approval.[414]

In view of this analysis, it is not surprising that Dorit Beinisch, the ninth
president of the Supreme Court of Israel (and considered to be a liberal
judge)—in a discussion of the book on May 20, 2021 organized by Miner-
va Center of Human Rights—pointed out that the Supreme Court cannot
be separated from Israeli society and its ethos. Meni Mazuz, a judge of the
Supreme Court who resigned in 2021, claims that *"the Supreme Court, sitting as the High Court of Justice, is authorizing illegal acts"*, accepting blindly
arguments of the security figures. Moreover, in a recent interview in television, after the burial ceremony of the former Supreme Court president
Miriam Naor, she said *"She* (Miriam Naor), *like her teacher and mentor [the
late Supreme Court President Moshe] Landau, who was Jewish, nationalist and principles, also respected settlement, but not on private [Palestinian]
land. That was the legacy of Supreme Court President Landau, that private
property is not to be harmed for the purpose of settlement. And I think it's a
great injustice to describe Justice Landau as someone who acted against the
state's most important values and its national-Jewish character."* We learn
from her remarks that the legacy of Israel's Supreme Court is to respect
"the settlement" (that is according to the international law illegal settlements) —as long as it isn't on private Palestinian land. Moreover, Naor
describes "the settlement" as part of *"the state's most important values and
its national-Jewish character."* Here we find an explicit admission that the
Supreme Court—when sitting as a constitutional court—has served and
does serve as a legitimizing Israeli highest legal court for the trampling of
human rights and international law in the territories, especially in regard
to the establishment and expansion of the settlement enterprise.[415] In spite
of these observations, the continuous attacks on the Supreme Court led
to the dramatic diminishment in the trust of the court, among the rightist
population—while in 2003 about 60% of the rightists expressed trust in
the Supreme Court, in 2020 only 38% expressed trust in it. Among leftists
and centrists, the level of trust in these times remained above 70%. Thus,
we learn that the majority of the Israeli Jews accepted the delegitimization
campaign of the Supreme Court.

A few years earlier, in August 2017, when Justice Minister Ayelet Shaked
was asked what her greatest achievement was, she replied that there were
two that were particularly salient—the first was the appointment of doz-

ens of conservative judges in the various courts, and the second was the responses by the Supreme Court attorneys regarding the settlements in the occupied territories, which were *"different than what they appeared to be in the past. Zionism, and I say it here, does not have to continue, and should not continue to bow its head to a system of universal individual rights disconnected from Knesset history and from legislation that we all know about."*[416] The words and deeds of Shaked as justice minister are another example of the institutional change in the legal system as one more stage in the increasing hegemony of the conflict culture.

Shaked, like many rightwing leaders, increasingly justified her actions as "serving democracy," since, in her opinion, she was expressing the majority political viewpoints. This is a narrow view of the essence of a democratic government, ignoring a central principle at the very heart of a democratic regime: protection of minority rights. In its absence, the regime is not democratic, but rather a tyranny of the majority.

The Supreme Court justices on May 5, 2020, in a vote 11 to 0 approved a possibility that a prime minster under indictment for corruption charges may form a government. This indeed happened when Netanyahu formed a government in November 2022. The Israeli law prevents a minister under indictment to take office. But the court was not brave enough to apply the law to the office of prime minister.

Harm to Pluralism and Freedom of Expression

One of the severest blows to a democratic government is the attempt to instill totalitarian thought in contradiction to the central principles of democracy—pluralism and freedom of expression.[417] In Israel, this is unavoidable because as already noted, if the government has decided to continue the conflict and the occupation, it must make ongoing institutional efforts to instill Jewish society members with conflict supporting narratives in order to mobilize the nation to support a continuation of the conflict and the occupation, and even to take an active part in its perpetuation. At the same time the government, with the aid of official and unofficial supportive institutions, must suppress the flow of information that contradicts these narratives. Thus, from the very nature of this process, freedom of expression, free flow of information, and freedom to be exposed to alternative information are negatively affected. In other words, an important foundation of democracy is certain to be abused.

Specifically, in the State of Israel, the leaders of the right and even the political center attempt to block legitimate freedom of expression from the left by delegitimizing it. Thus, in a long process that had already begun in the late 1990s, the label "left" became illegitimate in Israeli public discourse. The lack of openness to alternative information intensified during the 2000s, and the control that prevents freedom of expression and obstructs the free flow of information has not only penetrated the political system, but it has also infiltrated the cultural and educational systems. In addition, as we have already seen in the previous chapter, the rightwing uses all the tools in its arsenal by virtue of its governmental status, trying to block information disseminated by various human rights organizations who document the injustices done by the security forces, various government branches, settlers, and other organizations. This information details unnecessary killing of Palestinians, illegal arrests, collective punishments, abuse of Palestinians, harsh detriments to human rights, and more. These organizations have been persecuted by state institutions, parties, leaders, and associations established precisely for that purpose, and even the general public. This has even received support from the Supreme Court on 5 November 2019, which approved the expulsion of the senior representative in Israel of the human rights organization, Human Rights Watch, and thus, gave even greater authorization to the occupation, as it prevented the voicing of legitimate criticism of Israeli behavior in the occupied territories. The justification for the expulsion was that Human Rights Watch supports BDS (Boycott, Divestment, Sanctions) and should be banned from Israel. And again, this pattern of ostracization can be distinguished: boycott of the settlements by those who oppose the occupation and ostracizing those who call for these boycotts by the Israeli government. Polls show that Israeli Jews view the activities of the Israeli human rights NGOs rather negatively—a poll taken in 2021 showed that only 48% of Israeli Jews evaluate their activity favorably, but when asked about their collaboration with the Palestinians the percentage drops to 19%.[418]

In this reality, the citizens, both individuals, but primarily, those who hold government positions or private citizens who depend on their customers, are afraid to express opinions contradicting the hegemonic narrative for fear that they will be socially and economically punished. Punishments like those we have described in the previous chapter have succeeded in imposing a climate of fear in Israeli society. They arouse a sense of "let everyone see and beware." Naturally, only a small minority are willing to pay a heavy personal price for expressing independent positions, while most people force themselves into conformism, obedience, or even self-censorship—another result of the hegemonic conflict culture.

Monopolization of Patriotism

The state of affairs that we have described in detail has led to a monopolization of patriotism in Israel. This occurs when a group or groups lead a change in the definition of the concept of patriotism that is accepted by society, usually by adding certain conditions such as support for a certain ideology, for particular policies, or for a certain leadership. This enables them to exclude groups who are unwilling to adopt these conditions.[419]

In Israel, for right-wingers, only those who accept basic rightist assumptions are considered patriots. Accordingly, the concept of patriotism has become a mechanism enabling the expulsion of certain groups. Binyamin Netanyahu, as the leader of the rightwing, has had a decisive influence in creating this atmosphere. Following his election as prime minister of Israel in 1996, he began a general process of delegitimization of the left. In 1997, he was recorded while whispering in Rabbi Kadoorie's ear, "The left has forgotten what it is to be Jewish. They think that our security should be put in the hands of Arabs. Arabs will take care of it—Give them a part of the country and they will take care of us." At the end of 2016, he declared, *"Politicians from leftwing parties and television commentators took great pleasure in the anti-Israeli decision of the United Nations, almost as much as the Palestinian Authority and Hamas did. In fact, some of them even focused on an attack on … the Israeli government."* With these sentiments, Netanyahu has eliminated people on the left from the Jewish community; he negates their Jewish identity and presents them as dominating the media and other centers of power, as Arab-lovers, and as anti-Israelis, and he even represents them as a foreign power aiming to take control of the country. In the summer of 2018, just after the Nation-State Law was passed, Netanyahu, again in his status as prime minister, stated, *"The attacks (on the law) coming from the left, which calls itself Zionist, are absurd and expose the low point to which the left has descended … The Israeli left must submit itself to self-examination. It must ask itself why the basic concept of Zionism—the state of the Jewish nation, of the nation of Israel in its own land—has become a vulgarity, a word of obscenity, a principle that we should be ashamed of. We are not ashamed of being Zionist."* And in other words, only those who agree with his opinion and his actions are national patriots, and those who do not agree are not.

Accordingly, only those who support the leader, Binyamin Netanyahu and his policies, only those who support the idea of Greater Israel, only those who support the worldview of the rightwing about what democracy is—those are Zionist patriots. In this way, the right and the government accept only blind patriotism and reject patriotism coming from the desire of people to repair the damage which, in their opinion, is being done in Israeli society and in the state.

One of the most striking examples of the penetration of this view into Israeli social life is the adoption of the worldview and the messages of the rightwing parties by leaders of the center-left opposition parties. Yitzchak Herzog and Yair Lapid, and later, Benny Ganz (and earlier, Shelley Yachimovich), who were the heads of opposition parties, softened the rightist messages and entered the realm of political discourse that Netanyahu and the heads of the rightwing parties had marked as legitimate. It was sad to find that, in 2018, even the chairperson of the (dovish leaning) Mahane Ha-Tsioni (Zionist Camp) Party, Avi Gabai, repeated the accusations that Prime Minister Binyamin Netanyahu had made to Rav Kadoori in 1997.[420] Although Gabai later apologized, the legitimization that he had given to these views is difficult to erase. The delegitimization of the left was sharply and saliently emphasized during the election campaigns of 2019 and 2020, when the right used all its power to highlight the difference between themselves and rival parties of the center by attaching the label of "leftist" to them, in an attempt to distinguish between nationalist and patriotic parties that care about the interests of Israel, and parties that do not. This line was also used against any person (media personality, artist, cultural figure, academic, public figure, and even a senior army officer) who does not agree with the opinions of the rightwing and criticizes Prime Minister Netanyahu. The paradoxical peak of delegitimization was reached when Avigdor Liberman, a well-known right-winger, was denounced as a leftist by Netanyahu following the elections of April 2019, because Liberman had thwarted the establishment of a rightwing government with Netanyahu at its head. In fact, the concept of "left" has come to be an expression of delegitimization used by the right to damn political rivals just as the word "Zionist" has come to be an expression of dishonor among Arabs. In the change government headed by Bennett and Lapid in 2021-2022 this delegitimization was weakened because the leftist party, Meretz, and an Arab party participated in the coalition.

Thus, after many years of unceasing incitement, the term "left" as a political opinion is perceived by most of the Jewish public in Israel as unpatriotic, as supportive of the interests of Palestinians who are untrustworthy and violent, as advancing a peace that would endanger the future of Israel, as disseminating false information about Israel (injustices carried out by Israel against the Palestinians and the immorality of the occupation) and harming Israel and the IDF by transmitting information abroad. It is no wonder that all political parties except for Meretz do everything in their power to flee from the label which tarnishes them in the eyes of the Jewish public and to prove their determination to fight against the Palestinian enemy. It is no wonder that, according to the Peace Index of November 2016, about half (48%) of the Jewish public thought that the left was disloyal to the state because of the criticism it leveled against the Israeli government and its policies.[421]

Failure to Uphold the Law

Upholding the law represents an additional principle in a democratic regime. Failure to uphold the law and the absence of equal protection under the law constitute fatal harm to a democracy and its society. In fact, no regime can exist without safeguarding the law. Failure to uphold the law, particularly by state institutions, causes anarchy, in which every individual does what s/he sees fit. In the State of Israel, due to the occupation and the desire to settle in the occupied territories, the failure to uphold both state and international laws, primarily on the part of state institutions, "illegalism" has become widespread and has led to selective law enforcement.[422] The need to construct a reality that will seemingly appear to be moral and lawful, at a time when the state actually wants to control the Palestinians and to steal their land, leads the state to law violations, to ignoring criminal offenses, and to creating institutionalized falsehoods. Already in years past, researchers noticed the persistent non-legalism in Israeli society, indicating that the rule of law is not the highest value but rather, a principle that can also be ignored.[423] The political culture that has developed in Israel through the years since its establishment does not negate breaking the law, and as the years have passed, the norm that, for leaders, the law is just a behavioral suggestion has even strengthened. In the second decade of the twenty-first century, this norm has become dominant among the ruling echelons.

The attempt to gain control of Palestinian land is a paradigmatic example of violating laws and lying with the willing blind eyes of the Supreme

Court. It will be presented in the next section.

Taking over Palestinian Land

Immediately following the Six-Day War in 1967, settlement in the occupied territories was only permitted for military needs. However, in time, Israel turned the security consideration into an excuse that enabled the sudden appearance of numerous civilian settlements.[424] Between 1967 and 2014, 1,150 military orders were signed enabling the seizure of more than 24,710 acres, most of which were owned privately by West Bank Palestinian residents. An examination of these areas reveals that almost half of them (47%) directly serve the needs of the settler population—not the needs of the army. This makes an important statement about how the interpretation that Israel has accorded to the concept of "military needs" has been completely subjugated to the political interests of "Judaizing" the West Bank. Moreover, even considering the areas that have been appropriated but do not serve the settlers, about 45% of the land is also not actually used by the army. In other words, as a rough estimate, only a quarter of the areas defined as being used for military needs are actually in use by the army. Considering the rest of the areas, the designation of "army needs" is nothing but an excuse.

It should be noted that these legal "tricks" are in stark opposition to international law, which defines in detail the rights and responsibilities of a state, controlling territory that has been subdued under conditions of belligerent occupation—precisely defining the status of the West Bank, as it is understood by the Israeli Supreme Court. According to international law, taking control of such privately owned land is necessarily temporary, and only for pressing security needs, while the army must return the land it has taken after using it.[425] But Israel has created its own legal realities and, in order to justify land expropriation, several practices have been developed, although their connection to international law is totally nonexistent. One of these was the false claim that army officers have used when testifying to the Supreme Court, asserting that the lands taken over were needed for military purposes; the Supreme Court accepted these claims, while, in reality, the land was actually meant for civilian settlements. That was the case of Elon Moreh, except that the lie was exposed due to the honesty of one of the settlers,[426] Menachem Felix, who truthfully testified that his seed group had settled on the spot in 1979 due to God's commandment and not as a result of security considerations. That was the only time since the Six-Day War that the Supreme Court ruled against the settlers.

David Kretzmer (a law professor at Hebrew University) and Gershom Gorenberg (a journalist and researcher) investigated this issue in 2015.[427] They found that, although the normative framework used by the Supreme Court to investigate the activities of the Israeli authorities in the occupied territories is that of "belligerent occupation," that is, demanding attention to only two considerations—overt military needs and the good of the local population—in uncountable cases, the policy of the government in the territories deviates from these considerations. In other words, the government does not operate according to the rules determined by the Supreme Court. The investigation by these two researchers, which focused on official documents and testimony of officeholders regarding three cases (the Pithat Rafiah affair, the case of the Electric Company in Hebron, and the Highway 443 affair) whose immunity of 30 years had expired, revealed several interesting findings. These included the fact that the authorities made an effort to cover up the real political background that had motivated their activities, had concealed relevant facts from the court, and had invented fraudulent legal explanations in order to manipulate the Supreme Court into deciding what the government wanted it to decide. The researchers argue that these are not isolated cases. The authorities have regularly resorted to lying to the Supreme Court. Only in rare cases has the court uncovered the actual situation and has then not based their decisions on the legal justifications presented to it.

In the context of the West Bank settlement project, I will relate to unlawful conduct employed to gain control over private Palestinian lands. According to the rightwing NGO, Regavim, from May 2015, about 2,026 homes in approximately 25 Jewish settlements have been built illegally on private Palestinian land.[428] However, in August 2017, it became clear from the data issued by the Civil Administration that, in the Israeli settlements of the West Bank, 3,455 homes and public buildings had been built on private Palestinian land.[429] The courts and the government echelons had supported this construction and aided it. Not only were 222,395 acres of privately and collectively owned Palestinian land appropriated based on the declaration, dubiously rooted in Ottoman law, that these were state lands, but also, Jewish homes were built on this private Palestinian land in a clear and usually intentional violation of the law. Here is described the case of Amona, where, at the end of the 1990s, settlers' houses were illegally built on private Palestinian land with the aid of the Housing Ministry, which funded the settlement infrastructure. As early as 2004, the Civil Administration issued a demolition order and later, it also became clear that the settlers' documents had been counterfeit. In 2014 the Supreme Court ruled that the outpost must be evacuated within two years. However, the executive branch did everything in its power not to carry out the ruling. When, finally, after many postponements, 42 families were evacuated on 1 February 2017, they received 130 million shekels towards their resettlement at another spot.[430]

In addition, it was discovered that the Settlement Division of the Jewish Agency had, in several cases, taken control of lands over which it had no authority, some of which was privately owned, and advanced the establishment of settlements on these lands, a criminal offense under Israeli law. An investigation by Haaretz newspaper in October 2018 found that the Settlement Division had granted dozens of loans for the illegal establishment and development of outposts, agricultural farms and vineyards throughout the West Bank.[431] In this way, it had aided the funding of new illegal outposts—that is, in violation of the laws of the state itself. In addition, the division had transferred to contractors or settlers state lands which had never been allocated to it—land over which the division had no authority—sometimes lands that were privately owned by Palestinians— in order to advance the creation of settlements, also in violation of the law.[432] Illegal activity has also been conducted by the regional councils in the territories. For example, the Mateh Binyamin Regional Council in the occupied territories distributed more than 55 million shekels to various political associations operating in the region instead of transferring them to welfare, education and sports. It is no wonder that the West Bank has been referred to as the "wild west" of Israel because of the great amount of violence and the fact that the law is not upheld by the state or by the Jewish settlers.

Adding insult to injury, when the state was finally forced to evacuate settlers who had knowingly taken control of private Palestinian lands, an act that the state had ignored—the government compensated the settlers by granting them millions of shekels. Another case came to light in June 2018, when the state admitted that it had transferred a complete neighborhood of 700 people in the Palestinian village Silwan to the Ateret

Cohanim religious settlers' NGO, via a public trustee of the Ministry of Justice. This was done without making the effort to inform the Palestinians who were living there and without checking essential questions that had arisen about the sacred character of the property or about structures which had, in truth, not existed for a long time. Finally, it is important to mention that, in 2017, the Knesset enacted the Judea and Samaria Settlement Regulation Law, enabling expropriation of private Palestinian land rights on which Jewish houses have been built.[433] The very enactment of this legislation contradicts international law as it has been legislated by the Israeli Knesset, which is the legislative arm of the Israeli state, but enacted for an area under its control, but not under its sovereignty.

To the list of violations of Israeli and international law, we may add the establishment of dozens of illegal outposts without official approval from the authorities, but with covert and public government assistance in providing infrastructure, while the army provides security to the settlers. All of these actions were documented in the Sasson Report in 2005, which was submitted to Prime Minister Ariel Sharon.[434] The report supplied detailed information indicating that state and civil authorities (including the Ministry of Construction and Housing, the Defense Ministry, and the Settlement Division of the Zionist Organization) sweepingly violated state laws in order to respond to political pressure by the settlers. We may summarize by saying that the settlement project was conducted in part by counterfeiting documents, by leading the authorities astray, and by relentless law violations, while the government funnels public funds to the settlements, far from the public eye, and ignores violations of the law.

Torture

An additional example of law breaking, lies and deception relates to the legal, defense, and medical systems. For many years, hundreds of Palestinians have complained about being arrested by the security forces who recorded their confessions using torture. Considering these claims, a "mini-trial" was conducted in which these claims were investigated. General Security Service (*Shabak*) investigators, army representatives and doctors testified at the trials. The verdicts found that Palestinian claims of torture were untrue.[435] It must be mentioned that there have been relatively few of these trials, since GSS investigators try to avoid testifying and the prosecution prefers to reach a plea bargain with the defendant.[436]

Nevertheless, in 1987, a government commission under former Supreme Court Chief Justice Moshe Landau submitted a report that determined that the GSS had developed a culture of lies—investigators tortured and lied, supported by the higher echelons, and then their fraudulent claims were supported by doctors representing the GSS, yielding corresponding court rulings. Thus, it may be assumed that hundreds of people who were witnesses to this torture testified fraudulently in court. GSS workers, including investigators, lawyers, and doctors engaged in self-censorship, on the one hand, and demonstrated obedience to the defense system on the other hand, so that it could continue to use improper procedures which violated both Israeli and international law. Even today, there is evidence, despite the appointment of a GSS ombudsman, that torture still continues and simultaneously, there is still willingness to conceal it.[437] In 2016, hundreds of complaints were made by Palestinians who underwent torture in the course of their interrogation, and in not one of these incidents was the investigator placed on trial.[438]

In summary, we may say that the desire to control the Palestinians and to settle Jewish citizens in the occupied territories has necessarily led to the disintegration of democracy, as these objectives have overshadowed the principle of upholding the law.

Moral Deterioration

The conflict also leads to moral deterioration of society, in addition to the decline of democracy. The principle guiding the Israeli government for many years in the past and up to now has been that, in order to achieve security for the state, the government may take any action without consideration of its moral costs. And from the moment that safeguarding security was posed as the only consideration, processes of moral disengagement and moral entitlement have developed, and these have changed the face of the society and of the country beyond recognition. Moral disengagement makes it possible to ignore moral norms because we were traditionally victims throughout history. Moral entitlement makes it possible to harm those who threaten us, because victims (that is, Jews), by virtue of their very victimhood, may use any violent method to prevent any additional harm to themselves. Another principle may be added to these two: moral silencing, which states that other nations have no right to rebuke us as we have been victims, and primarily because they did not take any steps to save Jews during the Holocaust. Thus, criticism of Israeli government policies is perceived as immoral, if not an expression of absolute anti-Semitism against the Jewish state. This principle was succinctly expressed by Golda Meir, prime minister in 1973: *"European nations which did not help us during the Holocaust, do not have the right to preach to us."*

In the context of moral deterioration, the governments of Israel have supported the most disreputable governments in the world, such as the Shah of Iran, the Argentinian junta, the Pinochet government in Chile, the regime of the Colonels in Greece; Israel even had business dealings with the Apartheid government in South Africa. In the 1970s, when Jews in Argentina, who had been arrested and tortured applied to Israel for help, Israel officially refused to aid them due to its relations with the junta. Israel has also supplied arms to nations which have committed horrible crimes, like Argentina, Chile, Congo, Eritrea, Bosnia, Nigeria, Rwanda, Myanmar, and South Sudan. Some of these regimes are even guilty of genocide. What they all have in common is that the business dealings that Israel carried on with them were always concealed in deep secrecy—there were gag orders preventing knowledge of their details in order to neutralize any public debate about their morality.

Through the years, Israel has been involved in military meddling in various states by supporting sides in conflict. Here are some examples which have come to light—Israeli tried to destabilize Egypt in 1954 with violent undercover activities. Israel participated in the 1956 war in Egypt, conquering Sinai and advancing towards the Suez Canal, and taking advantage of the British and French attempt to save their spheres of influence. Israel also helped the Yemenis, supporting the royal military against revolutionary republicans in the civil war of 1962–1967. It was involved in the secret war in Sudan, assisting the Christian military in the south. It has had relations with Morocco for many years, granting intelligence and military help in its struggle against the Polisario Front (a military resistance organization) in occupied Western Sahara. Israel was also involved in the war in Iraq, helping Kurds in their battle against Iraq between 1963–1975. It saved the Jordanian kingdom in September 1970, during the violence between Jordanian soldiers and Palestinians. It was deeply involved in the Lebanese civil war, helping Maronite Christians from 1975 on.[439] All these examples show that Israel has not been isolated as it claims, and it has used various opportunities to play a negative role in destabilizing the states in the region.

Moreover, in recent years, Israel has become an international leader in exporting systems for spying on civilians. Technological industries, in many cases, taking advantage of those who have served in the army intelligence elite unit, 8200, supply despotic regimes with the possibility of listening in on human rights activists, penetrating their private correspondence and enjoying free access to content saved on their private telephones. It is difficult to assume that these companies are operating without the acquiescence of Israeli authorities. The particular story of the company NSO, selling the Pegasus program of surveillance, made news around the world because it has been used in different states for surveilling leaders and opposition activists.[440]

The processes of moral disengagement, moral entitlement, and moral silencing represent a slippery slope. In recent years, Netanyahu has made an informal agreement with the Eastern European states, like Hungary, Poland, the Czech Republic, and Slovakia, whose regimes are authoritarian-nationalistic and who even exhibit clear signs of anti-Semitism. In each of these states, the regime has narrowed democratic space by legislation, limits on civil society, delegitimization of the opposition, and control over the communications media and the courts. In Hungary, Prime Minister Viktor Orbán, who originated the concept of "non-liberal democracy," has led a personal campaign of incitement with clear anti-Semitism against the Jewish billionaire George Soros. Soros has consistently contributed to human rights organizations and defenders of democracy. The poisonous campaign was created, *inter alia*, by "matchmaking" conducted by Netanyahu, between Orbán and Netanyahu's own personal advisors, who formulated the plan, while the Israeli prime minister supported him and even took an active part, justifying his pronouncements and those of his representatives against Soros.[441] Similarly, to advance nationalist aims of the Polish regime, the Israeli government abandoned the memory of the Holocaust for a dubious agreement with the government of Poland, which was meant to clear the Poles of their part in handing over Jews and killing them during the Nazi occupation government. It should be noted that the political rationale behind Netanyahu's support of the Eastern European rightwing, along with the rest of the Israeli rightwing, is the desire to drive a wedge between the European community countries in order to weaken the liberal states of Western Europe. Binyamin Netanyahu also had very close relations with the defeated president of the United States, Donald Trump, whose actions trampled the democratic principles of the superpower. He supported him, ignoring expressions of racism and even antisemitism that appeared in Trump's surroundings. In addition, the Israeli rightwing has developed relations with racist-extreme nationalistic parties in Italy and Austria.

The State of Israel is also ready to join authoritarian leaders, even those to whom the concept of "democracy" is foreign, and for whom human rights abuse is an inseparable part of their policies. Those who are friends of Israel include Rodrigo Duterte, president of the Philippines, who has praised Hitler, Jair Bolsonaro, president of Brazil, who has justified torture and killing of opposition politicians, and Idriss Deby, president of Chad, who has had unlimited rule as dictator of his country for 29 years. All these relationships indicate how the government of Israel is distancing itself from a moral and democratic path. As Miguel de Cervantes wrote: "Show me who your friends are, and I'll tell you who you are."

If, in the past, Israel was perceived as an outstanding example of a small and determined society which built a vibrant state out of nothing in the shortest possible time, and thus, earned the respect of many in the Western world, today it spearheads the Western world in granting legitimacy to autocratic or otherwise dreadful regimes and their recognition.

SUMMARY: WHY DOES SOCIETY BEAR THE COSTS?

Ultimately, we must ask why there is almost no public discussion in Israel about the costs of the conflict and the occupation. The costs are tremendous in terms of human life, mental health, economic hardship, weakening democracy, difficulties in international status among nations, and moral deterioration. But Israeli Jews do not find these themes of interest, and practice denial and repression, although the themes do appear in academic writings and, from time to time, in journalism and documentary films. The following is an attempt to provide an explanation citing several causes. Some of them have already been discussed in different chapters in this book.

First, Israeli society has developed from the beginning within the context of wars and violent activities. Living in such a context created the need to develop strong patriotism that requires ongoing mobilization and routinization, enabling society to cope with the challenges posed by lasting bloody confrontations. From the establishment of the state and even before, Jews have become accustomed to sacrificing lives for the state, enduring economic hardship, living in chronic fear, and even tolerating autocratic regimes—all for survival, and these costs have been presented as necessary by the leadership and by formal institutions, constructing rationalizing narratives. These rationalizing narratives were weakened in the late 1970s following the peace agreement with Egypt, but from the 2000s they have again been strengthened and have become hegemonic, with the failure of the peace process with the Palestinians. Despite the opposition of an existing minority who have deviated from mainstream thinking, routinization of the conflict has become a way of life. Thus, it is one of the factors responsible for the fact that society does not perceive the costs and maintains a normalized way of life that is necessary in view of the existential threats.

Second, as already described, the leadership and state formal institutions prevent a free flow of information and debate and try to thwart messages that contradict the hegemonic narrative they propagate. In this hegemonic narrative the occupation does not exist; the nation is doomed to live by the sword, democracy is functioning well, and the costs are part of the national effort to cope with the threats. Thus, free debate about the costs is discouraged and the majority of the media reiterate this message. As a result, Israeli society is characterized by obedience, conformity, and self-censorship when it comes to issues of security and occupation. Most society members, who are aware of the costs incurred, prefer not to endanger society by open discussion and/or are afraid of the negative sanctions that may be used by national institutions or even their own social circles for expressing societal or political criticism.

Third, because the system of education in most schools avoids discussing the complexity of living under the shadow of a conflict and does not deal with the meaning of living in a democratic state, the great majority of the younger generation have grown up accepting the costs borne by society without question. The hegemonic narratives fulfill the functions of satisfying primary needs and new generations learn to live with routinization. Research shows that the new generation of young people is more hawkish and religious. Many of them are proud to serve in the Israeli army and volunteer to serve in combat units stationed in the occupied territories,

Finally, the readers must understand that Israeli society, not including the ultraorthodox sector, is a kind of Spartan society. Young men and women serve their mandatory army or national service and later, men serve in the reserves for about a month or more every year, for approximately an additional 20 years or longer. That means that the military is a people's army and a society in uniform. As a result, most of the secular, traditional and even religious families have strong ties to military service and avoid any criticism that touches upon loss of human life or wounds (physical or mental health) in the actual conflict as well as in military spending.

All these determinants are gloomy consequences of living in the conflict context for many decades, without the present leadership and a majority of the Israeli Jews even considering the possibility of resolving the conflict peacefully. Eventually, by freezing their hegemonic narratives justifying the conflict, its continuation itself becomes a need, with fear of taking even a small risk to change the bloody context. The next two chapters will elaborate on this psychological situation, because a conflict begins in the minds of the people and its end depends on changing those minds.

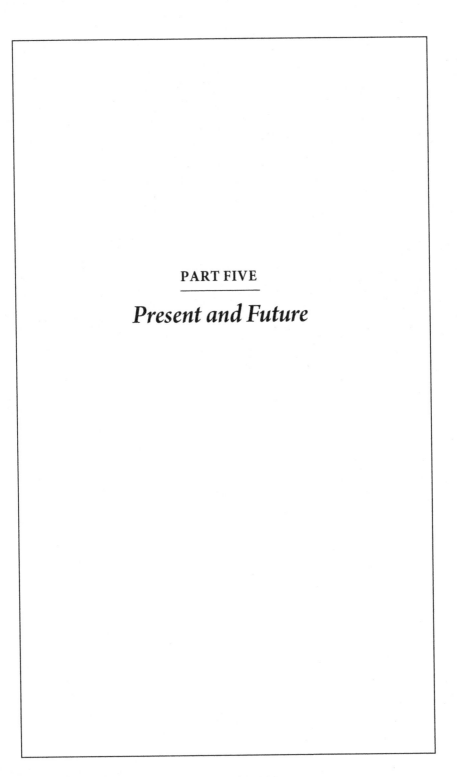

PART FIVE

Present and Future

CHAPTER 10

Where Do We Stand Now?

Information, Reality, and the Perception of Reality

Via a deep process of instilling institutionalized knowledge by the political rightwing, while consistently, methodically and systematically using undercover practices and misrepresenting them as pluralism, equality and freedom of speech, a society has evolved in Israel, in which most members accept the basic rightwing assumptions. Construction of this perception of reality and structuring of personal and collective consciousness are achieved by using considerable resources to control official institutions, with the aid of many non-governmental organizations and, of course, in the context of the presence of real threats. These assumptions exaggerate the severity of the dangers to the existence of the Jewish nation, consider Palestinians as no partners for negotiations; glorify Jewish society, undermine the principles of freedom of expression, freedom to organize, and the free flow of information, and intensify prejudice against Arabs, citizens of the state, justifying discrimination against them. The acceptance of these assumptions has established a conscious, stable infrastructure among the majority of Israeli Jews, who do not believe in the ability to reach a peaceful end to the conflict, are not interested in ending the occupation, hold that democracy is expressed only by elections and by majority rule, and do not think that democratic principles are the correct compass by which the state should be navigated. In addition to the socialization practices, there is also a demographic trend with the very high birth rate of the ultra-orthodoxical Jewish closed community, to which democratic principles are alien and the ideas of Greater Israel have become part of their religious dogma.

These attitudes dominate, even though there is ample information in Israel clarifying reality differently than what has been provided by the government, information which is not only different but sometimes is the complete antithesis. This information appears in some of the media, in cultural products, in academic and non-academic journals and magazines, and it is disseminated by civil and political organizations, and of course, can be found abundantly in sources abroad, and even on Wikipedia in English. However, the general public remains almost completely unexposed to this information—usually by choice—and when information does come to light, it is attacked by defensive denial that has developed through decades of indoctrination. The result, in practice, is that this copious amount of information does not break down the existing views, and, in fact, the opposite is true—its very appearance reinforces earlier assumptions with the perception that information, which is incongruent with previously held beliefs, is biased and erroneous, like, for example, information about the illegality of Israeli settlements in the West Bank (which just leads to an intensification of bitterness against the sources of this information). The existence of alternative information in Israel ultimately serves the government and the public, who use it just to demonstrate that the state is actually democratic. I can say with confidence that the great majority of Israeli Jews accept the narratives propagated by the government and, as a result, are ignorant in their knowledge about the conflict. Those who have the power to impart and maintain narratives also have the power over society members to impose the policies and actions regarding the conflict and the occupation that correspond to these narratives.

Although most of the Israeli public have internalized messages provided by the leadership, to the extent that they are completely blinded to the realities of the occupation, Israeli Jews nevertheless enjoy a self-image as those who aspire to peace. Netanyahu himself had, time after time, repeated the mantra that "our hands are outstretched in peace," but these are words that have completely lost their meaning. Most Jews in Israel would like to see negotiations being carried on—a fact that is also in line with their self-perception. By the end of the 1980s surveys were already showing that the Jewish public was supportive of negotiations with the Palestine Liberation Organization (PLO), and even today, more than 50% of the public support negotiations with Hamas. The Peace Index, as well, starting from 1994, shows support for negotiations—it has found that most of the Jewish public in Israel clearly and stably support negotiations with Palestinians. To illustrate, in August 2019, 54% of the respondents supported this possibility.[442]

However, what the negotiations will yield—that is another question. For many years, an increasing majority of respondents have answered that they do not at all believe that negotiations will lead to peace between Israelis and Palestinians. In August 2019, for example, only 17% replied that they believed that negotiations would lead to peace. Moreover, although about half of the Jewish population support the solution of two states for two peoples, when viewing this response in more detail, it becomes clear that they are not willing to pay the unavoidable price demanded by this solution, even considering the most minimal of demands. The Peace Index of August 2018, for example, showed that 63% of the Jewish public were opposed to the determination of East Jerusalem as the capital of a Palestinian state, and 70% opposed the evacuation of all of the isolated settlements in Judea and Samaria.[443] There are many people, including those on the right and in the center, who state that they are ready to make the most painful compromises, including the division of Jerusalem, but they immediately add that it is impossible to reach a solution with the Palestinians because they cannot be trusted and still aspire to destroy the State of Israel.

Did You Know?

In a poll of both nations, entitled "The Palestinian-Israeli Pulse," conducted by the Center for Peace Research of the University of Tel Aviv and the Palestinian Center for Policy and Survey Research (PSR) in Ramallah in July 2018, one of the interesting findings was that 47% of Israelis and 56% of Palestinians feel that the settlements in the occupied territories have increased to the extent that the two-state solution is no longer viable. The same survey also found that a large majority of both nations believe that the other side is not trustworthy (89% among Palestinians and 61% of Israeli Jews). The findings also indicate that only about 35% of both nations believe that the other side really wants peace. Finally, only one third of Israelis and Palestinians would agree to a package of solutions to the various issues in dispute that could lead to a general agreement. In October 2020, the same poll revealed that only 43% of Palestinians and 42% of Israeli Jews support the concept of the two-state solution; 56% of Palestinians and 46% of Israeli Jews are opposed. Like surveys of the Peace Index, this line of surveys has been conducted through the years; and it demonstrates that both Israelis and Palestinians have become pessimistic as time has passed; they have lost trust in the other side, they have become hardened in their attitudes and have lost hope for a solution to the conflict.

If, for a moment, we set aside trends in the Palestinian public, which diverge from the discussion framework, we may determine how the perception that there is no alternative to life by the sword has penetrated deeply into the Israeli public and how strongly it is believed that only military might will ensure the existence of the State of Israel. Although there are deep roots to these narrative tendencies in Jewish society, they have been institutionalized by recent rightwing governments in a way that has been unprecedented, and this has had a great effect on public attitudes. The Likud Central Committee has voted to unanimously support annexation of the West Bank.[444] Even in Meretz, the farthest left of Israeli political parties, about 14% support annexation of Area C. In summer 2020, then-Prime Minister Netanyahu openly promised annexation of Area C. But the intervention of President Trump and the peace agreement with United Arab Emirates postponed the formal step, leaving informal acts that are continuously carried out. In retrospect, it appears that what may have been possible to accomplish in the 1990s or even at the beginning of the 2000s, will be much more difficult to achieve in the present. Both Israelis and Palestinians have dug into their own narratives, and the psychological gaps between the two nations, which function as powerful obstacles, have greatly expanded.

The new government which assembled in November 2022 elections, an extreme, ultra-right, fundamentalist coalition, openly promotes sovereign rights of self-determination exclusively for the Jewish people on the entire landmass between the Jordan River and the Mediterranean Sea. The fiction of a "temporary" occupation is over, as well as the lip service paid to the "peace process." not because "there is no partner" and not because of security needs but because it is seen as a God-ordained imperative.

This is not only an expression of outlook, of theory or of ideas. For the Palestinians, their situation has grown worse beyond recognition during these years. The economic realities of their daily lives have worsened as, during the 1970s and 1980s, Palestinians could freely find jobs in Israel (and about 300,000 were permanent workers) and travel openly throughout the West Bank. However, since the Oslo Agreements, Palestinian society has been divided and pulverized by the division of the West Bank into three separate areas cut off from one another—the West Bank, Gaza, and East Jerusalem. The settlements and outposts have greatly expanded, often involving blatant land theft. Economic development, including digging wells for water, is dependent on Israeli approval. The Israeli Defense Forces are considered an army of occupation, often perceived as hostile to the Palestinian population. They freely enter all the West Bank cities and villages to arrest suspects and often, just to show their presence. The settlers have greatly increased their antagonistic acts towards Palestinians, with physical injuries and damage to their possessions, deeds often ignored by the army. The security apparatus has also strongly deepened their inroads into every level of Palestinian society, using ever-present means of supervision and control. The regime of work permits and entry into Israel including for health treatment has become a tool for control and abuse. Any expression of protest against the occupation is considered an act of terror and results in arrests; over four thousand Palestinians are imprisoned in Israeli jails; and even though some of them have participated in terrorist acts against the civilian population, they are considered freedom fighters by the Palestinians. Hundreds of thousands have been arrested due to their opposition to the occupation and thousands have been killed or wounded; harm to Palestinian children has also greatly increased. Naturally, living under these conditions has greatly intensified the hatred, the distrust, and the hostility towards the occupying nation.

On the other hand, the hope among Jews that the peace process would lead to an end to violence did not come about, and the immense number of the dead during the second intifada, more than one thousand, clarified that the violent struggle is far from ending. Palestinian violence and terror, which persisted during the following years, continues to serve as a reminder. However, in contrast to the Palestinians, for whom the occupation is an inseparable part of their daily lives, for the Israelis, the possibility always existed to repress, to deny and to distance oneself from the realities in the territories, even though they may have been living only several kilometers away from the Green Line. Although, from time to time, signs of violence on the part of the Palestinians have appeared, these are considered by Jewish society as tolerable and under control, certainly in comparison to the horrors of the second intifada. The violence of the present time is mostly in West Bank and does not reach the boundary of the state. Thus, the population of Israel either represses the threat or does not pay attention to it. At the same time, the violent events, like the Gaza-based Operation Protective Edge in 2014, the stabbings of the "knife *intifada*" in 2015, or rockets fired from Gaza, all served as proof—of the negative intentions of the Palestinians. In such a reality, development and acceptance of an alternate narrative to the conflict supporting one is a most difficult challenge. It would necessarily require a halt to the violence, or at least, a dramatic decrease. However, this cannot come into being due to the vicious circle in which we are trapped—narratives justifying the violence lead to more violence, which only intensifies the narratives justifying violence, and the cycle continues. This is a terrifying circle and the chances of breaching it diminish from year to year. A similar reality existed in Northern Ireland as well as in the Basque Country in Spain. However, determined leaders knew how to break the circle and to reach a peace agreement even while the violence was continuing.

Breaking this circle has become even more complex if we consider the particular values which are at the focus of the rightwing belief system. As we have already shown, for most of the nation, these values touch upon goals which benefit the kinship ingroup. In the case of Israeli Jews , these hegemonic values express worry about the future existence and security of Jewish society in Israel, and emphasize the importance of the group, members' loyalty to it, and the value of tradition and respect for its cultural heritage. These values are naturally accepted by society as they operate on the sense of concern for the kinship group—a primordial evolutionary principle enabling the survival of the group. This feeling is accompanied by the sense that Israel is a very small state, existing in isolation with a siege mentality that has characterized Jews for many generations. The ethos of conflict faithfully expresses these particular values and thus, the members of Jewish society accept them willingly and openly.

The Narrow View of Democracy

In comparison to those particular values, universal values, which direct attention to humankind in general, are perceived as secondary or at times, even competitive, as values such as equality, freedom of expression, human and civil rights clash with the human tendency to define private identity through membership in an ethnic group. This tendency, which may be termed ethnocentrism, is implanted deeply in human nature. Human beings by nature demand the good of their group—they are concerned first of all with the poor of their own city. It is no wonder that most of the Jewish public in Israel ignore the suffering of Palestinians, are ready to exclude and discriminate against Israeli Arabs, and to do harm to asylum seekers, most of whom have come from Africa. The Jewish public does not relate to principles of human rights that are meant to direct Jewish treatment of others, in accord with the Jewish moral codex, expressed accurately by Hillel the Elder, who lived in the first century BCE and coined the "golden rule": *That which is hateful to you, do not do to your fellow man. That is the whole Torah* … This narrow view of democracy and the practices that Israel instigates and implements have led to the view by more than few of the scholars who have investigated the state that Israel is "an ethnocracy," "an ethnic regime," "an illiberal democracy," "an undemocratic regime," and even "an apartheid regime."[445]

With reference to Jews, it is difficult to imagine that this is a nation that only 80 years ago was on the verge of extermination in Europe, victims of the racism and extreme nationalism of the German nation. For two thousand years, Jews were scattered among other nations and suffered from discriminatory edicts, abuse, inequity, and even pogroms and murders, only because of their Jewishness—being foreign and alien to other nations. And now, when they have acquired their own land, and have become a state with a powerful army, they have forgotten the lessons they should have learned and have themselves become a nation which discriminates against and represses others. In Israel, many do not even see the injustice that is being done to other groups and have become those who stand aside and look elsewhere, just as what they had experienced so many times in their own history. Apparently, nations don't learn from their own history as victims, to be compassionate, empathetic, merciful, humane, and moral. The moment they are empowered, they begin to act without these qualities, like many other nations, even when they preserve the memory of their own suffering.

In Israel, tolerance for values expressed in the 1948 Universal Declaration of Human Rights is now at a low point. The worldview of the rightwing that dictates public discourse in Israel in recent years sharply and totally defines its boundaries. Israeli discourse emphasizes the rule of the majority, national democracy, and nothing more. As we have already described, even on the procedural level, the separation of powers is faulty, the law is not being upheld, and harm is being done to institutions and position holders that might serve to block motivations of power and avarice, and the propensity for authoritarianism and unrestrained extreme nationalism. Those who support rightwing worldviews about democracy and the conflict are considered valid members of Jewish society and those who oppose them are situated outside society. The conservative rightwing does not recognize pluralism of opinions or freedom of expression as fundamental principles of a democratic regime, but rather defines this regime according to narrow formal principles, and primarily, a free vote for representation in state institutions, determined once every defined period. And then, after the elections, there is only one directive: The majority has determined, and now, they have the right to dictate their demands. This worldview determines that not only the Palestinians, citizens of Israel, are outside Israeli society, but leftists are also excluded since their worldview is opposed to that of the rightwing. Moreover, many rightists also do not accept the universal definitions in questions of human rights, equality and liberty. Thus, the Palestinians in the occupied territories are not entitled to basic human rights, and as a result, these rights are methodically trampled upon on a daily basis. Indeed, the Peace Index of May 2021 shows that 89% of the Jews in Israel oppose the establishment of one binational state with equal rights for Jews and Palestinians, but about 52% oppose the establishment of an independent Palestinian state side by side with the State of Israel.

With regard to democracy, the 2020 Democracy Index by the Israel Democracy Institute shows that 54% prefer a strong leader who will not take into account the views of the Knesset (Parliament), media, or public opinion, and 50% think that the state should cut financial assistance to cultural institutions or to any artist who strongly criticizes the state. A survey by Professor Sammy Smooha regarding Jewish-Arab relations in 2018 (the Index of Jewish-Arab Relations, 2018) showed that 75% of the Jews in Israel think that fateful decisions about peace and security issues should be made only by a Jewish majority; 67% think that Israel needs a law that determines that democracy in Israel should exist only if it does not harm the Jewish character of the state; and 49% suggest that Israel should deny voting rights to anyone who does not agree to declare that Israel is the national state of the Jewish people. These findings indicate that a significant portion of the Israeli Jewish population views democracy through a narrow lens, and is ready to disregard its basic principles of equality and freedom.

But when there are blows directed against Jews in the diaspora (for example, acts of antisemitism in various countries, prohibitions against immigration to Israel, as during communist rule in the USSR, or limitations on Jewish organizing in communist countries during the Cold War), both the government and the Jewish majority in Israel demand the implementation of democratic and moral principles in order to relieve the distress of their brothers and sisters living among other nations. When Jews are making these demands, they raise universal principles such as equality, human rights, or liberty.

Some of the difficulty in changing attitudes is a result of the narrow perception of democracy which is spreading and putting down roots in Israel. Education for democracy in Israel has been superficial for decades, in a determined attempt to supply the bare minimum and no more. Ministers of Education, who have long been chosen from the ranks of religious Zionism or from the nationalistic rightwing, do not accept the need to inculcate the coming generation with the principles of democracy in the liberal sense of the term. Thus, they reduce the importance of the value of "education for democracy" by lowering budget allocations, selectively determining content, and appointing people who support a very narrow view of democracy to senior positions in civics teaching. In contrast, civics now includes an expanded section of Jewish learning in the religious sense. (The civics curriculum covers only one year and is the only source of democracy studies, while using a book with no small number of flaws in its presentation.) It seems clear that this is one of the main reasons that many Israeli citizens consider the existence of free elections as the epitome of democracy.

Accordingly, it follows that the government leaders chosen in the elections have the right to rule as they see fit, without any other checks and balances. The will of the majority is the only compass determining the direction of the state and of society. This attitude has taken root among the Jewish public in Israel for obvious reasons. In addition, the principles of democracy do not interest most of the public and are not considered when evaluating the state of society or of the nation and are absent in the judgment of what goes on in the occupied territories—whether by ignorance and indifference or by considering short term narrow interests. The result is that most of the public are also not aware of the effects of the occupation on Israeli society, especially with regard to the narrowing of democratic space, as discussed in previous chapters. The recent elections show that Israel is distancing itself from a model of democracy and is coming closer to an authoritarian model, supporting nationalistic, racist and religious values. In general, it can be said that only a small minority of society members consider the importance of safeguarding liberal democracy in Israel.

Consensual Assumptions

Israeli Jewish discourse is delineated by basic assumptions which will now be detailed. We may say that most of the Jewish public in Israel—all the rightwing, a good part of the center, and even parts of the leftwing—agree with most, if not all of these. And they are:

1. The land of Israel is the exclusive homeland of the Jewish people. It was created there, existed for hundreds of years, and Jewish culture was established within its borders. The Jews were exiled from Israel, returned after great suffering in the diaspora, and built a state that ensures their survival.

2. Nevertheless, existential danger still threatens the State of Israel and the Jewish nation living in the country. The danger is perpetual, as Israel is surrounded by Arab nations which will never accept Jewish nationhood in general and specifically, deny the presence of a Jewish state in the region. In addition, the region is home to nations for which violence is a significant part of their characters and that is an additional reason explaining why there is no stability. In this view of reality, Israel encounters many dangers, while it itself constitutes an island of stability, a "villa in the jungle." It is true that some of the Arab states accept the reality of the existence of the powerful Jewish state, but this is a realistic viewpoint, while wishes are different.

3. The Jewish nation is the sole victim of the conflict.

4. The Palestinian nation does not want a peace agreement that will obligate them to compromise, but rather aspire to reach all their goals, and as such, Palestinian leaders are not partners to a peace process. They are not ready to make significant concessions; as proof, it is clear they have missed every opportunity for years.

5. Considering the difficult situation in the region, and the characters of neighboring nations and their actions, Israel must avoid any steps which may involve risk taking and uncertainty, including advancing peace negotiations with the Palestinians.

6. The principle of "divide and rule" should direct policy towards the Gaza Strip under Hamas and the West Bank under Fatah.

7. Military power must be used for deterrence and defense and also

to punish violence. However, Israel uses violence only when it must, and maintains a high level of morality.

8. In addition to being the sole victim of the conflict, the Jewish nation is also a permanent victim of anti-Semitic and anti-Jewish forces, who have been victims of persecution for the past 2000 years. The victimization reached its peak during Holocaust, when a methodical attempt was made to annihilate the Jewish nation completely, while other nations stood aside, at best, or took an active part in the annihilation, at worst.

9. Even today, anti-Semitic and anti-Jewish forces, aspiring to destroy the Jewish state, exist in many nations of the world.

10. Other nations cannot be depended on and therefore, maintaining Israeli security must be entrusted only to the State of Israel itself.

11. The state and its army should not be criticized, especially abroad, but even in Israel itself, as criticism provides ammunition to the Arab enemies of Israel, and to anti-Semitism in a variety of countries. In addition, it impairs morale, mobilization and the ability to stand up to the enemy.

These assumptions saliently appeared in the wide-ranging study carried out in 2002–03 and was noted earlier.[446] We will not discuss the validity of these assumptions, which are not relevant to the issues specifically under dispute in the Israeli-Palestinian conflict, such as Jerusalem, borders, and settlements, but we do maintain that most of these make support for a peace process impossible. That has not prevented these attitudes from achieving wide consensus in Jewish Israeli society. Two of them have even been elevated to the status of axioms among most of the Israeli Jewish public. The first is that the Jews of Israel are facing a real existential danger from enemies who want to destroy their state (to the point of the danger of another Holocaust), so that we must be prepared to defend Israel by every means possible. The second axiom is the designation of Arabs in the most repugnant terms, and the belief that they should not, under any condition, be trusted, as their basic characters are consistently negative and that cannot be changed. These axioms combine to create a concrete wall blocking any possibility to end the conflict.

It cannot be denied that real-time events sustain these two assumptions, but it is no exaggeration to say that they are inconsequential in comparison to the well-oiled systems—social, political, educational, and cultural—which totally reinforce them. In the last analysis, fear and the sense of insecurity, together with the chronic distrust of Palestinians, not only paralyze every possibility for change, but also reduce autonomous thinking, narrow horizons, and restrict critical reflection to a minimum among Israelis, in their attitudes to the conflict. It is not by chance that Franklin Delano Roosevelt, the 32nd president of the United States, famously stated, "…[T]he only thing we have to fear is fear itself—nameless, unreasoning, unjustified terror which paralyzes needed efforts to convert retreat into advance."

Every attempt to change the attitudes of the Jewish public in Israel will have to involve a change of these basic assumptions.

The politicians who have been leading the country for many years bear responsibility for this state of affairs which is obviously and clearly linked to the conflict and the occupation.[447] It may be said with cynicism that a successful leader is one who identifies the needs of the nation and gives society the feeling that s/he is satisfying these needs. Netanyahu, naturally, fulfilled these criteria perfectly. He even reinforced these needs among the Jewish population—primarily intensifying insecurity as well as strengthening the sense of Jewish ethnic superiority to the Arabs and other foreigners. In this way, he tied politics to ethnicity and religion, and nationalism to extremism, using rhetoric which was directed at the continuation of the conflict.

From the moment investigation files were opened against Netanyahu, in order to avoid a possible trial and sentence, he began to attack the Israeli legal institutions, making various accusations and even slandering them. Only one hour after the attorney general announced that he would serve bills of indictment against Netanyahu, the then-prime minister issued an unprecedented attack against the law enforcement institutions, saying, "We are witnessing an attempted coup against a prime minister on trumped-up charges and a tainted and tendentious investigation process … The tainted investigation process, including inventing new crimes, has reached its apex today … This tainted process raises questions among the public about the police's investigations and the prosecution … It must be demanded: investigate the investigators." This was a significant blow to the underpinnings of a democratic regime, as the trust for these institutions by Netanyahu supporters has diminished even more—while the resilience of democracy, any democracy, rests on the trust felt by the wider public in its institutions. That is the glue that connects the foundations of the regime. His actions gained Netanyahu two advantages, a kind of "killing two birds with one stone": He established support for himself despite suspicions of corruption, and increased dependence on himself as a "powerful leader." Through the years he has successfully built a base that accepts his words as holy truth with blind loyalty. And all of this comes at the expense of the survivability of democratic principles in Israel.

The previous government of Naftali Bennett, the leader of the rightist party, and Yair Lapid, the leader of the centrist party, announced that Israel would not hold peace talks with the Palestinians.[448] This statement is not surprising when one looks at the distribution of Israeli Jewish voters that stabilized 20 years ago—the Peace Index of November 2021 showed that 63% of the Israeli Jews categorized themselves as rightist, 21% centrists, and 14% leftists. We need to remember that even the past government included at least four leaders: Prime Minister Naftali Bennet, Justice Minister Gideon Saar, Interior Minister Ayelet Shaked and Minister of Education Yifat Shasha-Biton who are rightist nationalists, supporters of continuing the occupation and extending Jewish settlements in the occupied territories, rejecting the establishment of a Palestinian state and opposing political negotiation to settle the conflict. It is thus not surprising that Netanyahu won the elections, having bloc of rightists and extreme rightists' coalition. The present government consists of a coalition of ultra-rightists, nationalistic, religious and racist forces united in the wish to transform Israel into a totalitarian entity.

Meanwhile, on the Left

In order to correctly understand the depths of distress in which the left-wing camp finds itself and to comprehend the extent of opposition to its ideas, we must also discuss both sides of the political equation in Israel—not only the strength of the right, but also the weakness of the left.

The multidimensional activity by the right against the left, which we have detailed in previous chapters, has succeeded more than could possibly be expected. One of its effects is that centrists who wish to distinguish themselves from the left, harm it by using disparaging expressions against it, time after time, and thus, contributing to its exclusion. Only in the present unique circumstances, when the desire to get rid of Netanyahu overcame all other considerations, was a new coalition built with the leftist Jewish sector, including one Arab party. But this coalition decided not to deal with the cancer of the lasting occupation, and the left was caught in the honeytrap too.

Ehud Barak, in his words and acts, dealt a lethal blow to the left as we have described in Chapter 3. As time passed, the attacks from the right and from the center greatly accelerated the disintegration of the left and the peace camp. This sector fell apart without creating a unified body and began to function as a decentralized, disorganized and sporadic movement, with no central narrative and without presenting an ideological alternative that could fulfill the nation's needs. In some cases, leftist organizations which have remained, have adopted rightwing messages, without maintaining a critical approach. For example, leftwing parties, like the Zionist Union, have taken up the rightwing narrative regarding the illegitimacy of the Arab parties, to the point of refusing to cooperate with them. (On the other hand, it should be noted that the Arab parties bear no small responsibility for the impediments to cooperation with the Jewish parties).

In addition, as we have shown, people on the left are viewed as arrogant, as Arab lovers, and as harming the state of Israel by openly publicizing immoral acts carried out by Jews. They are also perceived as unpatriotic and insensitive to the basic psychological needs of the Jews, which also characterize other nations. These perceptions are put forward by the right methodically and incessantly, as a permanent mantra, and then are absorbed by the public at large and are accepted as actually defining the left. In addition, I have no doubt that the left has erred in the content of its own narratives. Justified and legitimate as their views may be, they must consider the needs of their nation, if they aspire to broaden the small circle of their supporters, that mainly are directed by universal values.

As a result, the left today is split into dozens of peace and human rights organizations, with different goals and different strategies. Cooperation between them is very minor, and many of them, for various reasons, prefer to act alone. Entire population groups, such as the business sector, professional organizations, or associations do not participate in the peace camp struggle, primarily due to its delegitimization by the rightwing. Many public struggles have emerged, starting with the separation of religion and state, the orthodox appropriation of religious institutions in the country and the process of religionization; continuing the battle against tycoons who have gained control over state resources; and ending in the campaign against state corruption. All these campaigns have consciously avoided tagging themselves as leftist struggles, even considering the clear relationship between their messages and the world of leftwing values and principles. Thus, those who are grappling with these issues have not succeeded in creating a common basis to realistically challenge the regime and the existing order, and have remained divided and isolated, and dispersed at random in space. In addition, the right has succeeded in defining "political struggle" as negative and as striving to undermine the basis of the state, while support for state policies and programs are not political actions but rather acts of patriotism. This perspective has also been transmitted to the educational process in the schools, in which any criticism or discussion of disputed issues is termed by many teachers and students "political" with negative connotations, while the school curriculum, which is by nature political, is not considered as such.

The left is not a passive actor in this tragedy. However, many of its supporters tend towards intellectualization, adopting rational arguments, and avoiding emotional expression, while exclusively stressing universal values, clarifying nuances, dissecting and constructing each idea in detail. Thus, they do not succeed in constructing a simple alternative narrative which will fulfill the basic and genuine needs of the Jewish public and outline a comprehensible image of the conflict which supplies hope for its peaceful solution. In contrast, rightwing supporters prefer to unambiguously and consistently promote the concept of "a strong leader" who evokes strong emotions and proposes a simple narrative that fulfills the basic needs of the Jewish ingroup. The focus by the left on the harm done to the Palestinians, the desire for peace or the blows to Israeli democracy cannot be the main focus of an alternative narrative, as it does not fulfill the basic needs of most of the nation. On this point, justice does not go together with wisdom, which comes with accumulated knowledge of social change. The principle that the left should be emphasizing is concern for the state and society in the sense of the statement by the well-known American general and senator, Carl Schurz, in the second half of the nineteenth century who stated: "My country, right or wrong; if right, to be kept right; and if wrong, to be set right." For some reason, only the first half of the sentence has penetrated the general consciousness, and it has been interpreted to express blind patriotism. But it was not by chance that Schurz added the second half, which states that, for love of one's country, we must struggle to alter its ways if we identify a deviation from the correct path. So that is the obligation of the Israeli left—with concern for the fate of the state and society, they must struggle against the occupation and in favor of democracy to achieve the welfare and success of the nation. This is not a narrow and ethnocentric approach, but rather, the wide-ranging perception that, as long as life is not good for your neighbors, it will not be good for you. The occupiers are subjugated no less than are the occupied. The subjugation of another nation is also self-subjugation at a very high cost, as we have shown throughout this book. A long period of subjugation deepens the harm to the occupiers; therefore, we must end our complete control over the subjugated for the benefit of both nations. In addition, the left must not neglect the struggle for equal and just economic and social rights, as well as broad welfare networks.

But the last elections showed that not many remained from the true leftists. The issue of occupation does not preoccupy many Jewish leftists and centrists. The disappearance of the Meretz party from the new elected Knesset testifies to this observation. In contrast, the issue of democracy with all its implications is focal among the centrist group and the leftist parties. The research confirms this view. In a study carried out, it was found that for Jews who opposed Netanyahu, the costs of losing democracy were unacceptable.

The Tenor of the Time – Right Orientation!

The image of Israel that we have outlined until now is not an optimistic one. Most worrying is the fact that it has joined a number of other nations on a similar path in recent times: Poland, Hungary, Slovakia, and the Czech Republic. All of these countries have had democratic liberal regimes in the past, even if for some, only for a short time. In recent years, they have all exhibited clear signs of authoritarianism, racism, extreme nationalism, and persecution of the opposition. In all, there has been harm to democratic institutions, especially to the judicial branch, delegitimization of a free media, and the advance of totalitarian thought. Even states like Turkey, India, the Philippines, and Brazil, where democratic traditions have long been weaker for other reasons, are distancing themselves even more from being characterized as democratic regimes. In Philippine and in Brazil the autocratic sectors is very strong but the autocratic leaders lost the elections The United States is a more complex example, but more worrying, as it is a superpower which influences many other states and it is also perceived as a leader of the free world: a country in which the democratic regime and its democratic institutions were once considered stable, but which suffered a heavy blow with the election of Donald Trump as president in 2016. Fortunately, in 2020 he was defeated in the election and Joe Biden, a Democrat, entered the White House, trying to repair the damage created by his predecessor. The United States has changed direction again, within a short time, and no doubt this change has also had an effect on the world and specifically on the relationship between the U.S. and Israel. This also includes Jewish citizens of the United States who overwhelmingly support the Democratic party and its liberal values. Change is not easy, as Trump left a well-established anti-democratic heritage in the Republican party that still is powerful. The mid-term elections in November 2022 left a balance between the Republicans and Democrats to the disappointment of the Republican party that hoped to take the Senate and the House of Representatives. In addition, the authoritarian rightwing has even gained strength in Western Europe, where up to now, the liberal democracies were not significantly affected. Countries affected include France, England, Germany, Italy, Austria, and even the Scandinavian countries. These changes are evidence of the *zeitgeist*, the spirit of the times, a factor which also grants legitimization to the rightwing in Israel. But the last two years have brought the wind of change—in all the five Nordic states and in Germany, leftist social democratic leaders were elected, and so too in Chile, Mexico, Peru, Bolivia, and Honduras. It may signal that the circle is moving.

Even though the present policies of Israel fit the authoritarian spirit of the times, this international trend has existed only for a few years. However, there have been many previous years of occupation—and that is probably the factor that has most strongly dominated Israeli politics, policies and economics through these years. What could have come about if there had not been such a difficult conflict at the center of Israeli experience? Would they, in any case, have developed a strong anti-democratic political culture? Naturally it is difficult to answer that question. But we may certainly remember the prophecy of Professor Leibowitz in 1967 and risk expressing the determination that it is the occupation that has made a significant contribution to the deterioration of democracy in Israel.

Creeping Annexation and Public Apathy

The occupation is not static; through the years it has undergone changes. One of these has taken place recently—the state of Israel is, at present, clearly advancing towards a policy of annexation. This is indirectly being implemented gradually and cumulatively, by legislation, court rulings and activity on the ground. The most striking action in this context has been the enactment in 2017 of a law whose title was laundered to Law for the Regulation of Settlement in Judea and Samaria. As already mentioned, this law enables the expropriation of private Palestinian land by the state and legally resolves illegal construction in Jewish settlements and outposts in the occupied territories. The legal opinion presented by the then-State Attorney General Avichai Mandelblit in 2017 simply permitted expropriation of private Palestinian land on which settlement structures had been built, since this was ostensibly a transaction that had been made seemingly "in good faith."[449] Then in the last week of being in office, in January 2022, Avichai Mandelblit approved the reestablishment of the Evyatar settlement. This outpost was built illegally in 2021, on the site of the former settlement in 2005 in the heart of a Palestinian rural area south of Nablus that was evacuated in the 2005 disengagement process carried by Ariel Sharon.[450]

An additional factor facilitating the implementation of de facto annexation is the informal policy of zero permits for Palestinians living in Area C, and that includes building permits, business licenses or approval to set up a factory. As a result, methodical destruction of Palestinian houses is routinely carried out in this area, apparently with the understanding that ultimately, Israeli law will be instituted. Leading up to the elections of March 2020, Naftali Bennett, who had been appointed Minister of Defense, announced the establishment of a system to strengthen Jewish settlements in Area C.[451] Following the 2020 elections and the publication of Trump's peace plan, which included approval for selective annexation, the political right made every effort to implement the annexation program before the presidential elections, which were to be held in the United States in November 2020. **But with the election of the new government in Israel we will witness practices that will speed the annexation. Thus, the State of Israel, if it does not see the error of its ways, is moving implacably towards apartheid, which will cause immense harm to society and to the nation, which wanted to be a secure shelter for the Jews of the world.**

It is important to note, I detect that in fact, instead of Israel annexing the occupied territories, the occupation is annexing the Israeli state. The practices carried out in the occupied territories permeate into the state, crossing the Green Line that was erased decades ago. These practices can now be observed within the state: delegitimization of those who struggle against the occupation, forbidding human rights NGOs from entering schools, violence committed by the police at leftist demonstrations, and even brutal army reactions towards Jewish leftists who try to help Palestinians in the West Bank, among others.[452]

Two prime ministers in Israel who were rightwing leaders during the 1980s and 1990s, Ariel Sharon and Ehud Olmert, later diagnosed the dangers and made clear statements in reference to the occupation: Ex-Prime Minister Ariel Sharon concluded that *"it is impossible to hold 3.5 million Palestinians under occupation ... my view is that it is wrong"* and that *"the occupation cannot continue"* (author's emphasis). (Meeting of the Likud faction in the Knesset on 26 May 2003). About five years later, in April 2008, then Prime Minister Ehud Olmert spoke to soldiers serving in the occupied territory in the West Bank:

> *We must understand that a very large population of Palestinians are living here and we must find the wisest and the most decisive mechanism so that, until that happens (the withdrawal from the West Bank), we will have maximum security. But we will not leave them in tatters and darken the rest of the lives of our future generations. Take a fifty-year-old [Palestinian] man living here, someone who has lived the crucial part of his life—forty years of his life, since he was a child of 10—under the custody of an Israeli soldier. That soldier is carrying a rifle—for the most justified of reasons. But that is this man's narrative. Take those who have been undressed at roadblocks, only because perhaps there is a terrorist among them. Take those who must wait for hours at roadblocks out of the fear that perhaps a car bomb might pass through. That could be a boiling pot that might explode and cause terrible burns, and it could be something else, depending only on your understanding and your ability to act wisely and decisively.[453]*

In opposition to these outlooks, the present leadership of Israel is marching in the opposite direction. The desire to annex the West Bank or parts of it has not yet been implemented in legislation (only East Jerusalem has been annexed). However, intentions to do so have already been openly expressed, although actually, there is no real need to do that in the present

Israeli realities. But apartheid is not dependent on the legislation. It appears with the development of a regime that actively consolidates Jewish domination of the West Bank and East Jerusalem through the operation of a two-tiered, ethnicity-based system that privileges Jews and oppresses Palestinians. The International Convention on the Suppression and Punishment of the Crime of Apartheid, adopted by the UN General Assembly in November 1973, defines apartheid as *"inhumane acts committed for the purpose of establishing and maintaining domination by one racial group of persons over any other racial group of persons and systematically oppressing them."* The Rome Statute of the International Criminal Court (ICC) concludes that apartheid constitutes *"inhumane acts ... committed in the context of an institutionalized regime of systematic oppression and domination by one racial group over any other racial group or groups and committed with the intention of maintaining that regime."*

The great majority of Jewish society in Israel is almost completely cut off from what is taking place in the territories. In the present state of affairs, Israeli society members live relatively comfortable lives. The economic status of the upper-middle class is very good and even parts of the middle class are satisfied. Findings show that Israelis were in eleventh place in the World Happiness Survey of 2018.[454] Restaurants are full in Tel Aviv and in other places in the country, and cultural and entertainment performances fill halls; hundreds of thousands were taking trips abroad each year before the pandemic. All these signs indicate satisfaction with their lives among most Jewish Israelis. **Whatever is happening a few kilometers eastward or southward in the West Bank or the Gaza Strip does not reach most of the Jewish public. Most are indifferent and repress or find rationalizations to justify the situation. A recent national survey carried out by NGO Zulat in February 2021 shows that 38% of Jews think that Israel is safeguarding human rights of the Palestinians in the occupied territories, 38% are neutral, and only 24% think that Israel is not safeguarding them.[455]**

In addition, the anti-democratic processes experienced by society are considered as not directly affecting Israelis or their quality of life— and perhaps they are right. These are intangible and long-term developments which are not immediately and openly experienced. At the same time, the "good old" conflict supporting narratives supply the essential needs for this public. Most Israelis do not comprehend the

full significance of the far-reaching changes that have occurred in the political-social spheres of the country and the national changes in the character of the country. Safeguarding the status quo has therefore become a prime need. On the other hand, the public does comprehend the leadership's messages about the threats and dangers awaiting them if a chance at peace arises. Simultaneously, they ignore the costs that society has been paying and the potential gains to be had if peace were to come. Only very few are able to see into the far future; most are satisfied with a short-term view in the spirit of "Let us drink today and leave the future to our children."

Appraisal of the Future

Processes of change in Israeli society are at their peak. The State of Israel is rapidly changing before our very eyes. But we may assume that the direction of this shift will not continue forever, both in Israel and in the world. It will evolve and forces of progress will come to the surface again. At least, that is what we hope. And if that happens, it will be very difficult for Israel to continue the occupation, considering the serious damage to human rights that it entails.

The age of prophets in our region has ended and we cannot risk indulging in prophecy. However, I would like to outline a reasoned evaluation, which in my opinion, is not even daring—in another decade or two, and maybe more, the State of Israel will be perceived in the same way that South Africa was until 1994—ostracized and isolated, even though their economy was strong and the country was blessed with enormous natural resources. In this context, the dynamics of how South Africa underwent isolation should be remembered. On the one hand, the process took dozens of years, slowly and cumulatively. On the other hand, events that led to political change in the country were quick and surprising. The basic assumption is that the countries of the world will not agree to an apartheid regime being a member of their community, especially a society that presents itself as "a light unto the nations," a cradle of universal morality, a pillar of Western civilization. And when that happens, the costs that we have cited will be dwarfed by those that will be demanded, almost immediately, from Israel and from its Jewish society. It is also difficult to imagine that the Palestinians will indefinitely accept their fate as a conquered nation.

Israel already has ruled the Palestinian nation for more than 50 years and has settled Jews on Palestinian land. It can be said, in general, that after its victories in the War of Independence and the Six-Day War, Israel had no intention of solving the Palestinian problem, in all of its complexities, ignoring the aspirations of the Palestinians and even refusing to take into account the Security Council resolutions in 1967 (242), 1973 (336), 1979 (452), and 2016 (2334), relating to withdrawal from the occupied territories and rejecting the legality of settling Jews in them.[456] **Almost all of the plans developed in Israel since 1967 by government leaders, have been intended to eat into the occupied territories, section by section, and to settle Jews in these territories for a range of reasons and justifications. Four windows were opened to advance the peace process with the Palestinians. Two were closed with unnatural events and one with human failure. Rabin was murdered by a Jew and the peace process ended. Sharon fell into a coma and died, while Olmert was indicted for bribery and put on trial. Barak blew his opportunity.** During the negotiations in Taba during Barak's term in January 2001 between Israeli and Palestinian representatives on the highest level and those between Prime Minister Olmert and Abu Mazen in 2008, a solution to the conflict was never even approached, but these two peace processes were never realized for a variety of reasons. But most of the time from 1967 till today the Prime Ministers who served in the office were not interested in settling the conflict that required major withdrawal from the West Bank and dismantlement of at least some of the Jewish settlements in the occupied territory.

This all takes place according to the universal rule that no society willingly gives up territory, resources, status, or prestige to another society, even if it has taken these by immoral means. Through the years, Israeli governments have not intended to permit Palestinians to establish an independent state on all the West Bank and the Gaza Strip with its capital in East Jerusalem.[457] In recent years, Israeli governments have become fixated on the desire to maintain the status quo or to annex sections of the West Bank while expanding the settlement project. This state of affairs has developed not only due to the persistent rightwing governments and their increasing popular support, but also due to significant changes in the world, as have been described.

History has shown that nations have waited even hundreds of years for independence. The Irish, Poles, Serbs, and Slovenes, among oth-

ers, have not given up their aspirations for self-determination and for the establishment of an independent state. They have revolted, been suppressed, revolted again, until their aspirations have been fulfilled. This has also taken place among nations under colonial occupation for decades and hundreds of years. Many have gained independence after violent struggles. In my opinion, this will also ultimately take place for the Palestinians, even if the international community does not force Israel to solve the conflict or to give Palestinians full rights. But that could happen in years or decades or perhaps even more.

Taking a philosophical-historical viewpoint, I believe that civilization is marching towards inclusion of moral and democratic norms, even if this does not take place consistently or quickly—two steps forwards and one step backwards. A long-term view of thousands of years of civilization makes it possible to distinguish progress in the realm of moral values, behavioral norms and governing principles. Even an advanced society like Greece, 2,500 years ago, did not consider human beings equal and excluded slaves and women from the right to choose and to be chosen. Great Britain, as well, was in a similar situation 400 years ago. Concepts which defined human conduct, such as liberty, equality or rights, appeared only 250 years ago. Women received the right to vote in many countries only about 100 years ago. Just 71 years ago the Declaration of Human Rights set out and the Fourth Geneva Convention, mandating the protection of a civilian population during wars between states or occupations in conflict, was adopted only 70 years ago. In addition, only in 2002 did the Rome Convention come into force, defining acts that are considered crimes and are meant to be judged by the International Criminal Court in The Hague: genocide, crimes against humanity, war crimes, and crimes of aggression. Although about 138 nations have signed the convention, including Israel, only 123 had ratified it by November 2019, when Israel and the United States stated that they would not ratify it. That is interesting since the whole process of establishing the International Criminal Court was initiated to prevent genocides like the 1940s Holocaust.

Only a little more than 50 years ago, the states of the world began to unite against the apartheid regime in South Africa, intending to eliminate it. And yet, it must be recognized that in the last century, one of the greatest acts of injustice that the world has known took place as a result of racism, extreme nationalism, and totalitarianism. Even today, there are many occasions of strong nations using military power in contradiction to what accepted moral and democratic behavior is in the civilized world. In quite a few countries that consider themselves democratic, there is still institutionalized and sometimes even legal discrimination, harm to values and democratic principles, and impairment of human rights. In addition, there are states that have overthrown democratic regimes which are not to their liking for economic or political interests. These all testify to the difficult and complex path of moral progress. However, civilization has succeeded in progressing from absolute monarchies which ruled for many hundreds of years by incessant violent conquests, while controlling populations with no rights at all, like slaves or women—to states with democratic regimes, and liberal values. Despite the retreat of the present period, the future looks promising to us.

For decades, Israel made an effort to conceal the story of the occupation, in Israel and in the world. In Israel, the attempt has been successful and even the term "occupation" has been suppressed. The world has now become more interested in different crises like those in Syria or Yemen, and since 2020, attention has been held by the pandemic that has threatened the well-being of the world. But on December 20, 2019, the chief prosecutor of the International Criminal Court (ICC), Fatou Bensouda, announced an investigation into Israeli and Palestinian war crimes allegedly committed in the Palestinian territories. Israel has been accused of illegally establishing West Bank settlements and violating the laws of war during the 2014 Gaza War, including claims of targeting Red Cross installations. On February 5, 2021, the court *"decided, by majority, that the Court's territorial jurisdiction in the Situation in Palestine, a State party to the ICC Rome Statute, extends to the territories occupied by Israel since 1967, namely Gaza and the West Bank, including East Jerusalem."* Judges ruled that the court does have jurisdiction, rejecting Israel's argument that it lacks such authority to do so. In May 2021, the United Nations Human Rights Council decided to investigate crimes against humanity during the Gaza war in May 2021 by Israel and Hamas, as well as systematic violations in the Occupied Palestinian Territory, including East Jerusalem and in Israel.[458] In November 2022 the Special Political and Decolonization Committee of United Nation recommended to refer the case of investigating occupation to the International Court of Justice in Hague. Thus, the story of the occupation is returning to public attention. It is slow, moves one step forward and then stalls for a while but it is progressing. **This analysis points to the**

fact that the fate of the Palestinians has not yet been sealed. There is a high probability that they will achieve their aspiration to live with full human and civil rights.

There is no doubt that the present leadership of Israel does not share this appraisal. And of course, I too do not know with certainty what the future will bring. But it is possible to say with confidence that, at present, a considerable percentage of Jewish society in Israel and in the Jewish worldview the costs we have detailed as intolerable. This leads inevitably to social rift and polarization—and that is one of the highest costs that we must pay for the occupation and, according to all signs for the future, this polarization will only increase. I personally believe that 50 years from now, perhaps more, perhaps less, the new saga of a march of folly will be written about Israel and its occupation, like what was originally written in Barbara Tuchman's *March of Folly* about Trojans, Renaissance popes, English King George III, and Americans in their Vietnam War. All these pursued policies and actions contrary to their own interests and harmed their countries dramatically.[459] The list of such marches is a long one and nations duplicate them without learning the lessons, as the United States did in its wars in Iraq and Afghanistan.

CHAPTER 11

A Look into the Future

S ome will say that this picture of reality is too pessimistic—and perhaps they are right. Therefore, a question should be asked that, in any case, remains open—what can be done to resolve the conflict and end the occupation?

There are any number of plans on the table at the moment to end the conflict between the Israelis and the Palestinians—both one-sided and reciprocal, but this is not the place to enter into the nitty-gritty of specific initiatives. Moreover—and this is the heart of the matter—I believe that a much more comprehensive societal change is needed than the advancement of another technical document, primarily when it comes to the questions in dispute (Jerusalem, borders, refugees, and others). So instead of the question asked above, let me ask another, broader one—How can we build an infrastructure that will enable us, when the time comes, to achieve the conclusion of a peace process with the Palestinians?

There are a number of necessary conditions to create a suitable climate which will advance a peace process. The most important among them, in the spirit of this book, is the replacement of conflict-supporting narratives with narratives supporting negotiations to achieve a peace agreement which will fulfill the primary needs of society members. The leaders (and not just them) must aim for a change in society's narratives in order to win its support, and to prepare it for an era of peace. The peace-supporting narrative has to begin with the recognition that Palestinians are partners for peace negotiations as a legitimate side. Trust has to be built in this primary process in which the delegitimization has to be stopped and a new worldview must be constructed, admitting that both sides have been victims of the conflict. Then, of primary importance, new goals must be set that also recognize the needs of the Palestinians. The violations of human rights have to cease. Negotiations must determine how to bring an end to the occupation and achieve a conflict resolution that the majority of both sides will accept. It is hard to imagine that the great majority of both societies will accept any solution that satisfies both Israeli Jews and Palestinians. There will probably be a minority that will reject any proposed settlement that does not involve a zero-sum solution in their favor. But, as in other conflict settlements, a legitimate majority could reach a satisfactory agreement.

This effort must require leaders to prepare society for the difficulties expected during the transition period, which will probably be characterized by continual violence while negotiations are being carried on, and even later. History teaches us that a transition is a period of duality, during which signs of conflict and signs of peace appear simultaneously. Leaders who have chosen to aim for peace must be willing to fight destructive groups who resolutely oppose a peace agreement for a variety of reasons and who will use any available means—including violence—to sabotage its achievement.[460] The State of Israel has already faced such groups and experienced this type of activity. **But first of all, a change is needed in political processes and in the political structure that has created and determined the conflict culture. Thus, media channels must be open to enable information to flow freely and the slander of individuals, organizations and institutions that bring alternative information must end. Pluralism must be developed to enable freedom of expression and to bring about an end to the delegitimization of those who hold other views, namely, to parties and organizations who speak about possible partners for peace and about the costs of the occupation, the injustices in its wake and the benefits of peace. Especially important must be returning democracy to its former status—a democracy that sanctifies human and minority rights, that poses values and respects them, that esteems the law and supports the separation of powers, and that strengthens checks and balances in order for democracy to flourish. This would mean a social-political change of the highest order. Finally, the Israeli-Palestinian conflict requires leaders on both sides that are motivated to reach peace, as charismatic, legitimate and determined as in South Africa, in France during the Algerian war, or in Israel and Egypt during the Israeli-Egyptian peace process. In divided societies such as those in the Middle East conflict, the internal change requires such leadership.**

Some critics may suggest that I place too much weight on the mind processes and there should also be emphasis on the change of reality such a decrease of violence, decline of violation of human rights, or improvement of life conditions. I claim that all these steps begin with ideas that drive de-escalation of the conflict. Searching all the cases of resolved conflicts as well as unresolved ones through my mind I find a determinative weight of ideas that lead either to peace making or maintaining and also escalating a conflict. Thus there is no question what comes first, the chicken or the egg. The idea to begin a conflict or to end it comes first, but then in order to move in one direction, the idea has to be complemented by action in order to have an effect.

What Are the Chances of an Internal Social Change?

Even a change of narratives cannot take place in the space of a day *ex nihilo*. Change can exist only in conjunction with another necessary condition for the development of real movement in the direction of peace—a deep internal societal change. A society immersed in a conflict could undergo such a change in two ways—when leadership with vision initiates and leads a peace campaign (a top-down process), as developed in France during the Algerian War, or change in the wake of pressure by civil society (a bottom-up process), as occurred to a certain extent in Northern Ireland. The first case—a preferable one for the Israeli-Palestinian conflict—is usually based on leaders who have changed their viewpoints and have led the nation into a peace process, like Menachem Begin in the context of the peace agreement with Egypt, and Yitzchak Rabin and Shimon Peres with the Oslo Agreements.

In asymmetric conflicts, when one side is a state and the other is an opposition group, ethnic or ideological, the initiative for negotiations usually comes from the stronger side—as in the French-Algerian War or in South Africa. That was also the case with negotiations between Israel and the Palestine Liberation Organization. The stronger side has the assets, the abilities and the resources to enable it to take the first steps towards solving a conflict by peaceful means. Accordingly, leaders of the stronger side have more significant opportunities to lead to change, on the condition that they are not afraid to take the risk. Steps taken by de Gaulle in Algeria or de Klerk in South Africa are paradigmatic examples of acts by such leaders. In comparison, the second, bottom-up case is one in which a well-organized civil society with strong institutions, exerts significant pressure on the leadership to take the road to peace, as occurred in Northern Ireland during the 1990s, with the joint pressure of Protestant and Catholic civil organizations. Ultimately, however, politicians are the ones who negotiate, and they must be the ones to reach an agreement, so even pressure from "below" is directed towards leaders who must change their own views and initiate a peace process.

Thus, a step towards internal change is to a certain extent linked to a change in society's narratives. In the case of congruence between conflict-supporting narratives in the leadership and those of most society members, there is no internal source of power capable of leading the nation to a peace process. For that to happen, there must be a sharp change of views among the leadership (which could occur quickly, as epitomized by the rapid change in de Gaulle's position regarding the end of the conflict between France and Algeria, or Menachem Begin's shift of views about the Israeli-Egyptian conflict), or the public's becoming convinced of the need for a peace process, translated into pressure on the leadership to initiate such a process (usually occurring much more slowly, but possible, as occurred in Northern Ireland). Another possibility might be a peace process beginning as a result of demands from a third party or broad pressure from the international community (as in the case of South Africa). In the end, there is an even more optimistic possibility: that the two battling sides ultimately reach the conclusion that the conflict is leading to a dead end with high costs and that neither side can be victorious and so they just decide to make the effort to end it. That is what happened in El Salvador and Guatemala during an internal conflict. A motivation for achieving one of these scenarios could be an unexpected constitutive event, that would accelerate an internal change of attitudes—among leaders and among the public—leading towards a solution, just as the fall of the Soviet Union motivated the Palestine Liberation Organization to reach an agreement with Israel.

Only belief in the path to peace, which is, in essence, fraught with uncertainty and risk, and the firm decision to employ every possible strategy necessary to advance that goal, will bring about the long-awaited peace. And because the birth of the conflict took place in the minds of human beings, making peace must also begin in their minds, as a desired objective whose achievement is important for the welfare of the society in which they are living. These ideas are not foreign to Jewish society. They have already taken hold in Israel, first, at the end of the 1970s, on the eve of the peace treaty with Egypt, and the second time, at the beginning of the 1990s, with the start of the Oslo negotiations. Prime Minister Yitzhak Rabin gave expression to these aims in his speech at the signing of the Cairo Agreement with the Palestine Liberation Organization, on 4 May 1994:

> *We are convinced that our two peoples can live on the same patch of territory, "every man under his vine and under his fig tree," as the Prophets foretold, and bring to this country - a land of rocks and of tombstones—the taste of milk and honey that it deserves. [...] On this day, I turn to you, the Palestinian people, and say: Our Palestinian neighbors, A century of bloodshed has forged in us a core of mutual enmity [...] Today we are both extending a hand in peace. Today we are inaugurating a new age...*

Especially interesting is the case of Ehud Olmert who served as Prime Minister of Israel from 2006–2009. For many years he had been one of the prominent hawks on the political map as a member of the Likud Party. For years he had attacked every move that hinted at compromise or agreement, and had opposed the peace agreement with Egypt and, of course, the Oslo agreements. But through the years, in a long process, he changed his attitudes when he understood that the price for continuing the conflict with the Palestinians was destructive to the state of Israel. Expressing this change, he spoke at the opening session of the Knesset in 2007:

> *I know that Israel has excellent excuses with which to justify a stalemate between us and the Palestinians. The Hamas and Islamic Jihad's murderous attacks from the Gaza border are intolerable, and we have no intention of acquiescing to them. The firing of rockets on the southern communities cannot continue indefinitely, and the Political-Security Cabinet will soon discuss the proposals by the Minister of Defense and the military system to put an end to these attacks.*
>
> *The terror elements, headed by Hamas and Islamic Jihad, continue to be active in Judea and Samaria, and had it not been for the vigilance of our security forces, the IDF, the security service and the Israel Police, which foil terror attempts on a daily basis, the situation in this sector as well would have been entirely different from what it looks like today....*
>
> *Knowing all these facts, I still wish to announce here, in the most explicit terms—**I have no intention of seeking ex-***

cuses to avoid a political process. I am firm and determined in my desire to create a momentum and provide a chance for the success of a substantive political process, in partnership with the President of the Palestinian Authority Abu Mazen. Any other option means a demographic battle, drowned in blood and tears, which does not serve the State of Israel in any way. (Emphasis added by the authors). *This November, an international meeting is expected to be held in the United States, with the aim of providing a backing to the process of dialogue between us and the Palestinians. I wish to clarify in the most explicit terms: The November meeting is not a conference which will replace bilateral, direct negotiations between us and the Palestinians. This meeting is intended to provide backing and encouragement and create a comprehensive umbrella of support for the direct process between us and them.* (Olmert, 8 October 2007)

In almost every case of significant societal change in movements towards peace, large swaths of society have felt a sense of loss and have blamed the leadership. After a sharp change in political positions by the leadership, a gap has often occurred between the new narrative espoused by the leadership and the one which has been accepted by at least part of the nation—the narrative that has been hegemonic until now. That is what took place for example in communist Poland, in Northern Ireland during the conflict, and in the United States in the 1960s and 1970s, during the war in Viet Nam. As far as we know, there are no ingenious solutions either in social or political psychology, that may instigate an overnight change in the narrative structure held by the public, or alternatively, in the narrative espoused by the leadership, without the occurrence of dramatic events. It would be unreasonable to expect anything so accelerated. Thus, what is certain is that this must be a long-term process—a broad and continuous development in civil society, binding and externally directed. It must be remembered that in many cases in history, the minority has succeeded in convincing the majority, but it takes many years and does not necessarily advance sequentially, but rather in a pattern of advance and regression. The principles of such change have been outlined previously.

How Can Rapid Change Take Place?

Considering what has been said above, a rapid change could take place in Israel under the following conditions:

1. A change in attitudes among leaders who will understand that continuing conflict is causing grave damage to society or the emergence of leaders who have the standing to navigate the Israeli Jews to the peaceful resolution of the conflict.

2. Powerful constitutive events (global, regional, or internal-Israeli) which will influence the public and lead it to reconsider its fundamental principles.

3. Palestinian steps which will exact a heavy price in Israel.

4. The effects and pressure in various ways and methods by a third party.

At present, in Israel, these conditions do not exist. The leadership is convinced (and convincing) that the aims at the basis of the conflict, such as the existence of greater Israel including the West Bank and its Jewish settlements, are sacred and cannot be subject to compromise. The dominant approach is that a peace treaty cannot ensure the security of Israel and of the Jewish nation; that democratic values are subservient to particularistic Jewish values; and that, from a practical standpoint, time works to the advantage of Israel since it has the human and material resources necessary for withstanding a lengthy conflict. This approach assumes that the international community of nations is motivated principally by economic, technological, military and political interests which can be provided by Israel, while moral values and human rights have only peripheral importance for the policies adopted by other states. In addition, the present situation of Israel seen from every angle looks very good to the Israeli Jewish citizens—the level of threats from neighboring Arab states is extremely low; Israel successfully expands the relationship and coordination with the Arab states that signed peace agreement; the Palestinian case has been moved to the periphery of attention in the international community because of other urgent issues like the Ukrainian war, the level of Palestinian violence moved to the negligible level; Palestinian leadership cooperates with the Israeli security, Israel has a tremendous advantage over the Palestinians on every measurable parameter; finally Israel achieved well recognizable status among key states with its political, military, economic and technological high standing. Moreover, the leadership feels that world Jewry, as well as Israel's international status, will prevent significant external pressure, and will protect it from international criticism; that support by the American nation and the U.S. Congress will not enable any threat to harm Israel; and that, in any case, Israel has the ability to withstand external pressure.

Israel's stable international status presently serves as an obstacle for far-reaching change in the region. Above and beyond the alliance between Israel and the United States, Israel's relations with Russia, China, and India also greatly improved during Netanyahu's terms of office. In addition, the country has established relations, both official and unofficial, with some Arab states, and especially with the Gulf States. It should also be noted that, through the years, international concern about the Israeli-Palestinian conflict has lessened to a significant extent due to the outbreak of other crises and disputes, demanding prompt and explicit attention—for example, in recent years, in Syria, Iraq, the Ukraine, North Korea, and others— in contrast to our conflict, which has been long-lasting and is perceived as chronic and unchanging. Furthermore, for several decades, the crisis with Iran has been occupying the nations of the world. Trump's loss in the United States elections and the ascendance to the presidency of Democratic President Joe Biden in 2021 will somewhat improve the relationship between the U.S. and the Palestinians. But no major move is expected as the new administration has many challenges in the internal and foreign arenas, especially as a result of the continuing polarization of the American society on many of the key issues.

Moreover, the alliance between Netanyahu and the Israeli right, and the extreme European rightwing, at the price of ignoring the spreading antisemitism there (on the basis of the Islamophobia common to both sides), along with the rapid empowerment of these rightwing forces, have supplied another safety net for Israel. This support comes even as, in most international states, public opinion about Israel is contradictory to that of the ruling leadership; the international public is critical of Israeli policies and supports Palestinian aspirations to establish an independent state. In the end, while this is being written, the entire world is embroiled in one of the most difficult crises in recent times, battling the pandemic, which has led to the deaths of more than five and a half million people by January 2022 and has paralyzed the economy in every country on earth. Even if the pandemic is defeated, its severe economic-social toll will occupy the human race for years to come. Finally, the "unexpected" war in Europe creates completely new geopolitical situation. The Russian invasion of Ukraine in 2022 created a new wide scope challenge with unknown consequences and implications. As this book is being completed it is almost impossible to predict the process and the results of the bloody conflict that involves united Western countries with the support of almost the entire world against Russia. In addition, the severe economic crisis that spread because of different reasons in the numerous states of the world poses a tremendous challenge that needs to overcome. Finally the global warming crisis is still not addressed properly and thus it became dangerous hazard to the world.

Like its leaders, the Jewish public in Israel certainly has no doubts about these basic assumptions and perceived reality. All these noted factors have caused to a new understanding of reality. Thus it is difficult to imagine that neither the leadership nor the society members will change their views of the conflict and the peace process. Also, at present it hard to imagine for the Israeli Jews an international pressure that could change reality in the visible future to move the country in the direction of peace.

In the present reality, there is no expectation that the Palestinians will change their behavior. First of all, a sector of Palestinian society now benefits from the status quo in material terms—the leadership echelon. At least some of these leaders are corrupt and, in any case, lean towards an authoritarian regime. In the wider circle, tens of thousands of families earn their livings as employees of the Palestinian Authority, which supplies the salaries of those who work in the public sector, like teachers, medical staff, workers in the security system, and additional service providers. Funding comes from a variety of countries and the present situation is convenient for many of these strata of Palestinian society.

An additional reason for the stagnation in Palestinian society is the all-encompassing system of control and supervision instituted by Israel, which penetrates every corner of Palestinian society both personally-technologically and by the use of Palestinian collaborators. No small number of people work for the Israeli authorities and, for various reasons, aid in the supervision of Palestinians. In principle, members of Palestinian society are dependent on the occupation authorities in many areas of their lives and there are those who are willing to serve these authorities. The split between the West Bank, controlled by the Fatah, and the Gaza Strip ruled by Hamas, and the rivalry between them, divides Palestinian society and that too leads to very serious outcomes. And finally, the Arab states, which have until recently served as important actors in the Israeli-Palestinian conflict, have more or less lost their interest in the fate of the Palestinians, and most of their official statements about the conflict are payment of lip service but nothing more. Furthermore, after Trump triumphed in the 2016 American elections, Saudi Arabia, as well as some of the Gulf States, have even started to criticize the Palestinians for what they term as refusal to make peace. Eventually some of the Arab states that include the United Arab Emirates, Bahrain, Sudan, and Morocco yielded to the American pressure and in return for promised benefits signed a peace agreement with Israel. Considering all these factors, it is difficult to imagine a rapid change in Palestinian society which will aid in initiating a peace process to end the conflict, even though, from a political and historical standpoint, these processes are constantly percolating under the surface and might suddenly erupt with great force. For example, that was how the first intifada broke out at the end of 1987.

However, the situation may change, perhaps even rapidly. What is apparently missing is a substantive event that will lead to a change in consciousness among the Israeli leadership, or alternatively, a change in Israeli public opinion. Events such as these develop gradually, and under the surface. On the other hand, sometimes they may appear all at once. The 2020 victory of Joe Biden, the Democratic candidate, in the U.S. elections of 2020—the complete antithesis of Donald Trump and the Republicans, in their attitude towards the Israeli-Palestinian conflict—might be the source of that event. The Republican Party, which is a strong supporter of the Israeli regime, has lost its control of the U.S. government. But it is hard to predict what will happen in the 2022 midterm elections, when the democrats may lose their narrow majority in Congress—and then nobody knows what the results of the elections in 2024 will be. Also unknown is how the war in Ukraine will affect the Middle Eastern conflict because in both of them, one side occupies the territory populated by the rival side. It could be that Russia's attempt to occupy the Ukraine will turn attention from the Israeli occupation. Maybe yes and maybe no. The international agenda will be also affected by the state of the pandemic and especially the economic situation around the world.

However, it is much more logical to assume that significant event related to the Israeli-Palestinian conflict, if it actually does occur, cannot really be expected at the moment; it will, by nature, be surprising and unexpected, like the appearance of the corona pandemic. But one thing is as sure as the sunrise every morning—the Palestinians are here in "Greater Israel" to stay. They will not move and will not be moved in spite of the dreams and wishes of some Jews. We will have to deal with this situation in line with the norms and values of a progressive civilization. But as Jeremy Pressman entitled his book, *The Sword is not Enough.*[461]

As public attitudes are anchored in the national culture of conflict, and as there is congruence between the fundamental assumptions of the nation and its leaders, with the leadership using every means available to reinforce these assumptions and convince the public that they are valid—there is very little chance for rapid social change by any usual methods of persuasion. Is it possible, for example, to persuade the ultraorthodox to abandon the sacred character of the Sabbath, or to convince the leftwing of the unimportance of the Declaration of Human Rights, using logical arguments, in the short term? Of course not!

Conditions for Political Change

How is it possible to motivate the Jewish public in Israel to support a solution to the conflict which will also respond to the reasonable needs of the Palestinian nation? In other words, how could the Jewish public in Israel be persuaded to accept the attitudes and ideas of the Israel leftwing? Could a minority change the opinions of the majority by a campaign of persuasion that would lead to support for a peace process and its realization?

This approach would demand, as already noted, adjustment of two fundamental positions, revised as follows: a. The understanding that the Palestinians, and even more so, their leaders, are partners for negotiations and for a peace agreement; b. The comprehension that a peace agreement will have to involve painful compromises, but these would not harm the security of the State of Israel. These two assumptions are fundamentally based on a sense of trust for Palestinians and on their legitimization, enabling Israeli Jews to perceive them as be-

longing to accepted and normative groups with which it is desirable to end conflict and develop peaceful relations. These adjustments provide the initial basis. Such trust might stem from utilitarian considerations and might be created even at a time of initial groping contacts between the two sides. It could perhaps be affected by some meaningful gesture (think about Jordanian King Hussein, bowing to the families of the seven young Israeli girls killed by a Jordanian soldier in 1997) or a surprising statement (consider the statement by Netanyahu after a meeting with Arafat in 1988: "I found a friend"). Some minimal amount of trust is necessary. Additionally, it may be assumed that, over time, humanization of the opponent will also evolve.

In order for these attitudes to develop in at least a good part of the public, we must recruit society members with determination and persistence. As we have explained more than once, establishing an alternative narrative is an especially difficult task, certainly in Jewish society, for which the point of departure is that the land of Israel has been "registered in its name in the land registry office." A solution to the conflict which demands giving up parts of the homeland does not necessitate a similar concession from the Palestinians or one that is equal in its scope, as they are "only on the receiving end." How can a compromise nevertheless be achieved? Agreements are signed when leaders consider that society may pay a very high price in the future for the cards it is holding, or when society reaches a general understanding that it is paying a very heavy price for continuing the conflict, or when resources to maintain the conflict are gone, which includes extreme psychological exhaustion. Sometimes, all three of these factors appear together; at times, two of them, and at other times, only one. There are no rules to govern these developments. They are only the proposals of two Israeli psychologists, Daniel Kahneman and Amos Tversky.

A penetrating look into the future costs of the conflict is likely to supply a source of optimism. Awareness of these costs at a time when the possibility exists of ending the conflict peacefully may be the most effective catalyst for a process of attitude change. To understand this, it is helpful to become acquainted with "prospect theory," formulated by the abovementioned Kahneman and Tversky. It theorizes that information about losses has a greater effect than information about profits, as it is more difficult for people to lose what they already have than not to gain something that they still don't have.[462] In psychological literature, most research using this approach centers on the context of merchandising and products. However, translation into conflict terminology also seems applicable. In the framework of research conducted by the author of this book with others in 2009, a detailed scenario which outlined the future costs to be paid by Israeli society in the framework of a one-state solution (first and foremost, the loss of the state's Jewish character), tipped the scales towards the choice of a two-state solution.[463] This is because the price of a two-state solution is lower than the potential losses of a one-state solution. The awareness of this price has caused people on the right, center and left to simultaneously support real compromise towards the solution of two states. This can teach us that the wording of the argument may have an effect on how the situation is evaluated. In this case, new and valid information about the real potential price, was effective to the point of reconsideration of beliefs and even serious thinking about new solutions which, up until then, had been thought to be completely unacceptable. **Thus, in accord with the formula suggested by Daniel Kahneman and Amos Tversky, a conflict ends when society understands that the price it is paying for a peace agreement is lower than the price it will pay for a continuation of the conflict in the future.**

This equation is particularly accurate in the Israeli case. The leadership's refusal to divide the country into two states at present may lead to a much heavier price for society to pay in the future. It will apparently have to deal with an impossible choice: to lose the democratic character of the state and remain Jewish by instituting an apartheid regime, or to lose its Jewish character by maintaining democracy. The assumption at the basis of this formulation is that about half of the inhabitants between the Jordan River and the Mediterranean Sea are Palestinians. Continuing to rule them will not make it possible to maintain a democratic state over time. As present realities indicate, even today, according to various appraisals, between the Jordan and the Mediterranean, the two populations, Jews and Palestinians, are more or less equal in number. Thus, to maintain democracy, Israel will have to give the Palestinians equal rights. And we are not the only ones who draw this conclusion. A similar understanding of the situation has, through the years, caused quite a few political figures to moderate their stances and to leave the political rightwing. These include Shlomo Lahat, Michael Eitan, Dan Meridor, Roni Milo, Ehud Olmert, and Tzipi Livni—all past high-ranking members of the Likud rightist party. But since this is a future price rather than an immediate one, and as the possibility has often been discussed, but has still not occurred—the Jewish public does not fear it. The public does not believe that it is real. Therefore, more and more public opinion makers and significant figures believe that the possibility of dividing the country for a two-state solution has passed and only a one state solution remained. It is difficult to determine at present whether Israel has missed the opportunity to save itself, but it is clear that any long delay of dividing the country, with continuation of the Jewish settlement of the occupied territory, will provide only a one-state solution. At present, Jewish and Palestinian populations are sliding down in their support of two-state solution. In March 2022, only 40% of Palestinians and 39% of Jews supported this solution, while in 2010, 71% of Jews and 57% of Palestinians supported it. Thus, the leadership has a short time to decide what is good for the State of Israel as was imagined by the founding fathers.

What are Effective Messages of Persuasion?

In general, messages of persuasion must fulfill two necessary conditions.

The first condition. As we are relating to conflict supporting narratives that society members have acquired at a young age, and which have been supported through the years by political leaders and the media, and have been reiterated many times throughout their lives, society members feel great security in their beliefs and their thinking about them is generally automatic. That means that they make judgments automatically, without investing great effort in examining them and without accumulating new knowledge. **Thus, as the first condition, in order for an individual to seriously consider a message directed at persuading him/her via a meaningful cognitive process and not spontaneously, the message must be strong, fresh, and credible. It must cause the individual to stop and reconsider the message deeply as though processing data. That is the first necessary condition. Of course, one message does not change viewpoints and attitudes that have been well anchored. This must involve the free flow of information, persistent, systematic, salient, and steady.**

The second condition: An individual must feel that the content of the message provides a response to his/her most basic needs, like the need for personal and collective security, the need for belonging

and positive identity, the need for justice and the need for a positive collective image. In recent years it has actually been the right wing that has succeeded in supplying these needs and convincing the public that it fulfils them more successfully. And because fulfilling these needs is irreplaceable, messages from the left must relate to them directly and without self-justification and must explain how these needs will be satisfied.

Subjects like personal and existential security are incorrectly identified with a rightwing worldview. But this is not necessarily so. It is possible to convince the public that there are a variety of ways to fulfill the need for security; that the reality of occupation harms existential security in the long term; that actually, peace is what will ultimately ensure the security of Israeli citizens as well as national security; that the settlements in occupied territories do not increase security, in contrast to what the right has insisted, but rather, intensify the friction with the Palestinians, reinforce the distrust and frustration, and increase the violence; that only signing a peace agreement will ensure the determination of permanent and secure borders for the State of Israel; and that, in time, violence will end, as it did in Northern Ireland and the Basque Country in Spain, even if that does not happen immediately. There are always extremist spoilers who think that the peace terms are not good enough—but since most people are interested in peace and quiet, the difficulties will fade away and in the long run, peace and quiet will be achieved. It is also important to persuade the public that, for this goal, which could, without exaggeration, be considered exalted, there is no reason not to take the risk, which, in the last analysis, is only a minor one. This risk is certainly not as great as what is argued by the rightwing, via descriptions of "the danger of destruction" or "a second holocaust." The public has already experienced the results of the peace agreement with Egypt, comprehending that occupying territories did not ensure security, while the agreement with the Egyptians has been in existence for 40 years and has ensured quiet on that border. And that was after Egypt had been considered the number one "Nazi" opponent of Israel for many years. In a period of long-distance rockets and other advanced technological alternatives, peace agreements can promise the security of Israelis to a greater extent than holding on to occupied territories and the need to suppress a conquered population to prevent them from rebelling.

In reality, the left has failed to transmit these messages, Take, for example, many dozens, maybe even many hundreds of defense professionals, serving in the security system at high level ranks—in the IDF, the General Security Services and the Mossad—who have, for years, carried the message that a continuation of the conflict and the rule over another nation have led to unceasing violence. However, the attempts of these respected security representatives have been to no avail. Their messages have not penetrated. Why is that? It is often because they have tended to go into the greatest detail about a possible future but have not proposed a general convincing narrative to clarify how the basic need for security of all Jews in Israel will be provided. This failure is even more striking against the backdrop of the very effective intimidation and continual fear mongering by Netanyahu and the right, which arouses and encourages feelings of fear, anxiety, and insecurity that, in time, have completely taken control of the discourse. The heads of the security system who have taken it upon themselves to refute these messages have not succeeded in clearing a path to the anxious minds of the Jews living in Israel, who have been trapped into thinking that only rightwing policies respond to the threats facing the state.

Persuasive messages must respect Jewish identity and tradition, and more than that, they must even base the reasons for the need to end the conflict on these two values. Jewish tradition includes no small number of messages expressing the yearning for peace which, in time, became the infrastructure of Western humanist thought. There are many examples, starting from the passage in Genesis, 1:26: "*Then God said, Let us make mankind in our image, in our likeness,*" establishing the principle that all people are created equal. In fact, Tomer Persico, an Israeli scholar of Jewish and Israeli studies, in his recent book, claims that the Jewish image of God has greatly influenced Western thought, starting from the era of Paul and lasting until today. It set the foundations for the principles of equality and freedom that are the pillars of democracy. Another biblical passage demands: "*When a foreigner resides among you in your land, do not mistreat them. The foreigner residing among you must be treated as your native-born. Love them as yourself, for you were foreigners in Egypt*" (Leviticus, 19:33-34). This passage establishes the obligation to safeguard the rights of members of other groups. "*Consecrate the fiftieth year and proclaim liberty throughout the land to all its inhabitants. It shall be a jubilee for you*" (Leviticus (25:10). This verse calls for the release of slaves after 50 years, but the occupation has existed for more than 53 years. "*He will judge between the nations and will settle disputes for many peoples. They will beat their swords into plowshares and their spears into pruning hooks. Nation will not take up sword against nation, nor will they train for war anymore"* (Isaiah 2:4). This passage is based on the independent aspiration for the imposition of peace. And finally, *"Whoever of you loves life and desires to see many good days, keep your tongue from evil and your lips from telling lies. Turn from evil and do good; seek peace and pursue it"* (Psalms 34: 12-15). Of course, this is only a small representative sample. We should not forget the Israeli Declaration of Independence, issued in 1948, containing the founding fathers' promise that the State of Israel *"will be based on freedom, justice and peace as envisaged by the prophets of Israel."*

Those who are struggling to make a change must understand that in the battle against the present situation, just pointing out the flaws of the present and the dangers of the future will not lead to a significant revision. They must present well formulated goals that are both clear and achievable and propose practical ways to accomplish them. In other words, the campaign cannot only be based on negativity, but rather on motivation to act. How? By presenting alternative objectives through which change will take place.

That is not a simple task. But despite the difficulties, we should not despair. Long-term resources should be invested in education, even if the Ministry of Education refuses to initiate a wide-ranging systematic program of its own. We must strive to distribute information, to persuade by establishing institutions and organizations whose representatives will go out into the general public from the northernmost to the southernmost tips of the country, in order to clarify reality in a way that can convince people of the justness of their objectives. The basis of this process must be joining forces, defining clear goals, formulating a strategy and gathering resources. This is possible and it must be done. As loyal patriots, who are concerned about the fate of society and of our country, it is clear that standing paralyzed from afar will lead to the destruction of everything our forefathers built and everything they sacrificed while struggling to establish the state.

The Positive Precedent

The development of a peace process is similar to the development of support for the conflict. Both are based on the formulation of a convincing narrative that is relevant and that fits reality. In our case, it must fulfill the basic needs of Jews in Israel. In the left camp, as noted, such a narrative does not exist. Narratives that are floating around the "market" do not meet the criteria of responding to the needs of society members. They do not answer needs for security; they are disconnected from Jewish identity, and they depend primarily on universal values, foreign to most of the Jewish public in Israel. Only an innovative, coherent narrative, expressed in the language spoken by the people, can develop the infrastructure for broad mobilization.

Fortunately, there is a precedent. The Jewish population in Israel has already been exposed to an alternative narrative in the past which maintained that peace with the Palestinians was possible. Until the 1960s, it received almost no support, but after that, it gradually increased in acceptance until, in the 1990s, it became fully established. And it should be remembered that those who invested great effort in its dissemination at the beginning of the 1970s were in a far worse set of circumstances than present realities. They had to face a society with far less openness to information that cast doubt on the hegemonic narrative than today, which meant that they were forced to deal with far harsher sanctions than one would face at present.

However, then as now, the peace camp had and still has to fight for the very legitimacy to express its positions. That is a basic right in a democratic regime, and it should never be dependent on conditions of one sort or another. We should not accept the present situation in which people are afraid to express their opinions. Necessary conditions for every change are the free unconditional flow of information, and openness and legitimacy in expressing criticism. During Rabin's government (1992–1995), the opposition received such freedom and used every means available (and sometimes those which deviated from legitimate tactics) to put a stop to government policy. The strength of society is not measured by conformity and obedience, but rather the ability to conduct multidirectional and open discussion about its course of action by those who hold a variety of opinions. The demand for blind patriotism is unjustified and wrong, even from a Jewish standpoint, not to mention from a democratic one.

If the development of a narrative which will constitute the epistemic basis for societal change is the first necessary condition for establishing a peace process, the second is the advance of a leader who can lead society from a state of conflict to a reality of agreement. Such a leader, as noted, must have courage, level-headedness, determination, a realistic worldview, and analytical ability, in addition to all the other positive qualities enfolded in the concept of "charisma," among which are the ability to correctly read society's needs and to find a way to fulfill them, and the ability to stand up to incitement and delegitimization. This does not mean searching for a messiah, but rather the development of authentic leadership from within society, in the first stage, and even the appearance of a group of leaders who, in time, will be able to deal with the difficult challenges posed by reality and will successfully stand up to the leadership of the rightwing.

Lacking constitutive events which integrate with reality, the persuasion process will be long and will not advance in a straight line. But history teaches us that intractable violent conflicts of the type that we are also involved in have ended exactly as a result of the fulfillment of the two conditions that we have described. All these conflicts were accompanied by high levels of hatred, hostility, and distrust. In all of them, a majority of victims came from the civilian population, and in each, determined forces led to their solution. However, in all these cases, the conflict ended only when a dominant majority among both societies considered that their needs had been met. When they are not, the flames of hatred continue to burn.

To the disappointment of the readers and to my own shame, I have no magic recipe to propose for a conflict solution, because there is no such thing. Although conflicts are dynamic, with similar foundations and psychological principles, each has its own specific context along with various activating forces. Researchers know the elements that lead to a peaceful end to conflicts in all cases that have succeeded and are also acquainted with the counterforces that have caused and are still causing failures to resolve other conflicts throughout the world. But forces which have led to success have operated at different levels for each conflict, and it is only after the successful conclusion of the conflict can the way these forces have operated be analyzed. In this book, I have proposed principles and factors that exist in every process of peacemaking. But it should be remembered that, in a peace process, there are many factors that operate together in a complex process of reciprocal effect, and it is extremely difficult to predict how the situation will develop. If there was one recipe or even a few which were certain to lead to a peace process, the world would be different, tens of thousands of lives would be saved, and human suffering and destruction would be greatly lightened. But homo sapiens, which literally means "wise human beings", are strange creatures, as the history of the past 10,000 years of civilization has proven. They create reasons for disputes in their heads, stick to them and in most cases, it is very hard to change their opinions about the objectives, the needs, the values, and their motives and beliefs.

When the two sides of the dispute in Northern Ireland (Catholics and Protestants) reached a settlement, known as the Good Friday Agreement, on 10 April 1998, with the assistance of the Irish Republic and Great Britain, it became clear that the agreement was almost identical in its details to proposals that were already circulating at the beginning of the 1970s. If the agreement had been made at that time, it would have saved a lot of blood, sweat and tears for Northern Ireland and for the British populations. The author of this book asked a friend, one of the important psychologists in Northern Ireland, Ed Cairns, why they had had to wait so long for an agreement when the divided Irish public had paid such a heavy price as the conflict continued. He answered that politicians were slow learners— and he was absolutely right. Not only do politicians learn slowly, but society members who have participated in conflicts are slow learners as well. And this also goes for members of Jewish society in Israel.

On the Importance of Hope

In addition to a narrative, leadership, programs, organization, unification of forces, and the right conditions, a minority group who believes in the feasibility of reaching a solution to the conflict must also believe in the possibility of achieving their objectives and consider that they are able to initiate change. In plain language—and in psychology—this is called "hope."

The story of the birth of the concept of hope in Greek mythology is very relevant to this idea. It suggests that the human race lived in a perfect world, without worry, until Pandora opened the forbidden box and released all of the disasters which are still an integral part of our world. She immediately hurried to close the box, but because the disasters had already escaped, she only made things worse since she imprisoned the hope that had also been enclosed in the box. Only after a long period of calamities, accompanied by despair, did Pandora reopen the box and allow hope to escape, finally granting people the possibility of enduring difficult periods with the help of optimistic thoughts about the future.

As becomes clear at the end of Pandora's story, hope is aroused when the expectation of achieving a concrete positive objective exists and in general, hope is the aspiration to be extricated from a negative situation. Hope, as we have presented it in the second chapter, includes cognitive elements, including setting objectives, planning to achieve these goals, evaluating difficulties, along with emotional elements, positive and negative. The positive elements lead to a favorable sense of accomplishment, enjoyment and satisfaction. But at times, achieving the final goal also involves bitter struggles, heavy personal costs and endurance, and thus, hope may be accompanied by a sense of fear and anxiety.

Did You Know?

The study by Leshem and Halperin studied hope by separating desire for peace (hope) and the belief in its likelihood, as well as appraisal of the rivals' (Israeli Jews and Palestinians) hope for peace, utilizing a large-scale survey administered in Israel, the West Bank, and the Gaza Strip in August 2017. The study showed that the vast majority of Israeli Jews and Palestinians support the idea of reciprocal peace that will address the basic needs of both groups, regardless of the final form of the solution (e.g., one state, two-state). But at the same time, approximately 80 percent of all participants underestimated their rival's wish for reciprocal peace. This underestimation has detrimental consequences on rivals' own hope and their support for peace. Specifically, members of both groups think that if the rival does not wish for peace, their own hope is reduced dramatically. In view of these findings the authors suggested what is needed. "*Direct communications through channels of public diplomacy and peoples-to-peoples encounters can expose group members to their rival's wishes for reciprocal peace and consequently increase their hopes and willingness to support peacebuilding. Conflict intervention through media campaigns can also be a channel by which citizens are exposed to the wish for peace of the rival party.*"[464]

The results of this study direct us again to the violent experiences of both groups and to the culture of conflict and the massive brainwashing that the two societies experience. The high distrust and mutual delegitimization show their power in the destruction of hope. We need to overcome the destructive climate with the public discourse expressed by leaders, most of the media and social networks that prolong the conflict.

It is not for nothing that one of the metaphors most identified with

hope is that of a light at the end of a dark tunnel. In contrast with fantasy, ideal, or utopia, hope must reflect the aspiration to achieve a concrete and sustainable goal. It may be seen as a kind of driving force activating the desire to change the existing situation: It creates expectation for change that, in turn, produces action. This psychological dynamic involves development of "scenarios" visualizing possible events in the future—positive ones, naturally. Thus, hope supplies motivation and energy, determination, obligation and perseverance for people who want to change their situation. A condition for the arousal of hope is belief that the present situation is capable of being changed. In other words, the situation is not permanent and frozen, but rather the outcome of factors which can be changed by action.

The special aspect of hope is that the individual does not distort reality as a result, but looks at it correctly, views the obstacles that it presents—and even so, decides to act. Thus, hope symbolizes readiness to take risks for something without the certainty that it will be achieved. But in avoiding risks, it is impossible to act for change in the present. Remaining a viewer in a state of inaction, apathy, and helplessness does not advance society members towards an objective. When individuals act out of hope, they take responsibility for themselves and their fate, and they are ready to cope with challenges posed by society. Only concern, involvement, volunteering, and readiness to sacrifice time and effort will advance society towards peace. That is our right, our obligation and our responsibility to future generations.

Hope gives us a reason for living. Without hope, we cannot struggle for a better future. Without hope we sink into a sense of helplessness, apathy, and escapism. Without hope we become submerged in despair and in fear, limiting the breadth and depth of our thinking. In actual terms, loss of hope may lead to emigration, to egocentrism, focusing on our personal lives, while repressing social life and turning to hedonism.

The minority in Jewish society, termed "the left," includes hundreds of thousands of people—at least a million adults, if we include the 20% of the Jewish public who express great support for leftwing positions on questions of democracy and peace in public opinion polls. On other issues that the left provides leadership, such as social justice and separation of state and religion, additional supporters can be counted. Of course, Arab citizens supporting the peace process can be added to this number and they constitute about 20% of the adult population in Israel. The result, no matter how you calculate it, is a very large public. And there are many talents and skills among them: the creative, the highly educated, the wise, the courageous, the daring, the dreamers, who can all contribute to a social change.

There is no reason to doubt that, ultimately, with their abilities, with our abilities, this change will come about to save our country. This should be also said regarding other existing conflicts that cause loss of life, destruction, and suffering as well. Humanity in its humane meaning must prevail and the struggle for it should preoccupy our civilization.

Epilogue

The book describes a specific case of Israeli Jewish society, engulfed in intractable conflict and occupation; it attempts to generalize the analysis to other intractable conflicts going through the same societal-political psychological crises. Thus, the book has analyzed the outbreak and development of the intractable conflict with its escalation, the peace process, its de-escalation and then, its re-escalation, reaching the present dead end. Israeli Jewish society is to a large extent embedded in the culture of conflict with its conflict supporting narratives that dictate the policies, actions, norms, laws, educational curricula, and public discourse. It has been in this situation since the beginning of the newly established Israel in 1948.

However, since the peace treaty with Egypt, signed on March 26, 1979, Israeli society has experienced different periods of moderation and extremization. Today, in spite of the hegemonic rightist (hawkish) views of the leadership and society members, there exists a stable and institutionalized minority within political spheres, civil society and society at large who, in spite of the setbacks, adhere to the leftist (dovish) views, believing that peace is possible, that withdrawal from the occupied territories is a must and that Jewish settlement in these territories is a disaster. But the dominant rightist majority tries by any means to delegitimize these views and their holders, and to maintain societal dominance.

Similar developments can be detected in present-day Turkey (Turkish-Kurdish conflict), Cyprus (Greek-Turkish Cypriot conflict), Russia (Russian-Chechen conflict and the ongoing Russian–Ukrainian conflict), Sri Lanka (Singhalese-Tamil conflict), Rwanda (Hutu-Tutsi conflict), India (Kashmir conflict) or Morocco (Western Sahara conflict). In some of these conflicts, one side has had a military victory over the other side, but even military success has not ended the conflicts because the grievances and contentions have remained unaddressed. And we know that conflicts can last decades and even centuries until either the deprivations are satisfied in the view of a majority of the deprived group, or one side is eliminated by genocide.

The Israeli-Palestinian conflict at present has not been resolved and no light appears at the end of the tunnel that signals the beginning of peacemaking. The last seven chapters of the present book have presented developments, consequences, and implications of the Israeli-Palestinian conflict with the attempt to predict its future development.

In the final pages of this book, I would like to move to a higher level of analysis by raising a question: **Is Israeli Jewish society unique in its behavior towards Palestinians within the context of the conflict and the occupation?**

This question relates to a very basic human issue discussed by hundreds of social scientists, psychologists, philosophers, historians, artists, writers, intellectuals, as well as practitioners. It invites at least two levels of response. The first is very general and refers to universal behavior of homo sapiens: denoting whether the obstructive, immoral and brutal behaviors of the Israeli Jews towards the Palestinians are unique in comparison to the actions of other human beings. The second level refers to the collective conduct of Israeli Jewish society towards a rival group in the context of conflict, that is, is Israeli Jewish society different from other societies in its behavior towards the Palestinians?

The first level response pertains to one of the most divisive questions—whether human beings are good or evil in their intergroup relationships or perhaps neither good nor evil, but rather always acting in context. This question cannot be answered exhaustively because of its complexity and due to considerable disagreement as to the response. Thus, I will briefly focus on the main point that I would like to pass on to readers.

Ordinary Men

This question has occupied the thoughts of many people from the earliest periods of human writings. Nevertheless, it received special attention following the evil-minded and genocidal behaviors of Germans during War World Two. The many thousands of pages that have been written about this issue have still not resolved this groundbreaking question because of its multi-complex challenge with multi-layer (i.e., political, philosophical, sociological, historical, and psychological) aspects. Observers of these horrific years in human history choose different perspectives, theories, and evidence. I myself have been tremendously influenced by the book *Ordinary Men: Reserve Police Battalion 101 and the Final Solution in Poland* by Holocaust historian Christopher R. Browning.[465] The book, based on documents and testimonies detailing actions of 500 soldiers of the battalion, concluded that the soldiers, coming from working class backgrounds of Hamburg, were not zealous ideological Nazis. They were recruited to the Order Police unit because they were found unfit to serve at the front. Their mission was to carry out mass murders of Polish Jews (men, women, the elderly and children) by shooting them or transporting them to the death camp of Treblinka. What is of importance for my argument relates to the fact that the commander of the battalion gave the soldiers a choice and did not force anyone to perform the murders. In fact, a few of the soldiers asked to be relieved from having to kill and were replaced. But the great majority became accustomed to the horrifying task, conformed and obeyed orders to participate in the mission. Though this unusual case became controversial, it still serves as support for my argument about human nature. Browning concludes by saying:

> *The behavior of any human being is, of course, a very complex phenomenon, and the historian who attempts to "explain" it is indulging a certain arrogance. When nearly 500 men are involved, to undertake any general explanation of these collective behaviors is even more hazardous ... The reserve policemen faced choices, and most committed terrible deeds. But those who killed cannot be absolved by the notion that anyone in the same situation would have done as they did. For even among them, some refused to kill and other stopped killing. Human responsibility is ultimately an individual matter.*

It is important of course to note that there were millions of Germans who had been poisoned by anti-Semitism and Nazi ideology and thus happily participated in the extermination of Jews.[466]

Milgram's Study of Obedience

Social psychology has contributed much to the understanding of human behavior in the seminal experiments performed by Stanley Milgram in New York in the 1960s. Milgram, as a Jew, was also preoccupied with the questions raised by the Holocaust which were at the basis of his experiment. The participants in the experiment were recruited through newspaper advertisement. Men of various professions volunteered to take part in the research project. The study was presented as a teaching experiment, and the volunteering participant in the study was paired with another volunteer. The former was always the teacher and the latter a learner. However, the learners were actors rather than experiment participants. The teacher was told to administer an electric shock every time the learner made a mistake in the learning task, increasing the level of shock each time. The learner was taken into a room with the teacher to see an electric shock generator with switches marked from 15 volts (Slight Shock) to 375 volts (Danger: Severe Shock) to 450 volts (XXX). The teacher was given a low voltage shock to expose him to the painful experience. But the learner did not really receive the "shocks" given by the teachers.

In the experiment, when the learner gave mainly wrong answers (on purpose), the teacher gave him an electric shock and heard prerecorded scream. When the teacher refused to administer a shock, the experimenter gave a series of orders/prods to ensure the continuation of the experiment. The surprising results showed that 65% (two-thirds) of participants (i.e., "teachers") continued to the highest level of 450 volts, even when the learner stopped reacting. All the participants continued up to 300 volts. These findings showed that ordinary people are likely to follow orders given by an authority figure, even to the extent of killing an innocent human being, without any consideration of its meaning or consequences. Milgram concluded his observations in his book years later, writing:

> *The dilemma posed by the conflict between conscience and authority inheres in the very nature of society and would be with us even if Nazi Germany had never existed. To deal with the problem only as it were a matter of history is to give it an illusory distance ... For the problem is not "authoritarianism" as a mode of political organization or a set of psychological attitudes but authority itself. Authoritarianism. may give way to democratic practice, but authority itself cannot be eliminated as along as society is to continue in the form we know.*[467]

This statement is of special significance. It says that individuals have the potential to behave in different ways depending on the particular situation. **The context together with human disposition determine the direction of human behavior**. Since situations differ, the same individual may be malicious in one situation and benevolent in another. Thus, on an individual level, we learn that individuals differ not only in their values, personality dispositions, emotions, and attitudes, but also in the particular situation they find themselves.

Importance of the Context

Contexts of intractable conflicts lead individuals to violent acts, including severe violations of moral codes and human rights by those who blindly follow orders. These are soldiers, fighters and sometimes even civilians who, without contemplating the moral meaning of the directive or even its legality, carry out orders to kill (even murder), destroy, and humiliate. That is one of the plagues of being human and its imprinting effects can be found in most atrocities, massacres, ethnic cleansings, and genocides. Intractable conflicts, being violent, provide numerous opportunities for human beings to exhibit this human characteristic with all its inhumane implications. Individuals obediently follow orders in line with the delegitimizing beliefs. This socio-psychological mechanism is carried out especially by active fighters in the conflict, whose role is to fight and withstand the enemy.

Israeli Jews are no different from other human beings and eventually each Israeli Jew chooses his/her behavior, depending on the disposition and circumstances. This is an important point, as history also clearly introduces individuals who have adhered to universal moral commandments, in spite of the group and situational pressure, and eventually some have paid with their lives for taking the responsibility for their choice.

Still, situations matter, and I would like to move from the first level to the collective level and focus on collective behavior in a specific context of bloody and protracted conflict that leads many human beings to engage in vicious violent behaviors wherever it occurs.

Socio-psychological View

In trying to explain normal human behavior, Kurt Lewin, the father of modern social psychology, proposed that the behavior of a group, like that of an individual, is greatly affected by the collective perception of the environment and the group's characteristics.[468] On the basis of this classical theoretical framework, I believe that understanding collective behaviors in intractable conflict requires an analysis of the **psychological conditions of the conflict's context** (i.e., an environment, a field) and the **collective psychological state** of the involved societies, which includes the *lasting psychological repertoire* of the collective as well as *immediate psychological response tendencies*.[469]

In addition to the deprivation detected in the context, societies in conflict must develop an epistemic basis for their goals. It serves as the **collective psychological state of the group. An epistemic basis consists of an elaborated system of narratives in the form of an ethos of conflict and collective memory that provide an explanation, rationalization, legitimization, and justification for the set of societal goals in the conflict.** The epistemic basis also presents ways and means to ensure a high likelihood of success in achieving these goals.

In addition to obedience, we note that violence is taking place especially against the others as enemies who are viewed as infiltrators, traitors, enemies, parasites, wolves, bugs, terrorists—the term is usually generalized to all group members including women and children. This process of delegitimization is directed towards the rival in conflict who may be a member of another nation, ethnic group, religion, race, or socioeconomic status, and even an ideological rival member of the same nation. **Delegitimization, as a collective psychological state of the societies involved in bloody conflict, is a powerful mechanism that provides the psychological permit to maltreat another group.**[470]

Intractable Conflict

This analysis implies that the lasting context of conflict and occupation provides rules for practices that are unique to these situations and together with the ideological dominant ethos, they guide behavior of members of the collective.[471] It may thus be assumed that many of the Israeli Jews who kill, murder, arrest, confiscate land, discriminate, torture, and attack Palestinians are also normal people, who fulfil their responsibilities and duties as settlers, soldiers, policemen, general security agents and even as Israeli Jewish citizens, who have grown up within the culture of conflict with its conflict supporting narratives at its foundation.

Specifically, the conflict supporting narratives that many Israeli Jews absorb tell them that Palestinians are their enemies who would try to annihilate the Jews if only they could, that the Palestinians desire to take their homeland, and therefore Jews perform defensive and deterrent acts to prevent realization of these intentions and to assure their survival in the jungle of the Middle East. In this vein, Israeli Jews believe that an existential threat exists, based on their collective memory and the present hostility to Israel by Palestinians, and some states and organizations in the Middle East. Moreover, they believe that European nations were much more brutal, during the period of colonialism. Only in the last decades have we learned what Belgians did to Congolese, British to Kenyans or French to Algerians and Dutch to Indonesians. Those were acts of extreme brutality in which hundreds of thousands of Africans and Asians were murdered, suffered discrimination, malnutrition and torture. But these practices have not disappeared.

Though World War Two was a violent climax with its millions upon millions of casualties in the twentieth century, even after its end and at present, we witness genocidal tendencies, atrocities, terror, mass killings, violations of human rights, and immoral behavior that causes human losses, suffering, refugees, and destruction (see Congo, Rwanda, Iraq, Cambodia, Vietnam, Syria, Myanmar, India, Yemen, Nigeria, China, Bosnia, or Armenia, as examples). Just recently, in February 2022, Russia invaded Ukraine causing harm, performing atrocities and seeding destruction. Thus, we see that societies continue violent struggles in which they commit brutal acts forbidden by international law. Moreover, acts of terror are an integral part of cycles of violence almost everywhere that intractable conflicts and wars for independence have taken place.

Rules of Power

I would like to return to direct attention to the lens of history, showing that no nation voluntarily returns territories, power, resources, even if taken immorally—these nations always construct narratives of justification to explain these the immoral acts. Thus, we find that almost every intergroup struggle to correct unjust and immoral situations necessarily involves violence, international pressure, boycotts, societal struggle and other means. But these are always viewed by the rival groups as illegitimate and unfair. The superpowers. as well as smaller states, ignore international laws and codes, when their goals and interests so demand.

In spite of the tremendous advancement of moral thought and international legal norms, nations often disregard their moral duties and do what is dictated by their wishes, aspirations, greed, interests, religious commands and ideological prescriptions. Clearly, violent conflicts and wars are underlined by economic interests, political aspirations, competition for power and status, and the wish for superiority. Orwell stated that *"war is not meant to be won, it is meant to be continuous"* and *"ev-*

ery war, when it comes, or before it comes, is represented not as a war but as an act of self-defense against a homicidal maniac". These motivations appear in many states, such as the United States, China, Russia, Turkey, Israel, and Iran. Think, for example, about the American and British invasion, aided by international forces, of Iraq in March 2003 under the false pretext "to disarm Iraq of weapons of mass destruction" that Iraq did not have. The real interests, never spelled out officially, were economic and political. In the war that lasted until 2011, hundreds of thousands of Iraqis were killed, mostly civilians, along with several thousand coalition soldiers. In this military operation, war crimes were performed by both the American and Iraqi military forces. Also, political considerations and economic interests often determine how third parties use double standards to judge the narratives and violence of various groups involved in different conflicts. They may support goals and violence of one group and reject justified goals and violent behavior of another.

Israeli behavior in the violent conflict with Palestinians is no different from the behavior of other nations in their violent conflicts. It desires to be a regional power with influence on the states of the Middle East and beyond. In this framework we should also view its conflict with states in the region, its intervention in internal matters in other states, its military activities in the region, and its regional alliances. Obviously, this narrative is not told to the citizens of Israel. The one that is always told relates to security of the state.

This is the place to quote Christopher Browning's conclusion to his book *Ordinary Men*:

> *There are many societies afflicted by traditions of racism and caught in the siege mentality of war or threat of war. Everywhere society conditions people to respect and defer to authority, and indeed could scarcely function otherwise. Everywhere people seek career advancement. In every modern society, the complexity of life and the resulting bureaucratization and specialization attenuate the sense of personal responsibility of those implementing official policy. Within virtually every social collective, the peer group exerts tremendous pressure on behavior and sets moral norms. If the men of Reserve Police Battalion 101 could become killers under such circumstance, what group of men cannot?[472]*

The Glorification of Violence

In order to understand the violence used by different societies, it is important to be aware that almost all nations glorify the violence of their own group and the heroes who maintain it, and this glorification is well embedded in their culture.[473] This should be seen as a paradoxical syndrome. Nations see violence as an important part of their collective memory, which they revere. This violence is, in most cases, initiated and carried out by the in-group and/or is conducted as defense against initiated violence of another group. Many nations glorify violence used to achieve their self-determination and independence; they celebrate wars initiated or imposed and they venerate violent expansions of their states. But the same nations object to the use of violence by various groups today that have the same goal of achieving equality, freedom, self-determination or independence.

Looking only at initiated violence, these are only a few examples: Americans glorify their war of independence and the conquest of the West, Russians glorify their expansion towards the Asian East, French glorify the Napoleonic wars, Israeli Jews glorify their violent resistance to the British mandate and its wars with Arabs, and we can cite nation after nation and find the same trend. **Obviously, all in-group violence is well justified in the national ethos, but I would like to claim that violence provides a fundamental ethos for the human being.** Children in almost every society learn about violence and all its implications from their early years in every group; these episodes are imbued with positive meaning as an inseparable part of every culture in its collective memory.

In summing the response to the posed question, it appears that, in their conflict with the Palestinians, Israeli Jews behave similarly to other nations engaged in violent conflict or war. Israel, as a regional superpower, struggling not only for survival, but also for regional domination, acts to solidify its hegemony in the region and beyond. Its violent struggle with the Palestinians and the occupation is part of this battle for supremacy. Israel, in its unresolvable conflict with Palestinians, aspires to strategic territorial depth, defensible boundaries, resources, water, cheap labor, markets for its goods, and expansion of the Jewish settlement beyond the borders of the Israeli state.

But the crucial point is what distinguishes the behavior of Israeli Jews from other nations. Israel, together with Morocco, are the only states that maintain a very long military occupation, without giving the occupied population equal rights (even only seemingly) in comparison to the occupying population. In 1967, Israel termed its conquest of the territories of the West Bank and Gaza Strip as "belligerent occupation" and military commanders assumed all governmental powers. The government decided that the Geneva Convention did not apply to the situation, but that the IDF would abide by its humanitarian provisions. Fifty-five years of the occupation and settlement of Jews in the occupied territories showed that not many humanitarian considerations have been taken into account. Occupation, by its nature, leads to immoral practices. The present book has described them in detail. Eventually the situation has deteriorated to "*inhuman acts committed for the purpose of establishing and maintaining domination by one racial group of persons over any other racial group of persons and systematically oppressing them*"[474]—called apartheid. The existence of this regime at least in the occupied territory of the West Bank has been validated by Human Right Watch, Amnesty, the British Labour Party, and the UN special rapporteur as an independent human rights expert, along with leading Israeli human rights NGOs.

Israeli apartheid transcends the discussed situation. It is unique in the present era. Obviously, the government denies it and discredits anyone who dares to label the state of discrimination as apartheid. This line of reaction is not unique to Israel. Every society denies collective wrongdoing against another group for as long as it can. Israeli society is no exception; it remains deeply in the comfort zone by overlooking the continuous malpractices of the occupying forces in the West Bank.

Conclusion

Intergroup intractable conflicts always involve a system of societal beliefs constructed in narratives that are used by the involved parties. The major reason for the construction of the narratives is that human beings in general need a reasoned, coherent and meaningful story that provides illumination, justification and explanation of the reality in which they live. This need is especially essential in situations of violent and lasting conflicts because they all involve human losses, injuries, destruction, suffering, misery, and hardship that lead unavoidably to uncertainty, helplessness, unpredictability, chronic stress, and distress. It is in these, as well as in less severe intergroup conflicts, that the narrative provides the needed enlightenment about the confrontational context. In addition to the fundamental need for meaningful and coherent understanding, the narratives also satisfy important needs for individuals and collectives for security, positive self-esteem, differentiation between the in-group and the rival, justice, social identity, and belonging, just to enumerate the most important ones.

Thus, in every intractable conflict, the involved parties construct a conflict supporting **collective hegemonic narrative** that that satisfies these needs.[475] It also explains the causes of the conflict, describes its nature, presents the image of the rival, portrays its own presentation, elaborates on the conditions needed to win the conflict, and others. The narrative provides the indispensable psychological tool that enables participation in the conflict. Without narratives, it would be impossible to mobilize society members to take an active part in it. Moreover, the narrative not only provides the psychological rationalization to sacrifice one's own life, but also supplies a psychological permit to carry out violent acts against the rival group. In this observation there is a clear reflection of psycho-political dynamics because they all refer to perceptions, cognitions, emotions, motivations and behaviors of individuals, groups, and societies.

Looking at intractable conflicts from socio-psychological perspective, all the conflict supporting narratives play a major role in the eruption of violent conflicts, in their long continuation, in the difficulties to solve them peacefully and in the use of violent means that often violate moral codes of accepted behaviors. They penetrate into the fabric of the societal socio-psychological infrastructure and serve as pillars of the developed culture of conflict. They also often serve as a foundation to socialize society members into closed minded societies. These narratives are imparted, or more accurately indoctrinated, into the minds of young society members as well to older members and they then become crucial.

This process has been taking place in the Israeli Jewish society again, after it was hegemonic in the fifties, sixties and half seventies- especially since the 2000s. It involves relaying collective hegemonic narrative with many supporting narratives that cover different topics regarding wars, specific battles, Palestinians, heroes, terror acts of Palestinians, the Holocaust, and so on. But in Israel are disregarded by majority of the Israeli Jews narratives about occupation and the mistreatment of the Palestinians. The hegemonic conflict encouraging narrative with the additional supporting narratives are viewed as representations of reality by them. This representation of reality is invalidated by hundreds of academic books and thousands of academic articles in English and Hebrew which present a very different account based on rigorous research of what is going in Israel and the occupied territories. It is possible to find them in libraries of the Israeli academic intuitions and on the Internet. Many of them were noted in the present book. But they are almost completely ignored by most of the leaders, governmental institutions, Israeli propaganda, mainstream media, social media, and schoolbooks. In this way two completely different realties have been constructed. The present book attempted to open the window to the alternative knowledge.

I would like state clearly in general that not all sides in all the bloody conflicts are immoral. I have noted that powerful states do not frequently yield to moral and just demands and then the only path left open for the harmed group is to resort to active protest with violence. As noted, all the liberation and decolonization movements, in addition to confrontations against injustice and discrimination, have made use of some degree of violence in their struggles. Throughout history, it is hard to identify any achievement by any disadvantaged group without a struggle that involved at least minimal violence. This is easily observed because the strong side always uses violence, a lot of violence, claiming that it is needed to make order.

Going beyond the intractable conflicts, I find it interesting that many societies construct narratives with manipulations and double standards. Manipulation is practiced because all societies, including those that try to achieve unjust goals, wrap the conflict supporting narrative in acceptable moral justifications, such as defending democracy, ensuring security or achieving justice. Use of double standards is apparent—societies judge and present a narrative that expresses their own goals and behaviors according to moral standards but delegitimize similar goals and behaviors of the rival society. They insist on deploring evil acts carried out against them, judging them according to moral standards, but tend to ignore similar evil acts committed by themselves, and at best rationalize them. Societies tend to be swamped in self-righteousness and have great difficulty looking in the mirror.

Israel's goals include preventing the establishment of a Palestinian independent state,[476] controlling and surveilling the Palestinians by all possible means to prevent their resistance to the occupation, settling as many Jews in the West Bank as possible, expelling Palestinians who live in area C, annexing to Israel at least 60% of the West Bank where most of the Jewish settlers live, reducing the number of Palestinians in the West Bank and dividing the different Palestinian groups under the principle "divide and rule." These goals are accepted by all leaders of the right and by many centrist leaders. They are also accepted by the majority of Israeli Jews in the hegemony of the right. Thus, Israel does not want to negotiate any peaceful settlement and is happy with the collaborative, authoritarian formal leader of the Palestinians, Mahmoud Abbas (Abu Mazen), elected in 2005 as the President of the Palestinian National Authority. These goals reflect the interest of Jews, as viewed by the governing leaders of Israel. These goals have nothing in common with any moral considerations nor are they in line with international laws and conventions. In fact, they negate them, and also negate the humanistic and moral Jewish tradition.

To end the book optimistically, I ask—Is this the only road for Israel and other states still engaged in intractable conflict? The response is unequivocal—NO!

The evidence clearly shows that other ways are possible. An examination of cases of intractable conflict that were resolved peacefully has shown that the change in the conflict occurred when at least a significant part of society changed the narratives they held during the conflict. This happened when a large portion of society realized that the price of the conflict was extremely detrimental to society: in human lives, in its development, and in its attempt to achieve prosperity. And in general, the narrative fuels the continuation of the conflict and blinds society in the most harmful way. It serves as a barrier to peace making when such an opportunity arises.[477]

When this understanding spreads and becomes legitimate, the insight that one can speak with the opponent arises, the same opponent who has been perceived as violent, with whom one does not negotiate. In other words, in order to enable the end of the conflict, it is important to change the way one looks at the opponent and the conflict. Those nations that have managed to end the conflict peacefully understood that one can achieve existential security, one can set constructive goals for society, and a sense of justice can be maintained, without continuing the conflict.[478] In Northern Ireland, as an example, the period preceding the peace agreement was not easy. The violence continued, but after both sides realized that it was not beneficial to continue with the conflict, that they would not achieve victory or security by using force, they turned to a negotiation process that lasted several years. Within the peacemaking process, the Protestants and the Catholics were able to overcome their mistrust of the other side and agree to compromises in order to end violence and create a new future. On April 10, 1998, a treaty between representatives of both sides was signed, and shortly thereafter the treaty was approved in a referendum.

I will quote excerpts from the Northern Ireland agreement:

- *"We, participants in the multi-sided negotiation, believe that the agreement offers an entirely new historical start."*

- *"The tragedies of the past have left us deeply sad regarding the suffering. We will not forget those who were killed or injured and their families. We will respect them with a new beginning and promise to achieve reconciliation, tolerance, mutual trust, respect and total defense of human rights."*

Catholics and Protestants in Northern Ireland also wanted to live normal lives like all human beings—lives of peace and security. Both sides realized that, instead of a violent competition about who was the better and who was the worse, one must use the possibilities for economic and social development that will bring prosperity to everyone. The agreement has held to this day, despite the difficulties and controversies that have come up over the years. The violence ceased shortly after the agreement and has almost completely disappeared. Over the years armed weapons vanished from the streets, and their place was taken by a new routine of tranquility and discourse.

The change in Northern Ireland was complex and prolonged, almost against all odds. Similar agreements were signed in Guatemala and Spain, Algeria and El-Salvador. One was also signed between Israel and Egypt. The latter was considered for 30 years by Israeli Jews as an ultimate enemy with Nazi intentions to exterminate the state and the Jews living there. The peace agreements provided security for both sides and a strong desire to keep them unbroken. Evidence that there is an alternative has been presented. The pain of who and what was lost remains, but the need to change the narrative to maintain life and provide genuine hope for security and tranquility has overcome the problems. We learn that there is another way!

The closing statement of the book, as the major lesson, is that narratives are constructed by human beings with their ideology and dispositions and then imparted to society members—whether are truthful, imagined or fictitious—serve as powerful mechanisms for establishing belief systems for the masses, directives for policies, and instructions for action. On the one hand, the constructed narratives may lead to violent conflict that brings misery of human losses, suffering and destruction. On the other hand, a contrasting narrative may lead to peaceful resolution of the conflict that brings security and prosperity. Human beings learn each of these narratives and have the ability to choose one of them. In this way they select the roads of their lives. This the focal theme of my next book that is in process.

Every major societal change must begin with the construction of new narratives. Societies that wish to set their direction towards democracy, humanizing the "other," peace, morality and justice must socialize their citizens with these values from a very early age. It is our responsibility and duty to show this road to the nations.

The alternative is to sink into the honey trap that leads to societal deterioration.

Endnotes

1 Euro-news. (2015, July 20). Turkey: Death toll climbs in Suruc attack. EuroNews. https://www.euronews.com/2015/07/20/turkey-death-toll -climbs-in-suruc-attack

2 Gurses, M. (2018). *Anatomy of civil war: Sociopolitical impacts of the Kurdish conflict in Turkey*. Ann Arbor: University of Michigan Press; Orhun, M. (2016). *Political violence and Kurds in Turkey*. London: Routledge.

3 Pettersson, T., & Oberg, M. (2020). Organized violence, 1989-2019. *Journal of Peace Research, 27,* 597-613.

4 Bar-Tal, D. (2013). *Intractable conflicts: Socio-psychological foundations and dynamics*. Cambridge University Press.

5 Bar-Tal, D., Halperin, E., & Oren, N. (2010). Socio-psychological barriers to peace making: The case of the Israeli Jewish society. *Social Issues and Policy Review, 4,* 63-109; Worchel, S. (1999). *Written in blood*. New York: Worth Publishers.

6 Bar-Tal, D. (2013). *Intractable conflicts: Socio-psychological foundations and dynamics*. Cambridge University Press.

7 Shaked, R. (2018). *Behind the kaffiyeh: The conflict from the Palestinian perspective* (in Hebrew). Rishon LeZion: Miskal Press.

8 Hollis, R. (2019). *Surviving the story: The narrative trap in Israel and Palestine*. London: Red Hawk Books; Mana, A., & Srour, A. (Eds.), (2020) *Israeli and Palestinian collective narratives in conflict: A tribute to Shifra Sagy and her work*. Cambridge: Cambridge Scholars Publishing: Rotberg, R. I. (Ed.), (2006). *Israeli and Palestinian narratives of conflict: History's double helix*. Bloomington, IN: Indiana University Press.

9 Khalidi, R. (1997). *Palestinian identity: The construction of modern national consciousness*. New York: Columbia University Press; Neville, M. (1976). *The Arabs and Zionism before World War I*. Berkeley: University of California Press; Shimoni, G. (1995). *The Zionist ideology*. Hanover, NH: Brandeis University Press; Vital, D. (1975). *The Origins of Zionism*. Oxford: Clarendon Press.

10 Azoury, N. (1905). *Le reveil de la Nation Arabe dans l'Asie Turque*. Paris: Plon-Nourrit.

11   Tessler, M. (2009). *A history of the Israeli-Palestinian conflict* (2nd ed.). Bloomington, IN: Indiana University Press.

12   Morris, B. (2001). *Righteous victims: A history of the Zionist-Arab conflict, 1881–2001*. New York: Vintage Books.

13   Golan, G. (2015). *Israeli peacemaking since 1967: Factors behind break-throughs and failures*. New York: Routledge; Podeh, E. (2015). *Chances for peace: Missed opportunities in the Arab-Israeli conflict*. Austin, TX: University of Texas Press.

14   Bar-Tal, D. (1990). *Group beliefs: A conception for analyzing group structure, processes and behavior.* New York: Springer-Verlag; Kruglanski, A. W. (1989). *Lay epistemics and human knowledge: Cognitive and motivational bases.* New York: Plenum.

15   Bar-Tal, D. (2000). *Shared beliefs in a society: Social psychological analysis.* Thousand Oaks, CA: Sage.

16   EU Peacebuilding Initiative (2021). *Mapping sources of mutual distrust in Palestinian and Israeli societies and politics: Role of education, daily life experiences, and exposure to violence.* Palestinain Center for Policy and Survey Research in Ramallah and Macro-the Center for Political Economics in Tel Aviv.

17   Friedman-Peleg, K. (2016). *PTSD and the politics of trauma in Israel: A nation on the couch.* Toronto: University of Toronto Press; Keynan, I. (2015). *Psychological war trauma and society: Like a hidden wound.* London: Routledge.

18   Lavi, I., & Bar-Tal, D. (2015). Violence in prolonged conflicts and its socio-psychological effects. In J. Lindert, & I. Levav, (Eds.), *Violence and mental health: Its manifod faces* (pp. 3-25). New York: Springer; Bleich, A., Gelkopf, M., & Solomon, Z. (2003). Exposure to terrorism, stress-related mental health symptoms, and coping behaviors among a nationally representative sample in Israel. *Journal of The American Medical Association, 290*, 612-620.

19   dataisrael.idi.org.il. Data of the national security and public opinion project stored by the Israel Democracy Institute.

20   dataisrael.idi.org.il.

21   Gluska, A. (2004). *Eshkol, give the order!* (in Hebrew). Tel Aviv:

Ma'arachot; Segev, T. (2005). *1967 and the country changed its face* (in Hebrew). Jerusalem: Keter Press.

22 https://www.haaretz.co.il/news/politics/.premium-1.3020979

23 Zertal, I., &. Eldar, A. (2007). *Lords of the land: The war over Israel's settlements in the occupied territories 1967-2007.* New York: Nation Books.

24 Liebman, C. S. (1978). Myth, tradition and values in Israeli society. *Midstream, 24*(1), 44–53. Luz, E. (1998). Through the Jewish historical prism: Overcoming a tradition of insecurity. In D. Bar-Tal, D. Jacobson & A. Klieman (Eds.), *Security concerns: Insights from the Israeli experience* (pp. 55-72). Stamford, CT: JAI Press; Stein, H. F. (1978). Judaism and the group-fantasy of martyrdom: The psycho-dynamic paradox of survival through persecution. *Journal of Psychohistory, 6,* 151-210.

25 Bar-Tal, D., & Bar-Tal, G. (2022). The Holocaust and its teaching in Israel in view of the conflict: General and pedagogical implications and lessons. In D. Yitzhaki, T. Gallagher, N. Aloni, A., & Z. Gross (Eds.). *Activist pedagogy and shared education in divided societies: International perspectives and next practices* (pp. 235-254). Leiden: Brill Publishers; Elon, A. (1971). *The Israelis: Founders and sons.* London: Weidenfeld & Nicolson.

26 Arian, A. (1995*). Security threatened.* Cambridge: Cambridge University Press; Bar-Tal, D., Jacobson, D., & Klieman, A. (Eds.) (1998). *Security concerns: Insights from the Israeli experience.* Stamford, CT: JAI. Horowitz, D. (1993). The Israeli concept of national security. In A. Yaniv (Ed.), *National security and democracy in Israel* (pp. 11-53). Boulder, CO: Lynne Rienner.

27 Quoted by: Pedatzur, R. (1998). Ben Gurion's enduring legacy. In D. Bar-Tal, D. Jacobson & A. Klieman (Eds.), *Security concerns: Insights from the Israeli experience* (pp. 139-164). Stamford, CT: JAI Press, p. 145.

28 Lazarus, R. S. (1991). *Emotion and adaptation.* New York: Oxford University Press. ; Smith, C. A., & Lazarus, R. S. (1993). Appraisal components, relational themes, and the emotion. *Cognition and Emotion, 7,* 233-269.

29 Bar-Tal, D., & Jacobson, D. (1998). The elusive concept of security and its expression in Israel. In D. Bar-Tal, D. Jacobson, & A. Klieman (Eds.), *Security concerns: Insights from the Israeli experience* (pp. 15-36). Stamford, CT: JAI.

30 Gray, J. A. (1989). *The psychology of fear and stress* (2nd ed.). Cambridge

University Press.; LeDoux, J. E. (1996). *The emotional brain: The mysterious underpinnings of emotional life.* New York: Touchstone.

31   Bar-Tal, D. (2001). Why does fear override hope in societies engulfed by intractable conflict, as it does in the Israeli society? *Political Psychology, 22,* 601-627.

32   Merom, G. (1998). Outside history? Israel's security dilemma in a comparative perspective. In D. Bar-Tal, D. Jacobson and A. Klieman (Eds.), Security concerns: Insights from the Israeli experience (pp. 37–52). Stamford, CT: JAI Press.

33   Ben-Meir, Y. (1995) *Civil-military relations in Israel.* New York: Columbia University Press.

34   Ben Eliezer, U. (1998). *The making of Israeli militarism.* (Bloomington: Indiana University Press; Kimmerling, B. (1985). *The interrupted system - Israeli civilians in war and routine times.* New Brunswick, NJ: Transaction Books.; Kimmerling, B. (1993). Patterns of militarism in Israel. *European Journal of Sociology, 34,* 196-223. Lissak, M. (Ed.). (1984). *Israeli society and its defence establishment.* London: Frank Cass.; Sheffer, G., & Barak, O. (Eds.). (2010). *Militarism and Israeli society.* Bloomington, IN: Indiana University Press.; Yaniv, A. (Ed.). (1993). *National security and democracy in Israel.* Boulder, CO: Lynne Rienner.

35   Bar-Tal, D., Jacobson, D., & Klieman, A. (Eds.) (1998). *Security concerns: Insights from the Israeli experience.* Stamford, CT: JAI.

36   Bar-Tal, D., & Hammack, P. L. (2012). Conflict, delegitimization and violence. In L. R. Tropp (Ed.), *The Oxford handbook of intergroup conflict* (pp.29-52). New York: Oxford University Press.

37   Bar-Tal, D., & Teichman, Y. (2005). *Stereotypes and prejudice in conflict: Representations of Arabs in Israeli Jewish society.* New York: Cambridge University Press.

38   dataisrael.idi.org.il.

39   Harkabi, Y. (1977). *Arab strategies and Israel's response.* New York: The Free Press.; Podeh, E. (2002). *The Arab-Israeli conflict in Israeli history textbooks, 1948-2000.* Wesport, CT: Bergin & Garvey; Segev, T. (2018). *1949 – The first Israelis.* New York: Free Press.

40   Segev, T. (2000) *The seventh million – The Israelis and the Holocaust.* New

York: St. Martin Press; Yurman, A. (2001). *Victimization of the Holocaust as a component of the cultural-political discourse in Israeli society between the years 1948-1998* (in Hebrew). PhD dissertation. Ramat Gan: Bar-Ilan University; Zertal, I. (2005). *Israel's Holocaust and the politics of nationhood.* Cambridge: Cambridge University Press.

41   Oren, N., & Bar-Tal, D. (2007). The detrimental dynamics of delegitimization in intractable conflicts: The Israeli-Palestinian case. *International Journal of Intercultural Relations, 31,* 111-126.

42   Allport, G. W. (1954). *The nature of prejudice.* Cambridge, MA: Addison-Wesley; Hewstone, M. (1996). Contact and categorization: Social interventions to change inter-group relations. In C. N. Macrae, C. Stangor & M. Hewston (Eds.), *Stereotype and stereotyping* (pp. 323–368). New York: Guilford Press.; Pettigrew, T. F. (1998). Intergroup contact theory. *Annual Review of Psychology, 19,* 185–209.

43   Almog, O. (1998). *The Sabre: A portrait.* Tel Aviv: Am Oved. (in Hebrew); David, O. (2012). *Sculpting the face of a nation: Jewish-Israeli identity in 20th century Hebrew readers.* Dor LeDor, 41. Tel Aviv: School of Education, Tel Aviv University (in Hebrew).

44   Meir, G. (1975). *My life.* New York: G. P. Putnam's Sons.

45   I. Peleg (ed.) (2019). Victimhood discourse in contemporary Israel. New York: Lexington Books.

46   Elon, A. (1971). *The Israelis: Founders and sons.* London: Weidenfeld & Nicolson.; Stein, H. F. (1978). Judaism and the group-fantasy of martyrdom: The psycho-dynamic par adox of survival through persecution. *Journal of Psychohistory, 6,* 151-210.

47   Stauber, R. (2007). *The Holocaust in Israeli public debate in the 1950s: Ideology and memory.* London: Vallentine, Mitchell.; Zertal, I. (2005). *Israel's Holocaust and the politics of nationhood.* Cambridge: Cambridge University Press.

48   Volkan, V. D. (2001). Transgenerational transmissions and chosen traumas: An aspect of large-group identity. *Group Analysis, 34*(1), 79–97.

49   Bar-Tal, D., & Bar-Tal, G. (2022). The Holocaust and its teaching in Israel in view of the conflict: General and pedagogical implications and lessons. In D. Yitzhaki, T. Gallagher, N. Aloni, A., & Z. Gross (Eds.). *Activist pedagogy and shared education in divided societies: International perspectives*

and next practices (pp. 235-254). Leiden: Brill Publishers.

50   Bar-Tal, D., & Bar-Tal, G. (2022). The Holocaust and its teaching in Israel in view of the conflict: General and pedagogical implications and lessons. In D. Yitzhaki, T. Gallagher, N. Aloni, A., & Z. Gross (Eds.). *Activist pedagogy and shared education in divided societies: International perspectives and next practices* (pp. 235-254). Leiden: Brill Publishers.

51   Bar-Tal, D., & Teichman, Y. (2005). *Stereotypes and prejudice in conflict: Representations of Arabs in Israeli Jewish society.* New York: Cambridge University Press; Zertal, I. (2005). *Israel's Holocaust and the politics of nationhood.* Cambridge: Cambridge University Press.

52   Bar-Tal, D., & Antebi, D. (1992). Siege mentality in Israel. *International Journal of Intercultural Relations, 16,* 251-275.

53   Schori-Eyal, N., Halperin, E., & Bar-Tal, D. (2014). Three layers of collective victimhood: Effects of multileveled victimhood on intergroup conflicts in the Israeli-Arab context. *Journal of Applied Social Psychology, 44,* 778-794.

54   Ben-Amos, A. & Bar-Tal, D. (Eds.). (2004). *Patriotism: We Love you motherland.* Tel Aviv: Hakibbutz. Hameuchad (in Hebrew).

55   Zerubavel, Y. (2004). Battle, sacrifice, victimhood: Changes in the ideology of patriotic sacrifice in Israel. In Ben-Amos, A. & Bar-Tal, D. (Eds.), *Patriotism: We love you motherland* (pp. 61-99). Tel Aviv: Hakibbutz Hameuchad (in Hebrew).

56   Staub, E. (1997). Blind versus constructive patriotism: Moving from embeddedness in the group to critical loyalty and action. In D. Bar-Tal & E. Staub (Eds.), *Patriotism in the lives of individuals and nations* (pp. 213–228). New York: Nelson-Hall.

57   Barzilai, G. (1996). *Wars, internal conflicts, and political order: A Jewish democracy in the Middle East.* Albany, NY: State University of New York Press.

58   Oren, N. (2019). *Israel's national identity: The changing ethos of conflict.* Boulder, CO: Lynne Rienner.

59   dataisrael.idi.org.il; Oren, N. (2019). *Israel's national identity: The changing ethos of conflict.* Boulder, CO: Lynne Rienner.

60   Yadgar, Y. (2006). A myth of peace: 'The vision of the new Middle East'

and Its transformations in the Israeli political and public spheres. *Journal of Peace Research, 43,* 297-312.

61   Bar-Tal, D. (2013). *Intractable conflicts: Socio-psychological foundations and dynamics.* Cambridge University Press; Halperin, E. (2016). *Emotions in conflict: Inhibitors and facilitators of peace making.* New York: Routledge.

62   Barzilai, G. (1996). State, society and national security: Mass media and wars. Ln Lisak, M. & Kenipaz, B. (Eds.), *Israel towards the 2000s: Society, politics and culture* (pp.176-194). Jerusalem: Magness (in Hebrew); Caspi, D., & Limor, Y. (1999), *The in/outsiders: The mass media in Israel.* Cresskill, NJ: Hampton Press.

63   Ben-Ezer, E. (Ed.) (1999). Sleepwalkers and other stories: The Arab in Hebrew fiction. Boulder, CO: Lynne Rienner: Cohen, A. (1985). *An ugly face in mirror: Reflection of the Jewish-Arab conflict in the Hebrew children's literature* Tel Aviv: Reshafim (in Hebrew). Govrin, N. (1989). Enemies or cousins? … Somewhere in between: The Arab problem and its reflection in Hebrew literature: Developments, trends, and examples. *Shofar, 7,* 13-23.; Shaked, G. (1989). The Arab in Israeli fiction. *Modern Hebrew Literature, 3,* 17-20.; Shohat, E. (1989). *Israeli cinema: East/west and the politics of representation.* Austin: University of Texas Press; Urian, D. (2013); Urian, D. (2013). The occupation as represented in the arts in Israel in Bar-Tal, D. & Schnell, I. (Eds.), *The Impact of lasting occupation: Lessons from the Israeli society* (pp. 438-470). New York: Oxford University Press.

64   https://www.haaretz.com/israel-news/.premium.HIGHLIGHT.MAGAZINE-classified-docs-reveal-deir-yassin-massacre-wasn-t-the-only-one-perpetrated-by-isra-1.10453626

65   Kipnis. Y. (2013). *The Golan Heights: Political history, settlement, and geography since 1949.* Oxon, UK: Routledge.

66   https://www.haaretz.com/israel-news/.premium.HIGHLIGHT.MAGAZINE-how-israel-tormented-arabs-in-its-first-decades-and-tried-to-cover-it-up-1.9433728

67   https://www.haaretz.com/israel-news/.premium-when-the-shin-bet-chief-warned-that-educated-arabs-are-a-problem-for-israel-1.10214323

68   Segev, T. (2019). *A state at any cost: The life of David Ben-Gurion.* New York: Farrar, Straus and Giroux.

69   Bar-Tal, D. (2019). Transforming conflicts: Barriers and overcoming

them. In M. Elman, C. Gerard, G. Golan, & L. Kriesberg (Eds.). *Overcoming intractable conflicts: New approaches to constructive transformation* (pp. 221-241). Lanham, MD: Rowman and Littlefield.

70   Snyder C. R. (Ed.) (2000). *Handbook of hope: Theory, measures, & applications.* San Diego: Academic Press.

71   Hermann, T. (2009). *The Israeli peace movement: A shattered dream.* Cambridge University Press.

72   Golan, G. (2015). *Israeli peacemaking since 1967: Factors behind breakthroughs and failures.* New York: Routledge; Kimmerling, B., & Migdal, Y. (2003). *The Palestinian people: A history.* Cambridge, MASS; Harvard University Press.; Morris, B. (1988). The new historiography: Israel confronts its past. *Tikkun, 3*(6), 19-23, 98-103; Segev, T. (2018). *1949 – The first Israelis.* New York: Free Press; Shlaim, A. (2001). *The iron wall: Israel and the Arab world.* New York: W.W. Norton.

73   Melman, Y. (1993). *The new Israelis.* Tel Aviv: Shoken (in Hebrew); Shapira, A. (1995). Politics and collective memory: The debate over new historians in Israel. *History and Memory, 7*(1), 9-40.

74   The Oslo Accords signed in 1995 divided the Palestinian territory into three temporary administrative sectors, Areas A, B, and C, which would exist until a final agreement would be signed. The three areas do not have territorial contiguity but are separated from each other and the division was made on the basis of various population areas and recognition of Israeli security demands: **Area A** (18% of the West Bank) includes all of the Palestinian cities and their surroundings, with no Israeli settlements. It is under full civilian and security control by the Palestinian Authority. **Area B** (21% of the West Bank) includes areas of many Palestinian cities, towns and villages, with no Israeli settlements. It is under civilian Palestinian control and under Israeli-Palestinian security control. **Area C** (61% of the West Bank) includes all Israeli settlements (cities, towns and villages) as well as 150,000 Palestinian residents. It is under full civilian and security control of Israel, except for Palestinian citizens.

75   Karpin, M. & Friedman, I. (1999). *Murder in the name of God: The plot to kill Yitzhak Rabin.* London: Granta Books; Kariv, D. (2016). *Words can kill: An untold story of the Rabin assassination, and the lessons for today.* South Carolina: CreateSpace Independent Publishing Platform.

76   **Hamas** [Islamic Resistance Movement]) is a Palestinian Sunni-Islam-

ic fundamentalist but pragmatic, militant, and nationalist organization. It opposes the secular approach of the Palestine Liberation Organization (PLO) to the Israeli-Palestinian conflict and rejects attempts to cede any part of Palestine. The origins of Hamas can be traced to the foundation of the Muslim Brotherhood. When Israel occupied the Palestinian territories in 1967, the Muslim Brotherhood members did not take an active part in the resistance, preferring to focus on social-religious reforms and on restoring Islamic values. The Israeli authorities encouraged these reforms as they saw Hamas as a useful counterbalance to the secular Palestine Liberation Organization. But in 1987 Hamas changed its ways and moved to violent struggle against Israel that has lasted until today. Mishal, S., & Sela, A. (2000). *The Palestinian Hamas, vision, violence, and coexistence.* New York: Columbia University Press.

77   The **Islamic Jihad Movement in Palestine** (known in the West as simply **Palestinian Islamic Jihad (PIJ)**, is a Damascus-based Palestinian Islamist organization formed in 1981. PIJ together with Hamas and six other factions are members of the Alliance of Palestinian Forces, which rejects the Oslo Accords and whose objective is the establishment of a sovereign Islamic Palestinian state. PIJ rejects a two-state solution and promotes the military destruction of Israel. Neither PIJ nor Hamas are members of the PLO. Dunning, T. (2016). *Hamas, Jihad and popular legitimacy: Reinterpreting resistance in Palestine.* New York: Routledge.

78   Rosler, N. (2016). Leadership and peacemaking: Yitzhak Rabin and the Oslo Accords. *International Journal of Intercultural Relations, 54,* 55-67.

79   Bar-Siman-Tov, Y., Lavie, E., Michael, K., & Bar-Tal, D. (2007). The Israeli-Palestinian violent confrontation: An Israeli perspective. In Y. Bar-Siman-Tov (Ed.), *The Israeli-Palestinian conflict: From conflict resolution to conflict management.* (pp. 69-100) Houndmills, England: Palgrave Macmillan.

80   Morris, B. (2001). Righteous *victims: A history of the Zionist-Arab conflict, 1881–2001.* New York: Vintage Books.

81   Bar-Tal, D. (2007). *Living with the conflict: Socio-psychological analysis of the Israeli-Jewish society.* Jerusalem: Carmel (in Hebrew).

82   Ehrlich, D. (1988, June 24). Haaret; Magal, T., Oren. N., Bar-Tal, D. & Halperin, E. (2013). Psychological legitimization-views of the Israeli occupation by Israeli Jews: Data and implications. In Bar-Tal, D. & Schnell,

I. (Eds.). *The impact of lasting occupation: Lessons from Israeli society* (pp. 122–185). New York: Oxford University Press.

83 Ben-Meir, Y. (1995) *Civil-military relations in Israel*. New York: Columbia University Press.

84 dataisrael.idi.org.il.

85 Halperin, E., Bar-Tal, D., Sharvit, K., Rosler, N. and Raviv, A. (2010). Socio-psychological implications for an occupying society: The case of Israel. *Journal of Peace Research, 47,* 59-70.

86 dataisrael.idi.org.il.

87 dataisrael.idi.org.il.

88 dataisrael.idi.org.il.

89 Bar-Tal, D. (2004) Nature, rationale and effectiveness of education for coexistence. *Journal of Social Issues, 60,* 253-271.

90 Podeh, E. (2002). *The Arab-Israeli conflict in Israeli history textbooks, 1948-2000.* Wesport, CT: Bergin & Garvey.

91 Adwan, S., Bar-Tal, D., & Wexler, B. (2016). Portrayal of the other in Palestinian and Israel schoolbooks: A comparative study. *Political Psychology, 37.* 201-217.

92 Bar-Tal, D. (2007). *Living with the conflict: Socio-psychological analysis of the Israeli-Jewish society.* Jerusalem: Carmel (in Hebrew); Wolfsfeld, G. (2004). *Media and the path to peace.* New York: Cambridge University Press.

93 Little, G. (1988). *Strong leadership: Thatcher, Reagan and the eminent person.* Melbourne: Oxford University Press.; Mutz, D. C. (1998). *Impersonal influence.* Cambridge: Cambridge University Press.; Norris, P., Kern, M., & Just, M. (2003). *Framing terrorism: The news media, the government and the public.* New York: Routledge.

94 Gitlin, T. (1980). *The whole world is watching.* Berkeley: University of California Press.

95 Peace Index, July 2000 (Peace Index is a longitudinal research report which measures the positions of the Israeli society towards peace and other issues. It began in 1994 by the Tami Steinmetz Center for Peace Re-

search of Tel Aviv university and in the late 2000 continued by the Israeli Democratic Institute and eventually by the Evans program in Conflict Resolution and Mediation of Tel Aviv University); Baltiansky, G. (2005, January 12th). In Y. Rahamim, (Ed.), *There isn't anyone to talk to: A critical perspective on the politics-media interaction*: Transcripts of a conference organized by the Haim Herzog Institute for Research of Politics, Media, and Society (pp:13-16). Tel Aviv: Tel Aviv University (in Hebrew).

96   Ben-Ami, S. (2006). *Scars of war, wounds of peace: The Israeli-Arab tragedy*. New York: Oxford University Press; Drucker, R. (2002). *Harakiri: Ehud Barak in the final test*. Tel Aviv: Yediot Aharonot (in Hebrew); Sher, G. (2006). *The Israeli-Palestinian peace negotiations, 1999-2001: Within reach*. London: Routledge.

97   Barak, E. (30 July, 2001). Israel needs a true partner for peace. *New York Times*. Beilin, Y. (2001); *Manual for a wounded dove*. Tel Aviv: Miskal (in Hebrew); Ben-Ami, S. (2004). *Frontline without backcountry: A journey to the boundaries of the peace process)*. Tel Aviv: Yediot Aharonot (in Hebrew); Edelist, R. (2003). *Ehud Barak: Fighting the demons*. Or Yehuda: Kinneret, Zmora-Bitan and Yedioth Ahronoth, Sifrei Hemed (in Hebrew). Morris, B. (13 June 2002). Camp David and after: An exchange. An interview with Ehud Barak, *The New York Review*, 49, no. 10; Ross, D., & Grinstein, G. (20 September 2001) Reply by Hussein Agha, Robert Malley Camp David. An Exchange, *The New York Review* 48, no. 14; Swisher, C. E. (2004). *The truth about Camp David: The untold story about the collapse of the Middle East peace process*. New York: Nation Books.

98   Barak, E. (30 July, 2001). Israel needs a true partner for peace. *New York Times*; Enderlin, C. (2003). *The shattered dreams: The failure of the peace process in the Middle East, 1995-2002*. New York: Other Press. Pressman, J. (2003). Vision in collision: What happened at Camp David and Taba? *International Security*, 28, 5-43; Swisher, C. E. (2004). *The truth about Camp David: The untold story about the collapse of the Middle East peace process*. New York: Nation Books; Wolfsfeld, G. (2004). *Media and the path to peace*. New York: Cambridge University Press.

99   Agha, H, & Malley, R. (9 August 2001). Camp David: The tragedy of errors. *The New York Review*, 48(13); Agha, H, & Malley, R. (27 June 2002). A reply to Ehud Barak. *The New York Review*, 49, no. 11; Barak, B. (2005). The failure of the Israeli-Palestinian peace process, 1993–2000, *Journal of Peace Research* 42(6) 719–736; Malley, R. (2001, July 8). Fictions about the failure at Camp David. *The New York Times*. Retrieved from www.ny

times.com; Pundak, R. & Arieli, S. (2004). *The territorial aspect of the Israeli-Palestinian final-status negotiations* Tel Aviv: Peres Center for Peace (in Hebrew); Sela, A. (2009) Difficult dialogue: The Oslo process in Israeli perspective. Macalester International: Vol. 23, Article 11, pp. 105-138. Available at http://digitalcommons.macalester.edu/macintl/vol23/iss1/11; Shamir, S., & Maddy-Weitzman, B. (Eds.), (2005).*The Camp David summit- What went wrong?* Brighton: Sussex Academic Press; Slater, J. (2001). What went wrong? The collapse of the Israeli-Palestinian peace process. *Political Science Quarterly, 116*(2), 171–199.

100 Malka, A. (2004). The regional system's stability is being tested. In Bar-Siman-Tov, Y. (Ed.), *Words of Generals: The collapse of the Oslo process and the violent Israeli-Palestinian conflict* (pp. 13-26). Jerusalem: The Leonard Davis Institute for International Relations (in Hebrew).

101 Steinberg, M. (September 12, 2002). *A "blessed" versus a "cursed" peace in the Palestinian–Israeli conflict.* Paper presented at Princeton University; Lavie, E. (June 13, 2004). Baseless conception-interview by Yoav Shtern, *Haaretz*, p. B3 (in Hebrew).

102 Klein, M. (2003). *The Jerusalem problem: The struggle for permanent status.* Gainesville, FL: University of Florida Press; Lehrs, L. (2011). *Peace talks over Jerusalem: A review of the Israeli-Palestinian negotiations concerning Jerusalem, 1993-2011* (in Hebrew). Jerusalem: The Jerusalem Institute for Policy Research.

103 Hassner, R. E. (2009). *War on sacred grounds.* Ithaca, NY: Cornell University Press; Matz, D. (2003). Trying to understand Taba talks. *Palestine Israel Journal, 10*(3), 96-105; Pundak, R. (2001). From Oslo to Taba: What went wrong? *Survival 43*(3), 31–45. I also draw on the findings of a research project conducted by the Davis Institute of the Hebrew University in 2002–2004 by a group of scholars, including myself. The project included interviews with more than twenty senior Israeli officials, including former PM Ehud Barak and leading negotiators of the Oslo process. The main attitudes and approaches to the Oslo process are summarized in Arie M. Kacowicz (2005). Rashomon in the Middle East: Clashing narratives, Images and frames in the Israeli-Palestinian conflict. *Cooperation and Conflict, 40*, 343–360.

104 Kaspit, B. (September 6, 2002). Israel is not a state that has an army but rather army that has a state attached to it. *Maariv* (Rosh Hashana Supplement), pp. 8-11, 32 (in Hebrew).

105 Drucker, R., & Shelah O. (2005). *Boomerang*. Tel Aviv: Keter (in Hebrew); Harel, A., & Isacharof, A. (2004). *The seventh war*. Tel Aviv: Miskal-Yedioth Ahronoth books and Chemed Books (in Hebrew); Hirsch, G. (2004). From "molten lead" to "another road": The campaign development in the Central Command 2000-2003. *Maarachot*, Issue No 393, pp. 26-31 (in Hebrew).

106 Kaspit, B. (13 September 2002). The army will decide and approve. *Ma'ariv*, pp. 6-10 of sabbath supplement; Drucker, R., & Shelah O. (2005). *Boomerang*. Tel Aviv: Keter (in Hebrew); Peri, Y. (2005). *Generals in the cabinet room: How the military shapes Israel's policy*. Washington D.C.: U.S. Institute of Peace.

107 Ben-Ami, S. (2004). *Frontline without backcountry: A journey to the boundaries of the peace process)*. Tel Aviv: Yediot Aharonot (in Hebrew); Drucker, R., & Shelah O. (2005). *Boomerang*. Tel Aviv: Keter (in Hebrew).

108 Ben-Ami, S. (2004). *Frontline without backcountry: A journey to the boundaries of the peace process)*. Tel Aviv: Yediot Aharonot. pp. 318-319; (in Hebrew).

109 Data regarding Palestinian casualties was taken from "Palestinian Red Cross Society," www.palestinerecs.org; while data regarding Israelis was taken Israel's Ministry of Foreign Affairs, www.mfa.gov.il, where short description of events can also be found.

110 There is considerable disagreement about the proportion of uninvolved civilians who were killed. Estimates range between 40 to 66 percent; www.palestinerecs.org.

111 Klein, M. (October 2, 2002) The origins of Intifada II and rescuing peace for Israelis and Palestinians. Lecture delivered in the foundation for Middle East Peace and the Middle East Institute. http://www.miftah.org/display.cfm?DocId=1813&CategoryId=5; Kaspit, B. (1 November, 2000). Israel will reveal top secret' Intelligence data as part of PR campaign. Ma'ariv (in Hebrew); Pressman, J. (2003). The Second Intifada: Background and causes of the Israeli-Palestinian conflict. Journal of Conflict Studies, 23(2), 114–141. Barnea, A. (2021). Israeli intelligence, the Second Intifada, and strategic surprise: A case of "intelligence to please?" International Journal of Intelligence and CounterIntelligence, 1-25. p. 19. https://doi.org/10.1080/08850607.2021.1994347.

112 Drucker, R., & Shelah O. (2005). *Boomerang*. Tel Aviv: Keter (in Hebrew); Klein, M. (October 2, 2002). The origins of Intifada II and rescuing peace for Israelis and Palestinians. Lecture delivered in the foundation for Middle East Peace and the Middle East Institute. http://www.miftah. org/display.cfm?DocId=1813&CategoryId=5; Kaspit, B. (1 November, 2000). Israel will reveal top secret Intelligence data as part of PR campaign. *Ma'ariv* (in Hebrew); Pressman, J. (2003). The Second Intifada: Background and causes of the Israeli-Palestinian conflict. *Journal of Conflict Studies, 23*(2), 114–141. *Report of the Sharm el-Sheikh Fact-Finding Committee* [hereinafter Mitchell Report], full text of the report completed on 30 April 2001 and published on 20 May 2001, http://www.state.gov /p/nea/rls/rpt/3060.htm, p. 7.

113 Ayalon, A. (2004). The dream and its demise: Analysis of the Israeli-Palestinian peace process In Bar-Siman-Tov, Y. (Ed.), *Words of Generals: The collapse of the Oslo process and the violent Israeli-Palestinian conflict* (pp. 5-12). p. 11. Jerusalem: The Leonard Davis Institute for International Relations (in Hebrew).

114 Malka, A. (2004). The regional system's stability is being tested. In Bar-Siman-Tov, Y. (Ed.), *Words of Generals: The collapse of the Oslo process and the violent Israeli-Palestinian conflict*_(pp. 13-26). p. 14. Jerusalem: The Leonard Davis Institute for International Relations (in Hebrew).

115 Ben-Ari, J. (April 4th, 2006), Haaretz.

116 Dichter, A. (2006, March 1). *Between choices and elections: Israel and the Palestinians*. A speech during the Chechik Award for Research on Israel's Security's ceremony. Tel Aviv: The Jaffe Center for Strategic Studies (in Hebrew).

117 Barnea, A. (2021). Israeli intelligence, the Second Intifada, and strategic surprise: A case of "intelligence to please?" *International Journal of Intelligence and CounterIntelligence*, 1-25.

118 Bar-Tal, D., & Sharvit, K. (2007). A psychological earthquake of the Israeli Jewish society: Changing opinions following the Camp David summit and the Al Aqsa Intifada. In Y. Bar-Siman-Tov (Ed.), *The Israeli-Palestinian conflict: From conflict resolution to conflict management*. (pp. 169-202) Houndmills, England: Palgrave Macmillan.

119 Bar-Tal, D., Raviv, A., & Abromovich, R. (2020). *In the head of the beholder: Views of the Israeli-Arab/Palestinian conflict by Israeli Jews*. Tel Aviv:

Tami Steinmetz Center for Peace Research, Tel Aviv University (in Hebrew).

120 Peace Index, November 2000.

121 Arian, A. (2002). *Israeli public opinion on national security 2002* (Memorandum No. 61). Tel Aviv: Jaffe Center for Strategic Studies, Tel Aviv University.

122 Peace Index, October 2000.

123 Yediot Aharonot, March 30, 2001.

124 Yuchtman-Yaar, E. (2017). The problem of trust in the Israeli-Palestinian conflict. In I. Alon, & D. Bar-Tal, (Eds.), *The role of trust in conflict resolution: The Israeli –Palestinian case and beyond* (pp. 149-167). Cham, Switzerland: Springer.

125 Arian, A. (2001). *Israeli public opinion on national security 2001* (Memorandum No. 60). Tel Aviv: Jaffe Center for Strategic Studies, Tel Aviv University. Arian, A. (2002). *Israeli public opinion on national security 2002* (Memorandum No. 61). Tel Aviv: Jaffe Center for Strategic Studies, Tel Aviv University.

126 Yuchtman-Yaar, E. (2017). The problem of trust in the Israeli-Palestinian conflict. In I. Alon, & D. Bar-Tal, (Eds.), *The role of trust in conflict resolution: The Israeli –Palestinian case and beyond* (pp. 149-167). Cham, Switzerland: Springer.

127 *Maariv*, 12 May 2002.

128 Peace Index, October 2019; Peace Index, March 2022.

129 Lavi, I., Canetti, D., Sharvit, K., Bar-Tal, D., & Hobfoll, S. (2014). Protected by ethos in a protracted conflict? A comparative study among Israelis and Palestinians in the West Bank, Gaza, and East Jerusalem. *Journal of Conflict Resolution, 58,* 68-92.

130 Hass, R. G. (1981). Effects of source characteristics on cognitive responses and persuasion. In R. E. Petty, T. M. Ostrom, & T. C. Brook (Eds.), *Cognitive responses in persuasion* (pp.141-172). Hillsdale, NJ: Lawrence Erlbaum.Hass, 1981; Hovland, C. I., Janis, I. L., & Kelley, H. H. (1953). *Communication and persuasion: Psychological studies of opinion change.* New Haven, CT: Yale University Press; Petty, R. E., & Wegener, D. T. (1998). Attitude change: Multiple roles for persuasion variables. In D. T.

Gilbert, S. T. Fiske & G. Lindzey (Eds.), *The handbook of social psychology* (4ᵗʰ ed., vol. 1, pp. 323-390). Boston: McGraw Hill.

131 Wolfsfeld, G. (2004). *Media and the path to peace.* New York; Cambridge University Press.

132 Bar-Siman-Tov, Y., Lavie, E., Michael, K., & Bar-Tal, D. (2007). The Israeli-Palestinian violent confrontation: An Israeli perspective. In Y. Bar-Siman-Tov (Ed.), *The Israeli-Palestinian conflict: From conflict resolution to conflict management* (pp. 69-100). Houndmills, England: Palgrave Macmillan.

133 Haaretz, June 14, 2004.

134 Shavit, A. (2004, October 7). In the name of his client. Haaretz (in Hebrew). https://www.haaretz.co.il/misc/1.1004558

135 Erlanger, S. (July 15, 2005). The Israeli settlers demolish greenhouses and Gaza jobs. *The New York Times;* Schwegel, J. (August 10, 2014). The Greenhouse propaganda–How Gazans history is being rewritten to dehumanize Palestinians. Mondoweiss. https://mondoweiss.net/2014/08/propaganda-dehumanize-palestinians/

136 Gisha. (2012, June). *Graphing 5 years of closure.* Gisha – Legal Center for Freedom of Movement. Retrieved from: http://www.gisha.org/UserFiles/File/publications/5years/5-to-the-closure-eng.pdf; Rynhold, J., & Waxman, D. (2013). Ideological change and Israel's disengagement from Gaza. *Political Science Quarterly, 123,* 11-37.

137 *Partial List of Items Prohibited/Permitted into the Gaza Strip* (May 2010). Gisha-Legal Center for Freedom Movement; *The Humanitarian Monitor* (April 2010). April Overview. Jerusalem: United Nations, Office for the Coordination of Humanitarian Affairs occupied Palestinian territory.

138 Hass, A. (October 26, 2010). Israel releases papers dealing with Gaza blockade. *Haaretz;* Hass, A. (October 17, 2012). 2,279 calories per person: How Israel made sure that Gaza didn't starve. *Haaretz.*

139 Butler, L. (2009). Gaza at glance. *Journal of Palestine Study, 38,* 93-97.

140 *Initial health assessment report Gaza Strip* (December 2012). Jerusalem: World Health Organization, Office of the occupied Palestinian territory; Prusher, R. I., & Al-Kahlout, S. (May 13, 2009). Pope's urging brings Gaza blockade to forefront. Christian Science Monitor; *Locked in: Stagnation or*

revival? Palestinian economic prospects (March 21, 2012) Economic Monitoring Report to the Ad Hoc Liaison Committee. World Bank. The *Humanitarian impact of two years of blockade on the Gaza strip* (August 2009). Jerusalem: United Nations, Office for the Coordination of Humanitarian Affairs occupied Palestinian territory; *Unraveling the closure of Gaza* (July 7, 2010). Gisha-Legal Center for Freedom Movement.

141 Pelham, N. (2012). Gaza's tunnel phenomenon: The unintended dynamics of Israel's siege. *Journal of Palestinian Studies, 41*, 6-31.

142 *Easing the blockade* (March 2011). Jerusalem: United Nations, Office for the Coordination of Humanitarian Affairs occupied Palestinian territory; *Strangled: Gaza collapsing in the grip of a humanitarian crisis* (May 2015). Geneva: Euro-Mediterranean Human Rights Monitor.

143 *Protection of Civilians Weekly Report – 290* (17-23 December 2008). Jerusalem: United Nations, Office for the Coordination of Humanitarian Affairs occupied Palestinian territory.

144 The Marker, August 17, 2018.

145 Booth, W. (February 13, 2015). War punishes Gaza. *Washington Post; Strangled: Gaza collapsing in the grip of a humanitarian crisis* (May 2015). Geneva: Euro-Mediterranean Human Rights Monitor.

146 Sharon, A. (2005, August 15th). Prime-Minister, Ariel Sharon, speech on the day of executing the Disengagement plan Prime-Minister Office (in Hebrew). Retrieved from: https://www.gov.il/he/departments/news/speech150805

147 Marciano, I. (2006, January 26th). Netanyahu: Hamas-Stan is being created before our eyes (in Hebrew). Ynet. https://www.ynet.co.il/articles/0,7340,L-3206983,00.html

148 Peace Index, October 2015.

149 Prime-Minister's Office, April 27, 2011.

150 Ramon, H. (2020). Against the wind. Jerusalem: Gefen (in Hebrew).

151 https://www.btselem.org/hebrew/statistics/fatalities/during-cast-lead/by-date-of-event; https://www.btselem.org/hebrew/press_releases/20160720_fatalities_in_gaza_conflict_2014

152 Peace Index, July 2006; Peace Index, December 2008; Peace Index, November 2012.

153 Peace Index, April 2018.

154 Ministry for Jerusalem and the Diaspora, 2015: p. 4.

155 Podeh, E. (2015). *Chances for peace: Missed opportunities in the Arab-Israeli conflict*. Austin, TX: University of Texas Press.

156 *Lessons of Arab-Israeli negotiating: Four negotiators look back and ahead* (April 25, 2005). Transcript of remarks delivered at the National Press Club, Washington D.C. Washington D.C.: Middle East Institute; Goldenberg, I. (2015). *Lessons from the 2013-2104 Israeli-Palestinian final status negotiations*. Washington: Center for a New American Security; Ramsbotham, O. (2018). When formal negotiations fail: Strategic negotiation ripens theory, and the Kerry initiative. *Negotiation and Conflict Management Research, 111*, 321-340.

157 Peace Index, May 2019.

158 Pliskin, R., Bar-Tal, D., Sheppes, G., & Halperin, E. (2014). Are leftists more emotion-driven than rightists?: The interactive influence of ideology and emotions on support for policies. *Personality and Social Psychology Bulletin, 40*, 1681–1697.

159 Bar-Tal, D. & Schnell, I. (Eds.), (2013). *The impact of lasting occupation: Lessons from Israeli society*. New York: Oxford University Press; Handel, A.)2009(. Chronology of the occupation regime. In A. Ophir, M. Givoni, & S. Hanafi (Ed.) *The power of inclusive exclusion: Anatomy of Israeli rule in the occupied Palestinian territories* (pp. 603–637). New York: Zone Books.

160 Benvenisti, E. (1993). *The international law of occupation*. Princeton, NJ: Princeton University Press, p. 4.

161 Bar-Tal, D. & Schnell, I. (Eds.), (2013). *The impact of lasting occupation: Lessons from Israeli society*. New York: Oxford University Press; Berda, Y. (2018). *Living emergency: Israel's permit regime in the occupied West Bank*. Stanford: Stanford University Press.

162 https://shovrimshtika.org/testimnies/database/649335; https://www.haaretz.co.il/news/law/.premium-1.8101364; https://www.haaretz.com/israel-news/.premium.MAGAZINE-stripped-beaen-tasered-palestinians-reveal-jerusalem-police-brutality-1.10491932

163 Hasson, N. (2019, November 11th). Common sense could have lowered the flames in Issawiya, but the police enhanced them (in Hebrew).

Haaretz. https://www.haaretz.co.il/news/law/.premium-1.8101364

164 Hass, A. (February 4, 2021). Why is the Israeli military exercising in these Palestinian villages, for the first time in 7 years? https://www.haaretz.com/israel-news/.premium.MAGAZINE-why-is-the-idf-exercising-in-these-palestinian-villages-for-first-time-since-2013-1.9509405

165 Shezaf, H., & Horodniceanu. (April 25, 2022). Israel's other justice system has rules of its own: Inside military courts for Palestinians, *Haaretz*. https://www.haaretz.com/israel-nws/.premium.MAGAZINE-israel-s-other-justice-system-has-rules-of-its-own-1.10762091

166 https://www.theguardian.com/world/2022/jun/24/shireen-abu-aqleh-palestinian-journalist-killed-by-israeli-bullet-un-says

167 Zunes, S., & Mundy, J. (2010). *Western Sahara: War, nationalism, and conflict irresolution*. Syracuse, NY: Syracuse University Press.

168 According to Global Firepower's in 2022 Israel is ranked 18 of 142 countries, while Palestine even does not appear in the ranking list. See the imbalance in https://www.trtworld.com/magazine/this-is-the-imbalance-of-power-between-israel-and-palestine-in-real-terms-46651

169 Shanahan, T. (2016). The definition of terrorism. In T, Shanahan (Ed.). *Routledge handbook of critical terrorism studies* (pp.103-113). New York: Routledge. p 110.

170 Karp, January 20, 2021: https://www.haaretz.com/opinion/.premium-how-israel-was-annexed-to-the-territories-1.9468702

171 Bar-Tal, D., & Schnell, I (2013). In Bar-Tal, D. & Schnell, I. (Eds.). *The impact of lasting occupation: Lessons from Israeli society* (pp. 1-28). New York: Oxford University Press.

172 Yefet, N. (January 27, 2022). *Haaretz*.

173 Worchel, S. (1999). *Written in blood*. New York: Worth Publishers.

174 Bar-Tal, D., & Schnell, I (2013). In Bar-Tal, D. & Schnell, I. (Eds.). *The impact of lasting occupation: Lessons from Israeli society* (pp. 1-28). New York: Oxford University Press.

175 Rosler, N., Bar-Tal, D., Sharvit, K., Halperin, E., & Raviv, A. (2009). Moral aspects of prolonged occupation: Implications for an occupying society. In S. Scuzzarello, C. Kinnvall, & K. R. Monroe (Eds.), *On behalf of*

others: The psychology of care in a global world (pp. 211-232). New York: Oxford University Press.

176 Allegra M., Handel A., & Maggor E. (2017). Normalizing occupation. The politics of everyday life in the West Bank settlements. Bloomington: IN. Indiana University Press; Aruri, N. A. (Ed.). (1989). *Occupation: Israel over Palestine* (2nd ed.). Belmont, Mass.: Association of Arab-American University Graduates; Berda, Y. (2018). *Living emergency: Israel's permit regime in the Occupied West Bank.* Stanford: Stanford University Press; Gordon, N. (2008). *Israel's occupation.* Berkeley, CA: University of California Press; Btselem Reports.https://www.btselem.org/publi cations?page=1, https:///www.haaretz.co.il/magazine/twilightzone/.pr emium-1.6723928; Levy, Y. (2020). Who controls the Israeli policing army? *Israel Studies Review, 35,* 58-76.

177 Halperin, E., Bar-Tal, D., Sharvit, K., Rosler, N. and Raviv, A. (2010). Socio-psychological implications for an occupying society: The case of Israel. *Journal of Peace Research, 47,* 59-70.

178 Dugard, J. (2006). Report of the special rapporteur on the situation of human rights in the Palestinian Territories occupied since 1967. Retrieved 31.3.2010 from http://documents-dds-ny.un.org/doc/UNDOC/GEN/G06/138/12/pdf/G0613812.pdf?OpenElement; Ophir, A., Givoni, M., & Hanafi, S. (Eds.), (2009). *Power of inclusive exclusion: Anatomy of Israeli rule in the occupied Palestinian territories.* New York: Zone Books; Makdisi, S. (2008). *Palestine inside out: An everyday occupation.* New York: W. W. Norton; Playfair, E. (Ed.). (1992). *International law and the administration of occupied territories.* Oxford: Clarendon Press; Roberts, A. (1990). Prolonged military occupation: The Israeli-occupied territories since 1967. *The American Journal of International Law, 84,* 44-103.

179 Halperin, E., Bar-Tal, D., Sharvit, K., Rosler, N. and Raviv, A. (2010). Socio-psychological implications for an occupying society: The case of Israel. *Journal of Peace Research, 47,* 59-70.

180 Rosler, N., Sharvit, K., & Bar-Tal, D. (2018). Perceptions of prolonged occupation as barriers to conflict resolution. *Political Psychology, 39,* 519-538.

181 Kadari-Ovadia, S. (2019, December 24). 37% of young Israeli-Jews view minority rights as especially important–lower than the average in the Arab world *Haaretz* (in Hebrew). https://www.haaretz.co.il/news/educ ation/.premium-1.8315479

182 The index for shared society progress in youth 2021. Jerusalem: Achord. https://en.achord.huji.ac.il/sites/default/files/achord/files/isspy_2021_exec_summary_english.pdf

183 Arieli, S. (2017). *Messianism meets reality: The Israeli settlement project in Judea and Samaria: Vision or illusion, 1967-2016.* Tel Aviv: Economic Cooperation Foundation; Greenbaum, D. (2016). *From the bravery of the spirit to the sanctification of power: Power and bravery in religious Zionism 1948-1967.* Ra'anana: Open University Press (in Hebrew); Naor, A. (2001). *Greater Eretz Israel: Beliefs and policy* Haifa: Haifa University Press (in Hebrew).

184 Aran, G. (1986). From religious Zionism to Zionist religion: The roots of Gush Emunim. *Studies in Contemporary Jewry, 2,* 116-143; Avruch, A. K. (1979). Traditionalizing Israeli nationalism: The development of Gush Emunim, *Political Psychology, 1,* 47-57; Barzel, N. (2017). *"Redemption now": The beliefs and activities of the Jewish settlers in the West Bank and the Israeli society):* Bnei Brak: Kibbutz Hameuhad (in Hebrew); Rubinstein, D. (1982). *Who's with God, to me: Gush Emunibm* Tel Aviv: Hakibbutz. Hameuchad (in Hebrew).

185 http://tikvahfund.org/wp-content/uploads/2021/06/Weinstein_44.pdf

186 *Harnoy, M. (1994). The settlers. Or Yehuda: Ma'ariv (in Hebrew);* Zertal, I., & Eldar, A. (2007). *Lords of the land: The war over Israel's settlements in the occupied territories 1967-2007.* New York: Nation Books.

187 Rabin, Y. (1996). *Yitzhak Rabin: The Rabin memoirs.* Berkeley, CA: University of California Press.

188 Cohen, Y. (1973). *The Alon plan* Tel Aviv: Hakibbutz Hameuhad (in Hebrew): Zertal, I., & Eldar, A. (2007). *Lords of the land: The war over Israel's settlements in the occupied territories 1967-2007.* New York: Nation Books.

189 Zertal, I., & Eldar, A. (2007). *Lords of the land: The war over Israel's settlements in the occupied territories 1967-2007.* New York: Nation Books.

190 Cohen, Y. (1973). *The Alon plan* Tel Aviv: Hakibbutz Hameuhad (in Hebrew): Rabin, Y. (1996). *Yitzhak Rabin: The Rabin memoirs.* Berkeley, CA: University of California Press.

191 Settlement Division. (1997, June). *The values in settlement of Judea and*

Samaria, Update 7664 Jerusalem: The Settlements' Division, World Zionist Organization (in Hebrew); Zertal, I., & Eldar, A. (2007). *Lords of the land: The war over Israel's settlements in the occupied territories 1967-2007.* New York: Nation Books.

192 Raz, A. (June 4, 2021) Four years before the Six Day War admitted in the General Staff: In a comfortable political situation we will be able to hold the occupied territories. *Magazine Haaretz*)in Hebrew). https://www.haaretz.co.il/magazine/the-edge/.premium.HIGHLIGHT-1.9867213

193 Settlement Division. (1997, June). *The values in settlement of Judea and Samaria, Update 7664* Jerusalem: The Settlements' Division, World Zionist Organization (in Hebrew); Zertal, I., & Eldar, A. (2007). *Lords of the land: The war over Israel's settlements in the occupied territories 1967-2007.* New York: Nation Books.

194 Schnell, Y. (2012). The strategy of settlement in the territories. In S. Hason (Ed.) *Space design in Israel* (pp.195-210). Jerusalem: Keter (in Hebrew).

195 Barzel, N. (2017). *"Redemption now": The beliefs and activities of the Jewish settlers in the West Bank and the Israeli society*): Bnei Brak: Kibbutz Hameuhad (in Hebrew); Cohen, S. A. (2013). *Divine service: Judaism and Israel armed forces.* Burlington, VT: Ashgate Publishing.

196 https://www.haaretz.co.il/opinions/.premium-1.10311268

197 Barzel, N. (2017). *"Redemption now": The beliefs and activities of the Jewish settlers in the West Bank and the Israeli society*): Bnei Brak: Kibbutz Hameuhad (in Hebrew); Zertal, I., & Eldar, A. (2007). *Lords of the land: The war over Israel's settlements in the occupied territories 1967-2007.* New York: Nation Books.

198 Levy, E., Shapira, T. & Baker, A. (2012, June 21). *Final report on the status of building in the Judea and Samaria region. The governmental examination committee regarding the status of building in the Judea and Samaria region* (in Hebrew) Retrieved from: https://www.gov.il/BlobFolder/news/spokeedmond090712/he/documents_doch090712.pdf; Sasson, T. (2005). *Advisory legal brief (intermediate) regarding unauthorized settlements* Jerusalem: Unknown publisher (in Hebrew). Retrieved from: http://www.nasserlaw.net/UserFiles/file/sason%20report.pdf

199 Lebel, U. (2013). Postmodern or conservative? Competing security communities over military doctrine: Israeli national-religious soldiers. In N.

Karakatsanis & J. Swartz (Eds.), *Political and military sociology: An annual review* (vol. 40). Piscataway: Transaction Publishers; Pedahzur, R. (2013). The occupation and its effect on the Israeli forces. In Bar-Tal, D. & Schnell, I. (Eds.). *The impact of lasting occupation: Lessons from Israeli society* (pp. 206-249). New York: Oxford University Press; https://www.washingtonpost.com/world/middle_east/west-bank-settlers-violence-attacks/2021/11/28/7de2f9d2-4bb7-11ec-a7b8-9ed28bf23929_story.html; https://www.breakingthesilence.org.il/inside/wp-content/uploads/2021/07/OnDuty-Testimonies-En.pdf

200 Ben-Ari, E., & Ben-Shalom, U. (2020). Israel's ground forces in the occupied territories: Policing and the juridification of soldiering. *Israel Studies Review, 35*, 37-57; Ben-Ishai, (2020). The missing policing: The absent concept of policing and its substitute in Israeli military doctrine. *Israel Studies Review, 35*, 9-36; Gazit, N. (2020). Military (mom [policing) in the occupied territories. *Israel Studies Review, 35*, 77-100.

201 Pedahzur, R. (2013). The occupation and its effect on the Israeli forces. In Bar-Tal, D. & Schnell, I. (Eds.). *The impact of lasting occupation: Lessons from Israeli society* (pp. 206-249). New York: Oxford University Press. https://www.haaretz.com/opinion/.premium-israel-s-policing-army-is-in-breach-of-contract-1.8029598

202 https://www.washingtonpost.com/world/middle_east/west-bank-settlers-violence-attacks/2021/11/28/7de2f9d2-4bb7-11ec-a7b8-9ed28bf23929_story.html

203 https://www.timesofisrael.com/settler-leaders-horrified-as-dozens-of-jewish-extremists-carry-out-w-bank-assault

204 https://www.washingtonpost.com/world/middle_east/west-bank-settlers-violence-attacks/2021/11/28/7de2f9d2-4bb7-11ec-a7b8-9ed28bf23929_story.html

205 https://www.haaretz.com/israel-news/.premium.MAGAZINE-charges-are-pressed-in-just-4-of-settler-violence-cases-1.10595783

206 On duty (2020), Haaretz.

207 Pedahzur, R. (2013) The occupation and its effect on the Israeli forces. In Bar-Tal, D. & Schnell, I. (Eds.). *The impact of lasting occupation: Lessons from Israeli society* (pp.206-249). New York: Oxford University Press; Ben Sasson-Gordis, A. (October 15, 2015). *Settlements damage Israel's security.*

Jerusalem: Molad- The Center for the Renewal of Israeli Democracy/ (in Hebrew)

208 http://en.cis.org.il/

209 Berger, Y. (2018, October 22). The settlement division assisted for 20 years in funding the construction of illegal outposts *Haaretz* (in Hebrew). https://www.haaretz.co.il/news/politics/.premium-1.6576695; Buso, N. (2015, January 2). This is how religious settlers' groups are trying to overtake Tel Aviv. *The Marker* (in Hebrew). https://www.themarker.com/markerweek/1.2527908; Feige, M. (2002). *One space, two places: Gush Emunim, Peace Now and the construction of Israeli space.* Jerusalem: Magness Press (in Hebrew); Settlement Division. (1997, June). *The values in settlement of Judea and Samaria, Update 7664* Jerusalem: The Settlements' Division, World Zionist Organization (in Hebrew); Zertal, I., & Eldar, A. (2007). *Lords of the land: The war over Israel's settlements in the occupied territories 1967-2007.* New York: Nation Books.

210 Rosen, M., & Roth, A. D. (2021). A progressive Jewish response to the discriminatory policies of KKL- JNF.

211 Del Sarto, A. R. (2017). *Israel under siege: The politics of insecurity and the rise of neo-revisionist right.* Washington, D.C.: Georgetown University Press. Feige, M. (2002). *One space, two places: Gush Emunim, Peace Now and the construction of Israeli space.* Jerusalem: Magness Press (in Hebrew); Schwartz, 2003.

212 Hermann, T. (2014). *The Nationalist-Religious camp in Israel* Jerusalem: The Israeli Democracy Institute (in Hebrew). Schwartz, D. (2003). *Religious Zionism: History and ideological chapters.* Tel Aviv: Broadcast University and Ministry of Defense (in Hebrew); Schwartz, D. (Ed.). (2018). *Religious Zionism: History, idea, society.* Ramat Gan: Bar-Ilan University Press (in Hebrew).

213 Holzer, E. (2009). *Double-edged sword: Military activism in the thought of Religious Zionism* Jerusalem: The Shalom Hartman Institute (in Hebrew).

214 file:///D:/Documents/Book%20in%20the%20comfort%20zone%20English/Addtions%20must/sattlers_report_eng.pdf; *Haaretz*, January 6th, 2020; Holzer, E. (2009). *Double-edged sword: Military activism in the thought of Religious Zionism* Jerusalem: The Shalom Hartman Institute (in Hebrew).

215 Schwartz, D. (Ed.). (2018). *Religious Zionism: History, idea, society.* Ramat Gan: Bar-Ilan University Press (in Hebrew); Schwartz, D. & Sagi, A. (Eds.). (2003). *One hundred years of religious Zionism* Ramat Gan: Bar-Ilan University Press (in Hebrew).

216 Moses, M. (2009). *There are several types of Religious Zionism* Unpublished PhD dissertation. Ramat Gan: Bar-Ilan University (in Hebrew).

217 Katsman, H. (2020). The hyphen cannot hold: Contemporary trends in religious Zionism. *Israel Studies Review, 35,* 154-174.

218 Arieli, S. (2017). Messianism against the anvil of reality: The settlement endeavor in Judea and Samaria Israel. unknown publisher (in Hebrew). Mendelsohn, B. (2016). Israel and its messianic right: Path dependency and state authority in international conflict. *International Studies Quarterly, 60,* 47–58; Roth, A. (2009). Religious Zionism in the statism test: From Maymon village to Amona in Bar-Siman-Tov, Y. (Ed.), *The Disengagement Plan: The idea and its breakdown* (in Hebrew). Jerusalem: The Jerusalem Institute for Policy Research.

219 Hellinger, M., Hershkowitz, I., & Susser, B. (2018). *Religious Zionism and the settlement project: Ideology, politics, and civil disobedience.* New York: SUNY Press; Peled, Y., & Peled. H. (September 2019). *Religious Zionism: The quest for hegemony.* Paper Presented at the European Consortium, for Political Research General Conference in Wroclaw, Poland; Schwartz, D. & Sagi, A. (Eds.). (2003). *One hundred years of religious Zionism* Ramat Gan: Bar-Ilan University Press (in Hebrew).

220 Cohen, S. A. (2013). *Divine service: Judaism and Israel armed forces.* Burlington, VT: Ashgate Publishing Levy, Y. (2014). The theocratization of the Israeli military. *Armed Forces and Society, 40,* 269-294; Gal, R. (Ed.). (2013). *Between the yarmulke and the beret: Religion, politics and the military in Israel.* Ben Shemen: Modan (in Hebrew); Harel, A. (2008, October 22). This is how the chief military Rabbi of the IDF converts the army to religiosity. *Haaretz* (in Hebrew). https://www.haaretz.co.il/news/education/1.1355654

221 Cohen, S. A. (2013). *Divine service: Judaism and Israel armed forces.* Burlington, VT: Ashgate Publishing; Levy, Y. (2015). *The divine commander: The theocratization of the Israeli military* Tel Aviv: Am Oved (in Hebrew).

222 Holzer, E. (2009). *Double-edged sword: Military activism in the thought of Religious Zionism.* Jerusalem: The Shalom Hartman Institute (in He-

brew); Levy, Y. (2015). *The divine commander: The theocratization of the Israeli military* Tel Aviv: Am Oved (in Hebrew).

223 Kaplan, R. (2018, June 16). They prefer faithless officers at IDF's top brass *Israel Hayom* (in Hebrew), https://www.israelhayom.co.il/article/563549; Kelner, G. (2017, June 28). Srugim. Retrieved from http://www.srugim.co.il/

224 Ben Simhon, K. (1 November 2014). When and why has the Israeli Army become so religious? *Haaretz* (in Hebrew). https://www.haaretz.co.il/magazine/.premium-1.2472342; Gal, R. (Ed.). (2013). *Between the yarmulke and the beret: Religion, politics and the military in Israel.* Ben Shemen: Modan (in Hebrew); Levy, Y. (17 January 2018). This is how Eisenkot institutionalized religious influences in the IDF (in Hebrew). Haaretz. https://www.haaretz.co.il/magazine/the-edge/.premium-1.5743689; Sheleg, Y. (2016, May 16). More religious soldiers in the Army: The boundary between "religious conversion" and suitability Makor Rishon/NRG (in Hebrew). https://www.makorrishon.co.il/nrg/online/11/ART2/777/284.html

225 Kashti, O. (17 July 2018). Despite promises by IDF's Chief of Staff: The volume of activity of religious organizations in the military has expanded *Haaretz* (in Hebrew). https://www.haaretz.co.il/news/education/1.6288100

226 Kashti, O. (17 July 2018). Despite promises by IDF's Chief of Staff: The volume of activity of religious organizations in the military has expanded *Haaretz* (in Hebrew). https://www.haaretz.co.il/news/education/1.6288100

227 August 23, 2018, *Haaretz.*

228 Winter, O. (2014, July 9). Commander's massage for battle, operation "Protective Edge" (in Hebrew). Retrieved from: https://www.haaretz.co.il/polopoly_fs/1.2373868.1405085600!/image/1605027746.png

229 Ya'ar, E. & Hermann, T. (2013). The Peace index, July 2013 (in Hebrew). The Peace Index website.

230 Ben-Meir, Y. & Bagno-Moldavsky O. (2013). *Voice of the people: Israeli public opinion on issues of national security.* Tel Aviv: Institute for National Security Studies (in Hebrew). p. 45.

231 Peled, Y., & Herman-Peled, H. (2018). *The religionization of Israeli society.*

New York: Routledge; Don-Yehiya, E. (2014). Messianism and politics: The ideological transformation of Religious Zionism. *Israel Studies, 19,* 239-63.

232 Feige, M. (2002). *One space, two places: Gush Emunim, Peace Now and the construction of Israeli space.* Jerusalem: Magness Press (in Hebrew); Klar, Y. (2014). From 'Do not arouse love or awaken love until it so desires' through 'Return to Zion' to 'Conquest of the Land': Paradigm shifts and sanctified reenactments in building of the Jewish state." *International Journal of Intercultural Relations, 43,* 87-99; Sagi, A. & Schwartz, D. (2018). *Religious Zionism and the Six-Day War: From realism to messianism.* New York: Routledge; Sivan, E., Almond, G. A., & Appleby, R. S. (2003). *Strong religions: The rise of fundamentalism around the world.* Chicago University Press.

233 Cohen, S. A., & Susser, B. (2000). *Israel and the politics of Jewish identity: The secular-religious impasse.* Baltimore: Johns Hopkins University Press; David, O., & Bar-Tal, D. (2009). A socio-psychological conception of collective identity: The case of national identity. *Personality and Social Psychology Review, 13,* 354-379.

234 Bar-Tal, D., & Bar-Tal, G. (2022). The Holocaust and its teaching in Israel in view of the conflict: General and pedagogical implications and lessons. In D. Yitzhaki, T. Gallagher, N. Aloni, A., & Z. Gross (Eds.). *Activist pedagogy and shared education in divided societies: International perspectives and next practices* (pp. 235-254). Leiden: Brill Publishers.

235 Schnell, I., & Bar-Tal, D. (2013). Conclusion: The occupied territories as cornerstone in the reconstruction of Israeli society. In Bar-Tal, D. & Schnell, I. (Eds.). *The impact of lasting occupation: Lessons from Israeli society* (pp. 507-539). New York: Oxford University Press.

236 Nasie, M., Diamond, A., & Bar-Tal, D. (2016). Young children in intractable conflicts: The Israel case *Personality and Social Psychology Review, 20,* 365-392.

237 Sommers, M. (2002). *Children, education and war: Reaching education for All (EFA) objectives in countries affected by conflict.* Conflict Prevention and Reconstruction Unit working paper. Washington D.C:. World Bank. Retrieved from http://documents.worldbank.org/curated/en/376921 468762874069/pdf/multi0page.pdf

238 Vered, S. (2018). *Peace education in Israel 2009-2013: Ministry of Educa-*

tion's policies and the challenges in the field. Unpublished PhD dissertation. Tel Aviv: Tel Aviv University (in Hebrew).

239 Scope, May 9, 2016, Haaretz; Haaretz, July 7, 2017; Kashti, O. January 21, 2016, Haaretz; Kashti, O. April 6, 2017 (in Hebrew).

240 Amsterdamski, S. (December 4, 2014). Institutionalized discrimination: Students in the state-religious education receive the highest funding *Calcalist* (in Hebrew). https://www.calcalist.co.il/local/articles/0,734 0,L-3646702,00.html; Davidson, M. (2002). *The Birth and implementation of the State Education Law, 1953: Politics and education in Israel during the tenure of Ben-Zion Dinur 1951-1955* (in Hebrew). Unpublished PhD dissertation. Tel Aviv: Tel Aviv University; Ilan, September 19, 2019, Calcalist (in Hebrew).

241 https://main.knesset.gov.il/News/PressReleases/pages/press17.07.18a. aspx

242 Interview with Minister of Education Rafi Peretz, in the supplement, Seven Days, *Yedioth Aharonoth,* January 10, 2020.

243 Ben-Amos, A. (in press). The representation of the occupied Palestinian Territories in the Israeli system of education: Between recognition and denial. In N. Tal & E. Naveh, (Eds). *Historical education: Arenas and connections,* Tel-Aviv: Moffet and Ha>Kibbutz Ha>Meuchad (in Hebrew).

244 Caspi, D. & Limor, Y. (1992). *The mediators: Mass media in Israel 1948-1990* Tel Aviv: Am Oved (in Hebrew).

245 Caspi, D. & Rubinstein, D. (2013). The wallkeepers: Monitoring the Israeli-Arab conflict. In Bar-Tal, D. & Schnell, I. (Eds.). *The impacts of lasting occupation: Lessons from Israeli society* (pp. 299-325). New York: Oxford University Press.

246 Elbaz, S. (2007). *Rethinking Israeli journalism.* New York: Israel Academic Press; Nossek, H. (1994). The narrative role of the holocaust and the state of Israel in the coverage of salient terrorist events in the Israeli press. *Journal of Narrative and Life History,* 4, 82-101. Roeh, Y., & Nir, R. (1990). Covering the intifada in the Israeli press: Popular and quality papers assume rhetoric of conformity. *Discourse and Society,* 3, 22-36.

247 Barzilai, G. (1996). *Wars, internal conflicts, and political order: A Jewish democracy in the Middle East.* Albany, NY: State University of New York Press; Elbaz, S. (2007). *Rethinking Israeli journalism.* New York: Israel Ac-

ademic Press Wolfsfeld, G. (1997). *Media and political conflict: News from the Middle East.* Cambridge University Press.

248 First, A. (1998). Who is the enemy? The portrayal of Arabs in Israeli news. *Gazette, 60,* 239-251; First, A. (July 2000). *The coverage of the enemy in Israeli TV news: The transitional nature of* representation. Paper presented at the annual meeting of the International Association of Mass Communication. Singapore. Levy, D. (1990). *Ideological functions of TV news: The case of the Intifada in Israeli television.* Unpublished MA thesis. Tel Aviv: Tel Aviv University (in Hebrew).

249 Elbaz, S. (2017). De-legitimization in Israeli news sites: Coverage of the 'other' before and during operation 'Protective Edge' *Public Sphere [Heb: Hamerhav HaTsiburi],* 12. (in Hebrew).

250 Elbaz, S. (2014). *Loyalty to the source: Media, ideology and political culture in Israel.* Tel Aviv: Resling (in Hebrew).

251 Elbaz, S. (2015). *Rethinking Israeli journalism: Core values & media revolution.* New Rochelle, NY: Israeli Academic Press.

252 The Civil Administration ordered 73 Palestinian members (including over 30 children) of the Khirbet Humsa community in the northern Jordan Valley to "voluntarily" uproot themselves from the area where they had been living for decades. Their shacks were demolished and their belongings confiscated.

253 Hass, A. (February 8, 2021). The silence of the Israeli media's occupation lambs. Haaretz. https://www.haaretz.com/israel-news/.premium-the-si lence-of-the-israeli-media-s-occupation-lambs-1.9520783.

254 Ingram, M., L. (2016). *Media under the influence? A comparative analysis of Israeli and Palestinian news coverage of the Israel–Palestine conflict.* Dissertation submitted to the Near and Middle Eastern Studies of the University of London. London: University of London.

255 https://www.maariv.co.il/news/politics/Article-57301

256 Netanyahu, B. (1995). *A place under the sun* Tel Aviv: Yediot Aharonot. (in Hebrew).

257 Rosler, N., Hagage Baikovich, H., & Bar-Tal, D. (2021). Rhetorical ex-

pressions of ethos of conflict and policymaking in intractable conflict by leaders: A comparative study of two Israeli Prime Ministers. *Peace and Conflict: Journal of Peace Psychology, 27,* 381-392.

258 Bar-Haim, G. (August 20, 2021). Interview with Shai Piron, 7 *Days, Yedioth Ahronoth,* p. 69 (in Hebrew).

259 Netanyahu, B. (2000). *A durable peace.* New York: Grand Central Publishing.

260 http://www.mako.co.il/news-military/politics-q1_2015/Article-466fe 8e5e99ea41004.htm

261 Kahana, A. (March 16, 2015). The Prime Minister: If I will win the election, a Palestinian state will not be created *Ma'ariv-NRG* (in Hebrew). Retrieved from: https://www.makorrishon.co.il/nrg/online/1/ART2/6 83/880.html

262 https://www.timesofisrael.com/likud-ministers-at-his-side-netanyahu-asserts-the-entire-right-is-on-trial/

263 Taber, S. C., & Lodge, M. (2006). Motivated skepticism in the evaluation of political beliefs. *American Journal of Political Science, 50,* 755–769, p. 746.

264 Oren, N., Nets-Zehngut, R., & Bar-Tal. D. (2015). Construction of the Israeli-Jewish conflict-supportive narrative and the struggle over its dominance. *Political Psychology, 36,* 215-230.

265 Caspi, D. & Rubinstein, D. (2013). The wallkeepers: Monitoring the Israeli-Arab conflict. In Bar-Tal, D. & Schnell, I. (Eds.). *The impacts of lasting occupation: Lessons from Israeli society* (pp. 299-325). New York: Oxford University Press.

266 Kubovich, Y. (August 18, 2021). *Haaretz.*

267 https://www.haaretz.com/israel-news/.premium.MAGAZINE-this-anti-bds-initiative-failed-so-israel-throws-another-100-million-nis-at-it-1.10565661

268 Azarov, V. (2013). *Institutionalized impunity: Israel's failure to combat settler violence in the occupied Palestinian territory.* Ramallah: Al-Haq.

269 *Haaretz,* October 21, 2015.

270　Gavriely-Nuri, D. (2013). *The normalization of war in the Israeli discourse* . Lanham, MD: Lexington Books.

271　Tsur, N. (2013). Vocabulary and the discourse on the 1967 territories. In Bar-Tal, D. & Schnell, I. (Eds.). *The impacts of lasting occupation: Lessons from Israeli society* (pp. 471-506). New York: Oxford University Press.

272　Oren, N., Nets-Zehngut, R., & Bar-Tal. D. (2015). Construction of the Israeli-Jewish conflict-supportive narrative and the struggle over its dominance. *Political Psychology, 36,* 215-230.

273　http://www.ynet.co.il/articles/0,7340,L-4011576,00.html

274　http://www.ynet.co.il/articles/0,7340,L-4577019,00.html

275　Democracy Index, 2017.

276　https://www.holocaustremembrance.com/antisemitism

277　https://www.holocaustremembrance.com/antisemitism

278　https://www.haaretz.com/isrel-news/2022-11-11/ty-article/.premium /shin-bet-admits-to-tracking-journalists-using-cell-phone-data/00 000184-6335-d879-a5d5-7bb5c9c90000

279　Boker, R. (June 9, 2015). Miri Regev to Norman Issa: "If you will not perform in the Jorden Valley settlements, we will reconsider our funding for your theatre." *Ynet* (in Hebrew). https://www.ynet.co.il/articles /0,7340,L-4666590,00.html; Boker, R. (June 16, 2015). Miri Regev freezes government funding for the El-Midan theatre. *Ynet* (in Hebrew). https://www.ynet.co.il/articles/0,7340,L-4669137,00.html

280　*Haaretz,* 28 March, 2017; *Haaretz,* March 3, 2017.

281　*Haaretz,* 25 October 25, 2016.

282　Bar-Tal, D., Nets-Zehngut, R., & Sharvit, K. (Eds.),(2017). *Self-censorship in contexts of conflict: Theory and research.* Cham, Switzerland: Springer.

283　https://www.haaretz.com/israel-news/.premium.HIGHLIGHT.MAG AZINE-war-crimes-and-unpleasantness-israel-s-censorship-list-1.1 0301458

284　Protocol, 2010, file:///D:/Documents/Book%20in%20the%20comfort %20zone%20English/Addtions%20must/Silencing-Akevot-Institute-Report-July-2019.pdf

285 Aderet, O. (August 19, 2016). Access to original documents in the National Archives has been blocked, and researchers are worried regarding future research *Haaretz* (in Hebrew). https://www.haaretz.co.il/news/education/.premium-1.3043261

286 Aderet, O. (2018, January 16). State Archiver accuses: Israel hides archival information in manner unbecoming a democratic country (in Hebrew). *Haaretz*. Aderet, O. (2018, January 16). State Archiver accuses: Israel hides archival information in manner unbecoming a democratic country. *Haaretz* (in Hebrew). https://www.haaretz.co.il/news/education/MAGAZINE-1; https://www.haaretz.co.il/news/education/MAGAZINE-.5742001

287 https://rsf.org/en/israel

288 *The New York Times*, August 24, 2021.

289 Haidt, J., Graham, J., & Joseph, C. (2009). Above and below left-right: Ideological narratives and moral foundations. *Psychological Inquiry, 20*, 110-119.

290 Hermann, T., Anabi, O. Cabison, W. & Heler, E. (2019). *The Israeli democracy index 2019*. Jerusalem: The Israeli Democracy Institute.

291 Hermann, T., Anabi, O. Cabison, W. & Heler, E. (2019). *The Israeli democracy index 2019*. Jerusalem: The Israeli Democracy Institute.

292 Bendet, S., Nahmias, O. & Altman, Y. (March 17, 2015). Netanyahu released a video: "The Arabs are moving in huge numbers to the voting posts." *Walla! News* (in Hebrew). http://elections.walla.co.il/item/2838603

293 Index of Israeli Foreign Policy (September 2019). Mitvim – The Israeli Institute for Regional Foreign Policies.

294 Peace Index, November 2015.

295 Hermann, T., Anabi, O. Cabison, W. & Heler, E. (2019). *The Israeli democracy index 2019*. Jerusalem: The Israeli Democracy Institute.

296 Bar-Tal, D., & Halperin, E. (2011). Socio-psychological barriers to conflict resolution. In D., Bar-Tal (Ed.), *Intergroup conflicts and their resolu-*

tion: A social psychological perspective (pp. 217-240). New York: Psychology Press.

297 Hirch-Hoefler, S., Canetti, D., Rapaport, C., & Hobfoll, E., S. (2014). Conflict will harden your heart: Exposure to violence, psychological distress, and peace barriers in Israel and Palestine. *British Journal of Political Sciences, 46,* 845-859.

298 *Haaretz,* October 26, 2019.

299 Bar-Tal, D., Magal, T., & Halperin, E. (2009). The paradox of security views in Israel: Socio-psychological explanation. In G. Sheffer & O. Barak (Eds.), *Existential threats and civil security relations* (pp. 219-247). Lanham MD: Lexington Books.

300 Bar-Tal, D. (2007). *Living with the conflict: Socio-psychological analysis of the Israeli-Jewish society.* Jerusalem: Carmel (in Hebrew).

301 Wohl, M. J. A., & Branscombe, N. R. (2008). Collective angst: How threats to the future vitality of the ingroup shape intergroup emotion. In H. Wayment, & J. Bauer (Eds.), *Transcending self-interest: Psychological explorations of the quiet ego* (pp. 171-181). Washington, D.C.: American Psychological Association.

302 Lam, A. (2018, March 28 2018). We are hereby warning *Yediot Aharonot* (in Hebrew). https://www.yediot.co.il/articles/0,7340,L-5202971,00.html

303 Bar-Tal. D. (2020). The essence of insecurity in Israel. In Keynan, I. & Harboun, I. (Eds.), *Reclaiming security: The civic aspects of securitization* (pp. 75-99). Haifa: Pardess Publishing (in Hebrew).

304 Bar-Tal, D., Nets-Zehngut, R., & Sharvit, K. (Eds), (2017). *Self-censorship in contexts of conflict: Theory and research.* Cham, Switzerland: Springer.

305 Bar-Tal, D., & Alon, I. (2016). Socio-psychological approach to trust (or distrust): Concluding comments. In Alon, I., & Bar-Tal, D. (Eds.), *The role of trust in conflict resolution: The Israeli–Palestinian case and beyond* (pp. 311-336). Cham, Switzerland: Springer. p. 312.

306 *EU Peacebuilding Initiative,* 2021.

307 Bar-Tal, D. (2013). *Intractable conflicts: Socio-psychological foundations and dynamics.* Cambridge University Press.

308 Nets-Zehngut, R., & Bar-Tal, D. (2017). The Israeli-Jewish collective memory of the Israeli-Arab/Palestinian conflict – Findings of a representative public survey regarding 23 major topics. In: Nets-Zehngut, R *The Israeli and Palestinian collective memory of conflict – Survey findings, analysis, comparison and collaboration* (pp. 14-50). Saabrücken, Germany: Lambert Academic Publishing.

309 Bar-Tal, D. (2007). *Living with the conflict: Socio-psychological analysis of the Israeli-Jewish society.* Jerusalem: Carmel (in Hebrew).

310 Rabin, Y. (April 27, 1987). In every generation. *Haaretz* (in Hebrew).

311 Canetti, D., Hirschberger, G. et al., (2018). Collective trauma from lab to the real world: The effects of the Holocaust on contemporary Israeli political cognitions. *Political Psychology, 39*, 3-21.

312 Halperin, E., Oren, N. & Bar-Tal, D. (2010). Socio-psychological barriers to resolving the Israeli-Palestinian conflict: An analysis of Jewish Israeli society. In Bar-Siman-Tov, Y. (Ed.), *Barriers to peace in the Israeli-Palestinian conflict* (28-57). Jerusalem: Konrad-Adenauer-Stiftung Israel & The Jerusalem Institute for Policy Studies.

313 Bar-Tal. D. (2020). The essence of insecurity in Israel. In Keynan, I. & Harboun, I. (Eds.), *Reclaiming security: The civic aspects of securitization* (pp. 75-99). Haifa: Pardess Publishing (in Hebrew).

314 Nasie, M., Diamond, A., & Bar-Tal, D. (2016). Young children in intractable conflicts: The Israel case *Personality and Social Psychology Review, 20*, 365-392.

315 Nasie M., & Bar-Tal, D. (2020). Political socialization in kindergartens: Observations of ceremonies of the Israeli Jewish holidays and memorial days. *European Journal of Social Psychology, 50*, 701-720

316 Adwan, S., Bar-Tal, D., & Wexler, B. (2016). Portrayal of the other in Palestinian and Israel schoolbooks: A comparative study. *Political Psychology, 37*. 201-217.

317 Sharvit, K. (2014). How conflict begets conflict: Activation of the ethos of conflict in times of distress in a society involved in an intractable conflict. *Journal of Experimental Social Psychology, 55*, 252-261.

318 Fuxman, S. (2012). *Learning the past, interpreting the present, and shaping the future: Israeli adolescents' narratives of the Israeli-Palestinian conflict.* Dis-

sertation submitted to Harvard University. Cambridge: Harvard University.

319 Zertal, I., & Eldar, A. (2007). *Lords of the land: The war over Israel's settlements in the occupied territories 1967-2007.* New York: Nation Books.

320 Bar-Tal, D., Abutbul, G., & Raviv, A. (2014). The culture of conflict and its routinization. In P. Nesbitt-Larking, C. Kinvall, T. Capelos, &. H. Dekker, (Eds.), *The Palgrave handbook of global political psychology* (pp. 369-387). Houndmills, UK: Palgrave Macmillan; Ochs, J. (2011). *Security & suspicion: An ethnography of everyday life in Israel.* Philadelphia, PA: University of Pennsylvania.

321 Vered, S., & Bar-Tal, D. (2014). Routinization of the Israeli-Arab conflict: The perspective of outsiders. *Israel Studies Review, 29,* 41-61.

322 Levinger, A. (1994). *Monuments to the fallen in Israel.* Tel Aviv; Hakibbutz Hamuahad (in Hebrew).

323 Oren, A. (2010). Shadows lands: The use of land resources for security needs in Israel (168-190). In G. Sheffer, & O. Barak (Eds.), *Militarism and Israeli society* (168-190). Bloomington, IN: Indiana University Press.

324 https://www.calcalist.co.il/local/articles/0,7340,L-3745611,00.html

325 https://finance.walla.co.il/item/2930566

326 Levy, Y. (2010). The tradeoff between force and casualties: Israel's wars In Gaza, 1987-2009. *Conflict Managements and Peace Science, 27,* 386-405.

327 Bleich, A., Gelkopf, M., & Solomon, Z. (2003). Exposure to terrorism, stress-related mental health symptoms, and coping behaviors among a nationally representative sample in Israel. *Journal of The American Medical Association, 290,* 612-620.

328 *Jerusalem Post,* October 17, 2018.

329 American Psychiatric Association, 2013.

330 http://news.walla.co.il/item/121822

331 Bleich, A., Gelkopf, M., Berger, R., & Solomon, Z. (2008). The psychological toll of the Intifada: Symptoms of distress and coping in Israeli soldiers. *Israel Medical Association Journal, 10,* 873-879.

332 http://www.nrg.co.il/online/1/ART1/726/072.html.

333 Greenbaum, W. C. & Elitzur, Y. (2013). The psychological and moral consequences for Israeli society of the occupation of Palestine land. In Bar-Tal, D. & Schnell, I. (Eds.). *The impacts of lasting occupation: Lessons from Israeli society* (pp. 380-408). New York: Oxford University Press; Shavit, N. & Katriel, T. (2009). "We Have Decided to Speak out": The testimonial project of Breaking the Silence as counter-discourse. *Israel Studies in Language and Society*, 2(2), 56-82 (in Hebrew).

334 Elizur, Y., & Yishav-Krien, N. (2009). Participation in atrocities among Israeli soldiers during the first Intifada: A qualitative analysis. *Journal of Peace Research*, 46(2), 251-267; Gelkopf, M., Berger, R., & Roe, D. (2016). Soldiers perpetrating or witnessing acts of humiliation: A community-based random sample study design. *Peace and Conflict*: Journal of *Peace Psychology*, 22(1), 84-90.

335 Shavit, N. & Katriel, T. (2009). "We Have Decided to Speak out": The testimonial project of Breaking the Silence as counter-discourse. *Israel Studies in Language and Society*, 2(2), 56-82 (in Hebrew).

336 Zarchovich. R. (2020). *The mental reaction of young Israelis which killed Palestinians during their military service – Quantitative and qualitative analysis* Unpublished doctoral dissertation. Tel Aviv: Tel Aviv University (in Hebrew).

337 Arian, A. (1995). *Security threatened: Surveying Israeli opinion on peace and war*. Cambridge, U. K: Cambridge University Press; Arian, A. (2001). *Israeli public opinion on national security 2001* (Memorandum No. 60). Tel Aviv: Jaffe Center for Strategic Studies, Tel Aviv University; Arian, A. (2002). *Israeli public opinion on national security 2002* (Memorandum No. 61). Tel Aviv: Jaffe Center for Strategic Studies, Tel Aviv University; Arian, A. (2003). *Israeli public opinion on national security 2003* (Memorandum No. 67). Tel Aviv: Jaffe Center for Strategic Studies, Tel Aviv University.

338 EU Peacebuilding Initiative (2021). *Mapping sources of mutual distrust in Palestinian and Israeli Societies and Politics: Role of education, daily life experiences, and exposure to violence*. Palestinian Center for Policy and Survey Research in Ramallah and Macro-the Center for Political Economics in Tel Aviv. http://www.macro.org.il/en/projects/?id=249

339 Friedman-Peleg, K. (2014). *The nation on the sofa: The politics of trauma in Israel* Jerusalem: Magness Press. (in Hebrew); Keynan, I. (2015). *Psychological war trauma and society: Like a hidden wound*. London: Routledge.

340 Zeira, J. (2021). *The Israeli economy: A story of success and costs.* Princeton, NJ: Princeton University Press.

341 https://www.israeldefense.co.il/he/node/33452

342 Calcalist, August 29, 2021 (in Hebrew).

343 http://www.economicsandpeace.org/

344 http://www.globes.co.il/news/article.aspx?did=1000585933

345 RAND (2015). *The costs of the Israeli-Palestinian conflict.* Retrieved from http://www.rand.org/content/dam/rand/pubs/research_reports/RR 700/RR740-1/RAND_RR740-1.pdf

346 Ben-Sasson-Gordis, A. (October 15, 2015). The Jewish settlements hurt the Israeli security. Molad (in Hebrew).

347 https://www.haaretz.co.il/news/politics/.premium-1.10643607

348 Waxman, A. (2019, December 17, 2019). Even without the Golan Heights: This year's investment in the settlements was the highest in the past decade. *The Marker* (in Hebrew). https://www.themarker.com/all-news/.premium-1.8282715

349 Shir, H. (2013). Economic costs of the occupation to Israel. In Bar-Tal, D. & Schnell, I. (Eds.). *The impacts of lasting occupation: Lessons from Israeli society* (pp. 380-408). New York: Oxford University Press.

350 Hermann, T., Anabi, O. Cabison, W. & Heler, E. (2019). *The Israeli democracy index 2019.* Jerusalem: The Israeli Democracy Institute. p. 148.

351 https://www.haaretz.co.il/opinions/.premium-1.10208450

352 Ezrahi, Y. (2013). The occupation and Israeli democracy. In Bar-Tal, D. & Schnell, I. (Eds.). *The impacts of lasting occupation: Lessons from Israeli society* (pp. 189-207). New York: Oxford University Press; Hermann, T., Anabi, O. Cabison, W. & Heler, E. (2019). *The Israeli democracy index 2019.* Jerusalem: The Israeli Democracy Institute.

353 Azoulay, A. & Ophir, A. (2012). *The one-state condition: Occupation and democracy in Israel/Palestine.* Stanford, CA: Stanford University Press.

354 March 21, 2018, Haaretz.

355 Ravid, B. (2021). *Summary of the Trump's peace*. Washington: Washington Press.

356 https://www.people-press.org/2018/01/23/republicans-and-democrats-grow-even-further-apart-in-views-of-israel-palestinians/

357 https://www.haaretz.com/us-news/netanyahu-favorite-leader-of-republicans-unpopular-among-democrats-1.6407965

358 https://news.gallup.com/poll/340331/americans-favor-israel-warming-palestinians.aspx

359 https://news.gallup.com/opinion/polling-matters/265898/american-jews-politics-israel.aspx

360 https://www.jewishvirtuallibrary.org/jewish-voting-record-in-u-s-presidential-elections

361 Wright, W., Saxe, L., & Wald, D., K. (2020). Is criticism disloyal? American Jews' attitudes toward Israel. *Politics and Religion*, 1-27. doi:10.1017/S1755048320000693.

362 http://www.inn.co.il/News/News.aspx/280615

363 http://www.ynet.co.il/articles/0,7340,L-4038587,00.html

364 http://www.calcalist.co.il/articles/0,7340,L-3396699,00.html

365 http://www.nrg.co.il/online/1/ART1/588/866.html

366 https://www.theguardian.com/world/2015/oct/27/uk-academics-boycott-universities-in-israel-to-fight-for-palestinians-rights

367 https://www.theguardian.com/world/2015/feb/13/cultural-boycott-israel-starts-tomorrow

368 http://www.haaretz.com/israel-news/culture/leisure/1.607866

369 Ezrahi, Y. (2013). The occupation and Israeli democracy. In Bar-Tal, D. & Schnell, I. (Eds.). *The impacts of lasting occupation: Lessons from Israeli society* (pp. 189-207). New York: Oxford University Press; Neuberger, B. (2019). Democratic and anti-democratic roots of the Israeli political system. *Israel Studies Review, 34*, 55-74.

370 Bar-Tal, D., & Magal, T. (2021). Socio-psychological analysis of the deterioration of democracy and the rise of authoritarianism: The role of

needs, values and context. In *Forgas, P. J., Crano, B., & Fiedler, K. (Eds.), The psychology of populism: 21st Volume of the Sydney Symposium of Social Psychology Series* pp. 42-61). London: Routledge.

371 https://www.haaretz.co.il/news/law/.premium-1.8328034

372 https://www.haaretz.com/opinion/.premium-those-loyal-to-democra cy-in-israel-must-wake-up-1.10639797

373 Dahl, R. A. (2000). *On democracy.* Hew Heaven, CT: Yale University Press; Neuberger, B. (2019). Democratic and anti-democratic roots of the Israeli political system. *Israel Studies Review, 34,* 55-74.

374 https://news.walla.co.il/item/3320754

375 Hermann, T., Anabi, O. Cabison, W. & Heler, E. (2019). *The Israeli democracy index 2019.* Jerusalem: The Israeli Democracy Institute, p. 148.

376 Ariely, G. (2021). *Israeli's regime untangled: Between democracy and apartheid.* New York: Cambridge University Press.

377 Ezrahi, Y. (2013). The occupation and Israeli democracy. In Bar-Tal, D. & Schnell, I. (Eds.). *The impacts of lasting occupation: Lessons from Israeli society* (pp. 189-207). New York: Oxford University Press; Hermann, T., Anabi, O. Cabison, W. & Heler, E. (2019). *The Israeli democracy index 2019.* Jerusalem: The Israeli Democracy Institute.

378 Bar-Tal, D., & Magal, T. (2021). Socio-psychological analysis of the deterioration of democracy and the rise of authoritarianism: The role of needs, values and context. In Forgas, P. J., Crano, B., & Fiedler, K. (Eds.), *The psychology of populism: 21st Volume of the Sydney Symposium of Social Psychology Series* (pp. 42-61). London: Routledge.

379 Kretzmer, D. (1990). *The legal status of the Arabs in Israel,* Boulder, CO: Westview; Lustick, I. (1980). *Arabs in the Jewish State: Israel's control of a national minority.* Austin, TX: University of Texas Press; Peled, Y. (1992). Ethnic democracy and the legal construction of citizenship: Arab citizens of the Jewish state. *American Political Science Review, 86,* 432-443; Peled, Y., & Navot, D. (2006). Ethnic democracy revisited. *Israel Studies Forum, 20,* 3-27; Rouhana N. (Ed.) (2017). *Israel and its Palestinian citizens: Ethnic privileges in the Jewish state.* Cambridge University Press, Cambridge.

380 Forman, G., & Kedar, A. (2004). From Arab land to "Israel Lands": the legal dispossession of the Palestinians displaced by Israel in the wake pf

1948. *Environment and Planning D: Society and Space, 22,* 809-830.

381   https://www.themarker.com/news/education/.premium-1.9457472

382   Yehuda et al (2014). *One rule, two legal systems: Israel's regime of laws in the West Bank.* Jerusalem: The Association for Civil Rights.

383   Azoulay, A. & Ophir, A. (2012). *The One-State condition: Occupation and democracy in Israel/Palestine.* Stanford, CA: Stanford University Press.

384   *Haaretz,* March 23, 2018.

385   *Haaretz,* March 23, 2018.

386   https://law.acri.org.il/en/2014/11/24/twosysreport/#:~:text=The%20 %E2%80%98One,the%20grocery%20store.

387   https://www.haaretz.com/opinion/editorial/2022-06-07/ty-article/ saar-looks-for-an-arab-to-blame/00000181-3f9c-dada-a9a7-ff9de-2fa0000

388   Sfard, M. (June 2020). The occupation of the West Bank and the crime of Apartheid. Tel Aviv: Yesh Din Volunteers for Human Rights.

389   https://www.btselem.org/publications/fulltext/202101_this_is_apart heid

390   https://www.hrw.org/report/2021/04/27/threshold-crossed/israe-li-authorities-and-crimes-apartheid-and-persecution

391   https://www.independent.co.uk/news/uk/politics/labour-confere nce-israel-palestine-apartheid-b1927830.html

392   https://www.amnesty.org/en/wp-content/uploads/2022/02/MDE 1551412022ENGLISH.pdf

393   https://news.un.org/en/story/2022/03/1114702

394   https://www.washingtonpost.com/politics/2021/09/17/academic-experts-believe-that-middle-east-politics-are-actually-getting-worse/

395   https://www.washingtonpost.com/politics/2021/05/08/critics-say-its-apartheid-do-israelis-palestinians-think-it-is/

396   https://www.haaretz.com/israel-news/2022-06-08/ty-article/.high light/under-settler-pressure-israel-extends-antiquities-authoritys-pow

ers-into-west-bank/00000181-42f8-df72-a5cb-c2ffa4660000

397 Peace Index, Sept. 2015.

398 Peace Index, Nov. 2016.

399 Peace Index, June 2016.

400 https://www.haaretz.com/israel-news/israeli-palestinian-conflict-solu tions/.premium-42-of-israelis-back-west-bank-annexation-including- two-state-supporters-1.7047313.

401 EU Peacebuilding Initiative (2021).

402 Jamal, A., & Kensicki, A. (2020). Theorizing half-statelessness: a case study of the Nation-State Law in Israel. *Citizenship Studies, 24*, 769-785. DOI: 10.1080/13621025.2020.1745152.

403 Peace Index, July 2018.

404 Kretzmer, D. (2005). The advisory opinion: The light treatment of inter- national humanitarian law. *The American Journal of International Law, 99*, 88-102; Kretzmer, D. (2013). The law of belligerent occupation as a sys- tem of control: Dressing up exploitation in respectable garb. In Bar-Tal, D. & Schnell, I. (Eds.). *The impacts of lasting occupation: Lessons from Israeli society* (pp. 31-60). New York: Oxford University Press.

405 Kretzmer, D., & Ronen, Y. (2021) *The occupation and justice: The Supreme Court of Israel and the occupied territories.* New York: Oxford University Press.

406 Kretzmer, D. (2002). *The occupation of justice: The supreme court of Isra- el and the occupied territories.* Albany, NY: State University of New York Press; Shamir, R. (1990). Landmark cases and the reproduction of legit- imacy: The Case of Israel's High Court of Justice. *Law and Society, 24*, 781-805.

407 Benvenisti, E. (2003). Case review: Ajuri et al. v. IDF Commander in the West Bank et. al. *European Public Law, 9*, 481-492; Kretzmer, D. (2002). *The occupation of justice: The supreme court of Israel and the occupied territo- ries.* Albany, NY: State University of New York Press.

408 Barzilai, G. (1998). The argument of "National Security" in politics and jurisprudence. In D. Bar-Tal, D. Jacobson & A., Klieman (Eds), *Security concerns: Insights from the Israeli* experience (pp. 243-265). Stamford, CT:

JAI Press; Kretzmer, D. (2002). *The occupation of justice: The supreme court of Israel and the occupied territories.* Albany, NY: State University of New York Press; Kretzmer, D. (2012). The law of belligerent occupation in the Supreme Court of Israel. *International Review of the Red Cross, 94,* 207-236; Procaccia, U. (September 5, 2018). The judicial system is fully enlisted in favor of the settlement enterprise *Haaretz* (in Hebrew). https://www.haaretz.co.il/opinions/.premium-1.6455313; Shamir, R. (1990). Landmark cases and the reproduction of legitimacy: The Case of Israel's High Court of Justice. *Law and Society, 24,* 781-805.

409 Barzilai, G. (1999). Courts as hegemonic institutions: The Israeli Supreme Court in a comparative perspective. In D. Levi-Faur, G. Sheffer & D. Vogel (Eds.), *Israel: The dynamics of change and continuity* (pp. 15-33). Portland, OR: Frank Cass; Shinar Levanon, O.)2016). *The ethos of the Israeli-Palestinian conflict as reflected by judgments of the Israel Supreme Court from 1948 until 2006.* Dissertation submitted to the Hebrew University of Jerusalem. Jerusalem: The Hebrew University of Jerusalem.

410 Kretzmer, D. (2012). The law of belligerent occupation in the Supreme Court of Israel. *International Review of the Red Cross, 94,* 207-236; Kretzmer, D. (2013). The law of belligerent occupation as a system of control: Dressing up exploitation in respectable garb. In Bar-Tal, D. & Schnell, I. (Eds.). *The impacts of lasting occupation: Lessons from Israeli society* (pp. 31-60). New York: Oxford University Press; Navot, D., & Peled, Y. (2009). Towards a constitutional counter–revolution in Israel. *Constellation, 16,* 429-444.

411 Fingher-Dasberg, R. (2020). *The role of the court in mediating the relationship between 'Equal Citizenship' and 'National Sovereignty.* Dissertation submitted to Tel Aviv University. Tel Aviv: Tel Aviv University.

412 https://www.yesh-din.org/en/hcj-petition-subject-military-searches-in-palestinians-homes-in-the-west-bank-to-judicial-review/

413 https://www.haaretz.com/opinion/editorial/israel-s-high-court-of-justice-the-occupation-s-rubber-stamp-1.10784957

414 Kretzmer, D., & Ronen, Y. (2021) *The occupation and justice: The Supreme Court of Israel and the occupied territories.* Oxford University Press. New York. pp. 489-490.

415 https://www.haaretz.com/opinion/for-most-israelis-including-bennett-occupation-is-legitimate-if-it-s-polite-1.10583692

416 Haaretz, August 20, 2017; Haaretz, August 30, 2017.

417 Dahl, R. A. (2000). *On democracy.* Hew Heaven, CT: Yale University Press; Raz, J. (1991). Free expression and personal identification. *Oxford Journal of Legal Studies, 11,* 303-324.

418 Chaitlin, J., Steinberg, S., & Steinberg, S. (2021). Jewish-Israeli attitudes toward human rights organizations and patriotism. *Ethnopollitics, 20,* 501-522.

419 Oren, N. & Bar-Tal, D. (2004). Monopolization of patriotism in the Israeli society. In Ben-Amos, A. & Bar-Tal, D. (Eds.), *Patriotism: We love you motherland* (pp. 363-398). Tel Aviv: Hakibbutz Hameuhad (in Hebrew).

420 Haaretz, November 14, 2017.

421 Peace Index, November 2016.

422 Sprinzak, E. (1986). *Whatever seems right: Illegality in the Israeli society* Tel Aviv: Sifriyat Hapoalim (in Hebrew).

423 Negbi, M. (2004). *We became like Sodom: On the slop from a rule-of-law state to a banana republic.* Jerusalem: Keter Press (in Hebrew); Sprinzak, E. (1986). *Whatever seems right: Illegality in the Israeli society* Tel Aviv: Sifriyat Hapoalim (in Hebrew).

424 Zertal, I., & Eldar, A. (2007). *Lords of the land: The war over Israel's settlements in the occupied territories 1967-2007.* New York: Nation Books.

425 Hass, 10 March 2019; Kretzmer, D. (2013). The law of belligerent occupation as a system of control: Dressing up exploitation in respectable garb. In Bar-Tal, D. & Schnell, I. (Eds.). *The impacts of lasting occupation: Lessons from Israeli society* (pp. 31-60). New York: Oxford University Press; Kretzmer & Gorenberg, 2015.

426 Zertal, I., & Eldar, A. (2007). *Lords of the land: The war over Israel's settlements in the occupied territories 1967-2007.* New York: Nation Books.

427 Kretzmer, D. & Gorenberg, G. (2015). Politics, Judiciary and the judicial process: The case of Israeli High Court of Justice and the territories *Judicial and Government* [Heb: Mishpat Umimshal], 17, 249-323 (in Hebrew).

428 Haaretz, May 3, 2015.

429 Berger, Y. (August 23, 2017). The civil administration: 3,455 buildings in the settlements are standing on private Palestinian lands *Haaretz* (in Hebrew).https://www.haaretz.co.il/news/local/.premium-1.4383049

430 Haaretz, March 3, 2017.

431 Berger, Y., (October 22, 2018). The settlement division assisted for 20 years in funding the construction of illegal outposts *Haaretz* (in Hebrew). https://www.haaretz.co.il/news/politics/.premium-1.6576695; Berger, 6 October 2015.

432 Berger, Y., (October 22, 2018). The settlement division assisted for 20 years in funding the construction of illegal outposts *Haaretz* (in Hebrew). https://www.haaretz.co.il/news/politics/.premium-1.6576695; Berger, 6 October 2015.

433 Haaretz, February 7, 2017.

434 Sasson, T. (2005). *Advisory legal brief (intermediate) regarding unauthorized settlements* Jerusalem: Unknown publisher (in Hebrew). Retrieved from: http://www.nasserlaw.net/UserFiles/file/sason%20report.pdf

435 Rahum, A. (1990). *The shabak affair.* Jerusalem: Carmel Press (in Hebrew).

436 Blass, I. (2015). *Jurists and torture in Israel post 1967: Denial, regulation or ban?* (in Hebrew). Retrieved from: https://www.thelawfilm.com/inside/hebrew/stories/denial-or-ban-on-jurists-and-torture-in-israel-post-1967

437 https://stoptorture.org.il/en/

438 Haaretz, December 7, 2016.

439 Podeh, E. (2021). *From mistress to known partner: Israel's secret relations with states and minorities in the Middle East, 1948-2020.* Tel Aviv: Am Oved (in Hebrew)

440 https://www.nytimes.com/2022/01/28/magazine/nso-group-israel-spyware.html

441 https://www.haaretz.co.il/news/world/europe/.premium-1.6868096

442 Peace Index, August 2019.

443 Peace Index, August 2018.

444   Haaretz, December 1, 2017.

445   Greenstein, R. (2012. Israel/Palestine and the apartheid analogy: Critics, apologists and strategic lessons. In A. Lim, (Ed.,) *The case for sanctions against Israel*. London: Verso; Jeenah, N. (2018). *Pretending democracy, Living ethnocracy*. In N. Jeenah, (Ed.,) *Pretending democracy: Israel, an ethnocratic state*. Johannesburg: Afro-Middle East Centre; Peleg, I. (2007). *Democratizing the hegemonic state: Political transformation in the age of identity*. Cambridge: Cambridge University Press. Smooha, S. (1997). Ethnic democracy: Israel as an archetype. *Israel Studies, 2*(2), 198–241; Yiftachel, O. (2006). *Ethnocracy: Land and identity politics in Israel/Palestine*. Philadelphia: University of Pennsylvania Press.

446   Bar-Tal, D., Raviv, A. & Abromovich, R. (2020). *In the head of the beholder: Views of Israeli Jews on theIsraeli-Arab/Palestinian conflict* (in Hebrew). Tel Aviv: Tami Steinmetz Center for Peace Research, Tel Aviv University (in Hebrew).

447   Sheffer, G., & Barak, O. (2010). *Militarism and Israeli society*. Bloomington, IN: Indiana University Press.

448   https://www.jpost.com/arab-israeli-conflict/article-691457

449   Berger, Y. (November 18, 2017). Mandelblit paves a way for the legalization of 13 illegal outposts in the West Bank *Haaretz* (in Hebrew). https://www.haaretz.co.il/news/politics/.premium-1.4608898

450   https://www.haaretz.com/israel-news/.premium-lapid-reveals-americans-warned-against-evyatar-settlement-s-reestablishment-1.10587315

451   https://www.haaretz.co.il/news/politics/.premium-1.8375436

452   Gordon, N. (2014). Human rights as a security threat: Lawfare and the campaign against human rights NGOs. *Law & Society Review, 48*(2), 311–344.

453   Verter, Y. (April 11, 2008). *Scruples*. Haaretz (in Hebrew).

454   https://www.ynet.co.il/articles/0,7340,L-5481839,00.html

455   https://zulat.org.il/human_rights_index_feb21/?utm_source=Newsletter&utm_medium=email&utm_content

456   Zanany, O. (2018). From a conflict management to a political settlement

managing: The Israeli security doctrine and the prospective Palestinian state. The Tami Steinmetz Center for Peace Research, Tel Aviv University (in Hebrew).

457 Golan, G. (2019). Deception and Israeli peacemaking since 1967. *Israel Studies Review, 34*, 1–26.

458 https://www.nytimes.com/2021/05/27/world/middleeast/israel-gaza-un-human-rights-council.html

459 Tuchman, B. (1984). *The march of folly: From Troy to Vietnam.* New York: Knopf.

460 Rosler, N. (2016). Containing duality: Leadership in the Israeli-Palestinian peace process. In K. Sharvit & E. Halperin (Eds.), *A social psychology perspective on the Israeli-Palestinian conflict: Celebrating the legacy of Daniel Bar-Tal* (Vol. 2, pp. 217-228). New York: Springer.

461 Pressman, J. (2020). *The sword is not enough: Arabs, Israelis and the limits of military force.* Manchester, UK: Manchester University Press.

462 Kahneman, D., & Tversky, A. (1979). Prospect theory: An analysis of decision under risk. *Econometrica, 47*, 263-291; Kahneman, D., & Tversky, A. (1984). Choices, values, and frames. *American Psychologist, 39*, 341-50.

463 Gayer, C. C., Landman, S., Halperin, E., & Bar-Tal, D. (2009). Overcoming psychological barriers to peaceful conflict resolution: The role of arguments about losses. *Journal of Conflict Resolution, 53*, 951-975.

464 Leshem, A., O., & Halperin, E. (2020). Hoping for peace during protracted conflict: Citizens' hope is based on inaccurate appraisals of their adversary's hope for peace, *Journal of Conflict Resolution, 64* (7-8), 1390-1417, p.1411.

465 Browning, R. C. (1992). Ordinary men: Reserve police battalion 101 and the final solution in Poland. New York: HarperCollins Publisher. p. 188-189.

466 Goldhagen, J. G. (1996). *Hitler's willing executioners: Ordinary Germans and the Holocaust.* New York: Alfred A. Knopf.

467 Milgram, S. (1974). *Obedience to authority: An experimental view.* New York: Harper and Row.

468 Lewin, K. (1947). Frontiers I group dynamics: I. *Human Relations, 1*, 5-41.

469 Bar-Tal, D., & Halperin, E. (2013). The psychology of intractable conflicts: Eruption, escalation, and peacemaking. In L. Huddy, D. O. Sears, & J. S. Levy (Eds.), *The Oxford handbook of political psychology* (2nd ed. pp. 923-956). New York: Oxford University Press.

470 Bar-Tal, D., & Hammack, P. L. (2012). Conflict, delegitimization and violence. In L. R. Tropp (Ed.), *The Oxford handbook of intergroup conflict* (pp.29-52). New York: Oxford University Press.

471 Bar-Tal, D. (2013). *Intractable conflicts: Socio-psychological foundations and dynamics.* Cambridge University Press.

472 Browning, R. C. (1992), Ordinary men: Reserve police battalion 101 and the final solution in Poland. New York: HarperCollins Publisher. pp. 188-189.

473 Bar-Tal, D. (2003). Collective memory of physical violence: Its contribution to the culture of violence. In E. Cairns & M. D. Roe (Eds.). *The role of memory in ethnic conflict* (pp.77-93). Houndmills, England: Palgrave Macmillan.

474 Text of the international convention on the suppression and punishment of the crime of apartheid (November 30, 1973) United Nation General Assembly.

475 Bar-Tal, D. (2013). *Intractable conflicts: Socio-psychological foundations and dynamics.* Cambridge University Press.

476 As of February 2020, 134 (69.4%) of the 193 member states of the United Nations have recognized the State of Palestine within the Palestinian territories, which are recognized by Israel to constitute a single territorial unit, and of which the West Bank is the core of the would-be state.

477 Bar-Tal, D., Oren, N., & Nets-Zehngut, R. (2014). Sociopsychological analysis of conflict-supporting narratives: A general framework. *Journal of Peace Research, 51*, 662-675.

478 Rosler, N., Hameiri, B., Sharvit, K., Wiener-Blotner, O., Idan, O., & Bar-Tal, D. (in press) The informative process model as a new intervention for attitude change in intractable conflicts: Theory and experimental evidence. *Frontiers in Psychology.*

Related Titles from Westphalia Press

The Limits of Moderation: Jimmy Carter and the Ironies of American Liberalism
by Leo P. Ribuffo

The Limits of Moderation: Jimmy Carter and the Ironies of American Liberalism is not a finished product. Yet, this book is a close and careful history of a short yet transformative period in American political history, when big changes were afoot. and continue to shape our world.

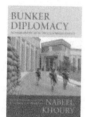

Bunker Diplomacy: An Arab-American in the U.S. Foreign Service
by Nabeel Khoury

After twenty-five years in the Foreign Service, Dr. Nabeel A. Khoury retired from the U.S. Department of State in 2013 with the rank of Minister Counselor. In his last overseas posting, Khoury served as deputy chief of mission at the U.S. embassy in Yemen (2004-2007).

Energy Law and Policy in a Climate-Constrained World
by Victor Byers Flatt, Alfonso López de la Osa Escribano, Aubin Nzaou-Kongo

This book presents reflections on concepts, foreign policy, regional and international cooperation, and the specific role the state is to play when it comes to such thing as energy law and policy.

The Zelensky Method
by Grant Farred

Locating Russian's war within a global context, The Zelensky Method is unsparing in its critique of those nations, who have refused to condemn Russia's invasion and are doing everything they can to prevent economic sanctions from being imposed on the Kremlin.

The Lord of the Desert: A Study of the Papers of the British Officer John B. Glubb in Jordan and Iraq
by Dr. Sa'ad Abudayeh

John Bajot Glubb, a British engineer officer, was sent to Iraq in 1920 to resolve the problems which erupted after the Iraqi revolt. He remained in the area for ten years, working with the Bedouins. In 1930, he moved to Jordan for twenty-six successful years. He invented what Dr. Abudayeh calls the Diplomacy of Desert.

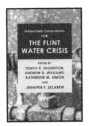

Managing Challenges for the Flint Water Crisis
Edited by Toyna E. Thornton, Andrew D. Williams, Katherine M. Simon, Jennifer F. Sklarew

This edited volume examines several public management and intergovernmental failures, with particular attention on social, political, and financial impacts. Understanding disaster meaning, even causality, is essential to the problem-solving process.

Resistance: Reflections on Survival, Hope and Love
Poetry by William Morris, Photography by Jackie Malden

Resistance is a book of poems with photographs or a book of photographs with poems depending on your perspective. The book is comprised of three sections titled respectively: On Survival, On Hope, and On Love.

Abortion and Informed Common Sense
by Max J. Skidmore

The controversy over a woman's "right to choose," as opposed to the numerous "rights" that abortion opponents decide should be assumed to exist for "unborn children," has always struck me as incomplete. Two missing elements of the argument seems obvious, yet they remain almost completely overlooked.

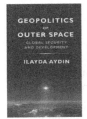

Geopolitics of Outer Space: Global Security and Development
by Ilayda Aydin

A desire for increased security and rapid development is driving nation-states to engage in an intensifying competition for the unique assets of space. This book analyses the Chinese-American space discourse from the lenses of international relations theory, history and political psychology to explore these questions.

The Athenian Year Primer: Attic Time-Reckoning and the Julian Calendar
by Christopher Planeaux

The ability to translate ancient Athenian calendar references into precise Julian-Gregorian dates will not only assist Ancient Historians and Classicists to date numerous historical events with much greater accuracy but also aid epigraphists in the restorations of numerous Attic inscriptions.

The Politics of Fiscal Responsibility: A Comparative Perspective
by Tonya E. Thornton and F. Stevens Redburn

Fiscal policy challenges following the Great Recession forced members of the Organisation for Economic Co-operation and Development (OECD) to implement a set of economic policies to manage public debt.

China & Europe: The Turning Point
by David Baverez

In creating five fictitious conversations between Xi Jinping and five European experts, David Baverez, who lives and works in Hong Kong, offers up a totally new vision of the relationship between China and Europe.

Issues in Maritime Cyber Security
Edited by Dr. Joe DiRenzo III, Dr. Nicole K. Drumhiller, and Dr. Fred S. Roberts

The complexity of making MTS safe from cyber attack is daunting and the need for all stakeholders in both government (at all levels) and private industry to be involved in cyber security is more significant than ever as the use of the MTS continues to grow.

Freemasonry, Heir to the Enlightenment
by Cécile Révauger

Modern Freemasonry may have mythical roots in Solomon's time but is really the heir to the Enlightenment. Ever since the early eighteenth century freemasons have endeavored to convey the values of the Enlightenment in the cultural, political and religious fields, in Europe, the American colonies and the emerging United States.

Growing Inequality: Bridging Complex Systems, Population Health, and Health Disparities
Editors: George A. Kaplan, Ana V. Diez Roux, Carl P. Simon, and Sandro Galea

Why is America's health is poorer than the health of other wealthy countries and why health inequities persist despite our efforts? In this book, researchers report on groundbreaking insights to simulate how these determinants come together to produce levels of population health and disparities and test new solutions.

Contests of Initiative: Countering China's Gray Zone Strategy in the East and South China Seas
by Dr. Raymond Kuo

China is engaged in a widespread assertion of sovereignty in the South and East China Seas. It employs a "gray zone" strategy: using coercive but sub-conventional military power to drive off challengers and prevent escalation, while simultaneously seizing territory and asserting maritime control.

Brought to Light: The Mysterious George Washington Masonic Cave
by Jason Williams, MD

The George Washington Masonic Cave near Charles Town, West Virginia, contains a signature carving of George Washington dated 1748. Although this inscription appears authentic, it has yet to be verified by historical accounts or scientific inquiry.

Frontline Diplomacy: A Memoir of a Foreign Service Officer in the Middle East
by William A. Rugh

In short vignettes, this book describes how American diplomats working in the Middle East dealt with a variety of challenges over the last decades of the 20th century. Each of the vignettes concludes with an insight about diplomatic practice derived from the experience.

westphaliapress.org

Policy Studies Organization

The Policy Studies Organization (PSO) is a publisher of academic journals and book series, sponsor of conferences, and producer of programs.

Policy Studies Organization publishes dozens of journals on a range of topics, such as European Policy Analysis, Journal of Elder Studies, Indian Politics & Polity, Journal of Critical Infrastructure Policy, and Popular Culture Review.

Additionally, Policy Studies Organization hosts numerous conferences. These conferences include the Middle East Dialogue, Space Education and Strategic Applications Conference, International Criminology Conference, Dupont Summit on Science, Technology and Environmental Policy, World Conference on Fraternalism, Freemasonry and History, and the Internet Policy & Politics Conference.

For more information on these projects, access videos of past events, and upcoming events, please visit us at:

www.ipsonet.org